M000238902

Human Information Interaction

Human Information Interaction: An Ecological Approach to Information Behavior

Raya Fidel

The MIT Press
Cambridge, Massachusetts
London, England

MIT Press books may be purchased at special quantity discounts for business or sales promotional use. For information, please email special_sales@mitpress.mit.edu or write to Special Sales Department, The MIT Press, 55 Hayward Street, Cambridge, MA 02142.

This book was set in Stone Sans and Stone Serif by Toppan Best-set Premedia Limited. Printed and bound in the United States of America.

Library of Congress Cataloging-in-Publication Data

Fidel, Raya, 1945–
Human information interaction : an ecological approach to information behavior / Raya Fidel.
    p.   cm.
Includes bibliographical references and index.
ISBN 978-0-262-01700-8 (alk. paper)
1. Information behavior. 2. Information storage and retrieval systems. 3. Information retrieval. I. Title.
ZA3075.F53   2012
025.5′24—dc23
2011026439

10   9   8   7   6   5   4   3   2   1

To Annelise Mark Pejtersen
for a wonderful ride

Contents

Preface

Life is complex. Every activity a person undertakes, whether physical or mental, is governed by rules, conventions, traditions, social position, personal preferences, the specific situation in which the activity takes place, and other constraints. Moreover, these factors interact with one another. While this complexity adds color to our lives, it confounds scholars' pursuit to understand human life. Clearly, researchers cannot identify and analyze all possible conditions under which an activity takes place and the effects of the various factors on the activity. As a result, much of human sciences' research tries to overlook complexity in order to make objects of study "researchable."

However, one of the leading threads in this book is the conviction that complexity *cannot* be overlooked if researchers wish to achieve a holistic understanding of humans, particularly if they hope to bring about changes that will improve the quality of human lives. Human information interaction (HII)—the area of study that investigates how humans interact with information—is no exception. The design of systems and services to support HII requires an understanding of human interaction in all its complexity. While this understanding is difficult enough to achieve, another major challenge emerges from the difficulties inherent in the translation of real-life and unstructured HII complexity into formal, linear structures necessary for systems design. While such translation is possible, it is a complex process in itself.

This book presents *cognitive work analysis* as an approach that addresses this challenge. Rather than avoiding complexity, this approach embraces it and, at the same time, provides a conceptual framework and tools to harness it to create design requirements. Cognitive work analysis is an ecological approach to design—one that analyzes the forces in the environment that shape human interaction with information.

The Motivation for the Book

This book is based on my research experience in the area of human information behavior (HIB) during the last three decades. HIB emerged as an established area in the field of library and information science about 40 years ago and has focused mainly on studying the behavior of people as they search for information. HIB is now joining other relatively new areas such as human-computer interaction, human factors, information retrieval, and social informatics; together, they make up the field of human information interaction. HII focuses on the interaction between humans and information with the support of any type of technology, be it face-to-face communication, paper, or advanced technology.

My research has been stimulated by the aspiration to create changes that would improve the quality of life. Although I enjoy abstract conversations and philosophizing, I have been attracted to approaches that are relevant to practice from the beginning of my research path. Throughout my research work, I have been engaged in qualitative field studies—often with collaborators—to investigate the information behavior of various groups of people. My study participants included librarians searching online bibliographic databases on behalf of users; engineers looking for information in various modes, including collaborative information retrieval; high school students searching the web to complete homework assignments; and sanitation workers using mobile technology in the field. Most of these studies contributed new insights and generated requirements for the design of information systems that could support the work of these groups. The various alternatives and options that I have considered and the conclusions I have drawn from this research experience have increased my confidence in the value of the ecological approach. I recognized that this approach is valuable not only to the study of human information behavior but also to the study of human information interaction in general.

The most obvious application of the ecological approach to an HIB study—and the approach that guided my research—is to grant a central role to the context in which information behavior takes place and to the way it shapes behavior. This view is rare in mainstream HIB research. While studies of the information behavior of specific groups of people in distinct contexts have become common since the late 1990s, they have almost never systematically investigated the contexts themselves and have seldom uncovered relationships between behavior and context.

This book is a critical analysis of HIB research from an ecological perspective with the goal of demonstrating how cognitive work analysis can increase the contribution of HIB studies to practice, and in particular, to the design of information systems.

My Philosophical Stance

My research has also been shaped by a philosophical stance. All researchers, whether working in the humanities, the natural sciences, or social sciences, have a philosophical stance, whether or not they recognize it. Even declaring a commitment to be objective, free of any philosophical approach, is a stance. My own approach is influenced primarily by Marxism and feminism, which have affected both my daily and professional life and activities. My research work is guided by dialectical materialism which I apply through systems thinking. In the context of my research, and in very general terms, dialectical materialism means to me:

• Material conditions and the economic system shape human lives on social, cultural, political, and individual levels. These lives also interact with the material conditions and the economic system, and even have an effect on them. But we cannot significantly improve human lives without changing the material conditions and the economic system that shaped them. Thus, an understanding of any aspect of human life requires an understanding of the material, social, cultural, and political conditions that shape it. An implication for the HII area might be, for instance, the understanding that we live in a profit-based system. Therefore, even when the changes that researchers make could meaningfully improve the quality of human interaction, their suggested improvements will not be implemented for general use unless there is a monetary profit to be made. As a result, research in the design of information systems is most often shaped by the opportunities that the market makes available for their implementation.

• The world is an integral whole in which elements are interdependent, rather than a collection of elements isolated from each other.

• The world is dynamic and in a constant state of change, and at the same time, has regularities that can be uncovered and identified.

• The dialectical approach explains that phenomena and artifacts are dialectical in nature: they include both an essential attribute and its opposite, such that one cannot exist without the other.[1] Development and forward movement in the world are achieved through dialectical processes in which a pair of dialectical opposites—thesis and antithesis—conflict with each other and lead to the emergence of a new attribute—synthesis. An example of a dialectical process is the development of research methods in the social sciences. The quantitative method (the thesis) was the first to be employed and was called the "scientific method." In reaction to the limitations of the quantitative method, researchers created its opposite: the qualitative method (the antithesis). The contradiction between the approaches has generated many methodological discussions in which proponents of one approach pointed to the weaknesses of the other and to the advantages of their approach. From these fierce discussions emerged a new approach—the mixed-methods approach (the synthesis)—which integrates methods from both approaches into one study, one supporting the other.

• Development is a process in which accumulations of small and sometimes undetectable quantitative changes bring about major, qualitative changes that take place suddenly and rapidly. For example, the incremental and steady increase in the possibilities for storing, managing, and analyzing large amounts of information rapidly brought about qualitative change in scientific research, medicine, economic analysis, police work, and, not the least, information retrieval.

I am also a feminist. In the context of my research work, feminism involves recognizing the relationship between gender roles and research agendas and approaches. For example, HIB, a field primarily populated by women researchers, is mostly conducted with the aim of helping and nurturing people, and with almost no consideration of the technology that can support it. HIB research is hardly known outside HIB circles, its approaches are frequently regarded as unscientific, and it attracts very little funding. On the other hand, the majority of researchers who focus on the design of computer-based technology to support HII are men.[2] They believe their systems satisfy human needs, but for the most part, researchers aim at constructing "cool" systems and have ignored "soft" research to uncover and understand these needs. Their research is highly appreciated by other scientists and by society, and is highly appealing to funding agencies. These relationships are not absolute: some HIB researchers do consider technology in their research, and some systems researchers see the importance of human research. In fact, these nonstandard trends are slowly strengthening, but they are still the exception. Moreover, gender is not the reason for this gap. Since women and men have equal intellectual abilities, the reason is found in the gender *roles* assigned by a society and its culture—roles that are shaped by the economic system in place.

Given my philosophical stance, I see two basic components that have helped me orient my work within the theoretical traditions in HII research: holism and realism.

The holistic view guides me to study a phenomenon along with the conditions that were necessary to create and sustain it. If the goal of research is to improve the quality of human lives, we need to understand the whole and its parts—without this, we cannot affect real change. Therefore, I find any philosophical stance that is reductionist, e.g., positivism, incompatible with my approach.

As a realist, I think that there is a reality that is independent of us—our perception of it and our relationship with it—and that it is knowable. In contrast, nonrealist approaches maintain that our perception of reality *is* reality. These include various traditions that were developed in light of the linguistic turn based on the assertion that different languages define different realities and that different cultures *are* different realities. Examples of such traditions are symbolic interactionism, constructionism, constructivism, and phenomenology, which, along with pragmatism, are nonrealist. Nonrealist traditions are not compatible with my stance.

While my position within the philosophical terrain is clear to me, I do not perceive it to be an exclusive one and recognize that in specific situations, parts of other traditions can be useful.

The Book and Its Intended Audience

Regardless of their philosophical stance, most HII researchers are motivated by a wish to improve the interaction between humans and information, whether by designing systems that could support it, or by advancing a certain aspect of the process, or by developing theories that can guide such advancements and design. The purpose of this book is to offer current and future researchers an effective approach that is not common in existing HII research. With this ecological approach, researchers will be able to increase the diversity of their analytical tools, which, in turn, will provide them an additional, alternative perspective for the design of research projects. The book is written for everyone interested in the study of human information interaction. I have done my best to avoid technical and professional jargon, and to explain such terms if their use was necessary. I have made no effort to cover the HIB literature comprehensively because such coverage is available in other books (e.g., Case 2007), and as a result, the list of references is selective.

The book's content is structured as a series of discussions on several topics that are relevant to both HIB research and systems design. These discussions lead to the presentation of cognitive work analysis, which is a context-based approach to the design of information systems—a design that is founded on an in-depth understanding of information behavior and its relationship with its context. The chapters are interconnected and presented in a useful order. Each chapter, however, is independent of the others and can be understood on its own.

The book is both descriptive and analytic. It can serve as an HIB textbook, as an introduction to an ecological approach in HII for students and researchers from various related fields, and as a window for design researchers to view the state of research in information behavior and its potential benefit to their work. I hope the book will serve as a springboard for new discussions in HIB and in other areas to which it is relevant.

Acknowledgments

The book is dedicated to Annelise Mark Pejtersen, who introduced me to cognitive work analysis and became a mentor, a friend, and a fellow traveler throughout my research journey. My friend and colleague Irene Travis contributed greatly to the book through her meticulous editing of drafts and highly constructive and useful comments. My collaborations with researchers from other fields—among them Susan Dumais, Jonathan Grudin, Steve Poltrock, and Jochen Scholl—have opened new intellectual and methodological doors to me. I have received much encouragement and stimulation through conversations with many of my friends and colleagues, among them Harry Bruce, Allyson Carlyle, Michael Crandall, Efthimis Efthimiadis, Hur-Li Lee, Jens-Erik Mai, Gary Marchionini, Cheryl Metoyer, Dagobert Soergel, and Tamara A. Turner. Special thanks go to Paula Woolley who copyedited the manuscript, and to my family—Yair, Racheli, Tal, and Netta—for their cheerful companionship throughout the book project.

Finally, many thanks to the doctoral students who have worked with me, particularly Kari Holland, Patricia Katopol, Liu Shuhua, and Kris Unsworth. Our conversations as well as their papers, dissertation proposals, and dissertations have provided an invaluable source of inspiration and a steady source of the latest in the scholarly literature.

I Introduction to Human Information Interaction

We interact with information during every waking moment and even in our dreams. The instant we open our eyes in the morning we see the furniture in the room and the pictures on its walls, we see whether the sun is shining and smell—or don't smell—the coffee. In fact, whenever we use any of our senses, we interact with information. The ubiquity of information demonstrates the important role it plays in our lives, which in turn underlines the need to understand human information interaction. Human information interaction is just beginning to emerge as an independent research area. It is helpful, therefore, to investigate its nature and structure.

Since information is ubiquitous, investigating how people interact with it requires the participation of all current and future disciplines and research fields. An all-encompassing study would consider the cognitive, physical, neurological, social, emotional, and economic aspects of the interaction, among others. Therefore, a comprehensive study of human information interaction is unattainable. This challenge, however, has not prevented human information interaction (HII) from developing into an active and dynamic research area.

HII is inherently a multidisciplinary field because it is problem-based. The idea of looking at HII as an object of study began to crystallize with the recognition of the problem of the "information explosion" and with the fast development of computer-based systems that were designed to help solve the problem. That is, HII is characterized by the problem it was created to investigate, unlike established disciplines that might be defined by a set of theories, methodologies, academic departments, or established academic journals. All problem-based fields are in the intersection of various disciplines—and thus inherently multidisciplinary—since real-life phenomena do not emerge within disciplinary boundaries. Thus, each discipline brings its own set of views to the HII research table. To add to the complexity typical of a multidisciplinary research, some basic concepts in HII have multiple definitions. The lack of agreed-upon, universal definitions presents challenges to collaborations among scholars from different disciplines, which are essential to multidisciplinary research. At the same time, real-life phenomena continue to exist, and each area that is a partner in the HII field employs its own analytical tools to address them with a few instances of collaboration and cross-fertilization.

From among the fields that have accepted HII as one of their areas, information science has been the most active,[1] with an extensive body of research in the area of human information behavior (HIB). Since I have been conducting HIB research for three decades, my view of HII is grounded in HIB; it is also based on the assumption that to design effective systems to support interaction with information requires an in-depth understanding of this interaction. Therefore, my interest in HII is motivated by my wish to contribute to the design of information systems, whether computer-based, sociotechnical, or purely human. This book analyzes research in HIB with a focus on its contribution to systems design, using the conceptual framework of *cognitive work analysis*. This framework is an ecological approach to the analysis of cognitive work that has been proven effective in transferring an in-depth understanding of information behavior and its environment into design requirements. Moreover, cognitive work analysis is relevant to human information behavior in general and therefore has the potential to be of interest to HII researchers in other fields.

The first part of the book briefly investigates the various manifestations of HII as a research area and opens with definitions and explanations of basic concepts.

1 Basic Concepts

Since human information interaction (HII) is a multidisciplinary field, it is not surprising that its basic concepts have various definitions and interpretations, with researchers giving these concepts the meanings common in their discipline. Yet the state of affairs is even more complex because researchers in the same discipline may differ in their construal of basic concepts.[1] It is useful, therefore, for researchers to explicitly state their personal interpretations of such concepts to avoid misunderstanding and confusion among their audience.

This chapter presents my understanding of some basic concepts relevant to this book. I first attend to concepts in HII and then to those in the systems approach that has provided analytical tools for this book and guided my research work.

1.1 Basic Concepts—Definitions

Scholars in the same area often put forward a variety of definitions for a single basic concept in HII. Thus, the definitions of basic concepts in HII have been a topic of discussion among scholars and will probably remain unresolved for the foreseeable future. Misunderstandings commonly occur in discussions among colleagues when participants do not clarify the meaning they attribute to basic concepts. To prevent confusion, I first present my interpretation of the basic concepts in the book's title: *human*, *information*, and the *ecological approach*.[2]

1.1.1 Human

In the context of HII, humans are people who interact with information. How to name such people has lately turned into a topic for discussion (e.g., Dervin 2006). In the context of information systems, people who interact with information through a system have been called *patrons* (in libraries), *clients* (in the corporate context), and *users* (in the information science and human-computer interaction fields). All these terms include only those who actually use a system and ignore potential users who may also benefit from using it. Because these terms are centered on a system and its patrons, clients, or users, they are useful when one investigates a certain system but are not accurate when one studies HII on a general level without focusing on a specific system. These terms are not useful for most HII studies, which aim at uncovering general, system-independent patterns even though they frequently examine people using a specific system—and at times even a system that was designed especially for the study.

Another term to signify the human participants in the interaction is *actor*. This term is the one used in this book.[3] The term *actor* has various advantages:

• It centers on the *participant* rather than on the *system*, as actors have an existence independent of information systems.

• It places interaction with information as part of a person's activities, rather than as an isolated process.

• It creates no division between actual users of a system and nonusers, and thus concentrates on the investigation of all participants who interact with information and may benefit from an information system. This approach is particularly important in cases where nonusers avoid the system because it does not fit their needs. Moreover, to identify such cases requires a study of users and nonusers as well, that is, a study of actors.

One important distinction from the term *people*, which is used in general studies, free of a specific system, is that the word *actor* emphasizes the *activities* aspect of humans when they interact with information. This emphasis highlights the view that HII takes place in a context of activities—a view that agrees with the ecological approach.

1.1.1.1 Community of Actors

A *community of actors* is a group of actors who operate in a certain type of environment, carrying out the same type of tasks.[4] Scholars have used other terms to represent this concept, such as *user group* and *users within context*, but these terms represent concepts that are broader than *community of actors*. The term *user group* has been employed intuitively without a specific definition. As such, it may bind all actors within a specific environment regardless of their tasks, or all actors conducting the same task regardless of the environment. It can also designate all users of a certain system. The term *users within context* refers to actors within a certain environment but by itself does not identify a task.[5]

Communities of actors are of various sizes. Students with no searching experience in an underfunded, inner-city high school searching the web to complete homework assignments for a course in which they have no interest and with the support and encouragement of both teacher and librarian are an example of a relatively small community of actors. Patrons of public libraries in a certain geographic region who are looking for "a good book to read" constitute a larger community, and North American customers of e-commerce interested in buying toys create an even larger one. It is relatively easy to see that the students and the library patrons define communities of actors. Their tasks are clearly identified and elements of the environment are explicitly delineated.

Considering the customers of the online toy stores as a community of actors is less clear. While it is obvious that they share a task—buying toys to be played with—their common environment is not that obvious.[6] An analysis of their environment, however, points to the various elements in it that they share, such as the economic system (e.g., buyer-seller relations, method of purchasing); the consumer-related tradition and culture of North America; methods of merchandise delivery; and a shortage of the latest fashionable toy.

The environment is an essential contributor to the definition of a community of actors, regardless of how specific the task is. Consider a search system for the retrieval of birth certificates, for instance, and its users. While the retrieval task is highly specific, the system users do not define a community. Even though they all search for birth certificates, they do not necessarily share an environment or a task for which information is required. Some are citizens looking for information about their family, others may be historians who look for evidence to support their claims, and yet others are designers who look for examples of old birth certificates to find old-fashioned elements in ornamental designs.

Positioning the environment at the center of the analysis is the basis for the ecological approach.

1.1.2 Information

When we say that whenever we use our senses we interact with information, we imply that anything that is felt by one of the five senses is information. Thus, patting a cat, smelling a rose, and searching the web are all examples of interaction with information. This construal of the concept *information* is highly inclusive and might therefore be attractive to scholars who are interested in metadisciplinary, abstract research. Such an understanding of the concept, however, is not likely to be useful for research that aims at producing implications for real-life practice because the information each sense supplies has its unique attributes. Information acquired by smell, for instance, is essentially different from that acquired by sight, if only because it cannot be articulated accurately. At the same time, principles for the design of systems that support interaction with information that cannot be articulated are different from those for information that can be expressed. Thus, studying human information interaction with the aim of improving it requires a well-bounded definition of the concept.

The concept *information* has been a source for many theoretical discussions.[7] Both the context in which it is used and the philosophical stance of the scholar who defines it shape the concept's construal. Vickery (1997, 459), for instance, explained that the meaning of the term when a person acquires information from the environment (a cognitive process) is different from its meaning when information is communicated from one person to another (a communicative process). It is reasonable, then, to accept *information* as a concept with various types, where each type caters to a certain context. My type of *information* stems from my interest in the design of information systems that improve HII. Therefore, I view information "as thing" (Buckland 1991).[8]

Information is a string of symbols that

1. has meaning,
2. is communicated,
3. has an effect, and
4. is used for decision making.

An *information system* is any system that supports human information interaction.

For a string of symbols to become information, it needs to have some meaning but not necessarily a single meaning, as people may ascribe various meanings to it.[9] The requirement for meaning indicates that, in addition to the generator of the symbols, there must be at least one other person who sees meaning in the symbols. Thus, *meaning* is construed in a communal sense rather than in an individual one. Considering the concept in an individual sense would present claims such as "person A finds meaning in the string of symbols X, and therefore it is information to him, while person B is clueless and the string is not information to her." That is, under my definition, a string of symbols has semantic value independent of whether or not a certain person recognizes that it has meaning.

Requiring that it be communicated indicates the transfer of the string from a source but does not imply intentionality, as a string of symbols may be communicated unbeknownst to the communicator. Neither does it imply that the string is received. The effect of a string of symbols is necessary for the definition of *information*—for it to inform the person who receives it. It can be a minimal effect, such as just knowing that the information exists even if it is redundant, or it may generate action. While it is challenging to point to a situation in which a string of symbols has a meaning and is communicated but does not affect the receiver of the string, explicitly stating that information has the potential to affect people highlights a focus on the relations between humans and information.

It is likely that many scholars in human information behavior (HIB) would be willing to include these three requirements on the concept *information* in their understanding of the concept. The requirement that information is for decision making, on the other hand, is not common, and it carries various implications. The concept *decision making* and the nature of the process itself have been the subject of much research and theorizing. An HIB researcher may consider this word too restrictive because it connotes work life, eliminating nonwork activities from consideration. My understanding of *decision making* is a broad one, however: A decision-making process is required when a person wants to move from state A to state B without knowing intuitively and immediately how to go about it.

In this definition, state A and state B can be any type of state: emotional, rational, physical, social, political, etc. Thus, a decision can be made, for instance, about how to do something, how to become happier, more informed, agile, popular, or powerful. This view of *information* places it in a secondary role in human life: People interact with information to support their decision making. This means that when actors interact with information, they had to stop the process of decision making or problem solving,[10] and then resume it once they feel they can continue the process. In other words, interacting with information is a way to overcome an obstacle in solving a problem. The requirement that interaction with information serves decision making also implies that it is not an end in itself. That is, the process of interaction is not a pastime activity, nor is it inherently carried out to achieve some kind of satisfaction.

HIB scholars who consider "information is for decision making" to be a limiting requirement are likely to disagree also with the view that information interaction interrupts another process and that it is not necessarily enjoyable. This requirement, however, is central to my definition of *information* and has shaped many of the ideas put forward in this book.

1.1.3   The Ecological Approach

Research in HIB is heavily influenced by a cognitive approach, which focuses on the cognitive processes during HII while ignoring the context in which these processes take place. Even when HIB scholars investigate information behavior in context they study the cognitive aspects of the behavior but not the attributes of the context.

The ecological approach takes a different stance. On a general level, the term *ecology* designates the study of the interactions between organisms and their environment. Focusing on humans, *ecology* is the study of the interactions between humans and their environment. Vicente (1999) explained that an *ecological approach* "starts with, and gives priority to, environment constraints" (6), which is different from the *cognitivist approach* "that starts with, and gives priority to, cognitive constraints" (5). The ecological approach does not ignore cognitive constraints but begins the investigation with a study of environmental constraints. In the context of HII, the ecological approach focuses on a community of actors, rather than on individuals or on all humans.

In an ecological design of an information system, the designer creates a virtual ecology that maps the interactions between humans and their environment onto the system.[11] The system is designed in such a way that actors readily understand what actions the system affords. One of the objectives of ecological design is to ensure that actors' "understanding [of the environment] corresponds, as closely as possible, to the actual behavior of the context with which they interact" (Vicente 1999, 55). Cognitive work analysis—the approach that is explained and advocated in this book—is an ecological approach that supports ecological design; it has originated from, and is based on, the systems approach.

1.2   The Systems Approach—A Few Basic Concepts

To account for the multidisciplinary nature of HII, my methodological and analytical work has been inspired by the systems approach, which is cross-disciplinary.[12]

The systems approach is built on the maxim that to understand and to develop insight into a phenomenon, it is useful to consider it as a system. While the concept *system* has various interpretations, Bánáthy (1997) explained that "In the most general sense, system means a configuration of parts connected and joined together by a web of relationships." Various categories of elements may form systems such as biological, electrical, social, physical, economic, or political systems. The systems approach has been utilized in a variety of disciplines, and it includes a range of schools of thought, specializations, and interpretations. Yet common to all is a holistic view of the studied phenomenon—a view that is in contrast with the reductionist view, which investigates elements in isolation. That is, systems thinkers study a system rather than an individual.[13] In addition, the systems approach is centered on the belief that every phenomenon can be viewed as a system—one with patterns and properties that can be understood.[14]

Although evidence of systems thinking has been found in ancient scholarship, the modern systems approach began to take root among scholars in the early1950s, after a few of its strands (e.g., operations research, cybernetics) were developed for military purposes during the Second World War. The first to systematically develop the principles of this approach was the biologist Ludwig von Bertalanffy, who began presenting his blueprints for the general theory of systems in the late 1930s and later published *General System Theory: Foundations, Development, Applications* (Bertalanffy 1968). One of his goals was to create one theory that would be applicable to all sciences—including the social sciences—and thus would unify them.

Many scholars have contributed to this area, among them leaders such as Kenneth E. Boulding, William Ross Ashby, Margaret Mead, Gregory Bateson, Béla H. Bánáthy, C. West Churchman, Russell L. Ackoff, Peter Checkland, and Jay Wright Forrester. It is beyond the scope of this section to offer an introduction to the systems approach; rather its purpose is to introduce a few basic concepts that are relevant to discussions in this book. Like any other person who applies systems thinking, I chose a certain interpretation to be most useful to my work. This interpretation was influenced primarily by the works of C. West Churchman (1971, 1979a, 1979b). One central principle in this view is that one studies systems to improve them; that is, to improve their ability to work effectively toward their goals.

1.2.1 What Is a System?

The definition of a system given above—"a configuration of parts connected and joined together by a web of relationships" (Bánáthy 1997)—captures the essence of the concept. However, it is not specific enough to define a specific system. To be able to observe a set of elements and determine if it is a system, or a part of a system, a more formal definition is required. Inspired by Churchman, I adapted the explanation that one can define a system under these conditions:

1. *One specifies a set of identifiable elements.*   The elements can be concrete or abstract, tangible or intangible, real or imaginary. In an academic department, for instance, one can designate curriculum, policies, classrooms, and administrative services as

identifiable elements, but the department's culture can be considered an element only if it is defined in a way that affords identification.

2. *One specifies identifiable relations among at least some of the elements.* For instance, administrative services are *governed* by policies.

3. *The elements specified are coordinated to accomplish a set of goals.* For example, policies govern administrative services to provide timely and effective support for students and faculty members.

Among the different types of systems it is useful to distinguish between *open* and *closed* systems, and between *teleological* and *emergent* systems:

• An open system continually interacts with its environment, and a closed one is isolated from it—that is, it has no environment.

• Elements in a teleological (purposeful) system interact with one another and the environment to achieve a set of goals, while in an emergent system the interactions create a new and emergent quality that affects the whole system.

In the context of HII, I see the systems we study as *open* and *teleological*. They are open because an information system, by any definition, interacts with its environment. They are teleological because information systems are designed with a goal of supporting certain activities, and because HII is always carried out for a purpose, be it fun, killing time, or retrieving useful information.[15] In addition, when technology takes part in HII activities, these systems are *sociotechnical* systems, that is, "system[s] composed of technical, psychological, and social elements" (Vicente 1999, 9).

In everyday language the term *system* is used much more freely and loosely than in the systems-approach vocabulary. The *weather system*, for instance, is not a "qualified" system in the teleological sense because it has no purpose. The U.S. *movie-rating system* (G, PG, PG-13, R, NC-17) is even less of a system because there are no interactions among its elements.

But even systems that can be defined with the three requirements above present challenges for their definition. Consider a computer lab in an academic unit, for example, as a system. The furniture, computers, the cable that connects to the Internet, the large screen, and the white board on the wall are some of its elements. "Computers *rest* on tables" and "computers *are connected to the Internet* with a cable" are examples of relationships among some of the elements. The main goal of the lab is to function well (probably according to some criteria).

A person may claim, however, that, for her, a computer lab is grounded in the reason for establishing one: to support an academic program. In this case, the elements of the lab are the support the computers afford to functions such as searching the Internet or carrying out statistical analyses, and those that the physical space facilitates such as collaborative work and interaction among students. The goal of the computer lab is then to satisfy effectively students' academic needs. Another view may include elements from both definitions to create yet another system. This situation raises the question: Which one is the "real" computer lab system?

The answer is: all and none. There is no "real" system. Systems are abstract, analytical constructs created by the investigator who wishes to study a real-life phenomenon. If the computer lab is analyzed to understand its physical functioning, the first system defined above is "the computer lab as a system." Similarly, if one wishes to analyze the contribution of the lab to the academic program, the second one is "the system." That is, systems do not exist in the real world; they are defined and created by researchers to advance their investigations.[16] A phenomenon can be defined as a system in various ways, some more useful to the purpose of an investigation than others. That is, one delineates the boundary of a system according to the purpose of the investigation for which it is constructed. The goals of the system itself determine which elements meet the criteria required to be included inside a system's boundary and which ones are eligible to be in the system's environment.[17]

1.2.1.1 *Functional Elements*

When defining an organization—whether formal or informal—as a system, it is reasonable and intuitive to identify its elements according to the organizational structure. An academic unit, for example, would include elements such as students, staff, faculty, and administrators. Similarly, a family might be composed of a mother, a father, and children. While it is essential to understand an organization's structure, elements in a teleological system are *functional* rather than *structural*. After all, the elements in a system are *acting* jointly to achieve the system's goals. A structure may be designed to support the activities that may lead to achieve a system's goal, but by itself it cannot bring goal attainment.

As an example, consider a family as a system with the goal of providing a safe and nourishing home for its members. In this case, *mother* would be a structural element. But the element *mother* includes parts that should not be in the system because they do not contribute to achieving the system's goal even when they interact with other elements—such as her learning style, the size of her shoes, and the score she received in her first math examination. The elements that can contribute to the creation of a safe and nourishing home are those that make it such a place. These are the activities in which the family members are engaged, such as conversing with other family members, participating in the children's life events, celebrating holidays, and cooking. These activities do not correspond to the structure of a family, as either the father or the mother can participate in them. Moreover, creating such a home does not necessarily require a "mother," for instance, as in single-parent families. But it would be almost impossible to have a nourishing home without conversations among family members and participation in the children's life events.

1.2.2 A System's Boundary: Its Environment and Constraints

To determine if an element is in the system under study, one examines whether the element's relations with some other system's elements are coordinated toward accomplishing the system's goals. Therefore, to identify the elements of a system, one has to first identify clearly the system's set of goals.

While elements that have no relations with any of the system's elements are clearly outside the system, not all those that have such relations are in the system. Since the investigator delineates the boundary of a system according to the investigation's goals (not those of the system), she may decide to place some elements outside the system she is constructing. Consider an instructor who wishes to investigate how he can use the computer lab to enhance the learning experience in his classes. Some elements in his system might be the software that is relevant to the class experience, the students' interaction with computers and the software, the policies guiding lab use, and the instruction students receive. Should he also include elements of the physical setting, such as the tables, the computers, and the Internet connection? That depends on his specific goals. He may decide, for example, that even though the lab computers interact with the software he may want to use, he will not include the actual physical setting in the system he defines because he is not interested in providing recommendations for physical changes, which might require resources that are not at his disposal. After all, the purpose of the investigation is to improve the system, and since improving the physical setting is not part of his goal set, there is no need to include the setting's elements in the system. That is, the faculty member considers the physical setting as a given that is fixed: It cannot be altered. This decision limits the range of improvements he will be able to recommend.

Elements that interact with a system's elements and are relevant to the system's goal set, but are outside the system—that is, the investigator considers them fixed or given—are called *constraints*. Being fixed and given, while at the same time interacting with the system's other elements, constraints restrict or limit possibilities with relation to the system's set of goals. While many elements that are outside a system do not relate to the system at all (e.g., the faculty club is outside the computer lab system), the constraints determine in part how the system performs. The set of a system's constraints creates the system's *environment*. From his holistic perspective, a systems thinker studies the environment of the system in question because elements in the environment shape the system processes. An example may point to the important role of the environment. Suppose the instructor who wants to improve the computer lab experience for students decides to place the physical setting outside the system and thus in the environment. He still needs to understand this setting in order to consider relevant software and the implementation of policies and to analyze student interaction with the lab computers. Similarly, the students' previous experience with computers cannot be part of the system because it cannot be improved (obviously, only current experience can be improved). Previous experience is a constraint, however, because it affects the students' actions when they interact with the computers in the lab and thus needs to be considered and understood when planning improved instruction.

1.2.2.1 A Note about Constraints

Constraints have a bad reputation because they limit our possibilities. In a society with a strong belief that everything is possible, a constraint can be viewed only in a negative way. Yet the fact is that constraints are essential to our lives; we would not be able to function without them. They are the given parameters within which we operate, and as such they are actually enablers of action. Without the constraint of gravity, for instance, we could not walk or dance and our bodies could not perform their functions. Imagine a workplace with no fixed mode of operation, where individuals can carry out any task that comes to their minds at any moment, and decisions that people make are free from the requirements of the tasks they perform. Obviously, such a place would not be functional. Likewise, how can design take place without specifications (i.e., constraints), or assignments be completed satisfactorily without instructions as to what is expected (i.e., constraints)?

Constraints *limit* the possibilities but they do not necessarily *hinder* action. In fact, they *enable* action. That is, they are dialectical entities: They limit and enable action at the same time.

1.2.3 A Systems Approach to HII

Systems thinking can be helpful to scholars who agree with three basic claims:

• *The purpose of HII research is to improve the interaction.* HII is a problem-based field and, thus, addressing HII problems is the reason for its existence. While theories and other conceptual constructs are necessary for the establishment of HII as a scholarly field and for the development of its practice, the final goal of these constructs is a contribution to addressing HII problems. Therefore, research projects that cannot point to the contribution they offer to research and practice in HII are not likely to affect the development of HII.

• *A holistic approach is required to understand HII.* HII is a complex process that is shaped by multiple elements, and some are bound to be regarded as constraints. Therefore, to understand the interaction process and the conditions that shaped it entails an investigation of both a system and its environment—that is, following a holistic approach. Isolating the process from its environment would lead to a partial understanding of it, which usually causes misunderstanding and possibly misleading conclusions.

• *An information system has goals.* An information system is the outcome of a design process, rather than the result of a random emergence. Every product is designed to serve a purpose, whether it is to organize one's personal files or to provide data for the Genome Project, and information systems are no exception. That is, information systems are teleological.

On the surface, the systems approach seems simple and straightforward: One defines a phenomenon as a system and takes it from there. Despite its simple appearance, the approach provides a solid basis for rich and complex investigations. Employing the systems approach continually, one gradually recognizes the great analytical power it provides for any investigation.

1.2.4 Context-Specific and General-Context Information Systems

A context-specific information system is designed for a particular community of actors. Designers who develop a system with no particular community in mind build a general-context information system. In other words, context-specific systems are customized, or tailored, to a specific community, while general-context ones are designed for all to use.[18] A search engine (and its interface) that is designed to support the high school students mentioned in section 1.1.1.1, as well as the one for a North American online toy store, are context-specific systems. A system to retrieve birth certificates, as well as many of the publicly available web search engines, is a general-context system.

A single context-specific system can be designed for a range of specific tasks. A system for the high school students, for example, may include two components, one for retrieving information for homework assignments and another to support teacher-student communication about the assignments. Moreover, a single such system may be designed to support more than one well-defined community—possibly through a modular structure—as is the case of an information system that is designed for high school students, their teachers, and the administrative staff. In the same vein, a general-context system can be designed for one specific task, as the birth certificates system demonstrates.

The design of a context-specific information system may rely on the use of general-context systems. Instead of creating a new system for a specific community, a designer may decide to create a system that is an assembly of several existing general-context systems modified and coordinated to satisfy the community's requirements.[19] While each general-context system is a system on its own, its assembly creates a new system in which it is a subsystem. A common example is the inclusion of a search engine in systems that support several specific functions such as shopping in addition to information retrieval, some of which may directly relate to retrieval. In addition, designers of general-context systems may create systems that can be easily modified and adjusted to the requirements of specific communities.

The distinction between context-specific and general-context information systems is fundamental to the discussions in this book because the book focuses on systems that require an ecological approach for their design (context-specific systems) and their relationship to those that are designed with other approaches (general-context systems).

1.3 Basic Concepts: Conclusions

Each scholar is guided by a certain interpretation of basic concepts in her field, tacitly or explicitly. Because of the variety in the meanings of basic concepts, it is important for a researcher to first explicitly recognize her reading of the concepts and then convey it to her audience. This clarity avoids misunderstanding and confusion. In this chapter I have provided my interpretation of some basic concepts in HII and in the systems approach in order to support a clear and straightforward understanding of the discussions in this book.

2 What Is Human Information Interaction?

Researchers in human information interaction investigate the interaction between people and information with its multiple forms and purposes. That is, they focus on the relationships between people and *information*, rather than on those between people and *technology* (as in human-computer interaction) or between people and the information *agency* (as in librarianship). As a research area, HII is of interest to scholars from various research traditions and disciplines, but it is still in its formative years, awaiting an initial consensus about its nature and attributes (e.g., W. Jones et al. 2006).

Human information interaction (HII) is inherently a multidisciplinary area, and the boundaries among the accounts of HII in various fields are usually fuzzy. Some examples illustrate the many contributors to HII.

The field of human-computer interaction (HCI) is an example of a relatively new field that is part of the HII area. It focuses on users of computers with the aim of defining principles and ways to present information that facilitate effective human information interaction. Computer interface is, therefore, the central object of study. HCI researchers develop models and theories of interaction, as well as methodologies and processes for designing interfaces and for implementing and evaluating them. In their work they rely on both technological developments and human sciences, such as psychology, physiology, organizational sciences, sociology, anthropology, and industrial design. The degree to which HCI researchers actually investigate HII varies. At the same time, the boundaries of HCI are elastic and constantly expanding.

Two other fields address HII with a focus on the machines used to support it: computer-supported cooperative work (CSCW) and human factors. Both fields concentrate on tools used at work, and both overlap with HCI.

Researchers in CSCW investigate how collaborative activities and their coordination can be supported by computer systems. Those with expertise in areas such as social psychology, sociology, and computer science study the ways people work in groups

to gain the understanding required for the design of technology to support cooperative work. While information is not a central concept in CSCW, it is central to collaborative work, which may require activities such as information sharing, collaborative
information retrieval, and negotiations about information interpretation. That is,
when HII is addressed in CSCW, it is investigated in the context of collaborative and
cooperative work.

Human factors, which covers a variety of issues, involves the study of all aspects
of the way humans relate to the world around them, with the aim of improving
operational performance and safety. Human factors, which is at times used synony-
mously with *ergonomics*, studies the human aspects of all designed devices. It does not
investigate the mechanisms of these devices—a study area which is in the realm of
human factors engineering. Developed primarily by psychologists and physiologists,
human factors studies have addressed problems faced by humans operating equipment, focusing on the cognitive and sensory-motor aspects. With the introduction of
computers, human factors studied the use of computerized systems. When a human
factors researcher studies an "information system," she studies a system that requires
information for its operation. Control panels, such as displays in an airplane cockpit,
are a typical example: Such panels provide information about the state of a machine's
parts and the physical environment to inform an operator's decision-making processes, and thus facilitate them. That is, human factors studies address HII as it takes
place when humans get information from tools they use, information that makes it
possible for them to use the tools efficiently and safely.

HII has been investigated on a purely cognitive level as well, without concern about
the technology that facilitates it. The study of decision making, for example, analyzes
how humans make decisions. Since information is an essential ingredient in the
process, any study that investigates decision making is bound to address HII. From a
cognitive perspective, the decision-making process is regarded as a process integrated
with the interaction with information about the environment. Cognitive studies
address questions such as, How do humans process information to facilitate a decision? How does a person's bias affect the selection of information to support a decision? Neuroscientists study the physical processes of the brain when it is processing
information.

In addition to cognitive aspects, social and organizational aspects play a role in HII.
Social informatics (SI) is a relatively new field that

examines social aspects of computerization—including the roles of information technology in
social and organizational change and the ways that the social organization of information technologies are influenced by social forces and social practices. SI includes studies and other analyses

that are labeled as social impacts of computing, social analysis of computing, studies of computer-mediate[d] communication (CMC), information policy, "computers and society," organizational informatics, interpretive informatics, and so on. (Kling 2009)

While analyzing social and organizational conditions, SI uncovers the human information interaction of individuals in a particular social and organizational context. In fact, many studies in SI analyze the HII of individuals in a particular context to reveal the ways in which the social organization of information technology, on the one hand, and social forces and practices, on the other, shape one another in that context.

Another discipline that incorporates HII studies from the organizational and social perspectives is management. Management studies that address HII include, for example, analysis of the flow of information in organizations and investigations of information sharing among members of an organization and with people outside of it. Such studies can focus on the public or private sectors, and may focus on both the human and technological components of the interaction. In contrast to other fields, some areas of management research study HII that takes place in human-to-human communication. A seemingly related area is management of information systems (MIS). A branch of business administration, MIS is primarily system-centric and is concerned with the design of information systems to support managers; as such, it rarely includes investigations of HII. Knowledge management is one area that has developed within MIS and was system-centric at its inception. Today, the area covers many subjects in various disciplines. As a result, its scope cannot be defined unambiguously and might include HII.

Among the fields that include HII in their domains, library and information science (LIS) is the only one that has granted it a significant position among its areas as the field of human information behavior (HIB). HIB is an established research area in LIS that investigates HII for its own sake and with multiple perspectives. Fisher, Erdelez, and McKechnie (2005) explained that HIB established itself as a distinct area of scholarship in the late 1990s; they defined it as the study of "how people need, seek, manage, give, and use information in different contexts" (xix).

While HIB can be considered the manifestation of HII in LIS, there are some critical differences between them. Most importantly, the HII domain is dynamic and open to including both existing and emerging research topics and traditions. Every form of interaction, once discovered and investigated, joins the HII domain. As a result, HII is a multidisciplinary field, with disciplines and forms of interaction linking in diverse ways. Certain forms may draw research scholars from a particular discipline into HII because the activities that generate these forms are typically studied by this discipline. At the same time, each form can be examined through various disciplinary lenses.

In contrast, HIB associates itself with certain research traditions, and, at this time, does not claim to include other traditions, such as those of human-computer interaction, communication, information policy, or management of information systems. Another characteristic of HIB is its tendency to define itself by naming the specific forms of interaction it recognizes as members of its domain. This membership has been expanding through its development, as Fisher, Erdelez, and McKechnie (2005) found, yet certain forms that attracted active research were not invited to join. For instance, most researchers who have addressed the topic of relevance—which looks at how people evaluate information—do not consider themselves HIB researchers, and are not considered as such by the LIS community.

HII and HIB can also be distinguished by the different connotations that the terms *interaction* and *behavior* carry and by the types of their definitions. To study *behavior* is to investigate external, observable acts and to have no claims on understanding internal, unobservable processes and perceptions. Tom Wilson (1994) introduced the term "information seeking behavior" to LIS, coining the phrase "'to identify those aspects of information-related activity that *did* appear to be identifiable, observable, and, hence, researchable" (16). This understanding of the concept is not new, and neither are ideas for alternative foci in social science research. Max Weber (1947), for example, based his approach on the view "that the social sciences study *meaningful action* as opposed to behaviour—movements which are the end results of a physical or biological causal chain" (Benton and Craib 2001, 77). Moreover, if associated with behaviorism, HIB connotes a positivist approach (see chapter 8) and an attitude in which investigators are analyzing the behavior of their subjects, who happen to be humans.[1] Although much of HIB research actually investigates behavior, quite a few studies aim at deeper analyses, and some are guided by traditions that are incompatible with positivism. These alternative approaches show that there is no reason to limit the study of HII in LIS, or in any other field, to behavioral approaches. The term *interaction*, on the other hand, is neutral with regard to the nature of the theoretical tradition of the investigator, to the phenomena to be investigated, and to the relations between the investigator and the participants in a study. In addition, *interaction* reflects the dynamic nature of the relationships between people and information—a connotation that is missing from the term *behavior*.[2]

The type of the definitions for HII and HIB is different as well. Fisher, Erdelez, and McKechnie's (2005, xix) definition of HIB is an *extensional* definition: It enumerates the entities that together form the defined object ("how people need, seek, manage, give, and use information"). Tom Wilson's (1994, 16) definition, similar to the definition of HII, is *intentional*: It provides criteria for deciding whether or not an entity belongs to the defined object ("those aspects of information-related activity that … [are] researchable"). The advantage of the *extensional* definition is that it explicitly delineates the boundaries of the field. When one wants to determine if a certain phenomenon is an HIB one, one has to see if it is on the list in the definition. *Evaluating* information, for example, is outside the HIB domain according to Fisher et al.'s definition. But this enumeration is also its weakness. HIB is a fast-growing field and its boundaries are constantly expanding as researchers investigate new information-related activities. This expansion makes the definition unstable, and the 2008 definition of HIB is different from, say, the one coined in 1995. The *intentional* definition is stable, on the other hand, but it requires that the meaning of the inclusion criteria be shared by most scholars in the field. Wilson's definition challenged this requirement when he introduced "researchable" activities as a criterion. The perception of whether or not an activity is researchable varies among HIB researchers, most often according to the theoretical traditions that guide their work.

Despite these differences, HIB can be considered a distinct and substantive part of HII, with a solid tradition and active research programs.

2.1   Areas of Research in Human Information Interaction

Analyzing all research areas in HII would be a monumental task, requiring a team of scholars from a number of disciplines. Here I address HII research with a library and information science lens, focusing primarily (but not exclusively) on research carried out by LIS researchers. This view by itself touches on a number of forms of interaction, and only a few are presented and discussed here.

2.1.1   Established Research Areas

Two HII research areas have already developed a set of agreed upon definitions and have established the methodologies they employ: information-seeking behavior (ISB) and information retrieval (IR). ISB scholars study how people look for information, and those in IR build and investigate retrieval models and mechanisms for computer-based systems that retrieve information in response to user requests. ISB has been the most active research area among HII studies in LIS, and most of this book focuses on it. While dominant in HIB research, ISB represents only one form of *acquiring information*—that is, only one way in which people get information. The area of IR is concerned with the design of systems that are used when acquiring information. Its aim is to design effective and efficient systems that satisfy their users. Even though IR and HIB have been investigating the same phenomena—people acquiring information—on the whole, they have a history of mutual avoidance and failure to collaborate. To emphasize the important role that IR plays in the study of HIB, and vice versa, its description is slightly expanded here in comparison to other areas. Chapter 10 analyzes the relationship between information retrieval and HIB.

2.1.1.1 Acquiring Information

The term *acquiring information* has been used by a handful of LIS scholars but is largely missing from the basic HIB vocabulary. HIB has recognized *seeking information* as the central form of interaction that people employ to get information. Although *seeking* means "looking for information," the term is used with a broader sense to mean "getting information." This expanded meaning is confusing, however. Research to date has shown that people may look at information with no intention of getting it (*surfing*), and they may get information without looking for it (*encountering*). Each of these three forms of interaction with information—seeking, surfing, and encountering—has a distinct motivation for its employment, a unique type of interaction, and a different outcome.

Seeking Information

When people seek information, they *purposely* look for information to support actual decision-making or to resolve an information problem. Most HIB research has focused on this phenomenon. In fact, many LIS researchers have perceived the scholarly fields of information-seeking behavior and human information behavior to be one and the same.

   To bring finer distinctions to this vast area, some scholars have distinguished between *seeking* and *searching* for information. T. D. Wilson (1999), for instance, explained that *seeking* is "particularly concerned with the variety of methods people employ to discover, and gain access to information resources," while *searching* is "a sub-set of information-seeking, particularly concerned with the interactions between an information user (with or without an intermediary) and computer-based information systems, of which information retrieval systems for textual data may be seen as one type" (263). I use *seeking* and *searching* interchangeably, depending on the context in which they are addressed, because I distinguish among types of information acquisition according to their *purpose*, rather than by the methods of acquiring information or the technology used.

The largest part of this book analyzes research in *information seeking*, since it is the most active research area. The other two areas are presented very briefly below.

Surfing

When people surf, they browse through a source of information just to see what it contains, *without reference to a particular decision*. Window shopping, skimming through the morning paper, and channel surfing on television or radio are examples of surfing, along with the well-liked pastime of web surfing. People surf to find out what is in a store—or in the newspaper, the television, the radio, or the web—to be informed in a general way without expecting to find information that might help them make specific decisions.

People acquire information while surfing, but the information is unanticipated and serves no ongoing, or expected, decision-making process. When I read the newspaper, I may learn that a powerful earthquake shook Indonesia last night, and that an international film festival is about to open in Toronto. These events are news to me—I didn't anticipate them, and they support no decision I have to make. While unplanned, surfing is not a completely random act. Even though it brings unpredicted information, it is directed. One decides which sections of the newspaper to read, which web link to click next, and which store window to view.

Surfing is one type of browsing, which is different from purposeful browsing. The latter is a strategy that can be used for information-seeking,[3] that is, for making a particular decision. Thus, browsing window stores to find out if the new style of jeans is out, or reading the newspaper to find items about the state of the economy is *browsing* but not *surfing*, because its purpose is to help in making a decision—whether or not to get the new jeans, or where to invest.

What differentiates purposeful browsing from surfing is that browsing *has* a purpose. While conceptually understandable, this critical distinction between the concepts is difficult to detect in empirical studies because the reasons for browsing are in a person's mind and are sometimes very difficult to articulate. Because most of HII research is empirical, it is reasonable to ask: Is the difference between these two kinds of browsing important enough to justify the efforts to uncover the reasons for browsing? Indeed, it is possible that researchers who describe how people acquire information, or develop theories about this process, prefer to forgo this characteristic of browsing in their attempt to be as general as possible. This distinction, however, is very important in empirical research that aims to inform the design of information systems.

Systems designed to support purposeful browsing are ineffective for surfing, and vice versa. Because browsing processes, by their very nature, are not guided by a plan, they may easily get off track. This tendency might be acceptable when surfing (it has no track), but it is challenging in purposeful browsing when the searcher is looking for information to solve a problem. Systems that support purposeful browsing, therefore, could help a user center the search and find promising directions for browsing. Surfing, on the other hand, calls for a wide display of what is available, and systems that support it could help a user to broaden the search and provide a wide selection of possible items of interest.

Despite its popularity, surfing has not been recognized as a research topic in HII. Yet it has been studied outside academe for a long time by market researchers and others who have examined this behavior to help businesses to advertise their products, so potential consumers will encounter them while surfing and be encouraged to buy them. Not only are such studies proprietary, and thus inaccessible to HII researchers, they are profit-centered and as such may have very little potential to enrich the human-centered understanding of the phenomenon which motivates HII research.

The closest concept to surfing that has been investigated in HII is what Savolainen (1995) called "seeking of orienting information." He defined *orienting information* as information "concerning current events," in contrast to *practical information*, "which serves as the solution to specific problems" (Savolainen 1995, 272). The purpose in *seeking of orienting information*, Savolainen argued, is to create a passive habitual monitoring system to focus on everyday matters by asking: How are things at this moment? Thus, while they are related, *seeking of orienting information* differs from *surfing* by definition. One other recognition of surfing is its entry in the *Online Dictionary of Library and Information Science* (Reitz 2007), which explains that to *surf* is to navigate the web with no definite purpose in mind. To date, the area of surfing—that is, browsing with no specific informational purpose—remains uncharted by HII researchers and ready for exploration.

Encountering

People encounter information when they "bump into" information they were not seeking at the time—information that can solve a particular information problem that presented itself in the past or is scheduled to be solved in the future. Finding a telephone number one will need tomorrow while surfing the web, or happening upon a nice toy store when going to a new movie theater, after unsuccessfully searching for a toy shop, or finding information when reading for pleasure (Ross 1999) are examples of *encountering information*. When the term was first coined by Sanda Erdelez,[4] the phenomenon had already been recognized and expressed by several names. Today, various terms are used, such as *serendipity, casual information-gathering, passive information-seeking, incidental information acquisition,* and *accidental discovery of information.* All these phrases mean *encountering,* but they are not synonymous, as each represents a slightly different approach and has a unique flavor. To add to this richness of concepts, even the definition of the term *encountering* is still evolving (Erdelez 2005).

The study of encountering information is in a very early stage of development. Researchers are still exploring it in order to understand what this form of information interaction is and how to investigate it. Among the scholars who coined these terms, Erdelez and Kristy Williamson (1998) are the only researchers who have focused on studying this form.[5] The motivation to study *encountering* came from anecdotal evidence, but also from researchers who encountered this form of interaction when they themselves were studying something else. By now it has been established that people encounter information more frequently than has been assumed, and some of them rely on this form to find information they need.

A major challenge for empirical investigations of the process of encountering information is pinning it down for observation because encountering occurs unexpectedly. As a result, most research findings are based only on participants' self-reporting of past encounters they had experienced. Researchers are continuing to investigate the phenomenon while simultaneously improving research designs to include a larger variety of research methods.

2.1.1.2 Evaluating Information

When people have acquired information as a response to their requests, they examine it to select the information that is relevant to the problem at hand. This process of evaluation is almost always necessary when retrieving information from computer-based information systems, such as library catalogs, bibliographic databases, or the web. Such systems, while providing access to large numbers of documents and amounts of information, cannot be sensitive to specific requirements that are not expressed by a query.[6] Moreover, not all documents or information retrieved by a system match the request presented to it, and not all the documents that match a request are retrieved. *Evaluating information* focuses on the judgment about whether or not a certain document is relevant to the problem the information seeker wants to solve. The main question for researchers and designers is: When we are designing retrieval mechanisms, how can we distinguish ahead of time between relevant and nonrelevant documents? Hence, *relevance* is the central issue—and the only one—that has been studied in relation to the process of *evaluating information.*

The concept *relevance* established its place on the information science scene when researchers began to consider the performance evaluation of computer-based information systems (Gull 1956).[7] While motivated by technological developments, the study of relevance has examined human aspects as well. In the area of information retrieval (IR), which focuses on the design of such systems, relevance has been associated with the performance evaluation of information systems. Other HII research, on the other hand, focuses on the study of human processes when people determine the relevance of a document, and the elements that shape these processes.

Relevance in Information Retrieval

The concept of *relevance*—which was first recognized in the 1950s by pioneers of IR research (e.g., Moores 1950; Gull 1956)—gained a central position, and drew much research after the Cranfield studies were completed and published (Cleverdon 1962, 1967; Cleverdon, Mills, and Keen 1966).[8] In this series of studies, which began in 1953, Cyril Cleverdon—librarian at what was then the College of Aeronautics in Cranfield, England—compared the efficiency of information systems using different indexing systems. He developed the standard research design for experiments to test system performance, and established *recall* and *precision* (Kent et al. 1955) as the standard measurements for that purpose. These measurements were developed with the assumption that, ideally, the most efficient system should retrieve all the relevant documents available, and only relevant documents. Thus, to measure the performance of a system in retrieving information for a request, *recall* measures what proportion of the relevant documents in the collection is retrieved, and *precision* measures the proportion of the retrieved documents that is relevant. That is, recall measures the ability of the system to *retrieve* relevant documents, and precision calculates its ability to *reject* nonrelevant documents. The Cranfield studies have had great impact on research in IR, and both their research design and the measurements employed are still dominant in IR research today.[9]

Some researchers consider relevance to be the fundamental and central concept in information science, the one that has signaled the formation of information science as a unique field (e.g., Froehlich 1994; Saracevic 1975; Schamber, Eisenberg, and Nilan 1990). This concept, however, is complex and difficult to define.

Most research projects about relevance have addressed it in the context of system evaluation, and many of them focused on the meaning of the concept and its shades. When systems are tested in an experimental setting, it is crucial to be able to determine for each document—whether retrieved or missed—whether or not it is relevant to the test request. Without such discrimination, neither precision nor recall can be measured. Because of its complexity, "how to determine relevance" has been a thorn in experimental pursuits, but fodder for conceptual and theoretical discussions. Researchers are still finding new, and possibly better, ways to assess relevance in their experiments, and continue to propose frameworks and models for the concept's analysis and its interpretation (e.g., Järvelin and Kekäläinen 2000). Several excellent articles have comprehensively reviewed this body of research and contributed new aspects for analysis (Borlund 2003a; Mizzaro 1997; Saracevic 1975, 2007a, 2007b; Schamber 1994), and others still continue the discussion about the nature of relevance (e.g., Hjørland 2010). Most performance evaluations are carried out under experimental conditions, either in laboratory or in operational settings. In the simplest designs, researchers conducting laboratory experiments run a set of queries through a system, analyze the retrieval to discriminate relevant from nonrelevant documents (this is usually done by judges rather than by the researchers), and measure precision and recall. Some combinations of the numerical scores for both measurements determine how well the system performs, and also make it possible to compare it with other systems. The most critical challenge in such experiments has been how to deal with relevance from the user's point of view.

The challenges that experimenters have faced with relevance have been discussed extensively in the literature. While these problems were pointed out in conceptual discussions, the existence of most of them has been detected in empirical investigations. The main source for these challenges is the realization that the judgment of relevance is subjective and dynamic, is not dichotomous, and has a specific target.

Relevance judgment is subjective. Studies to evaluate performance have been required to provide "objective" results. To achieve this goal, the relevance of each retrieved document needs to be determined "objectively." However, very early experiments quickly discovered that the discrimination between relevant and nonrelevant documents was not consistent among relevance judges (e.g., Gull 1956). This finding was not surprising since relevance judgment requires a human decision on what a document is about—and this decision may vary from one person to another. Clearly, participants cannot be controlled so they will all think alike during an experiment, and it is impossible to obtain "objective" relevance judgments. Recognizing that fact, IR researchers experimented with various ways to arrive as closely as possible to "objective" relevance judgments and to reduce inconsistencies among judges, but at the same time, continued to rely on subjective and inconsistent judgments.

Some IR researchers have asked: Does the inconsistency among judges affect the results of an evaluation? In other words, does it matter (Saracevic 2007b)? A couple of tests have indicated that the effect is not significant when comparing information systems or when ranking them by the level of their performance (e.g., Lesk and Salton 1968; Voorhees and Harman 2005). Because much of IR research today focuses on comparisons and rankings, it is possible that the subjective nature of relevance is not a challenge after all.

Relevance judgment is dynamic.   Even if additional studies would establish that subjectivity in judgment does not affect the measurement of performance, IR researchers still face the problem that relevance judgment is dynamic. Evaluation is a cognitive process; therefore, the argument goes, any new information, or even thinking, can change the view a person has on the information problem at hand, and the view of what is relevant as a consequence. This dynamism is especially critical when testing interactive systems, in which users can reformulate their queries. At what stage of the interaction should the relevance judgment be made? One answer is: It depends on the experimental design and the system evaluated, whether experimental or operational. An experimenter, for instance, may ask the judges to determine relevance at the end of each step of the interaction, and such judgments may at times guide the next iteration (e.g., studies of relevance feedback).[10] Another experimenter may ask the judges to limit their examination of documents to the final set.

Levels of relevance   Gull's (1956) experiment also discovered that the distinction between relevant and nonrelevant cannot always be determined accurately. He critically observed that past experiments "acted upon the assumption that there exists for each question a relatively well defined area of pertinent information and that the boundary between a high plateau of pertinancy and the surrounding lowland of irrelevant references can be located with considerable accuracy from the wording of the request" (326). If a clear distinction between relevant and nonrelevant documents cannot be made, how can researchers measure precision and recall, which require a dichotomous decision?

IR researchers who have considered this hurdle found means to make judges' relevance decisions easier, but they have not changed the dichotomous measurements. When judges can assign to a document a middle level, say "partially relevant," or use even a more refined set of levels, such as a seven-point scale, their judgments are closer to real-life situations than when they are confined to the dichotomous straitjacket. To measure performance, researchers then have to decide on a cutoff point above which documents are considered relevant, or they can provide several sets of precision and recall scores, each with a different cutoff point.

Relevant to what?   When researchers instruct judges on how to assess relevance, what is the object for which they determine the relevance of a document? Is it the query, the topic of the query, the user, or the decision that the information is to support? Answers to these and similar questions have been discussed extensively in the conceptual writings about the meaning of *relevance* and the types in which it is manifested, with no agreed-upon conclusion. Yet researchers have to answer these questions for each experiment. A common understanding seems to emerge from the literature: Algorithms and machines determine relevance to the *query* when they select the documents to be retrieved (called *system relevance*). People who judge relevance in experiments focus on the *topical relevance*—whether or not a document fit the topic of the query. Under special experimental conditions, relevance to the *user* and even to the *decision to be made* can be assessed. These will require that the study participants search for their own requests, and that the study concludes only after the information acquired through the search has been used.

Despite these challenges, IR research has been progressing steadily and improved retrieval systems have been developed. At the same time, these issues reflect the richness in the concept of *relevance* and its judgment, and have provided a fertile field for HII researchers to investigate.

Relevance in Human Information Interaction
Generally, most HII research about *evaluating information* and about *relevance* has been tightly connected to issues in IR experiments, rather than to matters deriving from HII research. Some research provided evidence that the issues indeed exist, and some have tried out ways to support IR experiments.

Relevance is subjective.   To substantiate Gull's (1956) findings with regard to the subjectivity of relevance judgments, several researchers conducted experiments in which each document was judged by more than one person. All studies found low consistency in judgments, ranging from 24% to 57% (e.g., Janes 1994; Lee, Belkin, and Krovitz 2006; Vakkari and Sormunen 2004). Other research projects aimed at uncovering variables that affect consistency, finding, for example, that unclear test requests decrease consistency (e.g., O'Connor 1967), while judges' subject knowledge and interest in the area increase it (e.g., Davidson 1977).

Relevance judgment is dynamic.   There is still no strong evidence that relevance judgment changes in time, even though intuition supports the idea that relevance judgment is dynamic. Testing this assumption, most studies measured changes in relevance judgments throughout the participants' projects—during which the information need itself is likely to change—rather than a single search process, but results were mixed. Smithson (1994) found that 84% of documents that were judged relevant at the beginning of a project were judged the same way in the final stage of the project. Similarly, several studies showed that the criteria people used to assess the relevance of documents were stable throughout their projects (e.g., Vakkari 2001). In contrast, one study found the opposite: Wang and White (1995) found that the number of criteria increased significantly during the project. Evidence that a user's notion of what is relevant alters during a single search process has not been easy to obtain, but some studies have suggested that such change may happen (e.g., Katzer and Snyder 1990; Robertson and Hancock-Beaulieu 1992).

Levels of relevance   Nondichotomous techniques to measure the level of relevance were proposed by various researchers. Katter (1968), among others, tested the effects of several techniques used to judge relevance—such as category assignment, ranking, rating comparison—and found that the results were not consistent among them, but no one technique stood out as the best.

Later experiments aimed at developing useful techniques, most prominently with continuous scales. Eisenberg (1988), for example, tested ranking along a 10 cm line and with an open scale,[11] and found that in both instances relevance judgments were easily made and cutoff points were simple to determine. Vakkari and Sormunen (2004) discovered an additional advantage of a nondichotomous relevance. Judges in their experiment were more consistent in their relevance judgment when they ranked it on a four-point scale (83%) than when they used a dichotomous scale (45%). Research on multiple-level rankings in IR experiments and their advantages is an area that continues to develop.

Other HII research projects related to relevance have not been associated with IR experiments but still have a potential to support system design, even though this influence has not yet materialized. These studies have investigated the factors that affect actors' relevance judgments and the criteria actors apply when making them. In her comprehensive review, Schamber (1994) listed 80 of the factors that had been revealed by HII researchers—combining both factors that shape relevance judgment and criteria that users employ when evaluating information (11). She organized them into six categories: judges (e.g., cognitive style, judgment attitude); documents (e.g., aboutness, style); Information System (e.g., browsability, physical accessibility); judgment conditions (e.g., definition of relevance, size of document set); and choice of scale (e.g., ease of use, kind of response required).

Clearly, these factors are not all the factors that have been discovered and, indeed, studies conducted since have uncovered new ones (e.g., Kim and Oh 2009). There were a few attempts to consolidate factors from various studies and to examine whether there were some central factors that have been identified in more than one study (e.g., Wang 1997; Barry and Schamber 1998). Results are tentative and suggestive at this point. In the same vein, some researchers wondered if relevance factors could be ranked by their importance to the user (e.g., Wang and Soergel 1998; Xu 2007). They found that *topicality* was the most important criteria for the users they studied. This result was supported by other studies, not all aimed at criteria ranking.

Almost all studies to uncover factors and criteria have been conducted in naturalistic settings where the researchers collected such factors through interviews and, at times, through observation as well. This research approach makes sense for two reasons: (1) under the artificial conditions of an experiment, participants are limited in the criteria that guide their relevance decisions, and may use criteria that may not be pertinent to them in real life; and (2) experiments are either devoid of context or create an artificial one, but common sense and evidence from multiple studies suggest that relevance judgment is contextual. Naturalistic research, on the other hand, is always carried out in a certain context, and therefore addresses the contextual nature of *evaluating information*.[12]

In most of the studies I reviewed, researchers have invited students or faculty, or both, to participate.[13] Because relevance judgments are contextual, one might think that this population is of special interest to HII researchers. It is reasonable to assume, however, that researchers selected this population because it was most accessible to them. Many researchers have ignored the specific context of the participants and seemed to have assumed implicitly that their results were generalizable even though their studies were limited to particular populations and contexts. Other studies were explicitly contextual, with no claims of generalizability. For example, Schamber (1991) studied professionals looking for weather information, Thomas (1993) studied new doctoral students as they interacted with an unfamiliar environment, Fidel and Crandall (1997) elicited criteria from engineers, and Hirsh (1999) examined fifth-grade students.

Evaluating Information: Conclusions

From a human point of view, judging relevance is equal in importance to other activities during the information-seeking process, such as identifying the problem, formulating the query, or selecting a search strategy. Relevance received its central position in information science because assessing it was necessary for measuring the performance of information systems. As a result, it was IR research that stimulated interest in the topic among HII researchers. Relevance became problematic because of the evaluation methods that were applied in IR research—experimental designs that yield purely quantitative results.

During the process of system design, designers of digital information systems evaluate various design solutions. Most often each solution is implemented by a certain algorithm. Although derived from theoretical principles, the "behavior" of an algorithm usually cannot be predicted to a certain level of specificity. In such cases only performance evaluations can inform the researcher on the nature of the outcome of using the algorithm. Therefore, evaluation is a central stage in the design process.

It is commonly believed that the best evaluations occur when researchers exercise the maximum control possible on the variables involved, so that the effect that changes in the independent variable—the algorithm—have on the dependent variables—whatever is used to measure the performance of the system—can be validly established. Therefore, experiments are usually employed for system evaluation. While experimenters cannot control either the criteria people use to assess relevance or other cognitive variables, researchers usually ask all participants to carry out their tasks under the same physical conditions, searching the same questions, and using the same system(s). They can also control the order in which questions and systems are searched, and the order in which results are displayed, among other variables. As a result, researchers can focus on variables they choose, assuming there are no intervening variables, and have the license to generalize the results. The control and generalizability of variables are crucial for the design of general-context systems.[14]

Quantitative results for performance evaluation are important for such systems as well. With each evaluation usually resulting in at most two scores[15]—precision and recall—researchers can detect improvements in performance resulting from a revised or new design, compare the performances of as many systems as they deem useful, and rank systems. While affording all these benefits, quantitative results do not tell researchers how to improve their systems. Suppose the system I tested ranked poorly on precision. How can I improve it? The score by itself gives me no information about why it is low, leaving me to speculate about what would enhance the system's performance.

Experimental design and quantitative results are not the only methods to evaluate information systems; systems can be evaluated in context and with a qualitative approach (see also T. K. Park 1994). In fact, while more labor intensive, such evaluations can add significant and vital contributions to systems design (see section 11.4

for an example of a qualitative evaluation approach that aims at contributing to design).

The vast literature on relevance has shown that its assessment is shaped by the actor's context. Participants in an experiment bring into the context of the experiment their individual habits and experiences, no matter how many variables an experiment design sets out to control. It is difficult to achieve significant results when the participant factors are not taken into account because it is not known if or how they affect a participant's searching. If each system were developed to serve actors in a different context, however, context would not be an issue "to deal with," but rather would be a guide. Within a context, it is possible to study the HII of its people in depth, and to tailor the design to their requirements.

While not suitable as a basis for comparisons and rankings, qualitative evaluations are very useful for system enhancement. Given a particular context, an evaluator can identify the dimensions along which the evaluation should proceed. Examples of such dimensions are the type of requests to which the system responds; the search strategies it supports; and the topical diversity of the documents in its collection. Research about the criteria people used in a particular context—such as fifth-grade students (Hirsh 1999), engineers (Fidel and Crandall 1997), or faculty members (Wang and White 1995)—has demonstrated that dimensions for evaluation that systems users deemed important can be identified. It has also shown that while some dimensions may be shared by several contexts, each context has its own dimension as well. For example, engineers preferred information items that have graphs and charts in them; they claimed that these tools helped them to get quickly to the information they needed (Fidel and Crandall 1997). A requirement for a retrieval system for such engineers can add this criterion to its relevance determination, and discriminate such items from the others. In addition, HII research about the *process* of relevance judgment, and how the actor's context shapes it, might further enlighten system evaluation.

With a few exceptions, IR research has not benefited from research in the HIB field. While there might be various reasons for the low level of collaboration between the two,[16] it is time for HII to expand its relevance research independent of systems design. With this autonomy, the definition of *relevance* might become almost irrelevant. HII research can then investigate *evaluating information*, focusing on the context of the process and its goals. It may address questions such as: What elements in a document are relevant to its evaluation? What contextual elements support the process of evaluation? How do people judge relevance to a topic, a decision, or a task? Schamber (1994) raised a similar idea when she suggested: "Perhaps as [HIB] becomes more holistic and situational in its perspectives, the everyday, intuitive meaning of the concept may become more common" (36). HII researchers may accept that relevance is a complex and rich concept that cannot be pinned down and agreed upon, and still expand their investigations into the process of evaluating information.

2.1.2   Advancing Research Areas

In recent years the topics that HIB covers have expanded. Most of these areas are still in their formative stage and have attracted only a few scholars. Two examples are described below: using information and sharing information.

2.1.2.1   Using Information

"Books are for use" is the first of the Five Laws of Library Science constructed by S. R. Ranganathan (1957), the most prominent scholar in classification theory. This law is the ultimate justification for the existence of libraries and other information systems. People usually interact with information in order to use it when they make decisions or solve problems, rather than for its own sake. Therefore, using information is a fundamental concept to any area related to information systems of any kind. Despite its significance, the area of using information has been mostly neglected in HIB research—particularly in comparison to research in information seeking. The term *use* has been employed chaotically to mean a large variety of activities and processes that are associated with the user, and at times it is a replacement for a term that could not be found. Definitional discussions have not been of much help, as researchers are still attempting to arrive at a consistent set of definitions for the concept of *use* (e.g., Kari 2007; Spink and Cole 2006; Taylor 1982; Todd 1999), and ways to detect it (e.g., Fisher, Durrance, and Hinton 2004). Meanwhile, only a few empirical studies in LIS investigated how people use information to resolve information problems.

The most prolific area of use-related research is bibliometrics—which is based on analyses of citations in scholarly publications and was introduced for purposes other than *use* studies. When one document cites another, a set of relationships between the two can be assumed. These relationships may indicate, for example, that both documents are on the same topic, and in combination with other cited and citing documents may reveal several types of associations among the documents' authors. While critics of bibliometrics claim that such relationships and associations cannot be inferred from citation analyses alone because the reason for a certain citation is not known, one relationship always exists: The author of a citing document used information from the cited one. Even though some researchers have applied bibliometric techniques to identify elements of information use (e.g., Biradar and Vijayalaxmi 1997; Hurd 1992), the purpose of most citation studies is to examine who has cited whom. Indeed, the contribution of most of these studies is to the area of the sociology of science. Through various techniques of analyzing citations, bibliometrics uncovers patterns and phenomena in the relationships among scholars—such as indications of interdisciplinary collaborations and identifying the leading researchers in a field.

Empirical researchers who were thoughtful and deliberate in employing the concept *use* have offered a range of interpretations of the concept, though not to the degree that prevails in conceptual discussions. Examples include the use of a certain information source or technology (e.g., Khalil and Elkordy 2005; Lamb, King, and Kling 2003; Nilsen 1998; Steinerova and Susol 2007), the frequency of using relevant information, the domain areas in which information was used for decision making (e.g., Adomi 2002), and when and for what purpose the information was used (Auster and Choo 1994; Mutshewa 2010).

Researchers who have investigated the actual use of information in decision making mostly observed the impact of using information. Not all studies looked at the same type of impact; rather, the context of a study formed the impact that was examined. In a study about the use of health information, for example, actors reported the degree to which information was helpful in a number of situations (Nicholas et al. 2003). In another study, the impact on learning outcomes was assessed for high school students (Limberg 1997).

Common to all studies of use, regardless of the meaning they attributed to *using information* and the method used, is the high level of contextuality. Unlike studies of relevance, these efforts are aimed not at generalizations but rather at an understanding of a specific community of actors when they use a particular type of information.[17] For instance, Komlodi, Marchionini, and Soergel (2007) investigated how attorneys and law librarians use search histories to improve their searches; Rothbauer (2004) studied how books with homosexual characters impact the personal and social identities of young self-identified lesbians; and Williamson and McGregor (2006) compared the impact of information used for an assignment on ancient history between secondary school students who plagiarized the most and those who plagiarized the least, and discovered themes that may help to illuminate the influences on information use in relation to plagiarism.

Using information is a highly complex process because it brings a host of new constraints in addition to those that shape the interactions that preceded use,[18] such as *seeking* or *evaluating information*. Therefore, studying it is a particularly challenging endeavor.

To get a notion of this complexity, consider the following simple scenario. Anna, a high school student, is looking for information about roses (constraint 1) to answer questions in a class assignment (constraint 2). Looking for information from home (constraint 3), she has access only to the web (constraint 4). Searching the web, she can get access mostly to web sites of nurseries (constraint 5), which she cannot regard as completely authoritative sources for the assignment at hand (constraint 6). Before working on the assignment—i.e., using the information—she collects all documents that might be useful and thinks about what information to use. When Anna does so, she considers the six constraints that have shaped her search activity. Examples are: She only uses information that can answer the assignment's questions (constraint 2); being at home (constraint 3) prevents her from turning to additional sources when she wants more information; she critically examines the credibility of the information posted by nurseries (constraint 6) and uses only facts that seem reliable to her, but uses all the information given by noncommercial sites.

Working on the assignment, she considers other constraints. The deadline for the assignment (constraint 7), for instance, compels her to ignore some of the longer documents she retrieved (i.e., *unusing* information). Most regrettably, she is not personally interested in flowers in general and in roses in particular, and the topic of the assignment was not her choice (constraint 8). For this reason, she is primarily concerned with the personal preferences of the teacher, rather than the benefit she might glean directly from the assignment. First, the teacher wants assignments to look as scholarly as possible (constraint 9), and Anna wants a high grade, so she uses Latin names whenever possible. Second, quality is more important to the teacher than quantity (constraint 10), which leads Anna to provide elaborate answers to questions for which she found credible information and leave a couple of questions unanswered because she lacks relevant information. At the same time, she aims at using information from as many sources as possible because another of the teacher's goals for the assignment is for his students to improve at web searching (constraint 11), which encourages her to show her ability to find many information sources. Lastly, he has highly developed aesthetic sensibilities (constraint 12) and Anna assumes, therefore, that the three pictures that were required by the assignment should be of high quality and have vibrant colors.

Given this example, it is easy to see that a study that focuses on the phenomenon without studying its environment, and that aims to arrive at context-free generalizations, would produce an incomplete understanding of the process, and may even lead to erroneous conclusions. In analyzing the case of the roses homework assignment, with no knowledge of Anna's physical constraints to information access, the attributes of the information on the web, or the teacher's personal preferences—and given that the information use of other students in the research sample exhibited the same pattern—a researcher might conclude that, in general, students use only information that is available on the web, they do not use all the information they find, they have no desire to complete their assignments, and they like to play around with images.[19] As we can see, to achieve an in-depth understanding of the process of *using information*, this complexity should be investigated together with the context in which it occurs.

It is not surprising that only a few LIS studies investigated how people use information to make decisions. The complexity of this activity, even within a highly specific context, requires the examination of many different issues, and the findings and conclusions of contextual studies cannot be made general—a highly desired attribute of studies—because they are anchored in a particular context.

Another challenge to research on information use is the fact that holistic, contextual research is work-intensive and resource-demanding, which makes it heavily dependent on funding. At the same time, its complexity and contextuality make research in using information unattractive to funding agencies. Most agencies prefer to support research projects that produce timely and efficient results that will be applicable beyond a particular context. The tendency to give priority to projects that support technology development, business, and industry also stands in the way of funding because LIS research in using information has not proven applicable to such purposes. Despite these obstacles, the number of LIS researchers who embark on use studies with contextual and holistic approaches is climbing up steadily, if gradually.

2.1.2.2 Sharing Information

Evidence that people are a rich source of information has been accumulating since early research in HII. Not only do people turn to other people for information, it is common for this source to be the first to which actors turn and the one used most frequently (e.g., T. Allen 1977; Byström and Järvelin 1995; Fidel and Green 2004). This has been found to be the case in both work-related and everyday-life activities. Savolainen (1995), for instance, found that both the workers and teachers who participated in his study primarily preferred personal communication when they needed information in their everyday life.

The complementary activity to getting information from people is sharing it. If person A gets information from person B, the latter shares information with the former. *Sharing information*, then, is another mode of human information interaction, and one that is common in people's lives.

This topic has been studied vigorously in management and in other areas that investigate the use of information and communication technology (ICT) in the workplace. This body of research includes several strands, and some examples are briefly reported here.

Researchers of the technological aspect of this topic have focused on ways to reduce communication noise during information sharing, thus increasing the efficiency of the information systems and ICT that are used to share information (e.g., Ackerman 1994; Pipek et al. 2003; Hendriks 1999; Marshall 1997). On the sociological side of the issue, an increasing number of researchers have begun to investigate the social interactions among information owners, seekers, and sharers (e.g., Levinthal and March 1993; McGrath and Argote 2001; Starbuck 1992; Walsh and Ungson 1991). The nature of the information that is being shared has also been an issue of interest. While ICT can support only the sharing of explicit information, studies have shown that actors frequently share tacit (implicit) information, to the benefit of all involved. Thus, researchers are looking for ways to externalize tacit information to make it explicit through the development of conversion protocols (e.g., Argote, McEvily, and Reagans 2003; Berends 2005; Herschel et al. 2001) and taxonomies (e.g., Zhao and Reisman 1992). Recently, a process-oriented approach led scholars to investigate the process of information sharing and the interactions embodied in the sharing process (e.g., Cook and Brown 1999).

LIS has used the term *giving* to represent *sharing information*. This concept was acknowledged in LIS research when Krikelas (1983) presented his model for information seeking. Although Krikelas construed *giving* as "the act of disseminating messages" (13), the concept usually connotes *helping*: people give information in order to help others, usually as an informal function. With this view, research may address questions such as why, how, and when people give information. How do they *know* what, when, and how to do it? What elements in the environment encourage or discourage them from doing so?

Karen Fisher (formerly Karen Pettigrew) introduced the phenomenon of *information giving* to LIS empirical research when she reported on her study of information flow among nurses and the elderly at neighborhood foot clinics (cited in Pettigrew 2000). While the nurses worked in a clinical capacity, they also informed their patients about the availability of local resources that could help them to improve their lives. Through a naturalistic, qualitative study, Fisher uncovered the reasons the nurses chose to give information, the types of information they gave, their strategies for giving it, and the affective aspects of the interaction.

The desire to help others is not the only motivation for giving information. People may do so to achieve other objectives (Barzilai-Nahon 2008a), such as getting information in exchange (e.g., Poltrock et al. 2003), promoting a certain idea or way of thinking (e.g., Althaus and Tewksbury 2002), or preserving a certain culture, whether ethnic (e.g., Metoyer-Duran 1993) or organizational (e.g., Katz, Tushman, and Allen 1995). Studies that have objectives other than informal help do not use the phrase *giving information*, and are commonly conducted to investigate another phenomenon: gatekeeping.

Coined in the area of sociology (Lewin 1951), the concept of *gatekeeping* has been adopted by other scholarly fields, receiving a range of interpretations. In the area of communication, for example, it is construed primarily as a selection process, while in the field of management it is seen as intermediation, and in other fields, as information control (Barzilai-Nahon 2008b). With this diversity in construal, gatekeeping does not always imply *giving information*, nor is it limited to an informal activity. When giving is involved, the focus is almost always on the gatekeeper himself and his role, rather than on the process of giving. Karine Barzilai-Nahon's (2008a) review of research questions in recent gatekeeping studies clearly illustrated this tendency. Examples of such questions are: How do gatekeepers make decisions? How has the gatekeeper role changed due to the Internet? How does one identify gatekeepers? How can one improve the gatekeeper role? What are the gatekeeper's information needs? What are the problems that gatekeepers may encounter in a decentralized context?

Some gatekeeping studies are directly relevant to *giving information* in the LIS sense, mostly through qualitative field research. Thomas Allen (1977) turned the HII community's attention to gatekeeping when he discovered that certain individuals serve as the information source for most members of their engineering teams. The role of these gatekeepers was informal and their motivation was to help their teammates (T. Allen 1977). In another groundbreaking gatekeeping study, Cheryl Metoyer-Duran (1993) built a taxonomy of information-seeking behaviors of gatekeepers in ethnolinguistic communities. Her study revealed not only the types of giving behavior, but also the context in which they manifested themselves, and their impact on the communities they served.

Information sharing is an integral part of the process of interaction among actors. Therefore, studies of the phenomenon in isolation are not likely to contribute much to either theory or practice. To productively study sharing requires an understanding of the context in which an actor asks for information from another actor (or gets information without asking for it), the motivation of the information seeker to turn to a person (rather than to another type of information source), and the motivation for the giver to share information. These requirements make the study of sharing information more difficult than studies of HII that involve machines, which might have contributed to the scarcity of sharing studies. To date, it is not clear what kind of contributions such studies may offer. It might be the time to start considering the phenomenon, so that conceptual and methodological foundations can be created to guide studies of sharing information, or to predict the type of contribution such studies may make.

2.1.3   Processes off the Research Chart

Among the examples of areas in HII offered here, a few processes are still on the sidelines of scholarly pursuits. Most of these processes have been discussed in other scholarly areas and from different aspects; hardly any studies have addressed their HII aspects.

2.1.3.1   Filtering Information

Filtering information is a close relative of *information retrieval*. The main difference between them is the direction of the information stream. While retrieval involves *pulling* from an information pool, filtering takes place when information is *pushed* toward an actor. In addition, the source from which information is retrieved may vary in time (e.g., the web, a digital library), while information is filtered from a designated and usually steady collection of sources. The relations between the two can also be explained in Savolainen's (1995) terms. *Filtering* might be useful for seeking what Savolainen calls "orienting information," that is, information "concerning current events." *Retrieval* is beneficial when seeking what he terms "practical information," that is, information that will solve a particular problem.

Up to the late 1980s filtering was carried out by librarians or other information professionals and was termed *selective dissemination of information* (SDI). In this system, a user provided a librarian with a "profile"—i.e., a list of concepts of interest to the user's work—and periodically received new documents that met the profile's requirements. A librarian selected these documents from the set of new ones just received by filtering out documents that he assumed were of no interest to the user. In the early 1990s, the task of filtering was delegated to computers, and various software programs have since been developed to facilitate the process.[20] The literature about filtering focuses primarily on algorithms for filtering, and is mostly published in computer science venues. To my knowledge, no study has examined filtering from the actor's point of view. Questions in this vein could lead to a fruitful area of study: What types of decisions does an actor make when browsing filtered documents? What elements shape these decisions? What forms of gatekeeping do different methods of filtering create?

2.1.3.2   Avoiding Information

Information is a very precious resource for individuals as well as organizations, particularly in the current information age. Most research in information science has been harnessed to answer the question of how to place this valuable resource in the hands of people who need it. To everyone's surprise, Elfreda Chatman (1987) discovered that people of some social communities avoided information even when it was accessible and potentially useful to them.[21] This discovery placed *avoiding information* on the HIB research map. It attracted much attention but stimulated almost no research to follow Chatman's work.

When Chatman's studies examined the social aspects of avoiding information, the concept was already in circulation but viewed from cognitive and organizational aspects. Avoiding information has been found to be one of the strategies for coping with information overload (Case 2007; P. Wilson 1995), and P. Wilson (1995) found another reason for avoidance in an empirical study: Actors in research and development units avoided using information because of organizational policies that deliberately excluded certain types of information. These three aspects—the social, the cognitive, and the organizational—have yet to be brought together in one study program.

2.1.3.3   Organizing Information

People organize information all the time whether or not they are cognizant of the process. We do so when we create categories in order to make sense of experiences (Lakoff 1987), and when we manage our personal information (Teevan, Jones, and Bederson 2006). Of most interest to the LIS community are processes that organize information for future retrieval. Personal information management (PIM) requires various processes, one of which is organizing personal documents and information (W. Jones 2008, 2010). As a scholarly area, PIM investigates how people manage their information in everyday life or on the job. PIM research has spread widely in the last decade but has left HIB almost untouched.

For some professionals—such as taxonomists and classificationists—organizing information is the very essence of their identity. Scientific taxonomists organize topics in their fields into structures that model the fields. According to current terminology, general taxonomists design structures to help people navigate when they look for information, and classificationists create classification schemes to provide access to documents.

Until very recently, no study has investigated how taxonomists or classificationists work—how they organize information—and how they interact with information when they build constructs. Part of the small body of literature about the topic includes a few project reports that described the processes that had taken place (e.g., Sutton 2004). The other part consists of advice to professionals, some of which was based on empirical research and experience. A common topic in this type of advice is the factors that are required for a successful design. Suggestions include user collaboration across the life cycle of system design, the contributions of expertise with library skills and the subject matter, and aptness of the system to the intended purpose (e.g., Wyllie, Skyrme, and Lelic 2003). The actual process of building a taxonomy or a classification scheme was studied for the first time by Oknam Park (2008) in a naturalistic study that investigated how, why, and when a team responsible for the development of a company's classification scheme was integrating knowledge about users in their work.

The area of organizing information is relevant to information seeking when it is conducted to support future retrieval. The way information is organized is one of the elements that shape how people look for information. An understanding of the process of *organizing* can usefully inform an in-depth analysis of how people acquire information.

2.1.3.4 *Representing Information*

When information is represented, it is always in a certain form. In fact, if one accepts that information, by its very definition, is communicated,[22] one must conclude that information always has some form of representation. Among the many forms, including information visualization (e.g., Card, Mackinlay, and Shneiderman 1999; Koshman 2006; Tufte 2001), only one is mentioned here—information represented through a surrogate—because of its close affinity to other areas in LIS.

Representing information through a surrogate is an LIS area which, unlike other areas, originated in LIS itself. The most common surrogates are abstracts, indices, and classification schemes. Actors interact with information when they write abstracts or index or classify documents. Though such surrogates are central to LIS, only two studies have been carried out to investigate how professionals create them. Brigitte Endres-Niggemeyer observed six expert abstractors thinking aloud while writing their abstracts, with the aim of explaining the knowledge-processing activities that occur during professional abstract writing (Endres-Niggemeyer, Maier, and Sigel 1995). She analyzed the data to create a model that represented the cognitive steps involved in the process, and used the model to design a system that simulated these steps (Endres-Niggemeyer 2000). Catalogers at work were the other population that was studied. Alenka Sauperl (2002) observed and interviewed 12 experienced catalogers in academic libraries to investigate how they determined the subject of a document for cataloging purposes.[23] The study found, for example, that the catalogers she observed were not able to incorporate the users' meaning in their work, even though they stated that the users' meaning was an important factor in subject cataloging. This example demonstrates the relevance of the topic of representing information to an in-depth understanding of the information-seeking process.

2.1.4   What Is Human Information Interaction? Conclusions

The few examples of current and potential areas of research show the complexity inherent to the topics related to human information interaction and to the multidisciplinary nature of HII. This complexity has constructed challenges to HII researchers in general and to HIB scholars in particular. Nevertheless, a large variety of research areas have been developed, and many enjoy a solid body of research with much still to be discovered. For HIB researchers, these examples also point to areas that may form potentially productive collaborations with information seeking, such as knowledge organization, information retrieval, human-computer interaction, and information and communication technologies.

II Conceptual Constructs and Themes in Information-Seeking Behavior

Researchers in library and information science (LIS) who study human information interaction (HII) focus on the area of human information behavior (HIB). Similar to scholars in most branches of the sciences, they wish to contribute to the understanding of the phenomenon. Research questions might be general, such as, Why do people look for information? How do they browse? What do they consider when they determine relevance? Or, questions can be highly specific, such as, How do female students from an inner-city high school look for health information about sleep deprivation? For a study to contribute to LIS, the researchers must have a clear understanding of the reasons for carrying out the project. That is, investigators want to have explicit and specific answers to the questions: Why am I asking this particular question, and what impact do I expect the study to have? In effective research projects, the answers to these questions shape the specific research questions and the research method employed.

Since LIS has one foot in theory and another in practice (and a big gap in between), an LIS researcher must be clear, for herself and others, where her contribution would lie—in research, practice, or in both—in order to provide a meaningful contribution. This is particularly important in this field because it does not have the characteristics of traditional disciplines. Such disciplines already have their own schools of thought and the research approaches associated with each. A researcher then needs only to identify the school to which he belongs, and his general goals and possible contributions become apparent. LIS, as a new field, has not yet developed stable research traditions; therefore, every research project has to define its purposes.

Moreover, several disciplines are defined by the type of their contributions and the set of research methodologies used. LIS—as an area within information science—is a problem-based field. Because its goal is to investigate the various facets of the interaction between people, information, and technology, the types of contributions to both research and practice and the research methodologies that can be used are numerous. This is one of the attractive attributes of LIS, but at the same time it requires high accuracy and clarity in the reasons for conducting a study and the expected contribution it will make to the field. Yet it is not uncommon for an LIS study to claim to increase our understanding of the studied HIB phenomenon, and justly so, but neither the researcher nor his audience can see how the study's insights actually contribute to research or to practice. "Deepening understanding" is a contribution only when it is clear what impact such an understanding has the potential to have on the field, regardless of the magnitude of the change it may bring—whether minuscule or groundbreaking.

To help define the area of HIB, various scholars have created conceptual constructs, focusing mostly on information-seeking behavior. The first chapter in this part is dedicated to some of these constructs. One building block in the definition of an area is the themes that are central to the field's scholarship. Central themes in HIB have been shaped by changes in both research techniques and information behavior that have been afforded by the introduction of digital technology.

The Effect of New Technologies on HIB Research

Since the introduction of digital information technology has arguably been the most important revolution since the invention of printing, scholars in several fields have been studying its effects on the individual and on society. The widespread use of this technology, and specifically that of the World Wide Web, brought new developments to research in HII as well. Most notable are the growth of new research areas and the increasing involvement in HII of researchers from various fields within computer science and engineering.

The field of information retrieval (IR), for example, was born when the prospect of using computers to store and retrieve information was first recognized, yet before it was operationally realized. Human-computer interaction (HCI) and personal information management (PIM) are other examples of fields that responded to phenomena related to the use of digital technologies;[1] both became increasingly relevant with its growth. In information science, the area of HIB established itself as a genuine field and received its name only after the spread of digital information systems, even though research in the area had been carried out before the introduction of new technologies. Within HIB, the study of information seeking in everyday life was established only after searching digital systems had become available to all, even though this area also addresses information seeking without the support of machines.

These changes, however, have not resolved all of the "old issues" in HIB, and several basic themes remained unaltered. Examples of unresolved questions are: How do actors evaluate information? What contextual elements shape the way actors organize information? And what motivates actors to look for information, use it, or share it? While the questions have remained the same, the methods employed to investigate them, and some of the answers, have been transformed. New technologies made it possible for researchers (a) to directly observe human information interaction when a machine was involved, and (b) to collect large amounts of data through instruments such as search logs and web-based surveys. These new possibilities have contributed to the shaping of the themes and trends of HIB research since the late 1970s.

These two new opportunities paved the way for additional approaches to HIB research, and they reinforced both qualitative and quantitative research. One method to collect data, for example, is to ask study participants to think aloud while they sit at a terminal and perform a search. Capturing such verbal protocols is highly difficult when participants interact with a manual or intellectual system, which usually entails movement among physical objects. This method, in turn, made it possible for qualitative researchers to collect rich data and for cognitive investigators to probe the participants' cognitive world.

This new situation also brought about the option of conducting experiments in searching behavior. Both qualitative and quantitative data can be collected in experiments, and they can even be limited to a certain context. Most of the HIB experiments, however, were quantitative and were carried out to establish facts that are general to all information seekers.[2] The opportunity to collect relatively large amounts of data through online surveys provided further encouragement for generalizations. The attention given to general results has also been supported by the digital search systems that are general-context systems and not tailored to particular communities of actors. This attention also amplified the interest in the study of cognitive aspects of HIB since it has been assumed that cognitive attributes are independent of the actor's context and therefore can be generalized.

In addition to its effects on research trends and methods, the introduction of digital technology shaped a shift in the conceptual scene. In particular, researchers have gradually begun to focus their attention on elements in the search *process* itself. Previously, their attention was exclusively directed at elements that surrounded the process—such as the information problem, the sources selected, and the task. An example of two concepts—*information need* and *search strategies*—demonstrates a typical shift in the centrality of research issues. The concept *information need* attracted much discussion among early researchers, who attempted to define it and analyze its attributes, but has been gradually dropping from its central place with the growing use of digital technology. Even though some scholars have claimed that information needs change during searches, the concept is usually not considered as part of the search process. On the other hand, the concept *search strategies*, which has become a popular topic for empirical research with the introduction of digital technology, is clearly a part of the search process, as it addresses the activities during a search. Moreover, while research on information need has been exclusively conceptual, that on search strategies has been empirical for the most part.

The last two chapters of this part of the book discuss these two concepts. The chapters focus on some of the limitations in the concepts' definitions and introduce definitions from another view—that of cognitive work analysis.

3 Theoretical Constructs and Models in Information-Seeking Behavior

The bazaar of conceptual constructs created and used in information-seeking behavior (ISB) research offers a great variety of these items, such as theoretical constructs, conceptual and methodological frameworks, guidelines for analysis, and models of various kinds. Among the theoretical constructs, theories occupy the highest rank in the hierarchy of conceptual constructs. Yet the majority of the conceptual constructs in ISB are models, followed by theoretical constructs, of which theories are a rarity.

The lack of "good" theories has been a constant source of frustration to LIS researchers and to those in the field of information science in general. This failing is lamented because, it is argued, a well-developed and stable body of theories is a sign of a mature scholarly field. While some scholars may believe that information science is indeed still immature, others explain that this weakness is the result of other factors, such as having roots in a practical field (Järvelin and Vakkari 1990), being a postmodern, problem-based science (Wersig 1993), and being interdisciplinary (Nolin 2007). These explanations make sense, and there probably are additional reasons waiting to be discovered. To date, no systematic investigation has been conducted to find the sources for the lack of theory: Is it inherent to information science or just a phase in its development?

In addition to their contribution to the development of the field, the use of theories in research has practical advantages. Such use has the potential to do the following:

- Provide explanations for a project's findings
- Open new research directions
- Help guide research design
- Point to central research questions
- Resolve difficulties when conducting a study
- Provide a basis for comparisons with other studies

• Facilitate the identification of implications for other phenomena
• Pave the way for placing a study in a broader context.

Several studies have attempted to assess the maturity of information science and measured the percentage of journal articles in the field that used or developed theories (e.g., Järvelin and Vakkari 1993). Pettigrew and McKechnie (2001) comprehensively reviewed these studies and reported on an investigation of their own on the role, transfer, growth, and use of theory in information science. Their findings were much more optimistic than those of previous studies: 34% of the articles they analyzed incorporated theory, while older studies had found a range of 10% to 21%. It would be encouraging to be able to attribute this difference to a growth in theory building and use. Regrettably, even if this were the case, these studies cannot point to such a trend because each one of them has its unique interpretation of what a theory is, and therefore their results cannot be compared or integrated. In addition, while the previous studies used various flavors of positivist views, Pettigrew and McKechnie (2001) employed a broad definition of *theory* to free their project from the limitations of these views.[1] As a result, more conceptual constructs qualified as theories in their study than would have been the case in the others, which may partly explain the relatively high proportion reported in their study.

Another contribution of Pettigrew and McKechnie's (2001) study was an increased refinement of the analysis. They examined how many theories were developed within and for information science, how many were imported from other fields and disciplines, and which information science theories were picked up by researchers in other fields. They found, for example, that the social sciences were the largest source of theories that information science researchers imported (45% of all imported theories), and that information science theory is not heavily cited in other fields.

Many definitions have been put forward for the concept *theory*, and most were influenced by the theoretical traditions to which their originators have subscribed—whether explicitly or implicitly. To discuss them is a considerable task that is beyond the scope of this work. The community of human information behavior (HIB) scholars has also used the concept with plenty of different meanings, and a definition unique to the field is unattainable (and probably not desirable). A specific definition, however, is useful for this discussion of the various conceptual constructs in ISB because it helps to organize the presentation of the discussion, identify the conceptual constructs that can be considered theories, and examine their roles. I prefer to use Benton and Craib's (2001) definition of *theory*:

The attempt to explain phenomena by going beyond our common sense, everyday explanations, and beyond our immediate experience. (186)

This meaning is used throughout this book. With this definition in mind, this chapter addresses various conceptual constructs, such as laws, models, and conceptual frameworks, in addition to theories.

Researchers have neglected to study the prevalence of other conceptual constructs that are discussed in this chapter, such as laws and models. Although some of these constructs were considered as theories, and thus were counted in prevalence studies, no studies investigated the nature of, say, laws and models in ISB. Nevertheless, some of these constructs, primarily models, have had a marked impact on ISB research.

Human information interaction is a complex and multifaceted phenomenon that is influenced, to varying degrees, by issues such as cognitive and affective states; organizational, cultural, environmental, and social aspects; and technology and the nature and structure of the information source(s). Research in ISB has taken into consideration some of these aspects, resulting in three strands of research that reflect the lens through which researchers view their work: the psychological, the social, and the in-context lenses.

The *psychological lens* focuses primarily on the study of cognitive and affective aspects of ISB. It typically aims at general statements about people looking for information.

The *social lens* focuses primarily on the study of social, cultural, organizational, and political aspects of ISB. It typically examines patterns of information seeking among people in a particular social, cultural, organizational, or political group.

The *in-context lens* focuses on actors and their context, addressing various aspects that are relevant to the actors' activities when looking for information.

To date, the psychological lens has dominated the field. The use of the in-context approach has been on a steady rise, and the social lens is of growing interest to scholars in other fields but has only a humble presence in ISB research.

3.1 Theories in Library and Information Science

The scarcity of "good" theories in information-seeking behavior (ISB) is not for a lack of trying. Many researchers have attempted to build new theories, and others have borrowed theories from other fields and applied them to ISB research.

3.1.1 "In-house" Theories

Although a number of LIS scholars have tried to develop theories in ISB that were unique to the field, only a few of these trials have yielded theories in the sense used in this book. Nevertheless, these trials at building theories have produced other conceptual constructs, such as laws and frameworks to guide research (see section 3.2), and their value for research is not affected by their conceptual status. An example of such a construct is Kuhlthau's (2004) "uncertainty principle," which makes the claim that uncertainty generates feelings of anxiety and a lack of confidence. This statement, however, reflects an immediate everyday experience, and for reflective people might even be in the realm of common sense. I am anxious when I am uncertain about the safety of a place I visit, or when I do not know how high the gas prices may climb before my summer vacation. When I prepare for teaching a new class and am uncertain about the students' reaction, I feel a lack of confidence. This principle, then, is better classified as a law, rather than a theory (see section 3.2.2).

Even though many constructs designated as theories by their originators do not qualify as such under the above definition, a few bona fide ones have grown in the field of ISB. Most of these theories were developed through years of empirical research, with each project guiding the development of a theory through validating or rejecting a statement, expanding or modifying it, or bringing to light new concepts and relationships.

Some examples are the works of Diane Nahl, Eliza Dresang, and Katriina Byström. Nahl's (2007) affective load theory, which has been 20 years in the making, identifies people's underlying habits of thinking and feeling while they are engaged in interaction with information. It explains seeking behavior from the actor's point of view, claiming that the thoughts and feelings of individuals affect observable behavior, such as selecting a search strategy or thinking about a synonym. Based on a string of research projects about the information behavior of children and young adults, Dresang (1999) constructed the radical change theory, which addresses the changes that have occurred in the digital age. This theory explains that information behavior in the digital age can be understood, or explained, by considering three principles: interactivity, connectivity, and access. Other theories are still in the development stage. Byström, for instance, is nurturing the progress of her theory on information activities in work tasks. She wants her research to be relevant to real-life work contexts and, therefore, studies the effects of various attributes of the task for which information is sought (e.g., task complexity) on searching behavior (Byström and Hansen 2002).

The most notable LIS theorist in HII was the late Elfreda Chatman, who centered her attention on the "information poor" (even those among members of the middle class) and their interaction with information in everyday use. Chatman examined HII as an integral part of the social lives of her participants; she saw HII as being shaped by people's social conditions, while also contributing to those conditions and their sustainability. The first researcher to consistently apply theories and methods from the social sciences, Chatman erected a theoretical structure in which the guidance of theories and concepts in conducting an empirical study has borne the seeds of new theories and concepts. Of particular significance to the development of the new constructs were the patterns she observed that could not be explained by the theories she used to analyze them. One of her most important contributions to the field is the empirical evidence that cultural and social norms affect the ways people interact with information or ignore it.

Chatman investigated particular groups of people: those who inhabited a "small world," which she defined as

[a] world in which everyday happenings occur with some degree of predictability ... [and] it allows for the presence of the "legitimized others." [That is,] people who share physical and/or conceptual space within a common landscape of cultural meaning. Within the contextual understanding of information behaviours, the legitimized others place narrow boundaries around the possibilities of these behaviours. (Chatman 2000, 3)

Because the information poor were the object of her studies, Chatman explored several small worlds, one after the other, in which people avoided information sources and information that directly addressed problematic situations they had experienced.[2] Each small world exposed its own social conditions and forces that had shaped the information behavior of its inhabitants, and brought to light new insights.

Poor women who had temporary employment as part of their participation in a training program composed the first small world she investigated (Chatman 1986). In this study Chatman applied diffusion theory from anthropology and sociology to the diffusion of information among the women. When she found that the theory did not explain all her findings, she focused on the cases that could not be explained. This investigation led to several observations, such as the competition among the women that served as a barrier to information sharing, and the discovery that some types of information decreased in relevance and value the longer they were in the process of being diffused.

Her next study participants were selected because they formed a stable small world that was convenient to study: janitors who worked at the university where she was a faculty member (Chatman 1987). Chatman followed the same barriers to information sharing she had discovered in the first study, and applied alienation theory—which emphasizes secrecy and self-protection—to the new study. This exercise led her to discover additional barriers. Furthermore, since the second small world was situated within a stable and long-term institutional setting, this environment raised her curiosity about the effects of the institution on the janitors' information behavior. To investigate this variable, she applied gratification theory. A clear issue stood out among her findings: The janitors avoided information sources even when the sources could potentially be helpful to them. They believed they did not need information because they felt that their lives were governed by fate, and there was nothing they could do to change things. This study broke new ground by introducing the concept of *avoiding information* to the vocabulary of HII research from the social perspective, a research area that up to that time had recognized only *seeking information*, assuming that people always look for information when they need it.

After completing the first two studies, Chatman thought that applying social network theory might provide new insights because of the prominence it gave to sharing among network participants. This time she studied aging middle-class women in an assisted living facility (Chatman 1992). Although the theory failed to provide new insights as expected, the result of the study encouraged her to begin building her own theories. She named the first theory a *theory of information poverty*, which she used to explain the ways people defined their life experiences in order to survive in a world of extreme distrust.

While no new theoretical insights were gained in the study of the aging women, it drew Chatman's attention to the importance of two concepts about life in a small world: *social norms* (the standards that determine acceptable behavior) and *self-protective behavior* (Chatman 1996). To further investigate these concepts, she embarked on a study of women in a maximum-security prison, exploring the information sources that identified and sustained "normative" life for the prisoners (Chatman 1999).

This investigation expanded and enriched her understanding of social norms and self-protective behavior and led to her next two theories. The first, a *theory of life in the round*, explained behavior in relation to three concepts: (1) social control (the element that binds the prisoners' small world together), (2) social types (the norms that govern one's public behavior), and (3) worldview (a collective perception that members of a social world hold in common regarding those things that are important and those deemed trivial or unimportant) (Chatman 2000). The second theory, *living life in the round*, included six propositions that explained various aspects of "life in the round," which is life that is taken for granted and with an enormous degree of imprecision but accepted levels of uncertainty. This theory explained the relationships and tradeoffs between social norms and self-protective behavior. Examples of the phenomena explained by the propositions include the results of establishing appropriate behavior, the effect that the force of social norms has on private behavior, and the conditions that have to be met in order for individuals to cross information boundaries (Chatman 2000).

Chatman's three theories had culminated in a more general theory: a *theory of normative behavior*. Four concepts played a central part in this theory:

1. "Social norms" (and their value for a small world),

2. "Worldview" (which is shaped by normative values),

3. "Social types" (the process of assigning people to a type according to their predictable behavior in everyday life), and

4. "Human information behavior" (which is shaped by what members of a small world believe is necessary to support a normative way of life).

In this context Chatman defined information behavior as "a state in which one may or may not act on the information received" (Chatman 2000, 12).

Although Chatman's work was stopped by her sudden death, her theories and conceptualizations have had a great impact on numerous researchers in LIS, many of whom employed them in their studies. Regrettably, at times her ideas have been applied too broadly, and researchers transferred her insights into other settings that might not correspond with the type of small worlds she studied. Chatman had clearly explained the nature of the context for which her theories and concepts had matured. While they offered robust explanations for the HII of the information poor, their potential to explain HII of the information rich is very limited, if relevant at all. The concept *small world* was associated with concepts such as *deception*, *secrecy*, *social control*, and *self-protective behavior*—concepts that would probably not be associated with, say, the world of a country club's members. In addition, Chatman targeted a well-defined type of information:

I am speaking of a particular type of information, one that is intended to respond to the needs of individuals within a specific social context. That is, the information sought to respond to problematic needs is a different type of information from that which is intended for everyday casual use. (Chatman 2000, 10)

Like many studies in the social sciences, Chatman's work was moored in a definite social context and cannot be meaningfully transferred to others, or to the cognitive realm, without conducting cautious and thorough investigations to demonstrate its applicability.

Chatman's contributions to research in LIS have moved the field forward significantly. She was among the first to use qualitative research methods that produced "thick descriptions"—narratives that richly describe the phenomenon of study—and to demonstrate the respect, genuine interest, and understanding that study participants deserve, especially when they are members of marginalized groups. She demonstrated the richness of description and insights to which investigations in context can lead, which "legitimatized" in-context studies and encouraged new researchers to consider them for their own work. Most notably, she offered a fine example for theory development through iterations between empirical and theoretical investigations.

Well-established theories that have guided researchers in ISB are in short supply. The theories that have been developed show that to develop a theory requires a long time and much intellectual effort, which can be materialized only with adequate support. Unfortunately, the area of ISB has not attracted funding at the level required for the in-depth empirical research that is the basis for theory development. Nevertheless, the few existing theories and those that are being built provide excellent examples of research processes that can lead to theory development.

3.1.2 Borrowed Theories

While Chatman employed theories from the social sciences to build theories in LIS, numerous researchers borrowed theories from other fields to guide their empirical research projects, most of which were not meant to lead to theoretical developments. Baker (1994), for example, employed monitoring-and-blunting theory from psychology, which explains behavior under stress, to study information seeking by women with multiple sclerosis. Limberg (1999) as well as Christine Bruce (1997) and Kirk (2002) applied phenomenography from the field of learning to their studies of information behavior. Limberg examined the information seeking and use of high school students, Bruce studied information literacy, and Kirk investigated the information use of managers. Another example of a borrowed theory is social positioning, which originated in psychology, and guided Given's (2002) research project about the information behavior of undergraduate students.

Not all researchers made the most of the theories they had imported. Picking and choosing elements of a theory, rather than using it holistically, is not that rare in ISB research. Generally speaking, one hopes that when a theory guides a research project, both the conception and methodology of the project fit the theory and that all of the project's components preserve the context, meaning, richness, and robustness of the theory. For instance, when using constructs from diffusion theory, it is best not to overlook the social context. Similarly, if researchers ignore the constraints on behavior in optimal foraging theory when they apply it to information seeking, they change the meaning of the borrowed concepts they use and reduce the reliability of the theory transfer.

In addition, at times, rich and complex theories are used to "discover" new insights that are rather commonsensical. For example, is it necessary to find empirical evidence to demonstrate that information seeking is a complex process or that experience in information seeking shapes a person's seeking behavior?[3] Although the determination of what is common sense and what requires evidence or theoretical backing is shaped by a researcher's experience and point of view, it is easy for researchers to ignore this issue, regardless of their approach. The differentiation between the obvious and a new insight is a particularly sensitive issue in ISB because of the relationships between the theoretical and the practical dimensions. Practitioners with experience in helping people when they look for information collect observations about this behavior, which are validated over time. Researchers who lack such experience may rediscover one of these observed behaviors and consider it to be a new insight. In such cases, experienced information professionals are likely to perceive such a "discovery" as additional evidence of the irrelevance of academic research to their work. Ignoring knowledge gained by practitioners thus affects the quality of research and widens the gap between theory and practice.

One exception to the patterns of theory use is the work of Marcia Bates, which has had a worldwide influence on HII research in LIS and in other fields. Unlike Chatman, who drew on theories from sociology and anthropology, Bates has been inspired by theories from a range of disciplines. Her work has been mostly conceptual and has focused on concepts and ideas central to information science in general and to ISB specifically. She was the first to examine basic concepts in the field, such as search and idea tactics (Bates 1979a, 1979b), and has analyzed the concept of information (Bates 2005), the nature of information science (Bates 1999), and the different roles that humans and machines can assume during an HII process (Bates 1990), along with the analysis of other concepts and phenomena. Her work has developed with a bit-at-a-time expansion of concepts covered and theories employed, which is typical for a "berrypicking" course—a pattern of searching she had identified (Bates 1989).

A few examples can illustrate Bates's use of theories. To propose a design model for subject access in online catalogs, Bates (1986) imported concepts from Heisenberg's "uncertainty principle" in physics' quantum theory (she used the original principle, which is very different from Kuhlthau's) and from Ashby's Law of Requisite Variety in cybernetics. Applying these concepts to searching and other activities such as cataloging, she concluded that generally "the system should help the searcher enter the system, get oriented, and generate the necessary variety" (Bates 1986, 12). Based on the specifics of her analysis she then offered suggestions for the design of some system components. In her keynote address at the Information Seeking in Context (ISIC) conference in 2002, Bates initiated an idea for an integrated model of information seeking and searching (Bates 2003). Her model calls for an understanding of several levels of human existence that intersect with various disciplines in the natural and social sciences as well as the humanities. Following an evolutionary tradition—manifested in approaches such as human behavioral ecology, evolutionary culture theory, and evolutionary psychology—she laid out in a hierarchical order the levels that required attention, starting with the chemical, physical, geological, and astronomical level, and reaching the top with the spiritual one. Bates (2007) also conducted an in-depth analysis of the search strategy *browsing* and constructed a new definition for it, for which she found support in research in psychology and behavioral ecology about visual search and about curiosity and exploratory behavior.[4]

The variety of theories that Bates used in her studies also distinguishes her work, for most of the other importers of theories in LIS preferred to use a single theory in their research. Typically, each theory was transferred and used by only one researcher. The geographic locations of the research importers are also few in number. Several theories have been imported for doctoral research projects at the University of Western Ontario in Canada, where the use of a theory in a dissertation is required, and the others took place in Europe and Australia, where a theoretical approach to research is common. The diversity among the theories that have been imported is great, and there seems to be no common conceptual thread among them. To date, we cannot point to one theory from another field that has had a major impact on ISB research.

3.2   Other Theoretical Constructs

Theoretical constructs are unique in the assortment of conceptual constructs because they have a direct association with the concept of theory—unlike other constructs, which may develop relations with theories but these theories are not essential to their being. Three types of theoretical constructs have emerged from ISB research: approaches, laws, and named concepts.

3.2.1   Approaches

When a theory is already in place, scholars may add other constructs to it and create an *approach*, which is a comprehensive view of a phenomenon (or the world) that implies a research methodology and tools. For example, after conducting some empirical studies guided by several theories, Diane Sonnenwald (1999) has created such an approach, which she named "information horizons." The theoretical framework included five propositions. Among these, the first proposition stated that human information behavior is shaped by and shapes individuals, social networks, situation, and contexts; and the fourth claimed that human information-seeking behavior might, ideally, be viewed as an individual's collaboration with information sources. She explained: "The information horizons theoretical framework and methodology proposes a universal, descriptive explanation of human information-seeking and use behavior, and data collection and analysis techniques to explore human information-seeking behavior in context" (Sonnenwald 2005, 191).

The concept *information horizons* is central to this approach because it constrains and enables information seeking.[5] Sonnenwald (2005) defined it in order to study issues such as the reasons that people access (or do not access) individuals and other information resources, or the impact of contexts and situations on the information-seeking process. The methodology included in this approach charts in detail the processes of data collection and analysis to be used in ISB studies.

A much more complex and refined approach has been developed by Brenda Dervin, who is a leading scholar in ISB. A scholar in the communication field, she has developed a "sense-making methodology"—the most comprehensive approach for simultaneously addressing methodology, method, metatheory, and substantive theory. Her approach has been applied widely by other researchers around the world to investigate various phenomena. Dervin's web site (http://communication.sbs.ohio-state.edu/sense-making/) shows that researchers in fields such as disability studies, telecommunication policy, pedagogy, and information seeking have applied her approach. Her chapter in the 1986 *Annual Review of International Science and Technology* (Dervin and Nilan 1986) is considered to mark the turning point from a system-centered to a user-centered approach (even though user-centered studies had been carried out before that date), and she is considered the instigator of what is called the "user-centered revolution."

Like Bates's work, Dervin's was influenced by many theories and theoretical traditions. Unlike Bates, however, her work has focused on one concept, that of *sense-making*, which emerged in the phenomenological tradition (Dervin and Naumer 2009). From this concept she has developed a full-blown approach (Dervin 1992), influenced by the works of several philosophers such as Bruner, Derrida, Dewey, and Foucault. Her work has centered on developing theoretical guidance on methods for such activities as theorizing and conducting empirical research. Sense-making focuses on how people understand information they receive within their life context, with factors such as the person's expertise, social position, and situation affecting their understanding. Dervin has been developing the approach over the last 30 years and continues to enrich and expand its conceptual construct.

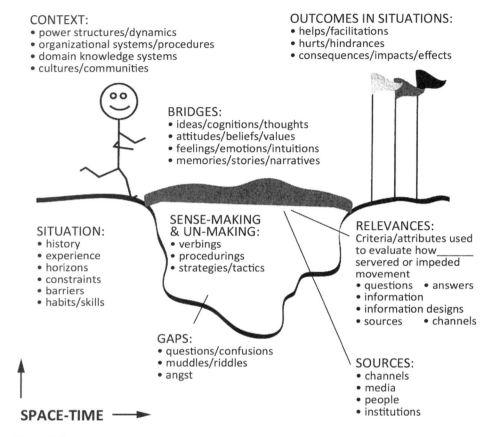

CONTEXT:
• power structures/dynamics
• organizational systems/procedures
• domain knowledge systems
• cultures/communities

OUTCOMES IN SITUATIONS:
• helps/facilitations
• hurts/hindrances
• consequences/impacts/effects

BRIDGES:
• ideas/cognitions/thoughts
• attitudes/beliefs/values
• feelings/emotions/intuitions
• memories/stories/narratives

SITUATION:
• history
• experience
• horizons
• constraints
• barriers
• habits/skills

SENSE-MAKING
& UN-MAKING:
• verbings
• procedurings
• strategies/tactics

RELEVANCES:
Criteria/attributes used
to evaluate how_____
servered or impeded
movement
• questions   • answers
• information
• information designs
• sources   • channels

GAPS:
• questions/confusions
• muddles/riddles
• angst

SOURCES:
• channels
• media
• people
• institutions

SPACE-TIME ⟶

Figure 3.1
Dervin's sense-making methodology metaphor. Reprinted with the permission of Brenda Dervin.

Figure 3.1 is a graphic presentation of the theoretical foundations of Dervin's approach. Simply put:

1. A person goes about her life, which is embedded in a certain dynamic context and situation, taking step after step through experiences.

2. A sense-making moment occurs when she arrives at a gap in the road: She cannot continue without changing her sense of the world or creating a new understanding of the world.

3. To move to a new situation, she needs to build a bridge, or she may decide to "unmake sense," that is, to change her sense of the world without building a bridge.

4. For that purpose she can get help from various sources of information.

The sense-making methodology is rich and complex. It cannot be summarized in one article, and definitely not in this chapter. However, no account of the approach can ignore the method Dervin (1992) developed for investigating information needs: the "micromoment timeline interview." Following this method, a researcher asks the participant in an interview to reconstruct a situation in terms of what happened, and then the researcher asks questions about the situation. The questions are directed by three major themes: how the person saw the situation, the gap, and the help she wanted. This method has been integrated into many studies in ISB and in various modes, as well as into research projects in other areas.

3.2.2 Laws

Laws have value as independent statements, but they can also serve as building blocks for a theory. In the positivist tradition, a law is defined as a regular event sequence. Following this definition, several of the constructs designated as theories become laws.

Kuhlthau's law regarding uncertainty, for example, has roots in her model, the information search process (see section 3.3.1), which examined the information seeker's feelings, thoughts, and actions at each stage of the search process (see figure 3.5). This model has guided several of the research projects that led her to develop a law—the uncertainty principle—which states that uncertainty (which is a cognitive state) generates feelings of anxiety and lack of confidence (Kuhlthau 2004). It should be noted that the use of the concept *uncertainty* is different from the one first introduced to information science; it was originally used in the context of the attempts to define *information* as that which reduces uncertainty. Kuhlthau explained that information did not always reduce uncertainty; in fact, at times it could create new uncertainties. She placed the concept in a dynamic context to reflect the cognitive uncertainty about the process and its success that people have when they look for information. Currently, the concept *uncertainty* is enjoying a revival, accepting various meanings and being discussed primarily among researchers with the in-context lens.

Other examples of laws can be derived from Sonnenwald's (2005) propositions. For instance, the first one ("human information behavior is shaped by and shapes individuals, social networks, situations, and contexts") claimed several regular sequences (Sonnenwald 2005, 192). That is, the social network of a person will shape his information behavior, and his information behavior will shape his social networks. This formulation of the laws can be repeated for the situations and the contexts in which a person is placed. The second proposition can be considered a law if we relax the definition of *laws* to include "tendencies of causal mechanisms—which may or may not be expressed in the form of observable regularities" (Benton and Craib 2001, 182).

The second proposition was, "Individuals or systems within a local situation and context may perceive, reflect, and/or evaluate change in others, self, and/or environment" (Sonnenwald 2005, 192). Reformulated as a law, it could claim that a tendency exists among individuals or systems to perceive, reflect, or evaluate changes around them when they are placed in a local situation and context.[6]

In the positivist sense, laws have predictive power, and therefore have explanatory power. With these powers they can guide and support studies carried out in the positivist tradition.[7]

3.2.3 Named Concepts

As an embryonic stage in building a theoretical construct, a scholar may define and name a concept and conduct studies about it, exposing its characteristics and importance. From among the variety of such concepts in ISB, three serve as examples.

The concept *imposed query* was introduced by Melissa Gross (1995). Imposed queries describe the situation when one person has an information problem and asks someone else to find the information that will resolve the problem. When a person searches for information to fulfill her mother's request, or when a librarian looks for information for a patron, they are executing searches for imposed queries. In her investigations of seeking behavior with such queries, Gross identified the variables that determine success in the resolution of imposed queries, defined the life cycle of impositions in the context of elementary school, and examined the implications of the imposed queries for the evaluation of library services (Gross 2005).

Two more recent concepts are *information grounds* and the *PAIN hypothesis*. Karen Fisher (formerly Pettigrew) borrowed the concept *grounds* from the lore of fishermen during her dissertation research project on community foot clinics for the elderly, in which nurses and other individuals shared health information. She defined *grounds* as "environment[s] temporarily created when people come together for a singular purpose but from whose behavior emerges a social atmosphere that fosters the spontaneous and serendipitous sharing of information" (Pettigrew 1999, 811). Through her subsequent research, Fisher identified seven concepts key to information grounds—*context rich*, *temporal setting*, and *social interaction*, among others. Her latest work has been dedicated to uncovering places that are information grounds and to finding the most common information grounds (Fisher, Naumer, et al. 2005).

Harry Bruce (2005) constructed the concept PAIN (personal anticipated information need) in the context of personal information management, to introduce the motivation and underpinning framework for information behavior in that context. More specifically, the PAIN hypothesis is related to a person's thoughts and actions when building and maintaining a personal information collection, which is the space individuals turn to first when they need to resolve an information need. A personal collection may include paper documents, notes, calendars, lists, website bookmarks, and people. PAIN has five propositions that Bruce introduced as a conceptual framework to propose that researchers engage in further study, continue to explore the concept, and validate or correct a proposition through empirical studies; hence the PAIN hypothesis.

When constructing concepts, scholars often neglect to ensure the rigor of their concept's definition. One such example (among quite a few others) is the concept of *imposed query*. Can the definition given by Gross discriminate between imposed queries and self-generated ones? As one example of an imposed query, Gross (2001) cites the queries students use to complete a class assignment. In this case, where does the information problem lie? Certainly not with the teacher; he does not expect the students' assignment to solve his problem. But, on the face of it, it does not lie with the students, either; they have not generated the information problem. On the other hand, one may claim that all students' queries are self-generated. They may look for information because they want to learn something new, to receive a high grade, to finish the assignment and get the teacher off their back, or to impress a classmate, among other reasons. All these goals are self-generated. Therefore, there are no impositions in this case, but rather constraints. The students, for instance, have to look for information that will help them satisfy the assignment's requirements; they may not be allowed to ask for help, and so forth. This constrained environment is not a special situation, as every information problem has its constraints. In sum, the definition of *imposed query* is not rigorous enough for other researchers to give it meaning and to use the concept in their work. Once rigorously defined, new concepts are seeds that may sprout and bloom into more complex theoretical constructs.

3.2.4 Theoretical Constructs: Conclusions

The area of ISB is blessed with many theoretical constructs of various types. It is possible that scholars took to heart the scarcity of "good" theories in this young field, rolled up their sleeves, and worked to move the field forward. These efforts, however, did not lead to a cumulative body that integrates constructs or defines relations among them. In this undertaking, it is easier for a scholar to find her own niche—create her own new concept, method, law, or theory—than to offer contributions to the perceptions of basic concepts in ISB that have already been investigated and theorized about. The map of theoretical work in the field indicates that many scholars opted for the easier road.

3.3   Action and Element Models

A *model* is defined here as a representation of a segment of reality. It may represent a real reality—for those who think that there is reality independent of our perceptions—or a perceived one.[8] A city map, for example, may be accepted as a representation of a city that exists whether or not we have ever heard its name, but Dervin's graphic presentation of the sense-making methodology metaphor (figure 3.1) is a representation of a concept—a thing that cannot exist independent of our perception. Similarly, a model can represent observable reality or one that is inaccessible to observation. One can observe, for instance, the thoughts of an actor when searching for information (by asking her to think aloud), but he cannot observe her general state of knowledge. Yet both can be represented in models.

The LIS community commonly assumes that models must have some type of graphic presentation. Indeed, most models in HIB are presented in a diagram form. As a representation of a segment of reality, however, a model may have various forms, such as mathematical formulas, artifact, or narrative text. In this sense of the concept *model*, most empirical studies in ISB create models because their findings represent a part of the actual reality of information-seeking behavior. Some represent behavior of people in general (common among cognitive studies) and others represent that of specific groups (identified by social and/or other context characteristics). The form researchers most often use to represent this reality is a narrative text, or research report. Such reports, which may also include drawings and formulas, are not labeled as "models" by their creators, even though they are models in the broad sense of the concept. This section addresses the limited interpretation of the concept and focuses on constructs that were identified as "models" by their originators. That is, the term *model* is limited in this section to this type.

Models in ISB can be divided according to the dimension of reality they represent: *action models* represent activities during information seeking and, at times, even before and after; *element models* represent elements that shape information seeking (or, to translate into positivist language: models that represent the variables affecting information seeking). Other models—*mixed models*—include both; some side by side, others in an integrated fashion. The method by which models were constructed is not uniform either. Similar to theoretical constructs, some of the models have been developed through empirical research, and others were based on theoretical foundations with plans to empirically test their relevance.

3.3.1 Action Models

Action models represent activities during information seeking in a variety of styles. Some represent the search process with ordered successive activities, others are two-dimensional diagrams that add a representation of the relations between the activities, and yet others list activities in no specific order.

The first prominent model was created by Robert Taylor (1968), who represented the flow of activities during a search process, mainly in the library context. This model focused on activities occurring before the actual direct interaction with information, with three decision points (the square boxes) in which the actor decides what to do next (figure 3.2). The main purpose of the model, which Taylor based on interviews with special librarians and on his own experience, was to help librarians to structure reference interviews. The next model he presented for that purpose delineated the five aspects that are necessary for understanding a query: (1) determination of subject; (2) objective and motivation; (3) personal characteristics of the inquirer; (4) relationships of inquiry description to file organization; and (5) anticipated or acceptable answers (Taylor 1968, 183). Taylor explained that the listing is approximately in the order of occurrence.

Michael Eisenberg and Robert Berkowitz (1990) developed a model of the same type—dubbed the *Big Six*—that included six successive steps guiding actors as they go through the process of solving an information problem. From beginning to end, the steps are: (1) task definition; (2) information-seeking strategies; (3) location and access; (4) use of information; (5) synthesis; (6) evaluation. This model was created to support teaching information literacy in elementary schools and was based on the creators' experience in addition to anecdotal and informal evidence. It has been expanded to other educational settings and is already used in the educational systems of several countries.

James Krikelas (1983) created a model similar to Taylor's graphic presentation of the first stages in information seeking. His is the first holistic model to be published that points to various information sources—including memory and observation—and that lays out the process from the need-creating event and environment to information gathering and giving (figure 3.3). Krikelas's model is also among the first to represent information seeking in general, stepping away from the traditional approach at the time, which had focused on libraries and educational settings, and providing the groundwork for future theories and models in ISB.

Dagobert Soergel (1985, 15) took a similar, general approach when he developed a model for the acquisition and use of information that analyzed information seeking in the context of decision making, which he perceived to be the goal of information

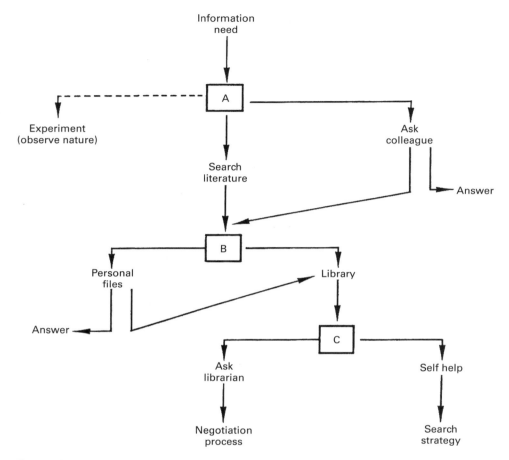

Figure 3.2
Taylor's (1968) model of prenegotiation decisions by the inquirer. Source: American Library Association.

seeking and use (figure 3.4). Because decision making is a cognitive process, the model placed the cognitive process in the center of human activities. Moreover, it explicitly recorded tacit activities during this process, such as the processing and interpretation of ideas and updating the seeker's image of both the actual and the desired states of affairs. Soergel's model expanded on the previous models in additional ways. Unlike earlier models, its aim was to be highly general in order to fit information seeking in both databases and text-retrieval systems.[9] In addition, it incorporated information use as an integral part of information seeking, since it represented situations in which

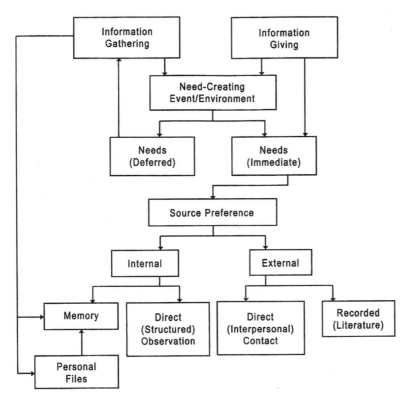

Figure 3.3
Krikelas's model of information seeking. From Krikelas (1983); reprinted with the permission of College of Information Science and Technology, Drexel University.

actors use information retrieved to continue the search. The model also covered situations in which a decision is made without looking for information at all, and in which an information need is resolved without the use of external information sources. At the time of its publication, it was the most universal and detailed model of seeking information.

These first models to represent a complete picture of the seeking process were based primarily on personal experience and laid out an ideal process with its alternatives. Kuhlthau (1991) was the first to study the seeking process empirically and systematically, with a beginning, a middle, and an end. Her model—the "information search process"—has drawn much attention and supported the work of a number of LIS scholars (see, for example, T. D. Wilson et al. 2000). She based the model on a

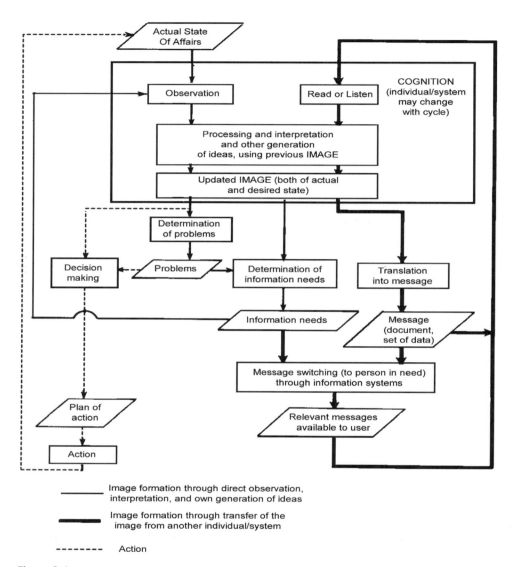

Figure 3.4

Soergel's model for the acquisition and use of information. From Soergel (1985), 15; reprinted with the permission of Elsevier.

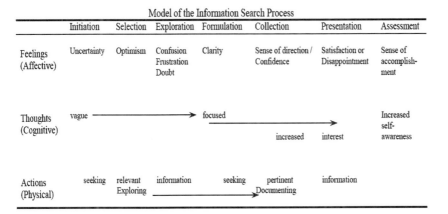

Figure 3.5
Kuhlthau's model of the information search process (ISP). Source: http://comminfo.rutgers
.edu/~kuhlthau/information_search_process.htm

longitudinal, term-long study of high school students who were in the process of writing a paper as a class assignment. Kuhlthau (1991) applied the work of the psychologist George Kelly on personal construct theory, which inspired her to study the actor's experience. The stages Kelly identified in the process of personal construction of meaning and the role of cognitive and affective aspects provided the basis for the empirical study that generated Kuhlthau's model (figure 3.5). Like Dervin, she continued to work on the concepts and relations she found in the first empirical study and went on to enrich it through several subsequent studies. This work led her to formulate the uncertainty principle.

Kuhlthau's novel contribution to ISB went beyond her linear description of the search process. In her studies she investigated the transformations of three facets within the progression of the search process: the affective (feelings), the cognitive (thoughts), and the physical (actions). Explaining that people experience the search process holistically, she presented the interplay of these three facets by following their transformation during the process along parallel lines. Unlike many of the previous models, hers was not purely a behavioral one since it represented feelings and thoughts.

One should note that the information search process model was based on a study of high school students in a distinct context: they searched for information to help them write a paper that was assigned in a specific class and that required the students to select a topic. Not surprisingly, the stages in the model reflect the process of preparation for writing such a paper, and thus may not reflect seeking processes in other situations. Although Kuhlthau did not claim the model to be general, quite a few researchers accepted it as a model that applies to any search process—possibly with the encouragement of the universal nature of its name. Also, a few researchers who were aware of the context tested the model on *university* students in similar situations and modified it to describe the college students' search processes (e.g., Vakkari 2001). Others had concluded that the model required modifications in order to be applied in the environments they studied (e.g., Hyldegård 2006; Rose 2006). Kuhlthau (1997) herself employed it in her study of the information behavior of a securities analyst. These studies may serve as the first steps in generalizing the information search process model. Because the model is context dependent, many additional tests in various other situations will be required to gradually build its generality.

Another departure from the traditional action models of information seeking was introduced by David Ellis (1993). Rather than representing seeking as a sequence of activities, he identified types of activities that may occur at any stage of the seeking process, such as chaining (following chains of citations or other forms of referential connection between materials), browsing (semidirected searching in an area of potential interest), surveying (familiarizing oneself with the literature of the area), and verifying (checking that information is correct). His first iteration of the model was the result of an empirical study of the information-seeking behavior of academic social scientists. He then expanded the model through studies of other actors, such as English literature researchers and physicists as well as engineers and research scientists in industry. Each study revealed the use of at least some of the activities in the initial model and added new ones. The model has become more general with each new group of actors Ellis has studied. It is purely behavioral, focusing on directly observable activities.

Action models in ISB have been molded in various forms, from a two-dimensional graphic representation of sequences and possible activities to the identification of types of activities. It is undesirable, however, and maybe impossible, to pull them all together into one grand model. Not only do the models have different forms, which raise barriers to blending, but integrating the activities would also result in a structure with internal conflicts and inconsistencies, and it might be too big to be relevant to the field.[10] But on a positive note, the plurality of models offers a diversity of choices for scholars who wish to consider action models in their work.

3.3.2 Element Models
Element models lay out those elements involved in information seeking that their creators deem central to the phenomenon. These elements may be ones that shape

the process, are shaped by it, or both. For instance, a model that indicates that information seeking is affected by the complexity of the decision for which information is required, and the urgency of the task for which the decision is required, is a model with two elements—in this case, two factors that shape information seeking. Only a few models represent elements of information seeking exclusively. Three such models have been heavily discussed in the ISB literature: Nickolas Belkin's (1980) model, which was purely cognitive; Peter Ingwersen's (1999) model, which was primarily cognitive but introduced some socio-organizational elements; and Gloria Leckie and Karen Fisher's model (Leckie and Pettigrew 1997), which was strongly socio-organizational.

Belkin's and Ingwersen's models were originally constructed for the information retrieval (IR) community and, therefore, used the term *information retrieval* instead of *information-seeking behavior*. Both models were cognitive and conceptually more comprehensive than other models; they represented information systems as well as information seeking, and dealt with them as equal partners.

In the *anomalous state of knowledge* (ASK) model, Belkin (1980) approached information seeking with the view that the process was initiated by the actors. To the questions of when and why actors look for information, he answered: when they have an anomalous state of knowledge (see figure 3.6), which occurs when a person's knowledge is not adequate to resolve an information problem. He further noted that most approaches in the field assumed that people knew what information they were seeking.

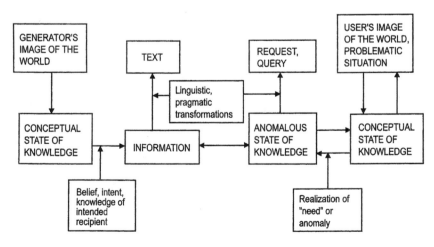

Figure 3.6
Belkin's ASK model. From Belkin (2005); reprinted with the permission of Information Today.

However, he claimed, most of the time people *don't know what they don't know* and cannot articulate their needs. Therefore, he recommended, we should view the seeking process at its very early inception, at ASK, and not assume that the process begins when people are able to spell out their information need or even when they are just able to determine its topic.

The ASK model bears similarities to other models, such as Taylor's (1968) model, which included the stages of the development of a need.[11] At the beginning of a need's formation, an individual feels a "vague sort of dissatisfaction ... [that is] inexpressible in linguistic terms" (182). Taylor named this the *visceral* stage. Later stages keep developing the need so that it can be presented to an information system. Clearly, the visceral stage and ASK represent the same state with different language and, as a result, slightly different meanings. Belkin's description of the concept *anomaly*—a state in which a person's knowledge is not adequate to resolve an information problem—is also very similar to Dervin's explanation of the "gap" that is created when a person's sense-making is not adequate to continue his journey through time and space. Here again, we have same situation—with different expressions and therefore varying meanings. Despite this similarity, sense-making methodology and ASK have developed in different directions. Basically, Dervin's model was set in context and was built to develop an overarching and rich methodology, while ASK was purely cognitive, independent of context, and was produced to support user-centered design of information systems.[12]

Another unique attribute of ASK is the level of analysis that it requires when applied in research. Belkin suggested that anomalies can be of different types that can be identified, both theoretically and in actual tests. No previous model had attempted to address cognitive processes to such a level of specificity. As a result of this approach, Belkin expanded the role of information systems: in addition to retrieving information, they should help users crystallize their need, much like the role the librarian fulfilled during reference interviews in Taylor's model. Belkin saw identifying the types of anomaly—and what information support they require—as a first step in designing systems that could fulfill this role.

Another model builder, Peter Ingwersen, is also a proponent of a cognitive view of information seeking that is closely associated with the design of information systems. Throughout the years, he has developed several models that he has continued to revise. His purely cognitive model, which represented the cognitive communication system for IR (Ingwersen 1999, 14), was similar to Belkin's approach in that both represented the actor as well as the system. Ingwersen, however, saw symmetry between the elements in the actor's and the system's contexts that made his model unique. Ingwersen's models were based on his view that during information retrieval an information system (whether human or machine) and a human actor are involved in an interaction that requires cognitive, and even emotional, processes in both participants. Therefore, a study of, say, users' seeking behavior that is divorced from an understanding of the system's retrieval behavior is incomplete. His *cognitive model in IR interaction* (Ingwersen 1996, 9), which is based on this same view, dealt most specifically with information seeking (figure 3.7). An expansion on the purely cognitive models, this model included elements such as the social and organizational environment and the work task or interest of the actor. The symmetry of actor and system is not as pronounced in this model; in fact, it is also incomplete since the system's environment (e.g., level of technological developments, policies, and laws) is absent.

While symmetry is attractive because of its elegance, it is still difficult to understand how the cognitive and emotional states of the designer affect the design of an information system, particularly when the design process spans a period longer than a day (which is usually the case), during which time both states may go through several transformations. Even when used metaphorically, viewing each algorithm as

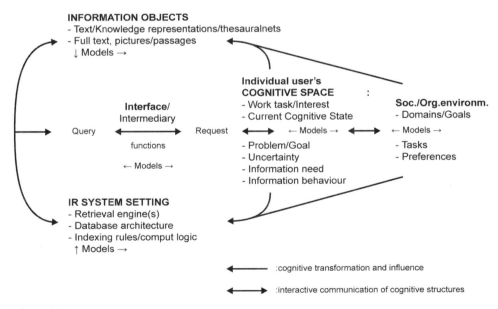

Figure 3.7
Ingwersen's cognitive model in IR interaction. From Ingwersen (1996); reprinted with the permission of Emerald Group Publishing Limited.

a cognitive state, it is not clear how these states shape the interaction. Moreover, the actor's cognitive and emotional states occur before and during each interaction. In contrast, information systems are designed for *all* interactions and their design is supposed to be stable for a period of time. To keep the symmetry, the system would have to choose an algorithm for each stage in a query. This capability has not come to be yet and is possibly a goal that is undesirable and cannot be achieved. Nevertheless, this theoretical view is appealing and may lead to new insights.

It is not surprising that both Belkin and Ingwersen have focused on the cognitive aspects of information seeking. Both developed their models for the IR community, which is composed primarily of computer scientists who aim to develop general-context systems.[13] In addition, the few IR researchers who have investigated information seeking have conducted laboratory experiments with computer-based information systems, which supported the design of general-context systems. Since cognitive aspects are considered common to all human beings, considering them may support the design of general-context systems. Moreover, because the cognitive state is considered to be independent of the context,[14] laboratory experiments are valid tools to study information behavior from the cognitive perspective. IR researchers have just begun to integrate cognitive aspects in their experiments. At this point, it is not clear to what degree such aspects can guide systems design. It is too early, therefore, to consider the integration of other factors, such as social and contextual ones, into the design of computer-based, general-context systems—those that are designed to successfully respond to queries submitted by any actor in any situation.

Choosing a different path from Belkin's and Ingwersen's general and cognitive approaches, Leckie, Pettigrew, and Sylvain (1996) chose to investigate information seeking on the job. Based on a literature review of professionals' seeking behavior in three fields (engineering, healthcare, and law), they created a basic model, much less detailed than the previous ones, of the elements that shape seeking behavior (figure 3.8). The model contributed two new elements: work roles and awareness of information. They explained that a task could not be considered without examining the role of the actor, whether, say, managerial, technical, or interpersonal. The task of writing a memo, for instance, will generate unique information needs for members of each of the three groups. This combination of the task and the role would generate the information need that had to be met to continue the work. The seeking process was shaped by three dynamically interlinked elements: sources of information, awareness of information (knowledge of the information sources and the search process), and the outcome of the seeking process. Leckie and Pettigrew (1997) explained that they intentionally selected simple and relatively abstract elements. They claimed that many

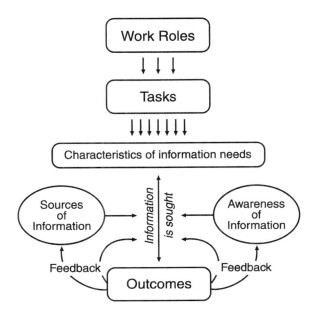

Figure 3.8
Leckie, Pettigrew, and Sylvain's model of the information seeking of professionals. From Leckie, Pettigrew, and Sylvain (1996); reprinted with the permission of University of Chicago Press.

of the specific elements that represented professionals' information-seeking behavior depended on local contexts, which made them improper for a general model. They replaced these specifics with broad, abstract elements for a general representation.

Element models can offer unique contributions both to research and design in information science. For research in the positivist tradition, these models propose variables and their possible associations ready for testing. They may also offer interpretive researchers some elements they may want to consider in their investigations. Creative designers of information systems and services can benefit by recognizing the constraints that limit and enable actors, as is argued in chapter 9.

3.3.3 Mixed Models

Several of the models representing information behavior are mixed ones, whether deliberately or inadvertently. The most integrative models represent activities in the seeking process and link these activities to the elements that shape each one of them. Two influential models show the nature of such models: one constructed by Tom Wilson (1997) and the other by Katriina Byström and Kalervo Järvelin (1995). A different type of mixed model, created by Reijo Savolainen (1995), could be called an embedded model, in which the activities are nested in several levels of elements that shape them.

Tom Wilson, who is one of the founders of the field of HIB and a most prolific writer, has developed an ever-evolving set of models.[15] The first were element models (e.g., Wilson 1981) based on his empirical research at a U.K. local-authority social services department (Wilson and Streatfield 1977; Streatfield and Wilson 1982). After additional empirical studies and further developments in the field, Wilson (1997) amalgamated his previous models and fused them with components of theories in fields such as psychology and education to build a new and revised model. In this model, as shown in figure 3.9, the first four columns represent elements (variables or theories) that all lead to information seeking, which is represented in the fifth column in one black box. The columns represent consecutive progression and thus, implicitly, stages in seeking. The first "Activating mechanism" box represents the decision to take action to satisfy an information need, and the second such box represents the decision to search information sources.

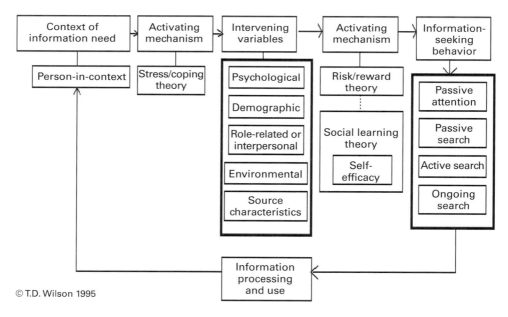

Figure 3.9
Wilson's general model of information-seeking behavior. Source: http://informationr.net/tdw/publ/papers/1999JDoc.html. Reprinted with the permission of Tom Wilson.

Wilson (2005) offered the model as a general framework for research in ISB. On the one hand, he shows that it is general enough to represent various HII situations, such as encountering information, which was represented by including boxes for passive attention and passive search. On the other, he claims, it can contribute to all research in ISB by drawing "the attention of the researcher to the totality of information behavior and showing how a specific piece of research may contribute to an understanding of the whole" (Wilson 2005, 35).

Byström and Järvelin (1995) picked up where Wilson's model closed; they opened the black box of information seeking in the context of the workplace. Their model, which was less ambitious than Wilson's, was constructed to guide their research project about the effects of task complexity on information behavior and use (figure 3.10). They derived the model from previous research and from models in HIB to

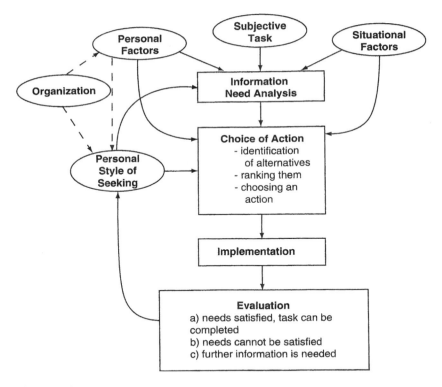

Figure 3.10
Byström and Järvelin's model of information seeking. From Byström and Järvelin (1995); reprinted with the permission of Elsevier. © 1995 Elsevier.

embody a process-in-context in which the task was a central element. Their model represented information seeking on two planes, each designated with its own graphical form— ellipsoids and boxes—one for the elements and the other for the activities carried out during a seeking process. An arrow from a box (designating an activity) led to the next stage in the process, and an arrow from an ellipsoid (designating an element) led to the stages it shaped. These explicit, many-to-many relationships between elements and activities are very rare in HIB models, which have usually represented the seeking process on a higher level of abstraction. However, the Byström and Järvelin model was built to lay out the assumed relationships that had guided their study. Its central goal was to serve as a source for formulating research questions and generating hypotheses—rather than to serve as a model to guide studies in general.

Whereas the Byström and Järvelin model represented information seeking in the work environment, Savolainen (1995) represented another facet of life in his model of *everyday-life information-seeking* (ELIS). The model was based on previous work in HIB and informed by "the theory of *habitus* developed by Pierre Bourdieu" (Savolainen 1995, 261). It provided a graphic representation of the process, with boxes nested in boxes, where elements in a box shaped those in the box nested in it, with some reciprocal relationships in the central box (figure 3.11). Factors that shape everyday life were laid out in the long box on the right-hand side of the center box. In the center were the elements in everyday life, all nesting the process of information seeking (in the bottom left-hand box). To fully understand the model requires reading the article that describes it because Savolainen created new concepts to represent daily life and people's approaches to it.

One of the contributions of the model is the representation of reciprocal and dynamic relations between activities and the elements that shape them. For instance, "problem-solving behavior" and "problematic situations of everyday life" shape one another. Clearly, a specific problematic situation would shape the way an actor solved the problem. At the same time, however, the process of solving the problem would create a new problematic situation, the shape of which would be influenced by the way the actor had solved the previous problem. The model is still continuing to evolve as Savolainen and other researchers have been testing it and discussing refinements.

3.3.4 Models: Conclusion

Most of the models presented here were heavily and productively used by other researchers for empirical as well as conceptual investigations. Yet their variety raises a question: Why is there a need for so many models? After all, they all represent the

EVERYDAY LIFE

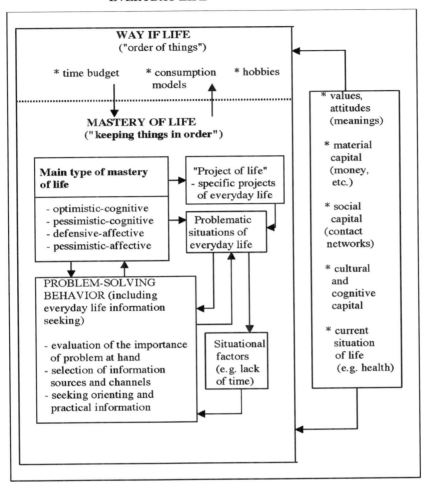

Figure 3.11
Savolainen's model of everyday-life information-seeking. From Savolainen (1995); reprinted with the permission of Elsevier. © 1995 Elsevier.

same reality (whether real or perceived): Why not aspire to create one grand model that includes them all? Some scholars believe that there is a need for such a model (e.g., Hepworth 2004; Kuhlthau 2005). Tom Wilson (1994), for example, argued:

[T]here is a need for an integrative model of information need, information-seeking behaviour and information use. That integrative model is already almost complete: it is a person-centered model, based largely on Dervin's 'sense-making' approach, but with extensions (actual and potential) into models of information-seeking behaviour, the multi-contextual character of information needs and the nature of user satisfaction. (42)

Wilson (1999) made a first step in this direction and tried to integrate three models without success (as described earlier). His failure was not a result of poor execution, but stemmed from the inherent impossibility of such an endeavor. It is also not clear whether the creation of a global, unified model is desirable.

Several reasons make the creation of a grand model almost impossible. The models are of different types (action, element, and mixed models) and on a different level of abstraction, and the number of elements and the level of specificity of the activity descriptions is very high, all of which result in a great number of components to integrate into one model. Furthermore, each new model introduces new elements, activities, and relations. If all were to be included in one model, the resultant construct would become unmanageable and probably almost impossible to understand. This barrier can be removed, however, if the grand model is much more abstract than the current models. This way, specific elements and activities would be subsumed under broader categories that might render the model manageable and coherent. The risk in building such a model is the possibility that its generality would make it useless—in other words, that the activities, elements, and their relations so broadly described could be ascertained with common sense alone.

More important than constructing one grand model is the nature of these individual models: Each one represents reality from its creator's point of view and her perception of it. Moreover, no "agreement" among creators can be expected, nor a complete overlap among models in the concepts they represent. Is it possible, then, to create an "objective" model? If yes, who would be qualified to build it? If no, whose view should guide the creation of the one grand model? It is highly unlikely that responses to these questions can be found. To overcome some of these difficulties, one may suggest that there might be several grand models, each with a different point of view. While theoretically possible, such an approach seems impractical for models of ISB since the creators' points of view are highly diverse as well and no dominant perspectives can be identified. This diversity emphasizes a creator's responsibility to explicitly explain what theories, ideas, and theoretical traditions have shaped his model, as such explanations increase the depth of readers' understanding of the model.

The lack of a grand model is not a loss to the field. In fact, I believe such a model is undesirable. While HIB models represent the same reality, their variety represents the diversity of research approaches in the area. A diverse research community has many advantages. For example, different approaches bring to light different aspects of the same object of study and new concepts. While this variety is a barrier to integration, it is a source of stimulation and cross-fertilization. Avoiding one dominant approach offers a space for researchers whose point of view differs from the dominant approach and creates the conditions for new developments. In addition, with so many models, it is likely that almost every researcher can identify an existing model that would support and guide her work.

3.4   Conceptual Constructs: Conclusions

The rate of growth of ISB conceptual constructs has accelerated in time. While at its inception the field saw one new construct every two or three years, quite a few of them have been sprouting each year in recent times.[16] This vigorous activity in building conceptual constructs can be partially explained by the lack of some generally accepted ones that can support research work. Some may explain the flood of constructs by claiming that ISB is a young field and as such is still in the process of building its conceptual foundations. In that case, it is not clear whether ISB research is on a constructive path for foundation building. While some constructs may accidentally complement one another, there have been no efforts to follow a cumulative process. A few constructs have been influential—such as those created by Taylor (1968), Dervin (1992), and Chatman (2000)—and have contributed to the development of other ISB constructs, but almost all of the many others were constructed with no reference to their equals and are completely independent of one another.

Having variety in conceptual constructs is necessary for a field to be open-minded and accepting of a diversity of viewpoints. But this variety is more likely to be productive with some self-control, whereas ISB constructs are out of control, pushing in many different directions. Most have been applied only by their creators, even though each one provides its own contribution. One hopes that future developments might lead to some convergence, resulting in a smaller number of constructs, each with implications that can nourish a variety of research strands. These could provide a solid conceptual foundation to ISB.

4 Information Need and the Decision Ladder

The concept *information need* is fundamental to human information interaction across all its areas of research. For instance, evaluating information is carried out in reference to an information need, and representing information is guided by predictions about the information needs of the actors for whom the representation is constructed. Similarly, sharing information takes place to satisfy an actor's information need, and filtering information is conducted to satisfy future needs. However, scholars in human information behavior (HIB), and in particular in information-seeking behavior (ISB), have studied this concept more than scholars in any other area. An information need is the foundation on which the seeking process rests, as all search decisions and activities—such as query formulation, relevance judgment, and ending a search—are guided by the need. This essential position is also reflected in HIB's cognitive models (see section 3.3), which all center on information need, although they present it at times by using different terms. Although an information need may change during the search process,[1] an information need is always present. By its very definition, a search for information takes place when there is a need; when there is no need, there is no search.[2]

Intuitively, the concept seems simple and straightforward, but when it is considered an object of study, *information need* becomes complex and slippery. One sticky issue is how we can define *need* in a way that distinguishes it from *non-needs*. Scholars in information science—and in other social sciences as well—have been discussing its definition for several decades with no agreed-upon conclusion. Even when a researcher has accepted a certain definition, it is not simple to empirically distinguish between a genuine information need and what seems to be one but is actually something else.

4.1 Definitional Challenges

Among HIB scholars, Robert S. Taylor was the most influential in the study of the information need. He followed Mackay's (1960) description of a state of need: "a certain incompleteness in [an actor's] picture of the world—an inadequacy in what we might call his 'state of readiness' to interact purposefully with the world around him" (cited in Taylor 1968, 180). Guided by this idea of an information need, Taylor identified four consecutive cognitive stages in which a need develops (he notes that not all needs complete their development at the time an actor interacts with an information system):

Q1—the actual, but unexpressed need for information (the *visceral* need);

Q2—the conscious, within-brain description of the need (the *conscious* need);

Q3—the formal statement of the need (the *formalized* need);

Q4—the question as presented to the information system (the *compromised* need). (Taylor 1968, 182)

That is, in the *visceral* stage, an actor feels a sense of uneasiness, vaguely recognizing a state of incompleteness. In the *conscious* stage, he can identify the area of incompleteness. If he continues to develop the information need, it would arrive at the *formalized* stage in which he describes the area in concrete terms, making it as explicit as possible. To submit the formalized information need to an information system, the actor is likely to present a *compromised* information need. Various conditions may call for a compromised version, such as the requirement to translate the need into the system's language, the tendency to ask for what one expects to be able to get, and a desire to protect privacy by concealing the "real" need, particularly when its subject is sensitive. This analysis of a need's formation has had great impact on conceptual developments in the cognitive approach of HIB, and its rigor and value are still being discussed (e.g., Nicolaisen 2009; Cole 2011), although much less frequently than in the early research period. Nevertheless, several definitions and views of *information need* have emerged independently.

4.1.1   The Shift from *Information Need* to *Task*

Naumer and Fisher (2009) reviewed and analyzed the concept of information need in the third edition of the *Encyclopedia of Library and Information Sciences*. They offered several examples of early definitions that echoed Taylor's construal of an information need:

Notable definitions of information need cited by Dervin and Nilan include: "a conceptual incongruity in which the person's cognitive structure is not adequate to a task" [Ford 1980], "when a person recognizes something wrong in his or her state of knowledge and wishes to resolve the anomaly" [Belkin 1978], "when the current state of possessed knowledge is less than needed" [Krikelas 1983], and "when internal sense runs out" [Dervin 1980]. (Naumer and Fisher 2009)

While not all the definitions above employed the term *information need*, the concept they defined included elements of Taylor's view.

Later definitions have related the concept of *information need* directly to the search process, expressing the need as the prelude to a search process. More specifically, information need was presented as the motivating force behind seeking information or as the trigger for it (e.g., H. Bruce 2005; T. D. Wilson 1981). With the spread of the context-sensitive approach, researchers have raised the notion that the context in which an actor is situated contributes to the shaping of an information need, because the motivation for information seeking is not only cognitive but contextual as well.[3]

The latest view—information needs are triggers for information seeking—together with the desire to identify specific needs in empirical studies, inspired some scholars to shift the center of research from the information need to the *task* that motivates searching for information. This move gained rapid acceptance not only because there was an increasing realization of the role of context, of which the task is a part, but also because it freed scholars from handling the somewhat amorphous concept of information need, an issue that had been particularly challenging in empirical studies. A clear example of this shift is the change in experiments in information retrieval driven by Borlund's (2000, 2003a, 2009) work. In such experiments it is now common to present participants with a task for which they are asked to search for information, rather than giving them an information need, which was the common practice in the past. Other attempts to move away from information need took various forms, such as the use of the term *information problem*, which seems to have gained popularity in recent writings.[4]

The transformation in scholars' understanding of the concept of *information need* was not accidental: It was brought about by the new possibilities that were afforded by new technologies to study the search *process*. In addition, Tuominen, Talja, and Savolainen (2002) explained that the definitional views of *information need* emanated from different theoretical traditions, with each view reflecting the dominant tradition of the day (see also Cronin 2008). They identified three consecutive traditions: the information-transfer, the constructivist, and the constructionist traditions.[5] These traditions correspond roughly to the physical, cognitive, and the social views.[6]

The substitutes for *information need* have made it easier to operationalize the concept. For instance, when conducting a naturalistic study, it is simpler to identify and explicitly delineate a task than to recognize an information need with all its dimensions. Such substitutes, however, carry new challenges, both conceptually and in their application in empirical studies.

Consider the concept *task*, for example, as a substitute for the concept *information need*. To agree on its definition is almost as complex as determining that of *information need* (see, e.g., Vakkari 2003). In addition, employing *task* as a substitute requires a particular view of the concept. The concept of task was introduced to include a contextual element that generates, motivates, or triggers information seeking. Yet the approach most researchers took to investigating task failed to lead to an understanding of how and why a task motivated information seeking. Scholars have focused on attributes of a task—such as complexity and flexibility—and some found association with variables in seeking behavior, but without addressing the triggering aspects of the task.[7] With this approach, *task* is another contextual element rather than a substitute for *information need*. What is missing is an understanding of how tasks should be analyzed, and what attributes should be investigated, for a task to serve a promising substitute for an information need. That is, selecting a substitute for information need that is applicable to empirical research calls for further analysis of the concept of *task*.

4.2 Operational Challenges

Since information need is a foundational concept on which information seeking rests, it is commonly agreed that a study of an information-seeking process requires the identification of the information needs that triggered it. This discovery has been considered challenging because it is assumed that most often it is difficult to discriminate between needs and non-needs that present themselves as needs. Indeed, most empirical researchers investigated information needs without regard to the definitional complexity. Challenges arose when scholars attempted to determine universal types of information needs.

4.2.1 Want, Demand, or Need?

In the early 1970s, after almost a decade of HIB research, some scholars raised the notion that needs are not researchable because they are in the actors' minds and therefore not observable. Yet user studies of that period identified the "information needs" of the population they had investigated. This contradiction gave rise to the concept *information demand*, that is, the information need as it is expressed by an actor—the only "need" that could had been observed in empirical studies. This new concept resolved the conflict to the degree that researchers could explain that they studied information demands, rather than information needs. Another concept, *information want*, was added to represent what an actor thinks he needs. The distinction among the concepts can be crudely described as

- Information *want*—what an actor thinks he needs
- Information *demand*—what an actor says he needs
- Information *need*—what an actor actually needs, objectively.[8]

The three concepts are not always different from one another; in specific situations, particularly simple ones, they might all be the same. When I search the web to find an address I need for sending a letter, for instance, my want, demand, and need are the same.

A simple example may demonstrate these concepts. Jonathan is a first-year student whose task is to choose an elective course. To decide whether or not to select a course in decorative plants, his information *want* is to know how good the instructor is. Having no colleagues who are familiar with the instructor, his information *demand* is to look at course evaluations, which he finds on the web. An experienced academic advisor would have suggested that his information *need* is the average grades the instructor gave in the last three years because Jonathan's implicit idea of a good instructor is one who grades generously.

The three concepts, and the interplay among them, stimulated scholarly discussions among early researchers (e.g., Brittain 1970; Crawford 1978; Faibisoff and Ely 1976)[9]—although they had very little impact on the way empirical studies have been conducted. One of the questions addressed whether there are "objective" needs and, if so, how they can be determined and who has the authority to determine what the objective need is.[10] Another question was whether an information system should provide the information an actor needs objectively or the information she requested. Discussion of the three concepts is rare now, as if the topic had lost its importance. Nevertheless, a reflective researcher who studies information needs may want to make a distinction among the concepts to accurately express the phenomenon of study.

4.2.2 Types of Information Needs

While studying the information behavior of engineers and scientists, early researchers—most of whom were not occupied with the definition of *information need*—attempted to discover types of information needs, presumably to then investigate how they shaped seeking behavior. Lipetz (1970) reported on one of the first such typologies that was recognized in the early 1960s and was tested and confirmed: current, specific, and exhaustive need. Lin and Garvey (1972) explained that most of the attempts to examine types of needs had focused on the channel dimension—e.g., libraries, audiovisual aids, and training programs—and only a few, small-scale studies had examined the type of material actors need, e.g., practical guides, review articles, or material of high relevance. Various attempts to construct a universal typology of needs have been made since then (e.g., Derr 1984; Ingwersen 1986; Meadow, Boyce, and Kraft 2000), but no cumulative construct has followed. Because interest in the topic has been waning, typological efforts have been rare in recent years. Although the idea is not explicitly expressed, it seems that the diversity among the typologies led to a conclusion that there might not be one universal typology. Needs come in all shapes and forms, and each researcher may catch only some of this richness. This leads to the notion that while needs cannot be typified on a universal level, each context may shape a set of typical needs.

Indeed, many studies of HIB in context investigated the information needs that were typical to each actor community they studied, even though most researchers were not attempting to create a typology. Although not attempted yet, a systematic integration of research results for a context may result in the context's typology of information needs.

4.3   The Decision Ladder

The accomplishment of a cognitive task is likely to require making at least one decision. Therefore, another approach to the identification of an information need is to identify the decision that generated it. In general, the construal of the concept *information need* is linked to the meaning one assigns to the concept *information*. Taylor's (1968) view of an information need and its development, for instance, is compatible with the definition of *information* as "that which reduces uncertainty." Guided by the systems approach, my definition of *information* is different and includes the basic assumption that information is for decision making[11]—that is, the need for information arises when a decision is to be made. Therefore, a closer understanding of the decision-making process is likely to result in a deeper understanding of the concept *information need*.

Much research has been conducted on decision making, and several models of the process have been created. One of these models is the *decision ladder* that Jens Rasmussen (1986) established when he and his colleagues developed the conceptual framework of cognitive work analysis (see chapters 11 and 12).

The decision ladder presents the process of decision making through three phases: (1) situation analysis, (2) evaluation, and (3) planning. Figure 4.1 introduces this model, in which the "situation analysis" phase is represented by the left leg of the ladder (climbing upward), "evaluation" by its top, and "planning" by the right leg (climbing down). In this presentation, "knowledge states" are indicated by circles and

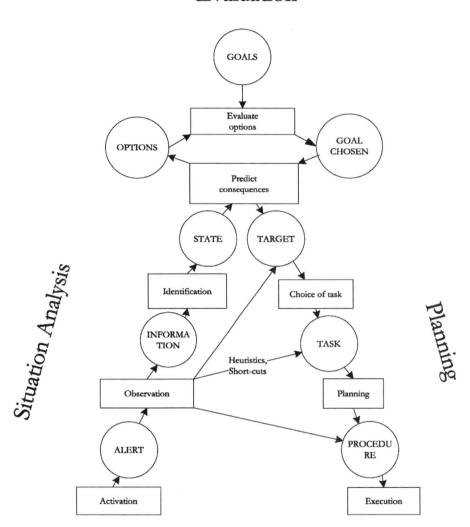

Figure 4.1
The decision ladder.

"information processing" actions by rectangular boxes. Knowledge states represent the knowledge the actors have on the state of affairs; arriving at each such state may require a certain category of information processing. For example, to understand how a problem fits into the general scheme of things (a knowledge state), one must observe, collect information, and analyze the environment in which one operates (information processing). Actors involved in a decision-making process traverse from one state of knowledge to another through information processing. Information seeking takes place during information processing, in that every time actors are involved in information processing that would lead them to a new knowledge state, they may seek information from sources external to themselves. That is, information needs arise during information processing.

Each phase in the decision ladder entails its own activities.

Situation analysis   In this phase, actors identify the current state of affairs and define the problem that requires a decision. This phase has various knowledge states and the information processing associated with it. During *activation* actors find out that a decision has to be made. This leads them to a new knowledge state in which they are *alert* to the new situation. Through *observation*, which may include various activities of information gathering and analysis in order to understand the situation, they arrive at a new state, *information*, in which they understand what information is relevant to the decision to be made. Processing the relevant information via *identification*, the actors can now proceed to the process of identifying what the problem is or what decision has to be made in the new knowledge *state*,[12] which is the final knowledge state in the situation analysis phase.

Evaluation   In the evaluation phase of the decision ladder, actors have defined the problem but have no solutions yet. During the process of evaluation they decide on the solution; that is, they decide what actions to take to solve the problem. To begin this process, actors *predict the consequences* of various possible solutions. Given the goals, constraints, and priorities of the task and the work context, as well as their own, they *evaluate options*. This process involves comparison and selection that will define the solution to the problem and the desired change in the state of affairs. During these iterative processes, several knowledge states are constantly updated: the knowledge the actors have about the *options* before them, the *goals* they should consider, and the goals they select to consider together with the solution they chose to pursue—that is, the *goal chosen*. At the end of the evaluation process, actors have a *target*, that is, the solution they would like to implement.

Planning   In the planning phase, actors plan the procedures that will implement the solution they decided on. Here the purpose is to identify the changes that need to be made in the current state of affairs so that the selected solution will be reached effectively. To arrive at a knowledge state in which they know what task is in front of them, actors have to make a *choice of task*. When making this choice, they consider the actions they can take, given the resources available, and the consequence of taking such actions. To develop the *procedure* to follow, they are engaged in a process of *planning* in which they plan the sequence of actions and how to support the actors who take these actions. The last process in the decision ladder is the actual *execution* of the solution.

A simple example can illustrate the decision ladder's phases.

Dave is a graduate student who always makes rational decisions. He missed classes last week because he was skiing in Canada, and he thinks that he will have to make some decisions about how to prepare for classes next week (*activation* and *alert*). He converses with some of his classmates (*observation*), and learns that the next assignment is to write a short paper. While the paper should be on a topic within the course's general subject, students can select specific topics to write about (*information*). With this information, Dave figures out what decision he needs to make (*identification*) and concludes that the first stage of the assignment is to select the paper's topic (*state*).

Once Dave realizes the decision he needs to make, he begins an iterative process to arrive at a "good" topic. Examining the course's textbook, his class notes, and a list of paper topics from the previous year, he selects some topics and for each analyzes what would be involved in its selection (*predict consequences*). To be able to carry out this analysis, Dave considers his personal goals for the assignment (e.g., spend as little time as possible on writing the paper, get a good grade, be innovative), the parameters indicated by the assignment (e.g., page limit, style, and citations requirements), the expectations for a graduate school paper (e.g., substantiating each claim, referring to scholarly sources, a clear structure), the instructor's preferences for papers (e.g., creativity, high relevance to the instructor's research work, and a prominent surprise factor), and the availability of scholarly writings about the topic. This process also requires him to choose the goals that he will consider (arriving at the *goal chosen* knowledge state), and to evaluate each possible topic in light of the chosen goals (*evaluate options*). As he continues with the iterative process, the number of options to consider (*options*) is reduced.

At some point, he selects a certain topic as the "best," given the goals and the constraints (*target*). Dave is ready to implement his decision, that is, to apply the selected topic to the paper. He considers the next step (*choice of task*) and plans to contact the instructor for topic approval (*task*). He plans to contact her by email (*planning*), and knows what procedure to follow for that purpose (*procedure*), which he carries out immediately (*execution*).

While the ladder seems to reflect rational decision-making, Rasmussen (1986) emphasizes that

> the decision-ladder is not a model of the decision processes of real-time decision-making but, instead, a framework representing the informationally logical relationships among states of knowledge and, as such, useful as a map upon which the decision processes can be represented. (12)

An actor may skip stages and proceed, for instance, from the *observation* directly to knowing the *procedure* she will follow to implement the decision. That is, processing information to understand what is needed to identify the decision may lead directly to the procedure that can be followed to execute it (see figure 4.1). Such heuristics and shortcuts are likely to take place when the actors making the decisions are experienced or experts in a decision's domain.

In a study about collaborative information retrieval (Fidel et al. 2004), our team found that the actors we investigated rarely followed this process sequentially.[13] At the same time, the ladder made it possible for us to understand how decision processes proceeded and the activities that were involved in each phase. We arrived at this understanding by mapping each activity during the decision-making process as a box in the model. Once the mapping was completed, we examined the actors' activities in each rectangular box to understand what information the actors needed in the various instances of information processing, how they collaboratively retrieved it, what information sources they used, and what helped their information retrieval and what hindered it. Given the complexity and the seemingly chaotic nature of the decision-making processes we investigated, analyzing them required some conceptual structure to guide the analysis, and the decision ladder provided a useful structure for this purpose.

Comparing *task* with *decision* as a substitute for *information need*, it is easy to see that a task may require more than one decision, and therefore is likely to trigger several information needs. That is, *decision* is a better substitute because it is the element in a task that causes information seeking to occur. Instead of asking questions about the task, empirical investigators can ask questions about a decision, such as, What is the decision for which information is sought? What are this decision's attributes, both inbuilt and contextual?

Replacing *information need* with *decision* makes the central concept easier to define, more observable, and thus, according to some theoretical traditions, more researchable. Yet no research (to my knowledge) has investigated decisions as a substitute for studying information needs.[14] It is possible that context-sensitive researchers consider *decision* as a purely cognitive element that excludes contextual consideration, and therefore have not included it as a part of *context*. Taylor's view, which is purely cognitive, comes closest to equating *information need* with *information needed to make a decision*. While making a decision is basically a cognitive process, the decisions to be made need to be investigated in their context. Without knowing the context, one cannot understand the *evaluation* process, for example, because the selection of a solution is based mainly on contextual elements, such as the implications of each solution, the goals of the decision makers, and the goals of the task that generated the decision-making process. It is not clear why each empirical study has considered a certain task as the trigger for an information search without analyzing the decisions involved.

What role does an information need play in a decision-making process? According to the decision ladder, an information need may arise when actors are involved in any stage of "information processing." That is, one decision may generate multiple information needs; moreover, each such stage has its own type of need. Vicente (1999, 187) provided some examples. In the *observation* stage, for instance, information is needed to answer questions of the type, What is going on? During *identification*, questions of the type "What lies behind it?" are likely to arise. When actors *evaluate options*, they are likely to benefit from information that leads to an answer to the question, Which goals should I choose? When *planning*, the most valuable information would answer the question, How should it be done?

That is, each decision may trigger more than one information need, and therefore *decision* cannot serve as a substitute to *information need*. Using *task* is even more problematic because a task may generate several decisions, each with its own information needs. Specific information needs can be identified in a naturalistic study only by analyzing each decision actors make when performing a task, identifying instances of "information processing," and investigating the needs for information they generate.

4.4   Information Need and the Decision Ladder: Conclusions

Typical of a foundational concept in information science, *information need* is challenging to define, and applying it in empirical research brings additional complications. Clearly, *information need* is a complex concept that is not given to simplification. Undoubtedly, for the sake of conceptual rigor some scholars will continue to discuss the meaning of information need with its variety of facets, but it is not clear if such discussions will occupy center stage or what effect they will have on empirical studies. To date, there is no evidence that the conceptual deliberations have shaped such studies one way or the other. Although the various approaches to the concept of *information need* have not affected empirical research projects, it is reasonable to ask whether these approaches could guide research in general and, in particular, whether they could guide research that supports the design of information systems.

The current approaches are not useful for design because they view an information need as a situational condition. Whether an information need is defined as an incomplete cognitive state or as a trigger for a search, it delineates an individual situational state under local conditions. Using these approaches, information need researchers may be able to uncover the needs that the people they studied had at the time they studied them, but not the information needs common to members of a community of actors. To identify information needs in general is even more demanding because it requires recording all the individual needs past, present, and future, which is obviously an impossible task. More generally, the current approaches to the concept of *information need* require a deterministic view in which one should be able to identify the specifics of a need. Applying this view to systems design calls for the prediction of future needs—a task that is impossible given the complexity involved in HIB.

More generally and from an empirical view, a researcher may ask: Is there any benefit in finding a universal, agreed-upon definition for the concept?

Some researchers have already raised this question. Tom Wilson (1981), for instance, pointed out that HIB studies "may never address the central question of 'information need,' that is, why the user decides to seek information, what purpose he believes it will serve and to what use it is actually put when received" (7). Therefore, he recommended that "it may be advisable to remove the term 'information needs' from our professional vocabulary and to speak instead of 'information seeking towards the satisfaction of needs'" (9). Information need, then, is a commonsensical concept that researchers may employ without attributing to it a well-defined meaning. From an actor-centered view, this conclusion may suggest that, since HIB research is focused on behavior during the search process, researchers can concentrate on the process leading toward a goal—which is a need's satisfaction—while ignoring the conditions, both cognitive and contextual, that paved the path for the need to emerge and the search to materialize. That is, even though the iterations during the process are shaped by the degree to which a need is satisfied, a study may concentrate on the process itself without recognizing the various facets of the goal or whether the goal is a need or a demand. However, while discussions on the concept of *information need* may leave empirical research unaffected, ignoring the context of search processes limits researchers' ability to understand the process.

A more useful approach was provided by Benton and Craib (2001) when they discussed the "needs" that must be met for a society as a whole to survive. In this context they presented a few interpretive views and noted:

Rather than talk about "needs," some thinkers talk about "conditions of existence"—which do not *cause* something to appear but which create space for its appearance and which interact with a multiplicity of other processes to produce whatever the outcome turns out to be. (89)

A crude translation to HIB vocabulary might be:

Rather than talk about "information needs," talk about elements in the context—which do not *cause* an information need to emerge but which create space for its emergence and which interact with a multiplicity of other processes to shape the search process that results.

According to this view, an analysis of the context, rather than a prediction of future information needs, is required to understand the search process. A simplified version of this approach that is relevant to design may claim: We are unlikely to be able to predict all the possible information needs because of their situational nature and the complexity involved, but given a certain context we can design a system that is based on elements in the context that afford searches in situations that may arise.

The decision ladder (section 4.3) is an example of an analysis that matches this approach. It shows that moving from one knowledge state to another requires information processing that *may* trigger information needs. Moreover, each information-processing activity during a decision-making process may trigger a certain type of needs, as Vicente (1999) explained. That is, considering the decision-making process as the context to a search for information, certain elements in the context of an information-seeking process "create space"—that is, create the conditions—for an information need to be triggered. Systems designers cannot predict the specific information needs that will be triggered, but their design can afford searches in a particular condition because the *type* of information need in each stage of the decision-making process can be assumed.

This approach to the concept *information need* opens a new way of viewing HIB in general. The concept has been essential to the user-centered approach in both the purely cognitive and the in-context views. These views are reductionist to varying degrees because they focus on studying users without systematically analyzing the context in which they act. A holistic and nondeterministic view of the concept *information need* focuses on the *context* that creates the conditions for an information need to emerge, that is, on the constraints that generate an information need and thus a search. Such a view is also likely to lead to the creation of formative models, which are those most useful for systems design (see chapter 9). This chain of reasoning suggests a new approach to the study of HIB in general: the *context-centered* approach. This approach is an ecological approach because it centers on the environment in which actor's activities take place (see section 1.1.4). It is discussed in chapters 11 and 12, which presents an example of a context-centered approach: the cognitive work analysis conceptual framework.

5 Five Search Strategies

The concept *search strategy* has been part of the vocabulary of human information behavior (HIB) since the earliest user studies. However, researchers only began to investigate search strategies after the development of digital technology, when the concept became a popular focus of study with the introduction of the World Wide Web. Unlike *information need*, which is relatively stable,[1] *search strategy* addresses the dynamic part of the search process itself. While an information need triggers a search process, search strategies reflect the activities during the search. In addition, strategies are considered to possess a great advantage as an object of study: While they are purely cognitive in nature, they are observable because their use—that is, the activities during a search—can be observed.[2] New research techniques that have been afforded by digital technology made it possible to investigate the search process itself, and thus its strategies.

Because the concept *search strategy* is relatively concrete and observable, its definition has not raised much discussion, but researchers have attributed to it a range of interpretations and definitions and have often overlooked the need to provide their construal even when search strategies were the focus of their studies. This chapter briefly provides a few examples of some of these definitions and proposes a view on search strategies that is relevant to the design of information systems.

5.1 What Is a Search Strategy?

Research into search strategies has been carried out since the late 1970s, but the interpretation of the concept *search strategies* has been highly fluid, and even today the concept is imbued with a plurality of meanings. HIB researchers have applied the term to signify any aspect of an information search process that lacks its own name. Most empirical researchers have also neglected to explain their understanding of the concept.

In some cases, the investigators' construal can be inferred from the specific search strategy they investigated. Only a few researchers provided explicit definitions for *search strategies*, and some others borrowed these definitions for their own studies.

5.1.1 Implicit Construal of *Search Strategy*

Examples of search strategies that have been discovered in web searching without the support of an explicit definition of the concept show that most address specific actions in a search process and are highly concrete, mechanical, and concerned with observable actions. Only a few implicit definitions enjoy some level of abstraction. Some researchers were inconsistent in the level of abstraction of the search strategies they investigated, identifying them along a range from highly concrete to the abstract.

The series of studies that Nigel Ford and his colleagues conducted is a typical example of a concrete and actions-based interpretation of the concept. Ford began his investigation of search strategies during the early period of bibliographical databases (e.g., Ford, Wood, and Walsh 1994). Examining his research reports, it seems that he understood search strategies to be the types of actions a searcher take to transform a query. A recent article about the use of search strategies provided 18 strategies (Ford, Eaglestone, and Madden 2009), such as *page down, remove Boolean operators, include quotation marks, reuse part of a query*, and *change operators only*. Other researchers—such as Martzoukou (2008) and Iivonen and White (2001)—recognized search strategies on the same level of abstraction, identifying, for example, *use Boolean operators* or *use subject directory*.

The concrete level of the search strategies' construal limits the range of their applicability because they are to a large degree determined by the technology being used. Search strategies that can be employed in best-match systems,[3] for instance, are different from those in systems with ranked output.[4] Moreover, some of the search strategies that were identified are based on specific technical attributes of the search system, such as the query language (e.g., *include quotation marks, use subject directory*) and query operators (e.g., *use Boolean operators*). As a result, the strategies that were discovered are pertinent to searches under the conditions in which they were discovered, but they may not be applicable to other modes of information searching, such as browsing the library shelves or asking a person for driving directions. The more abstract the level of definition, the more modes of searching it represents.

A few scholars interpreted search strategies on a somewhat abstract level. An example of such approach is the study by Ramirez et al. (2002) which examined the role of computers in mediating human-to-human communication, that is, information-seeking when the source of information is another human. It seems that they understood search strategies to be the relationship between the information seeker (the communicator) and the object of the information acquired (the target). They distinguished three main types of strategies (Ramirez et al. 2002, 219–221):

• *Interactive strategies* entail direct interaction between communicator and target during which different tactics are enabled to elicit desired information; for example, the communicator interrogates the target, discloses information designed to elicit reciprocal disclosure, and attempts to relax the target in order to acquire information.

• *Active strategies* involve acquiring information from other individuals but without direct interaction with the target, as is the case, for example, with the use of third-party information sources, such as acquiring information through email exchanges and chats with others familiar with the target.

• *Passive strategies* involve acquiring information about a target through unobtrusive observation, such as being "carbon copied" on messages, eavesdropping on a conversation, or lurking on a listserv.

Ramirez et al.'s classification demonstrates that universal, or abstract, construal of search strategies makes them independent of the technology used, and certainly free of association with technical attributes of an information system, whether a human or a machine.

In summary, the unsystematic nature of the use of the concept *search strategy*, supported by the lack of explicit understanding of the concept, created a muddled trail of research about search strategies in which only the term itself is common to all investigations.

5.1.2 Definitions of *Search Strategy*

Most explicit definitions of search strategies were universal and abstract in nature. The most universal one was offered by Belkin and his colleagues (Belkin, Marchetti, and Cool 1993; Belkin et al. 1995). They defined search strategies as the behaviors in which people engage when searching for information. One might claim that this definition is too general and actually represents the more general concept *information-seeking behavior* (ISB), thus making it difficult to differentiate between the two concepts. Nevertheless, using this approach, they presented four mutually exclusive dimensions (or facets) of strategies that together create search strategies. That is, each search strategy is a combination of elements drawn from the four facets. Each facet, in turn, includes a continuum of elements that Belkin et al. (1993) derived from informal analysis of empirical studies. For each dimension they listed the two extreme strategies.[5] The dimensions were method of interaction (from scanning to searching); goal of interaction (from learning to selecting); mode of retrieval (from recognition to specification); and resources considered (from information to metainformation).[6] These dimensions demonstrate a very broad construal of *search strategies*, and raise some questions. It is difficult to accept *goal of interaction*, for example, as a dimension of a strategy. A goal may provide a *reason* for selecting a certain search strategy but it is not a dimension of it. This is because strategies are usually associated with activities, whereas goals do not represent activities and are not even directly identified by them, since various activities may lead to the same goal and one activity may lead to the accomplishment of more than one goal. In addition, this broad definition cannot guide researchers in discovering other strategies, and thus limits the possible strategies to those Belkin et al. have defined.

A definition that is universal, yet in sync with the notion of *strategy* in everyday language, and the first one formulated in HIB, was offered by Marcia Bates (1981). She explained that a search strategy is: "An approach to or plan for a whole search. A search strategy is used to inform or to determine specific search formulation decisions; it operates at a level above term choice and command use" (142). This definition is not bounded by dimensions or technology, and places search strategies as a component of information-seeking behavior. An example of a strategy might be: First I'll try a couple of terms, and if I don't get good results, I'll look for better terms either by browsing the results or by thinking about the problem in light of what was retrieved.

Gary Marchionini (1995) construed *search strategies* in a similar way and also placed the concept in an abstraction hierarchy of concepts in searching behavior, in which each level is affected by the level above it. Marchionini's hierarchy moves from the concrete to the abstract:

• "*Moves* are finely grained actions manifested as discrete behavioral actions such as walking to a shelf, picking up a book, pressing a key, clicking a mouse, or touching an item from a menu" (74).

• "*Tactics* are discrete intellectual choices or prompts manifested as behavioral actions during an information-seeking session … for example, when restricting the search to a specific field or document type in order to narrow the search results" (74).

• "A *Strategy* is the approach that an information seeker takes to a problem. *Strategies* are those sets of ordered tactics that are consciously selected, applied, and monitored to solve an information problem" (72).

• "*Patterns* are sometimes conscious but most often reflect internalized behaviors that can be discerned over time and across different information problems and searches.

Patterns may be caused by chunked strategies or tactics that people internalize though repetition and experience" (72). One manifestation of *patterns* is, for example, an individual's *searching style*.

Iris Xie (2007) created a similar hierarchy with an understanding of search strategies that was more general than the previous definitions, and included the goals of a search. She explained:

Information-seeking *strategies* comprise *interactive intentions* and *retrieval tactics*. *Interactive intentions* refer to subgoals that a user has to achieve in the process of accomplishing his or her current search goal/search task. … *Retrieval tactics* are represented by *methods* and entities with attributes. *Methods* refer to the techniques users apply to interact with data/information, knowledge, concept/term, format, item/objects/site, process/status, location, system and humans. (Xie 2007, emphasis added)

These definitions have had an impact on other studies. Vakkari (1999), for example, used Belkin et al.'s (1993) dimensions among other constructs when he analyzed how an information problem's structure (i.e., structured versus ill-structured) affects search strategies, and Xie's (2007) definitions were inspired by the approaches of Belkin et al., Bates, and Marchionini in addition to other views. The definitions have guided empirical studies as well. Thatcher (2006), for example, employed Marchionini's hierarchy when he investigated the search strategies that were employed by 80 study participants. He identified 12 strategies, which he named "cognitive search strategies," including the following:

The participant went to a search engine that was known to them [*sic*]; participants used different search engines to conduct the same search; the participant deliberately opened multiple browser windows to conduct different searches simultaneously; the participant relied solely on hyperlinks from the homepage to get from one webpage to another. (Thatcher 2006, 1059-1063)

Thatcher's search strategies are different in nature and level of abstraction from those identified by Marchionini, who envisioned them to be laid out on a spectrum with opposite ends: the *analytical* and the *browsing* strategies. The analytical strategies are "planned, goal driven, deterministic, formal, and discrete," while the browsing strategies are "opportunistic, data driven, heuristic, informal, and continuous" (Marchionini 1995, 73).[7] While widely accepted (if not always correctly), the distinction between these two types of strategies is not compatible with the approach presented in this book. According to the view presented here, each search is driven by a goal (to solve an information problem) rather than by data, regardless of the strategies employed. In addition, every strategy is a plan. Thus, even a decision to start a search without a specific plan (i.e., browsing) is a plan. With these conceptions, Marchionini's definitions represent attributes of *searching* and *surfing* (see section 2.1.1.1). Since these are two modes of acquiring information, they are dichotomous, rather than the opposite ends of a spectrum.

In conclusion, definitions of search strategies are usually universal and abstract and can guide other researchers in identifying specific strategies, whether on a conceptual level or in empirical studies. But these definitions have had one drawback: Using them has generated an unruly repertoire of strategies in which each researcher has employed her own view on how to carve out strategies from an analysis of the literature or from the data at hand. In addition, the number of search strategies is growing constantly as new ones are discovered, usually without attempting to place them in relation to other strategies. Most concerning is the diversity in the levels of abstraction of the search strategies that have been generated, which ranged from the physical actions to plans of action.[8] This inconsistency points to fundamental differences among the interpretations of the concept. With the continually increasing number of strategies, it is useful to find a configuration that may contain them. One promising approach to reduce this confusion is to view a search strategy as a *category* of plans, general approaches, or interactive intentions (see section 5.4).

5.2   The Conditions That Shape the Use of a Strategy

Various studies identified the conditions that shape the use of a strategy, which are usually termed "factors affecting the choice of search strategies." Some of the findings of these studies were based on an analysis of previous studies (e.g., Vakkari 1999), and others on empirical research (e.g., Ford, Eaglestone, and Madden 2009; Rouet 2003). In a typical investigation the researcher selects a factor of interest and analyzes or tests its effect. Thus, Vakkari (1999) examined the effect of the structure of the information problem; Ford et al. (2009) looked at individual differences; and Rouet (2003) tested the effect of task specificity and prior knowledge.

Studies of this type face various challenges. For example, the definitions that researchers employed were unable to lead investigators to the variables that are likely to affect the selection of search strategies. It is difficult to think about a variable that may affect, say, the strategy "using quotation marks"—except for the obvious one: whether or not a searcher is familiar with the strategy. With these definitions, researchers have had to use a trial-and-error approach when they select the variables to be tested. Another challenge is the relatively large number of search strategies that were defined by researchers. Thus, even if investigators find a variable that may affect one strategy, the variable may leave the rest of the search strategies unaffected. Indeed, typical findings of such studies that tested an array of search strategies pointed to one or two strategies that were affected by the tested variables but found no factors that affected the other strategies. This way, one can state that an actor with high value on variable X is more likely to employ category A than an actor with low values, but the question "Which search strategies are an actor with low value is likely to select?" remains unanswered.[9] Considering search strategies as a category overcomes these and other challenges (see section 5.4.2).

5.3   Systems Designed to Support Strategies

Regardless of the definition of *search strategies*, most scholars agree that information systems that support the strategies are better than those that ignore them. Yet only a few researchers have provided systems requirements to support the strategies they unveiled or redefined. Most systematic among these researchers were Belkin, Marchetti, and Cool (1993). They methodically analyzed each strategy they had defined to identify the problems that one may encounter when employing it. Thinking about ways a system could alleviate the problems they identified, they generated 36 requirements for information systems interfaces (see section 10.3.3.1). They recommended, for example, that a system provide a "display of resources with explanations of link type," "direct retrieval of example information items from selected terms," and "structured representation of query and search" (Belkin et al. 1993, 330–331).

While Belkin et al. (1993) offered highly specific requirements, based on all the search strategies they had identified, Bates (2007) focused on one search strategy—browsing—and offered a much more general interface requirement. She explained that "[g]ood browsable interfaces would consist of rich scenes, full of potential objects of interest, that the eye can take in at once (*massively parallel processing*), then select items within the scene to give closer attention to." She also presented a model of such an interface that was developed by Toms (2000) as an example of a good interface.[10]

Both Belkin et al. (1993) and Bates (2007) offered implications for the design of universal systems, regardless of the characteristics of the searchers. Another approach is to focus on the searchers, identifying the strategy that would be useful to them, and then generate design requirements based on the actors' information behavior. It is unrealistic to design search systems for each individual, but it is reasonable to do so for a particular community of actors. In this case an analyst may ask, What strategies will play a central role in these actors' search for information? Once this question is answered, implications for design could also be based on the typical characteristics of the actors. Browsing support provided to scientists, for instance, should probably be different from that offered to youth looking for health information. This difference is required not only due to the dissimilarity in the actors' cognitive resources and context, but also due to the centrality of the browsing strategy for each community. While browsing is likely to be essential to youth looking for information in an unfamiliar area, scientists are not likely to employ it as a central strategy. Section 5.4.3 provides a comparison between two communities' strategy selections and the resulting design requirements as an example.

5.4   Search Strategy as a Category

A search strategy is cognitive in nature—because plans, general approaches, or interactive intentions are all hatched in the human mind—regardless of the contextual situation that shapes it. In my work I have applied the conceptual framework cognitive work analysis (CWA) to HIB (see chapters 11 and 12). CWA views strategies in association with decision-making processes (see section 11.1). Vicente (1999)—based on Rasmussen (1981)—defined a strategy as "a category of cognitive task procedures that transform an initial state of knowledge into a final state of knowledge" (220).

Rasmussen, Pejtersen, and Goodstein (1994) explained that cognitive processes within the same category—that is, the same strategy—"share important characteristics, such as a particular kind of mental model, a certain mode of interpretation of the observed evidence, and a coherent set of tactical planning rules" (70).[11] Vicente (1999) further explained that each strategy is "based on a different set of performance criteria, and requires a different kind of information support" (219).

Strategies can serve various decision processes, such as diagnosis, evaluation, or planning (Rasmussen et al. 1994).

5.4.1   Five Search Strategies

In the area of information science, field studies in information retrieval (IR) that were guided by CWA have defined strategies that are employed in the information search process.[12] More specifically, Pejtersen (1984) uncovered five distinct search strategies (Pejtersen 1979) in her study of fiction retrieval in public libraries. Later studies have observed the use of these strategies and found no additional ones.[13] Browsing and analytical strategies are included in this set, but their definitions are different from Marchionini's (1995). The strategies are presented in table 5.1

Although each search strategy is derived from a certain mental model, actors may switch strategy in the middle of a search.[14] One may use a library catalog employing the analytical strategy, for instance, to find the location of a book on a particular topic,

Table 5.1
Search strategies and their definitions

Search strategy	Definition
Browsing	Intuitive scanning following leads by association *without much planning ahead*
Analytical	*Explicit consideration* of attributes of the information problem and of the search system
Empirical	Based on previous experience, using *rules and tactics that were successful in the past*
Known site	Going *directly* to the place where the information is located
Similarity	Finding information based on a previous *example* that is similar to the current need

but browse the shelf for additional sources once that book has been located. Similarly, an actor may enter a complex search query but continue browsing through links when the results are not satisfactory. When conducting a study of searching behavior, it is sometimes difficult to detect a strategy shift. This difficulty is particularly the case when the analysis is based only on observation or on transaction logs. In fact, it is very difficult to identify search strategies without access to the cognitive processes involved in the specific search. A transaction log of a web search may show, for example, two terms in the search box followed by many clicks on links. Without understanding the mental model the actor had, it is impossible to determine if he employed the browsing or the analytical strategy. An awareness of the cognitive processes is required for the definition of *search strategies* because they reflect a mental model rather than specific procedures. Observation and analyses of transaction logs by themselves can identify only procedures and cannot provide insight to the mental model that is employed in a search.

5.4.1.1 *The Browsing Strategy*

The browsing strategy (intuitive scanning following leads by association *without much planning ahead*) had been identified long before computers began to be used for information retrieval. Although its most commonly recognized manifestation has been browsing bookshelves, the introduction of hypertext made browsing a highly viable strategy when searching digital information systems. A person who decides to browse in order to find information for making a decision might think: "Let me start here and see where it takes me." When searching the web, one might follow this decision by clicking on links or using a directory.

This view of *browsing* is different from Marchionini's (1995, 73) not only in meaning but also in type (he argued that browsing strategies are "opportunistic, data driven, heuristic, informal, and continuous"). His interpretation of the strategy is based on the category "elements that drive a search" (opportunistic, data driven) and on the category "manner in which the search progresses" (heuristic, informal, continuous). That is, while all these elements that define browsing are cognitive, they belong to different categories. In fact, according to the CWA definition, a browsing strategy can fit in Marchionini's analytical one because it can be goal driven, deterministic, and formal.

The browsing strategy has attracted more research interest than any other strategy, and has had the widest range of interpretations (see reviews of these in Chang and Rice 1993 and in Rice, McCreadie, and Chang 2001). One example of a thorough conceptual investigation into the concept is Bates's (2007) question: "What is browsing—really?" She placed the concept in human development and found that "most animals have a propensity toward exploratory behaviour." Viewing browsing in the context of this behavior led her to conclude that "browsing is a cognitive and behavioural expression of this exploratory behaviour," and that in humans, curiosity is "the in-built motivation for this exploratory behaviour." Thus, her definition is:

Browsing is the activity of engaging in a series of glimpses, each of which exposes the browser to objects of potential interest; depending on interest, the browser may or may not examine more closely one or more of the (physical or represented) objects; this examination, depending on interest, may or may not lead the browser to (physically or conceptually) acquire the object. (Bates 2007)[15]

On the empirical research front, Shan-Ju L. Chang (2005) carried out the most comprehensive series of studies on browsing. Besides identifying the dimensions that can support a description of browsing,[16] she created a multidimensional framework for understanding the influences on the process as well as the consequences of browsing.

In addition to being the most explored strategy, browsing is also the most pervasively used strategy in information searching. While it is a strategy on its own, it can also occur as a sequence when other strategies are employed. Retrieving a desired book from the library shelves, for example, requires some browsing on the shelf before the specific book can be located. Similarly, when one finds a web site, using any search strategy, that provides the needed information, one might click on additional links for further exploration. Despite its prevalence, no formal training about how to browse exists (to my knowledge),[17] and search engines provide no support for the strategy,[18] as evidenced by the common lost-in-cyberspace situation.

5.4.1.2 *The Analytical Strategy*
Using the analytical strategy, one explores the information need on the one hand and systems capabilities on the other.[19] The next step is to match the need and the system's attributes—or, translate the need into a query in the system's "language"— evaluate the options for search actions, and select the most promising one. This is the rational, decision-making and problem-solving strategy. In fact, it is considered almost the normative strategy, and training in searching for information usually involves instructions about how to employ the analytical strategy.[20] The use of advanced search options or of syntactical operators is typical of an analytical search on the web, as in any search for which a query is constructed with the aim of arriving directly at the desired information. Research about this strategy has been primarily focused on practical advice and suggestions on ways to apply it for efficient and effective results.

5.4.1.3 *The Empirical Strategy*
The empirical strategy can be used by actors who categorize previous experiences and generate rules and tactics. Then, when they face a new situation, they may intuitively recognize that it fits one of the previously defined categories, and apply the rules or tactics generated for it. An individual employing this strategy may think: "In a situation like this, this is what I usually do." An experienced web searcher may have a rule: "When I want to buy something, I just put it as a URL. For example, if I need to buy a flag, I'll enter www.flags.com."[21] Or: "When I need a homepage of a person or an organization, I just enter as many identifying terms as I can in the Google search box. Most of the times the homepage will appear at the top of the list of results." The empirical strategy is a shortcut to the analytical one and can be employed only if an actor has developed rules or tactics.

5.4.1.4 *The Known-Site Strategy*
In certain situations, an actor knows exactly where the desired information is located. The trivial case of this strategy is when an actor is led to the site, as is the case when one is given the URL of a site that has the information, or when one knows exactly where a book is on the library shelves. To employ this strategy in a nontrivial mode, however, one has to remember that certain sites exist as well as the information

included in them. To help them to locate known sites, people have created files and lists that include either the sites themselves—such as a file of physical documents—or an easy point of access to them—such as bookmarks or a list of favorites.

5.4.1.5 The Similarity Strategy

The similarity strategy is useful when an actor can best express an information need by presenting a specific item as a basis for retrieving another information item that is similar to the specific one. In the study of fiction retrieval (Pejtersen 1979), for example, readers sometimes could best articulate the kind of book they were after by presenting a book they had already read as an example of the type they wanted.

On the surface, it may appear that the similarity strategy is identical to the retrieval tactic query-by-example, in which the actor provides an exemplar of what is to be retrieved. Query-by-example, however, is a procedure, rather than a strategy. As such, it might be used when the similarity strategy is employed, but it can also support other strategies. Consider the case of an actor who wants to retrieve the musical scores of a song from which he knows only one tune. This situation requires the browsing strategy because entering the tune as an exemplar will retrieve all scores to songs that have a tune similar to the entered one. To find the relevant score, the actor will browse through the retrieved ones. Query-by-example can also be used when employing the analytical strategy, as would be the case if the actor knew the song and purposely considered which tune would be most effective in retrieving the song's scores. In other words, the query-by-example procedure may be employed when the actor searches for a specific document, while actors employ the similarity strategy when they do not know what documents would satisfy their need and they cannot articulate the documents' attributes.

To design a machine that can retrieve a similar item requires overcoming various hurdles. The main challenge in defining similarity is identifying appropriate metrics for its measurement. If an actor likes a certain picture of a tulip, say, and she wants a similar picture of a rose, how can the system figure out what attributes are most important to her? This strategy could be most effectively supported, therefore, when the attributes that actors employ to determine similarity are known and can be represented unambiguously, or with an interactive and iterative process that can effectively lead to the desired information without explicit similarity criteria. Pejtersen's (1989, 1992) BookHouse system is an example of an explicit consideration of similarity attributes. Based on her analysis of conversations between users and librarians, and on other data, Pejtersen (1992) designed this retrieval system for fiction in which the retrieval of similar books is based on a network of book attributes.

Although many search engines make it possible to search for similar items, most similarity searches facilitated by the engines are based on the topic or the author of the retrieved document and ignore other attributes that might play an important role in an actor's tacit criteria for similarity—such as the quality of graphs and charts, the intensity of an image's colors, or the technical level.[22] Measurements of similarity are also used in recommender systems (Resnick and Varian 1997), such as the familiar recommendation of electronic bookstores: "Others who bought this book also bought the following books." Recommender systems have not been used thus far to support the similarity search strategy in information retrieval. Thus, while the similarity strategy is a viable search strategy, most search systems today do not afford it.[23]

5.4.1.6 Five Search Strategies: Conclusions

The five strategies presented here are general enough to apply to any search regardless of the technology used. An example may illustrate this point.

The browsing strategy   Michael, a resident of a retirement home, won $1,000 toward buying a computer in a talent competition, and he wants to buy a laptop. He decides to search the web and find the best computer for him. He is not familiar with the web and knows very little about laptops and selects to enter "best laptop computer" in the search box and see where it leads him.

The analytical strategy   Susan is in the same situation, but she has some experience in web searching and knows a thing or two about laptops. Moreover, she needs a computer that can stand harsh conditions because it will accompany her on her field trips. She formulates a query with Boolean operators that include several synonyms for *harsh*, such as *rugged* and *rough*.

The empirical strategy   Steve has much experience with web shopping, and in particular with buying electronic devices. He has developed a tactic that worked well in the past. First he displays a list of all the electronic stores, deletes those that do not sell computers, and selects the web pages of those with which he had good experience in the past.

The known-site strategy   Dave has it best: He knows which store has the top computers and lowest prices, and he knows what computer he would like to get. He goes directly to the store's web site.

The similarity strategy   Rachel knows which computer she wants—the one her sister has—but it is too expensive for her. She likes working on it because it has a pleasing shape, the keyboard is sturdy, and the display is clear. She wishes she could enter the specifications of her sister's computer and ask for similar ones, so she could scan them and hopefully find one that fit her requirements.

Search strategies can also be used when looking for information from other people.

The browsing strategy   Allyson wishes to get a laptop. She decides to ask advice from her acquaintances, but she is not familiar with their computer expertise. After her yoga class she usually walks home with her classmate Ben. Asking him for help, she finds out he knows very little about computers and cannot help her. Walking her dog a week later, she meets her next-door neighbor who has never used a computer but knows that a neighbor down the street is an expert.

The analytical strategy   Natasha has many friends who are very familiar with computers, and so before she buys one, she wishes to consult with some of them. Nora might not be the best consultant because she doesn't listen well. Asking Kevin is not simple because he will insist on taking part in the buying process; to be independent, she will have to pretend that she is helping a friend who needs a laptop. Jesse might be the best person to ask because she listens well and does not interfere with others' lives, but she has not bought a new computer for a long time. Which one should she choose?

The empirical strategy   Haejin likes to talk to people and has many friends. When she has to make an important decision, such as what laptop to buy, she talks first with her closest friends and asks for their opinion. Next she turns to her classmates and her professor. She also calls her family in Korea. Armed with the advice and information she collected, she finally makes the decision.

The known-site strategy   Amir asks his wife, who is a computer expert, for recommendations.

The similarity strategy   Karen explains to the sales person that she would like to have a laptop that is similar to the desktop computer she has in her office.

These examples illustrate that under certain cognitive and contextual conditions a particular strategy, or a certain combination of strategies, is more promising than others. Moreover, defining *search strategy* as a category makes it possible to understand the conditions that shape the use of a strategy, and therefore supports informed design.

5.4.2   The Conditions That Shape the Use of a Strategy

The view of search strategies as categories of cognitive task procedures that are induced by a mental model makes it possible to infer which cognitive and contextual conditions motivate the use of a strategy. To illustrate this possibility, I present an examination of the relations between each strategy and a sample of resources an actor has:

- *Time*—how much time the actor has for a search
- *Prior knowledge* required for the employment of a strategy
- *Cognitive processes*—how much thinking is required when using a strategy
- *Search in memory*—how much human remembering is required for a strategy's use.[24]

This analysis does not rely on rigorous measurements, such as the number of minutes an actor has to perform a search. Instead, it assesses the level required from each condition to proceed with a strategy in comparison to the other strategies. For example, browsing requires much time, while the known-site strategy requires little time.

The browsing strategy Browsing is the easiest strategy to apply because it does not require previous knowledge, much thinking, or remembering. It is, however, the least efficient strategy to resolve an information problem because it rarely leads to the desired answer directly, and therefore requires more time than the other search strategies. In other words, a person who has little knowledge on the information problem, the subject domain, or web searching (or a combination of those), but has no strict time limits, would find the browsing strategy most useful.

The analytical strategy To be productive, this strategy requires some knowledge of the search system and its functionality and some knowledge of the subject domain. Search time is shorter than when using the browsing strategy, and some search in memory is required. On the other hand, to proceed with the strategy entails much thinking and analysis. It is most useful when an actor is searching for something new—such as a new topic or a variation on a topic—or is searching on a new system, and the actor has neither rules that can direct the search nor a site he knows will provide the needed information.

The empirical strategy This strategy requires analysis as well, but instead of comparing the information need with the system's capabilities, an actor compares the need with rules and tactics she has developed through previous searches. Even though the empirical strategy is, in a way, a shortcut to the analytical strategy, it has different requirements. While it saves time, it requires an actor to search her memory to a greater extent than the analytical strategy. In addition, only actors who have enough knowledge and experience and who have developed rules and tactics can employ it. The empirical strategy can be beneficial to actors who have

Table 5.2
A comparison of the resources required for each strategy

Strategy	Prior knowledge	Cognitive processing	Search in memory	Time spent on searching
Browsing	Little	Little	Little	Much
Analytical	Medium	Much	Little	Medium
Empirical	Much	Little	Much	Little
Known site	Much	Little	Much	Little
Similarity	Medium	Little	Little	Little

much experience in searching but have limited time and are looking for something new.

The known-site strategy   On the surface it seems that the known site is an ideal strategy: It is the most efficient, and it does not require much knowledge and analysis. Yet it can be employed only under very strict conditions. Not only must the actor remember a site that is likely to have the desired information, she must remember particular attributes of the site: those that can provide her with direct access to the information. Thus, while highly efficient, using the known-site strategy creates high memory load and requires an extensive search in memory.

The similarity strategy   This strategy is most useful when one cannot articulate the information problem but can present to the system information that is similar to what is needed. In fact, in many cases this might be the only strategy an actor can use because he cannot come up with terms that might lead him into a productive search. All that is required to apply this strategy is an item that can serve as an example. While the strategy requires little effort on the actor's part, it can be materialized only if the search system—whether human or machine—can carry out similarity searches successfully. Moreover, its efficiency depends on the ability of the search system to produce relevant results. The better the system, the less scanning is required.

Comparing the strategies   The relationships between conditions and strategies are summarized in table 5.2. The values *little*, *medium*, and *much* represent a relative amount in comparison to the other strategies.

What is the relevance of these relationships? Once we know what conditions are typical to a community of actors, we can anticipate what strategies they are likely to use, and therefore which strategies require most support. These predictions could guide the design of an information system that supports search strategies.

5.4.3   Systems Designed to Support Strategies

While the few researchers who analyzed strategy use and offered design requirements have focused on general-context search systems, a more extensive application of search strategy definitions and analysis can take place when an information system is designed for a particular community of actors. When focusing on a community, researchers are familiar with the actors' information behavior and can integrate this knowledge into design requirements. This approach is based on the assumption that an understanding of the searching behavior of a community's members is relevant to design that supports search strategies. A comparison between two communities of actors—high school students and engineers, both using the web to find information for their work—may serve as an example to demonstrate this approach.

Table 5.2 displays resources required for the application of each of the five strategies defined in section 5.4.1. With regard to these resources, an empirical study of high school students (Fidel et al. 1999) revealed that the participants had low levels in all resources but one: time. They were searching in a subject area of which they were completely uninformed, and thus had no prior knowledge. Their priority was to find the easiest way to complete the assignments, and thus they avoided heavy thinking efforts. Because they lacked web-searching experience as well as subject knowledge, they did not have to search in their memory. At the same time, they had plenty of time to complete the assignments. Examining table 5.2 shows that browsing is the most promising strategy for them. Indeed, this is the only search strategy we observed them to employ.

The designer of a search system for students with similar resources—and for other actors under the same conditions—would make a special effort to provide support for the browsing strategy. The specific support to be provided would depend on additional constraints that might be specific to each community of actors. In our study we discovered that the main challenge the students confronted was finding their place on the web space; that is, they "got lost in cyberspace" very easily. Therefore, providing means to quickly find where actors are and providing mechanisms for an easy access to pages visited earlier would have improved their interaction with the search system and its outcome.

Such support mechanisms are best when their design is based on the conditions under which the interaction takes place. The students we observed selected landmark pages during the search to help them find their way. At some point in their browsing they selected a certain web page that they used as a "home base," or a "starting point," from which to venture into the web space, expecting to come back to it if they needed to continue their explorations in a different direction.[25] Their greatest challenge was to find their home base when they wanted to get back to it. An interface to support this technique in browsing would offer an easy and fast way to return to a landmark, that is, to the home base.[26]

Search support may also address strategy shifts. The students who participated in our study became frustrated at times with the poor results they received through browsing. Their searches might have been more effective if they could have employed the analytical strategy. Their lack of subject knowledge and of experience in web searching, however, made it difficult for them to employ the strategy. A search system that at any time during browsing guides searchers in formulating their queries for the analytical strategy would have been highly useful to them.

The conditions under which engineers work, and the resources available to them, are unlike those of the high school students. Therefore, engineers require different types of support when searching the web. My studies of engineers searching the web (e.g., Fidel and Green 2004) revealed that they almost always have some level of prior knowledge of the subject matter, and they are not reluctant to think or to search their memory, which has been nourished by their experience in web searching. In most workplaces, however, time is in short supply and engineers are frequently under time pressure. With these levels of resources, the best strategies for engineers are the known-site and empirical strategies. The analytical strategy is also viable—particularly in searches in which the other two strategies cannot be applied—but requires additional time.

A search system to support engineers' web searching therefore would help them in applying these three strategies. Memory is the resource most in demand to carry out the known-site and empirical strategies; therefore, search systems for engineers could be designed to support them when they search their memory. For the known-site strategy, engineers need to remember addresses of web sites, and for the empirical one, they have to store their searching rules and tactics. The "bookmarks" (or "favorites") facility is already providing support for the known-site strategy and it could be a focus for improvements.[27] Facilities to store and organize search rules and tactics have not been developed yet (to my knowledge). The analytical strategy could receive support as well. The engineers who participated in our study almost always planned their search when they employed the analytical strategy. Most of them expressed their desire to have a facility that would make it possible for them to predict the search results during planning.

Thus, an analysis of the constraints under which actors look for information can reveal the search strategies that are likely to be most useful. An understanding of these constraints and the searching behavior of actors of a certain community can lead to the creation of system requirements that would support the use of these search strategies.

5.5 Five Search Strategies: Conclusions

The concept *search strategy* is associated with the search process and has become a regular object of research since the introduction of digital technology increased both the number of possibilities to employ search strategies and their visibility to researchers. Search strategies are considered essential to the analysis of a search process, and the many definitions of the concept were inspired by the views their creators have on the process. Most of the implicit understandings of the concept—that is, the use of the term *search strategy* without defining it—have been derived from observable search procedures, and their level of specificity has varied. Thus, strategies with very different levels of abstraction—such as *include quotation marks, rely solely on hyperlinks from the homepage to get from one webpage to another,* and *employ rules and tactics that were successful in the past*—were identified, mostly through empirical research. At the same time, most explicit definitions of the concept *search strategy* have been abstract. The plurality of ways to construe the concept and the continuous identification of new search strategies make cumulative research unattainable.[28] Therefore, it is necessary for the scholarly community to arrive at some common understanding of the concept if it wishes to reduce the fragmentation in search strategy research.

Most empirical research on search strategy has been dedicated to the study of the factors that might affect the selection of a strategy. Only a few researchers have addressed the implication of this research for design, that is, the design of information systems that support the use of search strategies. One of the challenges to such design stems from the reality that requirements based on the technology in use at the time of their generation are short lived and become obsolete when a new technology is introduced. Therefore, requirements that are likely to be stable over time should be independent of the technology in use. Yet both of the examples of design recommendations presented above (i.e., Belkin et al. 1993 and Bates 2007) are technology-dependent. Bates's (2007) suggestion that the interface for browsing "would consist of rich scenes, full of potential objects of interest, that the eye can take in at once" addresses browsing with the aid of digital technology. This requirement cannot be applied to browsing with other types of technology, such as books or file cabinets, and might bring serious design difficulties for systems with small screens such as cell phones.

Belkin et al.'s (1993) requirements were highly concrete and on the level of actions. As such, they were based on the search systems that were in place at the time of their research, and some of them are immaterial for web-based search systems. To generate these requirements, the researchers identified problems that might occur when carrying out several information-retrieval tasks and then offered a design requirement that would help to alleviate each problem. For example, one of the problems they identified that related to "search strategy formulation" (i.e., employing the analytical strategy) was the difficulty users had in understanding the use of the search logic. To alleviate this problem, the researchers suggested that the search interface should "mask logic from user." A contrary requirement may alleviate the problem to the same degree, however: Search interfaces could represent the logic, that of Boolean algebra for example, and lead users to enter Boolean statements by providing a structure in which query formulations are entered. Such a structure could be in the form of a table in which each term that is connected to another term with the "AND" operator is entered in a different column, and those associated with the "OR" operator are in the same column.

These examples show that defining search strategies on the actions level is unlikely to lead to the generation of useful design requirements. An individual search action might be supported by more than one possible design feature. Which one is the designer to choose? In addition, requirements based on a list of actions may at times contradict one another since an overall view, a direction, or an approach is missing. Moreover, actions are shaped by the technology in use, and some cannot be materialized with new technologies. Technology also limits the modes of information seeking in which a strategy can be employed. An action-level strategy that is identified in web searching, for instance, would not be applicable for searching in physical spaces, such as libraries and other people.

Defining strategies as categories of cognitive task procedures—rather than specific actions—resolves several challenges to producing stable and useful design requirements and thus makes the concept *search strategy* relevant for design. First, focusing on cognitive procedures—rather than on physical actions—results in requirements that are independent of technology. Having this focus is not foreign to search strategy scholars. Despite the large diversity in the construal of *search strategy*, most scholars would probably agree that it is cognitive in nature. Therefore, it is reasonable to focus on cognitive processes instead of recording the mechanics of actor-system interaction with no insight into the cognitive processes that generated it. Second, defining the different categories of search strategies enables a relatively comprehensive identification of possible search strategies. A design to support all possible actions-based strategies requires the identification of all possible actions-based strategies, which is an impossible task. On the other hand, the number of categories that cover possible procedures or actions is relatively small and stable, and does not require the identification of *all* possible actions. Third, viewing cognitive categories as a focal point opens a window to understanding the reasons for strategy selection that can guide the design of systems that cater to specific communities of actors, because the actual implementation of category-based search strategies is informed by the contextual constraints that shape them. That is, this approach is context-centered and beneficial to ecological design.

III Conceptual Traditions in Human Information Behavior

Human information behavior (HIB) is one of the most active research areas in library and information science (LIS). Since it became a recognized research field in the early 1960s, it has grown by leaps and bounds. A testimony to this growth is the number of documents covered in review articles about the area in the *Annual Review of Information Science and Technology* (*ARIST*). Whereas the first review (Menzel 1966) covered 23 documents, the fifth review (Lipetz 1970) covered 114 documents, most of which had been published in the previous year. The last review—titled "Information Behavior" (Fisher and Julien 2009)—was selective rather than inclusive and covered over 240 documents, excluding papers "that limited themselves to the use of a particular source or system, did not encompass broader concepts or principles, and [belonged to] other information subfields such as information retrieval, information literacy, and knowledge management" (317). Tom Wilson (1994) indicated that between the mid-1960s and the beginning of the 1990s, LIS literature included reports on several thousand HIB studies (15).

The rapid growth of the field is also reflected in the titles of the review articles in HIB. Until the 1990s the area was called *information needs and uses* by American scholars, who also used the phrase *user studies* to refer to empirical research projects.[1] The reviews that followed were much more specific. Some of them focused on a particular community of actors, such as managers (e.g., Katzer and Fletcher 1992; Choo and Auster 1993), or on the search and use of a specific type of sources, such as scholarly publications (e.g., King and Tenopir 1999). Others were dedicated to specific topics within the field, such as the browsing strategy (e.g., Chang and Rice 1993), task-based information-seeking (e.g., Vakkari 2003), context in information behavior research (e.g., Courtright 2007), collaborative information-seeking (Foster 2006), and design of an interface for information-seeking (Marchionini and Komlodi 1998). Some articles even found enough documents to complete a review about the methods and methodologies in HIB (e.g., Wang 1999; T. D. Wilson 2008).

Following the methodological and conceptual shifts in the social sciences, HIB research has experienced transitions of its own. In addition to its expansion, research standards have shifted with regard to four interrelated, basic methodological concepts:

• *Generalizability* has changed its status as the most important value of a study's findings. Other criteria were established and a research project is also valued according to its contributions to theory and practice, regardless of the level of its generality.

• The nature of the *expected results* has expanded to include not only "facts" (or knowledge claims), but also ideas and insights.

• The status of *variables* as the main (and at times the only) center of an investigation has been altered as researchers studied phenomena to understand them without focusing on their variability.

• Scholars have recognized the significant role of *context*, which is specific and particular to the studied phenomenon, and have included it in studies.

The concepts' transformation is commonly recognized as a shift from a system-centered approach to a user-centered one. This transformation created a distinction between two generations of research (the topic of chapter 6) and supported the growing interest in in-context research (see chapter 7). These shifts were gradual and were supported by relatively new theoretical traditions that have been developed in the social sciences. Moreover, the four major concepts are strongly shaped by the theoretical traditions researchers are following, whether or not the researchers are cognizant of the tradition they follow. The transition to a user-centered approach is still far from being complete.

6 Two Generations of Research

Human information behavior (HIB) made its first steps as a scholarly area in the early 1960s. Typical of an emerging field, it has undergone several transformations since then, the most noticeable of which was the shift from the first research generation to the second. First-generation projects typically focused on a defined group of users searching a context-specific system, and employed statistical analyses to uncover correlations among variables, primarily for the purpose of improving the information system and services at hand. In contrast, many projects in the second generation sought patterns of user behavior—some general and others specific—hoping to contribute in a variety of ways.

The two generations can be differentiated along various characteristics. From the methodological view, it is useful to examine two of the threads in research that made the difference: (1) the level of *generalizability* to which the field aspired, and (2) the nature of the *expected results*, including their projected contribution. These threads can be explained by their scales. At one extreme on the generalizability scale is a study that cannot be generalized beyond the single person in the local context in which she was investigated (e.g., a case study of an HIB event), and at the other extreme is a project that studies a behavior that is common to all humans. On the expected results scale, the possible emergence of a theme that may contribute to future research or to building a theory is on one end, and valid statistical correlations and evidence for causation that can be used for both building a theory and immediate application is on the other.

A typical research project in the first generation accepted limited generalizability and aimed at applicable results, while many projects in the second generation aimed at general results with a variety of contributions, often vaguely expressed. Related to these two threads, the transition from the first to the second generation brought to light new, more focused views of HIB: the cognitive and the in-context approaches.

6.1   The First Generation

Early researchers studied specific groups of users with the aim of generalizing for all members of the group, or over the same type of groups in any other location, and were not interested in other types of generalizations. In fact, numerous research projects were carried out to improve specific libraries and their services. These studies were motivated by the looming information explosion and the existing and potential capability of libraries and information centers to satisfy their users. Recognizing the significance of the issues, partly through their own experience, researchers had two main goals, which they sometimes addressed simultaneously: (1) to improve information services to certain groups of users, and (2) to advance the conceptual and methodological aspects of user-studies research. Intensive research was carried out by librarians as well as academicians in both the United States and England.

6.1.1   Studies of Scientists and Engineers

Early studies typically focused on identifying the type of documents and the information sources group members used, and how they used them. This limited scope is not surprising. Given that the studies' findings were supposed to improve libraries and information services, and given the nature of libraries before the digital age, the library component that could most easily be improved was the library collection.

Scientists and engineers were the first focus of research, which began in academic and special libraries, as well as in information centers. Regardless of the group studied, libraries and the services they provided were the center of interest, with very little attention paid to information sources outside libraries. In the United States, the most active research was conducted in research and development organizations within large corporations and government departments, primarily the Department of Defense (Paisley 1968). In England, early user-studies research focused on the use of academic libraries and was supported largely by government agencies, such as the British Library, the Advisory Council of Scientific Policy, and the Office of Scientific and Technical Information, each sponsoring large-scale studies. The first such study of social scientists—the INFROSS Project—began in England in 1968 (Brittain 1970; Line 1971), while in the United States, funds for research of scholars other than hard-core scientists were lacking (Line 1971). Crane (1971) reflected the attitude toward investing efforts in such scholars when she explained: "Information-seeking is probably more difficult in [social sciences] than in the basic sciences, but also perhaps *less imperative*" (6; emphasis added).

Studies of scientists and engineers focused largely on the information-seeking habits of users, investigating issues such as the type of material used most frequently (e.g., review articles, technical reports, colleagues) and the frequency at which actors used the library and information centers. In addition to recommending ways to improve a library's collection and services, some studies offered the scholarly community suggestions for future research. These proposals typically focused on specific aspects of information problems, such as needs and problems of a certain type of engineers or the use of patents.

Some scholars approached the information behavior of scientists and engineers from the viewpoint of the sociology of science. This approach made it possible to expand the research focus beyond the library and to include other aspects of human information interaction (HII) such as the creation, dissemination, and use of information (Crane 1971). While scholars investigated a limited range of topics, they enriched HIB research with a most important concept: "the invisible college" (Crane 1972), the informal network through which scientists exchange information with colleagues. This was the first instance of a large-scale, in-depth, and comprehensive study of humans as sources of information.[1] The concept of the invisible college and its attributes were developed by the psychologist William D. Garvey and his team at the Center for Research in Scientific Communication at Johns Hopkins University in the late 1960s (Garvey 1979). It was based on a series of systematic studies carried out by researchers from several disciplines and is possibly the most comprehensive series of explorative studies in HIB.

While scientists and engineers were first considered as one cohesive group, later studies showed that there was a need to study them separately. Engineers became a most popular target of study, and probably the most investigated user group. Not only are they still being investigated (e.g., Allard, Levine, and Tenopir 2009; Robinson 2010), but some groundbreaking HIB studies focused on this population (e.g., T. Allen 1977). First-generation HIB researchers ignored other professions by and large.

While most of the first-generation studies were focused on specific groups of users, after more than a decade of HIB research some scholars believed that there were enough data to draw some general observations. Among them were Faibisoff and Ely (1976), who carried their analysis of the HIB literature to the most desired type of research results at that time: They derived general recommendations for systems improvement. For example, analyzing the studies on scientists' information needs and uses, they concluded that, for an information system serving the group to be effective, a number of needs had to be met:

1. The need for more prompt dissemination of information …

2. The need for quality filtering of information …

3. The need for the right amount of information at the right time.

4. The need for receiving information in the desired form, usually oral or written, and in understandable language.

5. The need for active, selective switching of information …

6. The need to browse …

7. The need to get information easily and inexpensively …

8. The need for awareness of current literature, and the need to know of work in progress.

9. The need to know about how to use available information systems.

10. The need for synthesis of the literature, state of the art reviews, and introductory surveys of subjects. (Faibisoff and Ely 1976, 6)

Most of these requirements seem commonsense today, a few may seem obsolete (e.g., "the need for more prompt dissemination of information"), and others might have been commonsense when they were "discovered" (e.g., "the need to get information easily"). Nevertheless, these early studies provided a solid base for future research not only with their findings, but also through their pioneering methodological and conceptual developments.

Although they had fewer resources, several studies investigated the information needs of people outside the work context, and others explored how actors, primarily students, used library catalogs.

6.1.2 Information Needs and Uses of the Public

The shift in the view of public libraries from "warehouses" to "information centers" motivated research of the public they served. With the goal of improving library services, most studies investigated issues such as the topics in which residents of a certain region, neighborhood, or community were most interested; the degree to which their information needs were met; and the level to which the residents used community information sources that were available to them (e.g., Rieger and Anderson 1968). A few studies limited their focus to particular groups in the general public—such as civic organizations and voluntary groups (e.g., Kidd 1976)—or to a particular type of information service—such as information and referral service in urban areas (e.g., Long 1976). Other studies carried out their claim for generalizability to the maximum, investigating the information need of the "average citizen" (e.g., Chen and Hernon 1982; Dervin 1976).

The contribution of knowledge about the general information needs and uses of all residents of a country to the improvement of systems and services is limited because it can be achieved only on highly abstract levels. For example, one may hypothetically conclude that, in general, library services should increase their accessibility, but no generalizations can be made about how to improve it and at what rate. Even Faibisoff and Ely (1976), who attempted to arrive at generalizations and were successful for the scientific community, concluded in their analysis of general-public studies that the findings usually could not be generalized beyond the particular community that had been investigated.

6.1.3 Catalog Use Studies

The first study of catalog use was published in 1931, possibly the first study available to us in the field of HIB. Some additional studies followed, all for the purpose of improving library catalogs. The early 1980s saw a series of large-scale studies of the Online Public Access Catalogs (OPACs) carried out several years before the catalogs entered fully into use in large library systems. Catalog studies are still being conducted today, aiming at using advances in information technology to improve access to library documents.

Akers (1931) began a tradition in which researchers (most of whom were librarians) examined users' views of elements recorded on the catalog card. She surveyed undergraduate students about which elements they used, which were not useful, which ones the students did not understand, and which ones they would have liked to have seen. Other studies examined the elements that users had actually used when looking for information (e.g., Ayers et al. 1968; Kenney 1966; Tagliacozzo and Kochen 1970). While not limited to a professional group, such as engineers or chemists, these studies focused only on users of academic libraries.

The OPAC studies, on the other hand, investigated the use of catalogs in all types of libraries and offered researchers a variety of methods for data collection—methods that could not be employed when studying the use of card catalogs (Cochrane and Markey 1983). This set of studies was the first large-scale attempt to generalize the seeking of information across all users of one type of a system—the OPAC—and brought together researchers from both technical and human fields. These efforts to uncover general patterns were also carried out despite the fact that most scholars in previous research had concluded that useful large-scale generalizations could not be attained. The findings of the studies were numerous, and it is difficult to form a cohesive picture of how they have contributed to our understanding of searching OPACs. In addition, technological developments have created a new generation of OPACs which has made only a small portion of the studies' results relevant to the current design of library catalogs.

In spite of the resources invested in catalog use studies, it is not clear what contributions they offered to advance cataloging or OPAC design, which were their main purposes. It is possible that studies in a particular library helped improve its catalog or services, but there is no evidence these studies contributed to cataloging standards—such as the Anglo-American Cataloging Rules (AACR)[2]—or to the design of online catalogs.

6.1.4   Expanding the Range of Generalizability

A few researchers aimed to establish generalizations that would cover all contexts. Flowers (1965), for instance, surveyed physicists and chemists in various settings throughout England to identify the information sources they used. He concluded that there were no differences among scientists in diverse settings, finding that they all preferred to rely on reviews and original papers rather than on patents and they preferred information from the scientific literature over that from colleagues. On the other hand, several researchers found that generalizations cannot be made. Summarizing the large-scale INFROSS project, Line (1971) claimed researchers found it impossible to establish "any consistent general patterns of social science users" (430), and that "No major patterns were detected which could be of use for information system design purposes" (430). Reviewing HIB research in general, Crawford (1978) similarly explained that "observations based upon limited populations and divergent methodologies have restricted our abilities to generalize and to develop theory" (63–64). Later, the first set of studies of searching behavior of online searchers (Fenichel 1980, 1981) led researchers to the conclusion that individual differences overcame any other variable,[3] and thus made it impossible to find common patterns of behavior.

Nevertheless, Faibisoff and Ely (1976) identified 14 general patterns in information behavior when they analyzed the research literature at that time. Some examples of the patterns they found are:

• People tend to seek out information which is most accessible;

• People tend to follow habitual patterns when seeking information;

• Face-to-face communication is a primary source of information;[4]

• Different types of persons use different sources of information;

• The quantity of information often exceeds the capability of the individual to use it;

• An inverse relationship frequently exists between the quantity of information and its quality;

• When information is needed, it must be timely, accessible and relevant. (9–11)

Based on the general patterns they discovered, Faibisoff and Ely (1976) recommended guidelines for the designer of information systems, including that the designer should identify the user in relation to his discipline or environment, and the system should assume that the user has not articulated his information need (12–15). While some of the general patterns and guidelines for designers are outdated or have proven not to be useful, others have stood the test of time and are still valid today.

6.1.5 The First Generation: Conclusions

The early period of HIB was a time of conceptual and methodological exploration with an emphasis on the application of study results to operating information systems. During this stimulating period, researchers faced for the first time issues that were central to HIB and its investigation. The diversity of methods and scales that they used supported the development of the relatively stable methodologies that have been employed in later studies.

Although most present-day research is different from that of the past, the pioneering work of first-generation researchers laid the basis for the emergence of the second generation. Several large-scale studies by first-generation researchers unearthed some basic details about information-seeking behavior (ISB) that could not be arrived at by common sense alone. For example, they exposed the complexity in the ISB process and in some of the dimensions involved, the important role that informal sources play in information acquisition, the existence of habitual patterns in ISB, and the high significance of accessibility. They also introduced some of the central concepts in HIB, such as *information need* and *gatekeepers*. In addition, several study reports and analyses of such reports contributed directly to the growth of the second-generation methods and frameworks by experimenting with multifaceted research methods and beginning the exploration for conceptual frameworks.

6.2 The Second Generation

Based on the experience and results of HIB research during the first generation, scholars in the second generation moved in a conceptual direction in which study results were expected to contribute to future research, rather than to the improvement of a particular operating information system.[5] HIB research became a world of its own with an active internal life, free of the requirement of offering direct contributions to people and communities in the real world. Contributions to the HIB research world have taken the form of (a) actual suggestions for future research, (b) an increasing understanding of HIB phenomena, and (c) the creation of new conceptual constructs—ideally, models and theories—a contribution that has been greatly appreciated.

This focus on contributions to HIB research is typical of current research as well. The quest for conceptual developments is not new, however. As early as the 1960s, Paisley (1968) presented a conceptual framework for analyzing the HIB of scientists, and in the early 1970s, Lin and Garvey (1972) observed a growing realization among researchers of the need for a conceptual framework under which the various studies of scientists and engineers could be integrated. Yet the actual development of such frameworks began only after the transition into the second generation.

Since the transition, the number of user studies to improve a particular information system has been relatively small. Moreover, HIB studies that included some conceptual contributions have been perceived to be of higher value than those without such contributions. To arrive at the expected results, researchers in the second generation turned to one of the two extremes in generalizations:

1. Discovering properties of HIB in general, regardless of the actor's context and the system used. That is, focusing on the individual—rather than on a group of people, a profession, or a community—and carrying out research that leads to general results that are applicable to all human beings. With this focus, researchers have centered their efforts on studying the psychological aspects of the individual.

2. Investigating a group of people—which can be as small as one person—all in the same environment and acting under a particular situation, and arriving at findings that are applicable only to the members of the specific group. This brand of HIB research is called *in-context research* and has investigated individuals as representative of a group, but has also at times studied aspects of their social and environmental circumstances.

The search for general attributes relevant to HIB can take place in any type of study, including in-context research. Looking for general attributes that seem to be inherent to any person regardless of her environment and situation, a number of researchers turned to research in psychological factors, which has focused on the cognitive and affective aspects of information-seeking behavior (ISB).[6] In-context researchers have studied cognitive and affective aspects as well but not exclusively. They also have investigated facets other than work life, such as everyday life. Moreover, in-context research has moved beyond seeking behavior and has investigated other phenomena in HII such as information sharing, using, and evaluating.

This chapter focuses on research leading to general results. The following chapter (chapter 7) discusses in-context research.

6.2.1   The Cognitive Viewpoint

A cognitive approach to the study of HIB is highly attractive. After all, interaction with information is a cognitive process. Indeed, a great part of HIB research is conducted from a cognitive viewpoint and most of its models, as discussed in section 3.3, are cognitive. Pettigrew, Fidel, and Bruce (2001) explained:

> At the heart of the cognitive viewpoint rests the concept of knowledge structures. This concept has been borrowed from the cognitive sciences. Knowledge structures are the sets of concept relationships that comprise each individual's model of the world. It is this model of the world that is seen to mediate an individual's information behavior. Each person will apply the knowledge structures that are required to perceive, interpret, modify, or transfer information.... In information behavior research, the cognitive viewpoint focuses fundamentally upon the individual, on understanding the way each person thinks and behaves in response to information needs. (47)

The psychological sciences have provided the conceptual basis for this HIB viewpoint by offering conceptual constructs such as theories, approaches, and concepts. Researchers in these sciences, however, have diverse understandings and interpretations of such constructs, a diversity that has often caused controversies among them. To display this variety, Bryce Allen (1991a) provided an example from knowledge studies, which, he explained, was most relevant to HIB work: "Knowledge is sometimes characterized as 'mental representations,' 'mental models,' or 'cognitive structures'" (6). This list clearly opens the door to various approaches and interpretations of psychological concepts in HIB research. Although this multiplicity of interpretations has not been contentious in HIB investigations, it has stood in the way of building a cumulative body of research.

Whereas the cognitive viewpoint was already recognized in early HIB research, the development of these models was based on the personal experience of the researcher, anecdotal evidence, and intuition rather than on systematic research.[7] In contrast, the second-generation cognitive viewpoint was based on mature research and systematic investigations.

Cognitive research has several flavors. Some of it is based on the assumption that stable, innate human cognitive attributes—i.e., cognitive style—have an effect on ISB, and aims at finding out how each of these attributes affects searching behavior. Other parts explore cognitive attributes that have been acquired through learning and seek to find their effect on ISB. The majority of cognitive research, however, studies a variety of cognitive processes that are associated with ISB without considering individual styles or the effect of learning.

6.2.1.1 Cognitive Styles

Cognitive style is a term used in cognitive psychology to describe the way individuals perceive, process, and remember information, or their preferred approach to using such information to solve problems. While the term has various interpretations, it is perceived to be a constant, stable attribute of an individual's cognition. Cognitive style has various facets that were revealed through empirical studies—studies that not only uncovered these facets but also developed measurements and techniques to determine them. A measurement of a style may include several categories or present a continuum with emphasis on the extremes,[8] and one style may have more than one measurement. HIB researchers study how the cognitive style of an individual affects his ISB and, at times, the quality of search results.

Studies to investigate these effects are usually conducted as experiments. The researcher chooses the styles that seem most relevant, and applies the appropriate measurement to determine the cognitive style of each study participant. She then gives the participants searching tasks and measures elements in searching behavior; some studies also measure the quality of the results—usually applying the precision and recall measurements. Statistical analyses then select the significant correlations between cognitive style and ISB and/or performance. Some researchers looked at various combinations of two or more facets of cognitive style, and a few explored combinations with other variables such as gender, academic discipline, and searching experience.

The most commonly used measurement of cognitive style in HIB research has been the level of *field dependence*. Allen (1991a) explained that: "People who are field dependent tend to respond uncritically to environmental cues, while those who are independent will tend to orient themselves correctly in spite of environmental cues. Field dependence is associated with passivity, field independence with an active coping style" (21–22). Other measurements have been used as well, such as open-mindedness versus rigidity, holist versus serialist, and analytic versus undifferentiated. Other examples of cognitive style are visualizer versus verbalizer and impulsive versus reflective, but to my knowledge they have not been tested in HIB studies. Related to cognitive style are learning styles—such as the deep versus the surface approach and comprehension versus operation learning—and several researchers explored the effects of learning style on ISB. In studies of cognitive style and learning style, searching behavior (the dependent variables) has been measured along various variables, such as the following:

• Time required to complete the task

• The number of nodes traversed to locate a relevant item (on the web)

• The breadth of the search (narrow or comprehensive)

• Whether the participants employed Boolean search, best-match search, or a combination

• Perception of the utility and friendliness of various attributes of the search system (such as being able to display search history and ease of navigation)

• How confident the participant was about the results

• The preferred color of presentation.

These studies generated various findings, each according to its research questions. For example, a study of web searching found that field-independent participants had greater clarity of thinking than the field-dependent ones (Ford et al. 2002), and field dependents spent a longer time in order to visit more nodes than field independents did (Palmquist and Kim 2000; Wang, Hawk, and Tenopir 2000). Palmquist and Kim (2000), however, found this difference only among novice searchers. Strategy shift was also investigated. Ford, Wood, and Walsh (1994), for instance, discovered that field-independent searchers changed their strategies during different experimental conditions much more than the field dependents did. Investigating the effect of learning style on search performance, Logan (1990) found that searchers with a particular learning style called *concrete experience* achieved lower precision and recall than those with other styles.

More directed were studies relating to user interface. Exploring the effects of cognitive styles with the aim of improving user interface is common in the area of human-computer interaction (HCI). Several HIB researchers have followed this tradition, examining how to tailor the interface of information systems to individual cognitive styles. Chen and Ford (1998), for instance, found that field-dependent individuals primarily used the menu, while field independents progressed sequentially using the backward and forward buttons. Chen, Magoulas, and Dimakopoulos (2005) studied the display of web directories and found that field independents preferred the subject categories to be arranged alphabetically, while field dependents preferred them to be arranged according to relevance. In addition, field independents preferred deep ꝺ

category structure (i.e., few main categories but several levels underneath them), while field dependents preferred flat structure (i.e., many main categories).

One study that was conducted under semiexperimental conditions did not provide such crisp results. Vilar and Zumer (2008) asked participants to search their own requests and asked them to fill out several questionnaires before and after the search. Vilar and Zumer looked for correlations between individual characteristics (including cognitive style) and the perceived user-friendliness of the system. They could not identify simple overall patterns, but some single dimensions of individual characteristics could be linked to specific aspects of perception or preference.

This study and that of Palmquist and Kim (2000) provide the first indication that isolating cognitive style variables and testing their effect in the lab may not present results that are pertinent to real-life searching. In Palmquist and Kim's (2000) study, differences in cognitive style affected the web searching of novice searchers only. This finding can be interpreted to indicate that such differences may be overridden by experience. Vilar and Zumer's (2008) research demonstrated that once experimental conditions are loosened, it is difficult to discern the effects of cognitive styles. The main difference between this study and the ones with more typical conditions lies in the type of requests the participants searched. In experiments, all participants are typically asked to search the same set of made-up requests, while in this study the participants solved their own information problems. Vilar and Zumer (2008) introduced variability to the *context* of the search requests and thus were unable to observe the effects of the participants' cognitive styles. That is, context variables may also override those of cognitive style. Since every real-life search for information takes place in its own context, it is not clear whether a researcher who wishes his study results to be relevant to real-life conditions should focus on cognitive style.

Indeed, most cognitive style researchers did not see in their findings specific and direct implications for real life. They expressed their contribution as useful for the development of models of HIB, for showing the usefulness of an existing model, for the design of training for searching, or for providing hypotheses for future research.[9] One exception is the contribution to the user interface. Here the main premise has been that information systems should fit cognitive styles, and therefore the best user interface should have options for different styles. Some researchers did carry their studies further and developed prototypes of such interfaces.

Studies focusing on cognitive style constitute a definite part of research within the cognitive viewpoint. Less active but still within the realm of psychological sciences is research addressing personality traits and mental models. Both areas share their research approach with cognitive style studies.

6.2.1.2 Personality Traits

A relatively new area of research is the effect of personality traits on ISB. Citing Phares (1991), Jannica Heinström (2003) explained, "Personality is that pattern of characteristic thoughts, feelings, and behaviours that distinguishes one person from another and that persists over time and situation." This definition views cognitive style as a component of an individual's personality. Therefore, examining personality traits is, in a way, an expansion of the study of cognitive styles. Similar to cognitive styles, these traits are assumed to be innate to an individual and unchanging. The most comprehensive investigation was carried out by Heinström (2003), who set out to find whether "personality traits are likely to influence attitudes and behaviour ... in an information-seeking context." Personality researchers agree that there are five basic dimensions that can be used to describe differences in cognitive, affective and social behavior: neuroticism, extraversion, openness to experience, agreeableness, and conscientiousness. Heinström (2003) addressed all of them.

In a series of studies, each with a different population—all students—and at times with large samples, Heinström (2003, 2006) set out to find if there were correlations between the set of dimensions of personality traits and variables in information behavior, such as difficulties in relevance judgment, document selection criteria, experience of time pressure as a barrier to information, and effort used in information-seeking—all assessed by the participants themselves by describing their usual habits, mostly using a Likert-type scale. She found that information behavior can be connected to all five personality dimensions. Her results show, for example, that people with a low level of *neuroticism* have a positive attitude toward information-seeking and appreciate high recall; in addition, the more secure they are, the more actively they search for information (Heinström 2003).[10] A high level of neuroticism, on the contrary, implied difficulties in coping with unpredictability, disorder, and ambiguity in search systems (Hyldegård 2009). Another dimension, *competitiveness*, was related to experiencing lack of time as a barrier to information retrieval, problems with relevance judgment, and competence in critical analysis of information.

In another research project, Hyldegård (2009) could not confirm some of Heinström's findings. She carried out a naturalistic study of a group of people in an actual social situation, following students working in teams on a class assignment. Hyldegård observed them throughout the project with the purpose of finding out the effects of team members' personality traits on their information behavior within the team. She found, for example, that the participants had low levels of uncertainty during the project even though most of them had a high level of neuroticism. Attributing this seeming contradiction to the team situation, Hyldegård (2009) introduced the notion that social settings affect the manifestations of personality traits. That is, one cannot generalize about the ISB of people with certain personality traits across all social settings.

6.2.1.3 Mental Models

Among the cognitive attributes that have been acquired through learning, mental models are most commonly employed in relation to information systems, their design, and the training to use them. Borgman (1984a) defined a *mental model* as "a model of the system the user builds in his or her head" (37). Mental models are crystallized through experience, some of which may include systematic training. Borgman explored the creation of mental models through training to determine the effect of two styles of training on retrieval performance. One type trained subjects by presenting a conceptual model of the system, and the other presented the procedures one can follow. She found that complex questions that required exploration were searched more successfully by those who received conceptual training, but there was no difference between the styles when subjects searched simple questions (Borgman 1984b).

Other studies of mental models took different directions. Zhang (2008), for example, studied the types of mental models undergraduate students had of the web and the relationships of these models with ISB. Earlier, Dimitroff (1992) found that the more complete the subject's mental model of the retrieval system, the more likely she was to make fewer errors and to retrieve more items. On a more general level, Marchionini (1989) reported that the mental models students had of print encyclopedias were useful for their searching of online encyclopedias. Other studies investigated some factors that contribute to the building of mental models and their effect on ISB, such as the level of domain knowledge—that is, the degree to which a searcher is familiar with the subject domain of the request (B. Allen 1991b; Jacobsen and Fusani 1992)—and searching experience (Ford and Chen 2002).

6.2.1.4 Cognitive Processes

Most researchers who are guided by the cognitive viewpoint have focused on the study of ISB as a cognitive process that is common to information seeking in all contexts and situations—regardless of personal attributes such as age or gender. These processes were first attended to in the early HIB models, such as Taylor's (1968) stages of a need's development and Krikelas's (1983) model of the search process. In fact, most of the action models in ISB describe cognitive processes (see section 3.3.1), and the second-generation concepts that were introduced, such as sense-making (Dervin 1992) and anomalous stage of knowledge (ASK) (Belkin 1980), represent states in a cognitive process.

HIB researchers have investigated multiple aspects and processes. Some followed the information-seeking process from initiation to completion, and others focused on a particular state or activity. As the HIB models demonstrate, there is no one way to describe the seeking process. Each researcher outlines its stages according to her view, and no one description is generally better than the others.[11] While several models were based chiefly on the conceptual models and viewpoints of their creators, some have been based directly on systematic empirical research.[12] In a relatively early study, researchers analyzed the decisions that participants made during a search in an online catalog and concluded that their behavior resembled that of decision making in other contexts (Blackshaw and Fischhoff 1988). Another example is the pattern developed by Cole (1999), who identified five cognitive stages in the search process by collecting data from 45 students—beginning with "opening" and concluding with "effect of process."

Vakkari (1999), on the other hand, focused on one stage: He explored what triggers an individual to look for information. Based on studies of actors in workplaces, he concluded that the conditions that aroused this behavior were the nature of the problem to be resolved, the complexity of the task, and prior knowledge. On the other end of the spectrum, Berryman (2006) examined a much later stage in the search process and asked: How do people decide that they have enough information? Like Blackshaw and Fischhoff (1988), she concluded that the contextual factors she found to shape this decision are similar to those found by decision-making researchers.

The search process however, has not been the only focus of study. H. Bruce (1994), for instance, examined the dynamism of relevance judgment, and Spink and Park (2005) called attention to the multitasking that occurs in HIB, such as when an individual searches for information on two topics simultaneously, switching back and forth from one search to the other.

Identifying and measuring cognitive processes are challenging goals. Cognitive processes are not directly observable and do not present themselves in a quantitative form that can be directly transferred into measurements. Nevertheless, identifying and describing cognitive processes constitute a large share of HIB research, including in-context inquiries.

6.2.1.5 The Cognitive Viewpoint: Conclusions

The emergence of cognitive research signaled a step forward in HIB research. It is perceived to be more scholarly than previous research in several respects, including its heavy reliance on conceptual constructs (usually borrowed from psychological sciences), its investigation of details rather than a broad-brush approach, and its capacity to offer general results. In particular, progress has been made because cognitive research has aimed at *understanding* HIB rather than merely *describing* it.

Cognitive research has indeed offered many contributions to the HIB field, particularly to its conceptual developments. It has shown, for instance, that (1) a search is an adaptive process with stages that can be clearly defined; (2) looking at a search as a problem-solving process opens the possibility of applying the rich results from decision-making research—both conceptual and applied ones; and (3) there are factors external to the individual that affect cognitive processes during a search. Cognitive research can also be applicable to training and education relating to information behavior. Even though the cognitive viewpoint is considered to be progress compared to the studies in the first generation, it is not "better" or more "progressive" than other types of HIB research. Similar to any other viewpoint in HIB research, the cognitive viewpoint has its own limitations.

In particular, this research has offered very few relevant recommendations for the design of information systems because the suggestions it presented are too general. For example, suggestions that there should be flexible online help, multiple access points, and an interface that matches the learning style of the individual user cannot guide the system designer because they do not specify the way in which online help should be flexible or when to provide a certain type of access points. McKechnie et al. (2008) substantiated this observation. In their analysis of the 117 research reports that were presented in the Information Seeking in Context (ISIC) conferences from 1996 to 2006, they found that 59% of the reports included implications for practice, but 56.5% of these reports used vague, general or otherwise unclear statements rather than explicit delineation of implications for practice.

This gap is not surprising for several reasons, especially because cognitive studies are descriptive (see chapter 9). Determining an individual's cognitive (and personal) attributes is a challenging task. To identify cognitive, personality, or learning styles requires users to fill in questionnaires, at times rather lengthy ones. How can a system identify these styles for each user, and once they are identified, what should the system do in order to operate in a manner that matches a user's style? One area of research that has attempted to resolve these issues is that of *user modeling*. Its goal is to design information systems that create a model of each individual user and respond to her input accordingly. While this is an active area of research that touches upon various fields such as human-computer interaction (HCI) and information retrieval (IR), it seems to have produced results that are limited to certain activities—such as clustering web search results according to the user's area of interest—and various user's attri-butes—such as persistence in searching and long-term interest—none of which is a cognitive or personality trait.

Reservations about the benefit of cognitive studies to systems design were raised as early as the beginning of the 1980s when nonbibliographic information systems were first introduced. Huber (1983), for example, brought up questions about the value of cognitive style studies for the design of management information systems (MIS) and decision support systems (DSS). He concluded that cognitive-style research cannot "lead to operational guidelines for MIS and DSS designs" (567). Building on some of his arguments, I can offer the following explanations for his conclusion:

• Earlier literature concluded that other factors are better predictors of HIB. Huber quoted Chervany and Dickson (1978), who explained, "Researchers have not been able to predict consistently behavior/performance on the basis of individual personal-ity characteristics. Rather, behavior appears to be (to a very large degree) determined by the characteristics of the task in which the individual is involved" (Huber, 1983, 569). In addition, since the characteristics of a task reveal themselves not in the lab but only in naturalistic settings, results of lab experiments cannot scale up to real-life situations.

• Research has shown that other personality traits may be relevant to systems design, such as response to uncertainty, responsiveness to organizational norms of rationality, risk-taking propensity, dogmatism, and previous training. Clearly, personality charac-teristics do not necessarily correlate positively among themselves. Suppose studies find that a field-dependent individual would benefit from a certain design requirement, while a person with previous training would require the opposite design. How would a system be designed to support a field-dependent user who has rich experience? The only way to arrive at a "reasonable solution" is to test HIB for all possible combinations of personality traits and then design systems that support each one of them. The number of such combinations is so large that this "solution" is practically impossible.

• Designing systems that match a certain cognitive style is not always useful. As research has indicated, some cognitive styles create barriers to information retrieval, and so it would not be beneficial to design systems that match such a style. On the other hand, systems that are designed to complement this style are likely to be avoided by individuals who possess it. In short, it is not clear how to fit system design to a particular cognitive style in order to improve interaction and retrieval.

Most important is the question of whether a certain style, independent of the context, induces consistent behavior. Two studies have already indicated that it might not (e.g., Hyldegård 2009; Vilar and Zumer 2008). When studies were carried out without the controls commonly employed in a lab experiment, results were not clear-cut, which usually led researchers to conclude that some external conditions affect an individual's behavior more than his style. This repeated experience may lead to the conclusion that the findings of studies of style-induced behavior are valid for experimental conditions but may not be directly applicable to real-life settings. Researchers who are interested in contributions that can improve information systems may ask whether the cognitive viewpoint is relevant at this time or whether it is better to focus now on other attributes that clearly affect ISB and have the potential to guide design, such as the social environment and the nature of the task that motivated a search. Once systems can cater to these conditions, future research may add the cognitive viewpoint as icing on the cake.

Other limitations are the bounded realms the cognitive viewpoint has addressed and the justification for its generalizations. Almost all the conceptual contributions of this research were limited to the search process and have offered very little to the understanding of other realms in HII such as evaluating, organizing, or representing information.

In addition, generalizations are unwarranted for a considerable part of this body of research, and yet researchers have implicitly assumed that the effects of cognitive attributes are the same for nearly everyone and under any condition. The most obvious reason that the results cannot be generalized is the fact that the majority of the studies were carried out with students as participants. With the emerging evidence that searching behavior is also shaped by acquired cognitive attributes—such as mental models, subject knowledge, or experience—it becomes somewhat uncertain whether student behavior represents that of everyone else or even the same students when they, say, search the web for fun.

Furthermore, searching behavior is shaped by the functionality and interface of the search system. In fact, analyses in some studies heavily relied on the capabilities of the system employed in the experiment, so their results cannot be applied to the use of a different system. Findings from studies of searching traditional bibliographic databases, for instance, are not directly applicable to web searching. Some studies limited the experimental conditions to a degree that obviously defies any attempt at generalization. For example, how can a hypothetical study of LIS graduate students who search two factual questions on their school's web site be generalized beyond these conditions? Admittedly, most researchers in such cases mentioned in their research reports that their findings could not be generalized.[13] But the presentation of the findings usually states general facts without reminding the reader that all these new discoveries are relevant only to the participants in the experiment. To make matters worse, even when it is clear that no generalization can be made, readers feel free to integrate them into their own work as findings that apply universally.[14]

In conclusion, although there is no evidence of contribution to design, and there have been some dead-ends in terms of applications, the cognitive viewpoint has been a major contributor to conceptual developments in HIB research.

6.3 The Chase after Variables

HIB researchers are still looking for variables to study. The desire to identify which variables affect HIB was one of the main goals of the early large-scale studies. Paisley (1968), for instance, issued a call to researchers: "we now urgently need theories of information-processing behavior that will generate propositions concerning channel selection; amount of seeking; effects on productivity of information quality, quantity, currency, and diversity; the role of motivational and personality factors, etc." (3).

One means scholars have applied to find useful variables is collecting data through questionnaires that address the variables they decided to study with the hope that associations among them would reveal those that affect HIB. Mote's (1962) study is a typical example of the use of a questionnaire to find variables that affect information behavior. Conducting a survey and analyzing records about requests for information at an information center in an R&D department, Mote found relationships between the occupation of the professional staff and (a) the type of literature they required, (b) the number of requests for information, and (c) the time it took to respond to a query.[15] Staff members who worked on projects that employed a single well-defined subject scored lowest on the three variables, whereas staff whose work required a variety of subjects with fuzzy borders among them scored highest.

In a summary of these large-scale studies, Vickery (1973) discussed a total of 41 variables. For example, studies found that the volume of searching a person conducted related to various variables, such as the size of his work team, his age, the nature of his job, and his scientific productivity. Also, the success of a search related to variables such as the nature of the person's institution and the nature of his job.

The purpose of these studies was to support the design of libraries. They were based on the implicit assumption that once a designer ascertained the characteristics of the potential users, she could consult the studies and decide how to organize and manage the library and what services to provide. Obviously, this approach was unrealistic for the same reasons that variables representing cognitive styles are not likely to guide systems design: the number of possible variables and the interdependences among them is too large.[16] Moreover, because at that time enumerating the variables was based on the researchers' commonsense and creativity rather than on conceptual frameworks or on empirical research, there was always the possibility of missing variables that actually made a difference.

Second-generation researchers recognized the inefficiency in this trial-and-error method for uncovering influential variables and began to identify variables in a more systematic manner.[17] This task was made possible by the growing use of qualitative methods that were applied in naturalistic settings.

Accordingly, the central research question became "Which variables should we study?" rather than "What associations exist among a particular set of variables?" This new approach matches the common view that qualitative research should result in hypotheses that can then be quantitatively tested and generalized beyond the local context in which they were developed. Therefore, many studies asked the question: "What is the information behavior of X (a group of people defined by setting, life experience, profession, and various other aspects and their combinations)?" A large portion of these investigations employed an inductive approach—that is, building the answer from the bottom up without relying on a priori conceptual constructs.[18] The outcome of such studies was usually a list of factors that affect the participants' behavior—that is, a list of variables.

Another approach for generating relevant variables is to base their identification on previous research and conceptual constructs (e.g., Urquhart and Yeoman 2010). The studies in cognitive style, for instance, were all based on previous research in the cognitive sciences and on the measurements that were developed through some of these studies. Ingwersen and Järvelin (2005) also used previous empirical studies and models in HIB and IR as a basis for developing a model of information retrieval from which they derived variables. They went further and designed experiments to test the associations among these variables.

Despite some attempts to collect the variables that proved relevant to HIB, no core list of such variables exists—a fact that is still of concern to some HIB researchers. In fact, the multiplicity in approaches and methods that have been used to derive variables and test them makes it unfeasible to find a set of core variables that affect HIB. This situation is not surprising and is not likely to improve, given the complexity of HIB processes. Therefore, it might be the time for HIB scholars who favor general findings to limit the search for universal variables, and consider other types of useful generalizations (see section 7.3).

6.4   Lingering Issues

As early as 1967, Herner and Herner reviewed the literature about information needs and uses in science and technology and observed the following seven flaws in the research in that field:

1. The relatively few techniques used

2. The diversity of corpora of users to which these few techniques have been applied

3. The diversity and ambiguity of language in discussing the techniques that have been used and their results

4. The lack of innovation

5. The failure to build on past gains

6. The failure to profit from past mistakes

7. The frequent absence of rigorous experimental designs (Herner and Herner 1967, 2).

Their review, which was the second of its kind to be published, was based on 38 research reports, several of which were reports of large-scale studies. A year later, Paisley (1968), in a groundbreaking review article, added two additional requirements beyond the flaws noted by Herner and Herner: (1) the designers of information systems must recognize the need for user studies, and (2) theory must play a stronger role in research.

Does HIB research have the same failings 40 years later? Clearly, HIB research has matured and most of the issues raised by these authors disappeared or were shown to be irrelevant. Second-generation research employs a variety of techniques, and discussions about these usually follow a common standard and a relatively stable nomenclature, even when one concept has several interpretations, such as *the search process*. Theory plays an increasing role; researchers are frequently innovative, often on several levels; and the lack of rigorous experimental design is rare. In addition, the "diversity of corpora of users"[19] is not considered a flaw and is actually blooming with in-context research, which has provided valuable contributions. One flaw that still requires improvement is the rigor of research. In conducting surveys, for example, researchers accept low response rates even though such rates imply weak validity, and in naturalistic studies researchers ask participants to write a diary that details each information event, even though previous studies have revealed that participants find it difficult to integrate such activities into their work day. In addition, the gap between HIB and IR research still exists (see chapter 10).

The major lingering issue, however, is the lack of a cumulative body of research. Today, it is commonly considered advantageous among HIB researchers for each to create new ways of approaching research and to discover new concepts or phenomena. Although there are a few, relatively small, communities of scholars that share an approach or elements of it, numerous researchers have created their own individual lenses. Some have even created a research agenda that avoids a commitment to a certain view or to a stable type of actors and that tries on several lenses, one after the other. Further, even though most researchers are familiar with the literature related to their studies, it is not uncommon for investigators to fail to see the benefit they may gain from previous mistakes.

In summary, the list presented by Herner and Herner (1967) demonstrates that one of the main issues that plague HIB research today had already reared its head in the first HIB studies: Research is not cumulative. Contributing to this situation are (1) the failure to build on past gains and to profit from past mistakes, and (2) the diversity in approaches to research. The failure to learn from past research is a barrier not only on the path to cumulative research but also to conducting high-quality research. The diversity in approaches and methods, on the other hand, provides a richness that enhances the development of HIB research in spite of its drawbacks.[20] While it is unlikely (nor is it desirable) that one approach or technique would become the standard, one hopes that the coming together of the different approaches and techniques will result in the creation of fewer of them, but ones that are solid, useful, and central. Chapter 13 explains how the use of cognitive work analysis can support the conversion of diverse approaches.

6.5 Two Generations of Research—Conclusions: System-Centered versus User-Centered Research

The transition from the first to the second generation of HIB is often characterized as a shift from a system-centered to a user-centered view. On the surface it seems that the distinction between these views is clear and easy to determine: A study that focuses on a context-specific system is a system-centered one, while a user-centered investigation considers user attributes. Yet the distinction between the generations as reflected in these simple definitions is inaccurate and misleading. The term *user* by itself is system-centric because one looks at users of an information system. Without a system there are no users.[21] Moreover, it seems that studies conducted in the second generation are automatically considered user-centered unless they clearly focus on a context-specific system. For example, it is common to agree that studies in the first generation were system-centered because they investigated people using libraries and biblio-graphic databases. At the same time, studies of web searching, which began in the second generation, are considered user-centered. Does the difference lie in the type of system? Clearly, this distinction is not supportable. In addition, the claim that second-generation studies have heightened the focus on the user is not valid. First-generation studies investigated many user variables (if different from those studied in the second generation), as well as environmental variables.

Most HIB researchers today claim to subscribe to the user-centered view, and yet a considerable number of studies are actually system-centered because they investigate users interacting with particular systems (e.g., a library catalog, a medical help system). Typical user-centered studies had already been carried out in the early 1960s. Mote (1962), for example, identified three types of scientists at Shell Research Ltd. and found the type of information services each one required—e.g., a self-service library for one type and intensive user support for another. Project INISS (Wilson and Streatfield 1977; Wilson, Streatfield, and Mullings 1979) observed a typology of workers in social services departments that led to recommendations for information services for each type. Admittedly, such studies were rare at that time. It seems, therefore, that the concept *user-centered*, particularly when it is used to distinguish between the two research generations, still lacks a stable interpretation among scholars.

Dervin and Nilan's (1986) *ARIST* article is considered the milestone marking the transition from the first to the second generation.[22] Based on a review of both empiri-cal work and critical essays, they discerned an evolving position among scholars which recognized the need for a user-centered approach, that is, "to make information needs and uses a central focus of information systems, and … the central focus" (7). Dervin and Nilan's unique contribution to the definition of the shift lies in their explicit and systematic distinction between the system-centered and the user-centered approaches, and their call for the development of the latter. They described the essence of the transfer when they delineated several basic conceptual and methodological aspects that typified the differences between the system-centered and the user-centered approaches. I have presented these in table 6.1.

This comparison offers a definition of each approach that better fits our circum-stances than the common one. It indicates that the difference lies not in whether the study participants use a certain system or whether the goal of a study is to generate system-design requirements, but rather in the conceptual, theoretical, and methodological approach of the researcher. Under this definition, several contemporary research projects that are considered user-centered are actually system-centered.[23]

Table 6.1

A comparison between the system-centered and the user-centered approaches based on Dervin and Nilan (1986)

System-centered view	User-centered view
Information is objective; its meaning remains constant through the transfer from producer to receiver	The meaning of information is in the eye of the user
Users are passive recipients of information; they are informed when they receive documents	Users are purposive, self-controlling, and sense-making
User behavior can be predicted regardless of their situational context	User behavior is shaped by situational contexts
Studies focus only on the interaction between humans and systems	Studies are holistic, examining factors that do not relate directly to the interaction but that shape it, such as social and cognitive factors
Studies investigate external behavior	Studies investigate internal cognition
A consideration of individual attributes prevents prediction	Individuality can be studied systematically. People share common dimensions in constructing experience
Use of quantitative methods	Use of both quantitative and qualitative methods

Even though the work of Dervin and Nilan (1986) designated a generational transition, no precise date delineating one generation from the other can be specified because HIB development has not been linear. The difference between the generations and their shift in focus from systems to users is primarily epistemological (see chapter 8). Research projects today may have questions almost identical to those posed in the first HIB studies, and may even employ the same methodology. In addition, some second-generation "new" approaches had already been employed to varying degrees by first-generation researchers. The maturation process of HIB research has followed a spiral pattern with its threads gaining increased maturity, and with the first-generation research providing a solid basis for the second generation to thrive.

7   In-Context Research

As we have seen in chapter 6, first-generation research (considered system-centered) investigated contextual variables of users of certain systems, while second-generation research (considered user-centered) focused first on the person, regardless of the context. From these opposing views emerged a third view: in-context research that centered on a person in a context or situation. In-context research was formally established with the first Information Seeking Behavior in Context (ISIC) conference in 1996. This branch of research has grown significantly since then and has attracted the attention of researchers from fields other than library and information science (LIS), such as information retrieval (IR) and human-computer interaction (HCI) (Vakkari 2008).

It is commonly agreed among researchers that research investigating a particular context or situation cannot be generalized beyond the empirical setting. This "limitation" has caused various researchers in human information interaction (HII) to doubt in-context studies' ability to contribute to research and design. On the other hand, because it is confined to certain conditions, in-context research provides for in-depth analyses and the capacity to preserve some of the complexity that is typical of HII in real life—a depth and complexity that cannot be achieved in research aiming at generalizable results. Moreover, since there has been growing evidence that contextual elements shape HIB, it is more reasonable to consider context than to ignore it. Empirical in-context studies have ranged from case studies of one person in particular circumstances (e.g., Fidel et al. 2004; Kuhlthau 1997) to about 100 participants under a certain condition (e.g., George et al. 2006).

Today, even though a large portion of HIB scholarly work is in-context research, the community is still discussing the definition of *context*. Most empirical research, however, has overlooked this debate,[1] and the elements that are considered in the investigation in each research project draw de facto the boundaries of its context. One hypothetical study of the HIB of, say, inner-city high school students might include the librarian, the teachers, and the budget restrictions as its context, while the context of another study might be composed of the librarian, the school's relationship with the community, the state's graduation requirements, and the racial mix of the city. Some of the contexts that have been selected have been highly specific, and some even unique. While the richness in the interpretation of *context* provides for discussion and reflection, this ad hoc understanding of context stands in the way of building a cumulative body of research that may lead to generalizations. Clearly, if each study of a phenomenon such as inner-city high school students examines a different context, the findings are incompatible and cannot be aggregated into a coherent accumulation of results.[2]

7.1   What Do We Mean by *Context*?

Generally speaking, the term *context* is construed in different ways, depending on … the context. The *Oxford Dictionary of English* (2nd edition, revised) offers two meanings that are related to the concept *frame of reference*, which enhance our understanding:

• The circumstances that form the setting for an event, statement, or idea, and in terms of which it can be fully understood;

• The parts of something written or spoken that immediately precede and follow a word or passage and clarify its meaning.

This construal is not uncommon in LIS research, as Vakkari, Savolainen, and Dervin (1997) explained: "context constitutes necessary conditions for sufficient understanding of [the information needs and seeking] phenomena" (9). Another form of this interpretation is the idea that context creates meaning. Dervin (1997) argued that various epistemological views have created their own perception of the term. It is not surprising, therefore, that various scholars in HIB have their own understanding of what is meant by the term.[3]

Although not officially declared as such, in-context research began with the first user studies. First-generation researchers considered the context as the central force shaping HIB activities and conducted studies to find out its effects. While most did not use the term *context* and were not aware of the challenges to its definition, many of the independent variables they tested are likely to be considered today as part of context (see section 6.3). As early as the late 1960s, T. J. Allen (1969) reported on the contextual variables considered in previous studies that were found to affect HIB, such as the phase in the problem-solving process and the formal and informal structure of the organization. In addition, most first-generation researchers focused on well-defined groups of users—such as scientists in basic research and scientists working in research groups—and on additional contextual elements, including the nature of the subject domain in which scientists work (e.g., self-contained versus drawing on other domains) and the social organization among scientists (Crane 1971).

Moreover, several first-generation researchers suggested the dimensions of a context that would be relevant to information-seeking behavior (ISB). The first to put forward such a proposal was Paisley (1968), who laid out the context of the scientist as a person within "almost concentric" systems. These were (1) the culture, (2) a political system, (3) a membership group, (4) a reference group (i.e., other scientists with similar characteristics), (5) an invisible college, (6) a formal organization, (7) a work team, (8) the scientist's own head, (9) a legal/economic system, and (10) a formal information system (Paisley 1968, 3–6). Other scholars put forward other configurations of context (e.g., Lin and Garvey 1972; Taylor 1991; Vickery 1973, 34).

Today, when an empirical researcher is unconcerned with the complexity inherent in the interpretation of *context*, she usually understands it, in a somewhat vague way, to be the background in which actors operate. In contrast, HIB scholars who have explored the meaning of *context* have been highly precise in explaining their own construal. HIB scholars have different opinions about whether context is composed of identifiable and stable elements or is fluid and dynamic and about whether it is the real context that is relevant to HIB research or the one that is perceived by the actor.

7.1.1 Fluid and Dynamic versus Identifiable and Stable Context

First-generation researchers conceived the context to be a composition of mostly discrete elements that were stable, such as the size of the actor's team, its management style, and the nature of the institutions in which the actor works. To guide the design of stable information systems, they conducted studies to discover these elements and their effects on searching behavior.[4] Most empirical research projects today implicitly assume a stable context, but conceptual discussions about context tend to highlight its dynamic and ever-changing nature. These views represent the extreme ends of a spectrum, and portray a rift between theory and practice. On one end, the assumption that elements in reality are stable and unchanging has no acceptable conceptual leg to stand on. On the other, it is still not clear how empirical studies address a fluid and ever-changing world or how they can guide practical applications.[5]

Most scholars do not reside at the extreme ends of this spectrum. It would be difficult to find a researcher who claims that some elements in reality never change. It is equally difficult, if not impossible, for information systems and services to be dynamic and ever-changing to a degree that supports the fluid conditions under which HIB takes place. This system would have to update itself every time, say, a user updates her state of knowledge during a search process. The view of fluid context addresses the *situational* side of HIB, that is, it assumes that the actor's situation is in a constant state of change. At one moment a situation may be characterized by one set of conditions and in the next by another. Dervin's sense-making approach (see section 3.2.1), in which a person is viewed as going through life moving from one situation to another, is an example of this view.[6]

When one assumes that reality is dynamic but aims to conduct research that is applicable to practice, one can define *context*, as opposed to *situation*, to include regularities—that is, conditions that are relatively stable and evolve gradually—rather than those that change constantly.[7] Researchers can investigate patterns of processes and of the conditions involved with the recognition that specific applications to practice will be useful for a period of time, and new ones will have to be determined as practice evolves. In other words, when investigating HIB in context, a researcher takes a snapshot of the activities and the context, and analyzes the pertinent elements that are relatively stable to arrive at relevant applications. Once this analysis leads to the implementation of a new information system, a next round of improvements is planned. In this way, systems and services evolve with reality.

7.1.2   The Boundaries of a Context

The definition of *context* is not only a subject of discussion but also a practical matter. When conducting empirical in-context research, investigators define the context under study, that is, they define its boundaries by determining its composition. The boundaries have been defined through different methods: (a) ad hoc, (b) as a result of previous studies, or (c) with the guidance of conceptual constructs. A researcher who is the first to study the user group that is of interest to him often employs an ad hoc approach and is ready to discover its context.[8] In this case he approaches the investigation with the exploratory question: What elements external to the actors shape their HIB? As he applies qualitative, naturalistic methods with inductive analysis of the data, he develops findings that define the context for the target group. That is, "the setting" is being discovered by the research process and is not fully understood before data are analyzed.[9] Quite often, however, the researcher has access to previous studies that are relevant to his project. He can then use the contextual elements that have been discovered as a basis for his research or for other goals, such as testing, expanding, or refining the elements and thus redefining the context for the project's group.

Regardless of previous knowledge, a researcher may choose to be guided by conceptual constructs that lead to a definition of *context*. Fisher et al. (2004), for example, selected Granovetter's (1973) theory of the strength of weak ties, and the concept of *third place* (Oldenburg 1989) to develop the contextual concept of *information ground;* and Chatman (2000) grounded her concept of *small world* in several theories from sociology (see section 3.1.1). Similarly, Williamson's (2005) ecological theory of human information behavior was inspired by ecological theory, and the onion model of cognitive work analysis (Vicente 1999; also see chapters 11 and 13) has its roots in both systems thinking and ecological psychology.

One question that is relevant to determining the boundaries of a context has been neglected: What is the object of which we study the context? Most context-related discussions refer to HIB's context, but it is not clear whether the context is of the *person* who is carrying out HIB or of the *activities* involved. That is, is the context *structural* or *functional*? This difference has had a minimal presence in discussions about the definition of *context*. Researchers who wish to arrive at results that are applicable to practice, however, need to consider the choice between the two types.[10]

Paisley's (1968) construct of scientist-within-systems is a good example of a structural view of context. His systems within systems were carved out mostly from the organizational structure of the unit, and of more encompassing structures outside the organization, such as the political and legal systems. Another example is the conceptual model Baker (2004a) developed in the context of end-of-life care, in which a patient is enveloped first by the family group, which is then nested in the community. Both groups are then embedded in the cultural context and environment, which include several aspects, such as the physical, legal, economic, ethical/moral, and the health system.

To observe the differences between the structural and functional views of context, consider Baker's (2004a) model.[11] It is clear that family and community members affect the patient's HIB, and Baker's study has indeed shown that. But it is reasonable to assume that the *functions* that the family and community perform in relation to the patient are more likely to affect HIB than the family's *structure* or that of the community. Clearly, the structure of the family and the community contributes to shaping the functions they perform, and the functions in turn affect behavior. The nature of the relationship among family members, for example, may affect the patient's HIB. For instance, there might be a lack of communication and coordination that might make it difficult for the patient to get consistent information about the care of her children. What will shape her information behavior, however, is not the nature of the family relationships but the lack of access to consistent information. That is, the function "Have consistent access to information about child care" is a requirement for the design of information systems and services to improve the situation that can be operationalized, rather than being a vague injunction, like "Consider family relationships."[12]

Moreover, some functions are likely to have the same effect whether they were performed by a family member or a community member. For instance, when a patient wants to watch a health channel on television, whether her cable bill is paid by her family or a community member is not likely to affect the way she will look for information and use it. The function that did affect her HIB was that of providing access to the television channel. Thus, while on a conceptual level it might be important to understand, say, the relationships between a patient and her family, what is relevant to the design of information services is the finding that a television channel is a desired source of information, and knowing the ways in which it can be made available.

This view of context—which advocates its applicability to real life—leads to the idea that context should be perceived as being a context of *activities* rather than of a person's context. With this view, personal attributes that may shape HIB—such as experience, knowledge of subject domain, and values—belong to the context because they shape HIB activities.[13] With the person-centered view, these attributes will be part of the person rather than of his context.

7.1.3   Real versus Perceived Context

What is more important for HIB—the actual context, or the context that is perceived by the actor? HIB researchers have two views, each providing the opposite answer. On one side are scholars who believe that actual conditions in real life, whether or not they are perceived by the actor, are those that shape HIB. We can call them the *realists*.[14] On the other side, the *constructivists*[15] believe that "reality"—whether or not it exists independent of a person's perceptions—is relevant only when and as the actor perceives it. That is, only the actor's constructed reality is appropriate for the concept of context, whether it was constructed through individual views, social interaction, or both. After all, an actor's actions are guided by what she thinks the conditions are.

While all first-generation researchers were realists, constructivist approaches have been taking their place among HIB researchers' views since the mid-1990s.[16]

The actor-constructed view of context is supported in part by the observation that, without it, HIB studies could not explain the variability among people within the same context. This observed variability may be explained, the argument goes, by the diversity of user-constructed contexts. That is, there is no "objective" context with people in it; rather, each person creates his or her own context.[17] Thus, context and person are mutually dependent.

While there are various arguments to support a constructivist view of context, common to most is the observation that an actor-constructed context shapes an actor's behavior, which in turn shapes the context. An example may demonstrate this notion. Consider an actor who interacts with an information system. His perception of the system's functionality is an element in his context because the system is external to him and this perception shapes his HIB. Through interactions over time, however, the actor discovers new functionalities; that is, his perception of the system has changed and thus his context is changing. Namely, his HIB shaped his constructed context. In this way, context is fluid because it changes with any change of an actor's perceptions. As learning beings, humans constantly update their perceptions and, with them, their context.

A realist view, in contrast, is likely to perceive the context as relatively stable. A constructivist view focuses on the *person*'s context, and a realist view may focus on the context of the *activities*.[18] Centering on the person has been attractive to scholars who see personal attributes as the main trigger to HIB activities and to those who are focusing on situational conditions. There is no doubt that personal attributes play a role, and that actors constantly traverse from one situation to another. It seems, however, that if these personal attributes were the major constraints to shape HIB, creating systems and services to support HIB would have been unattainable.

Like any other approach to research, these two views are guided by the researcher's worldview, and neither is "objectively" preferred to the other. Nevertheless, if the purpose of a research project is to contribute to the improvement of HIB in the real world, a realist approach is more promising. Because they focus on the activities during the search process, realists consider actors' perceptions of the context as *part* of the context, rather than its totality.

7.1.4   What Do We Mean by *Context*? Conclusions

The work of context scholars who harness their theoretical tradition to provide a meaning for *context* that guides empirical research is essential to the development of in-context research. Conceptual constructs and empirical research in HIB are not completely divorced from one another. At the same time, it is not common for empirical researchers to be explicitly guided by conceptual constructs.[19] Moreover, it is not clear if or how conceptual discussions about context have supported empirical research that has provided applicable contributions to practice.

A view of context in HIB that can lead to practical applications construes context as composed of identifiable and relatively stable elements that exist in the real world. In addition, the context is a context of activities rather than of a person. Activities are shaped by the *level* and *type* of resources available to the actor, that is, by their constraints. Therefore, *constraints* are central to my understanding of *context*, and my construal of it is guided by my commitment to research that aims at offering relevant contributions to real-life conditions. In my view, context is created by the constraints that shape the HIB activities under study.

On the surface, this meaning of the concept assigns it to the category of "context as container" (Dervin 1997), that is, people (or activities) are contained within a context. This view is looked upon unfavorably by various context scholars (e.g., Dervin 1997; Dourish 2004; Talja, Keso, and Pietiläinen 1999) who focus on constructed context. However, my research experience and that of others—together with the dialectical materialism and the systems thinking approaches—have shown me that constraints may have prototypical, HIB-shaping elements that can be analyzed in empirical research, even if at times an actor does not perceive them. In fact, this pragmatic definition is relevant to the study of all aspects of HII: Context is created by the constraints that shape the HII phenomenon under study.

With this definition of *context*, one may ask: How is *context* different from *environment* since both are bounded by constraints? Indeed, researchers at times use the terms interchangeably. From a systems-thinking view, however, these concepts are different, and this difference highlights the unique nature of context. Environment is the set of a system's constraints and is essential to the definition of a system's boundaries.[20] *Context* is reserved for the constraints that actually shape HII activities taking place *in* a system. The time of day, for example, might be an element of the environment but not of the context if it does not shape the HII activities under study.[21]

With this interpretation, context is defined by the relationship it has with the studied phenomenon. While determining an environment is necessary in order to define a system's boundaries before a study commences,[22] the context of a phenomenon is left to be discovered as its investigation progresses.[23] That is, the discovery of the context of activities under certain circumstances evolves with the progression of an in-context study. In fact, for an in-context study to be relevant to practice, it should *investigate systematically* the context of HIB activities, rather than merely *describe* them, as is the common practice in current in-context research.

While most context scholars are likely to agree with this conclusion, in-context studies have often conclusively determined the HIB context before they began.

7.2   In-Context Studies

Most first-generation HIB studies investigated professionals in the workplace. The second generation brought a noticeable expansion in the range of actors studied. In addition to studying the HIB of nonprofessionals in the workplace, the field has experienced a growing interest in HIB in everyday life. This development has brought the advantage of opening up an almost endless range of user groups of actors and types of context in which researchers could apply their analytical instruments. But it has also raised new challenges with regard to defining the actors' context. The structure within which work takes place had served as a basis for context when studying HIB at the workplace, which usually is within an organization and operates according to policies and rules. Everyday life seems to be without a given structure and therefore provides no support for drawing a context's boundary. In addition, the large diversity of user groups and their conditions makes it difficult to discover some basic elements that are likely to be contextual for most everyday-life circumstances. Nevertheless, in-context studies have followed a similar methodological pattern regardless of the type of context.

7.2.1   The Role of Context in In-Context Studies

A minority of in-context research continues the tradition established by the first generation, collecting structured data from a relatively large sample of actors and analyzing them quantitatively (e.g., Eriksson-Backa 2008; Fikar and Keith 2004; Nicholas et al. 2009). In addition to exploratory investigations to determine a context's elements, many in-context studies set out to unearth the HIB of a group of users and are based on interviews—often semistructured—and, less frequently, on observation. Data are analyzed qualitatively, quantitatively, or both.

The study by George et al. (2006) is an example of a typical project studying the HIB of a group. The investigators studied the information-seeking behavior of graduate students from various disciplines at Carnegie Mellon University through in-depth, semistructured interviews with an untypically large sample of 100 students. The data were coded inductively as categories developed during the coding process. Because of the large sample, the researchers were able to provide both quantitative and qualitative results.

The quantitative results were descriptive statistics that compared responses among disciplines. The qualitative results described elements in the students' HIB: people who influenced their HIB (e.g., advisors, colleagues); their perceptions of the Internet as an information source; searching techniques (e.g., general, open-ended searches, citation chaining); the university library's online and print resources they used; and factors that affected their use of libraries (e.g., course requirements, need of convenience, speed). A summary of the findings showed that some of them were confirmed by results from previous studies, and a discussion provided suggestions for services academic libraries could provide to graduate students, such as providing more electronic resources, providing library instructions, and finding ways to increase awareness of the library and its resources.[24] The study report concluded with a strong statement about the need for more research.

This example demonstrates one of the major weaknesses of current in-context studies: Typically, researchers investigate the actors in a context, but not the context itself (see Courtright 2007;[25] Kari and Savolainen 2007).[26] Dervin (1997, 14) pointed to the lack of rigor with regard to context in empirical HIB research and explained that, most commonly, "Context has the potential to be virtually anything that *is not defined as the phenomenon of interest*" (emphasis added). Researchers perceive their studies to be in-context research because they study a relatively well-defined user group under certain conditions and conduct relatively in-depth investigations that cannot be generalized beyond the studied group. That is, the generalizability of the results is bound to a specific context. Such an approach generates descriptions of HIB but provides no means for understanding it.

In the study of graduate students, for example, an investigation of the constraints under which they look for information could have explained, say, their reasons for giving priority to people as information sources. These constraints may be created by the goals of the university and those of the students' departments, the standards of student-faculty relations and of the quality of students' work, or the level of access to technology.[27] Uncovering the constraints imposed on the students not only would have made it possible to understand their HIB, but would have created suggestions for improvements that were more likely to be effective. Let us assume that George et al. (2006) recommended that the library find ways to increase awareness of its services because the students in their study had not used the library to the level that could benefit them. It is possible, however, that students avoided the library not because they were unaware of its services but because it was not "cool" to use it. In this case, increasing awareness would not have been effective. Were the researchers investigating the context, they would be likely to learn about the constraint and as a result recommend ways to make the library seem "cool."

In summary, studies that investigate HIB without understanding its context, or the relationships between it and HIB, are limited in their potential contributions. They may find nuances in HIB that have not been observed before, but they are unlikely to induce progress either in conceptual understanding or in practice.

7.2.2 Types of Contexts

How does a researcher select what user group to study? Availability of funding might be a criterion, particularly since naturalistic, in-depth studies are highly resource-intensive. Researchers whose work is independent of funding, or those who have easy access to funding, may select a study's context according to their research agenda. But other personal and circumstantial criteria also play a role. With this plurality of criteria, user groups that have been selected for HIB studies are diverse, with some colorful ones in the mix. Many studies have investigated ordinary actors, whether at work or in their everyday life. Examples include the use of mobile information systems by police (D. K. Allen et al. 2008), information seeking on health issues by women in a rural area (Wathen and Harris 2006), searching electronic journals to support academic tasks (Vakkari and Talja 2006), and urban young adults seeking everyday information (Agosto and Hughes-Hassell 2005).

A good number of studies, however, have focused on actors that are special in one way or another. Two trends in the choice of such groups are typical in HIB research. One is motivated by the concern for marginalized, vulnerable communities or those under adverse conditions. Studies about the HIB of immigrants (e.g., Courtright 2004; Fisher, Durrance, and Hinton 2004; Fisher, Marcoux, et al. 2004; Shoham and Strauss 2008), gays and lesbians (e.g., Fikar and Keith 2004; Yeh 2008), abused and neglected children (e.g., Hersberger, Murray, and Sokoloff 2006), the elderly in a language minority (e.g., Eriksson-Backa 2008), people at the end of life (e.g., Baker 2004a), battered women (e.g., Dunne 2002; Westbrook 2009), people in a state of increasing dependence and disability (e.g., Williamson and Asla 2009), homeless parents (e.g., Hersberger 2001), and social scientists studying stateless nations (e.g., Meho and Haas 2001) are a few examples.

Another trend is to investigate unique groups, those not in the mainstream of HIB research. Some such studies focus on people seeking paranormal information (e.g., Kari 1998); female police officers involved in undercover prostitution work (e.g., Baker 2004b); Canadian women pregnant with twins seeking information about baby feeding (McKenzie 2006); people involved in gourmet cooking as a hobby (e.g., Hartel 2006);

sperm-donor offspring looking for information about their donors (Cushing 2010); and a public library knitting group (Prigoda and McKenzie 2007).[28] While some of these examples are studies of highly specialized and unique groups, others represent trendy, middle-class activities. This trend is one of the indicators that a portion of in-context researchers greatly value the uniqueness and unusual position of the actors they select to study. Given the crucial role of information in everyday life and at work, it is not clear how studies of such inimitable groups contribute to the well-being of society.

7.2.3   In-Context Studies: Conclusions

Many in-context researchers would probably agree that the ultimate goal of their empirical research is to improve, whether directly or indirectly, systems or services for HIB, rather than to engage only in intellectual exercises. Yet the in-context research literature does not reflect this aspiration; indeed, conceptual investigations that lack practical implications have a strong presence in in-context research.

This statement is supported by a cursory examination I conducted of the 42 articles reporting empirical research that were published in *Information Research* as the proceedings of the 2006 and 2008 Information Seeking in Context (ISIC) conferences. Almost half of the articles (48%) offered no contribution, either to research or to practice.[29] Each concluded with a summary of the results, and some stated that the study brought a deeper understanding of the HIB of the actors in question. Almost a quarter of the articles (24%) reported on studies that were carried out to prove that a certain conceptual construct was a useful guide for research.[30] About 20% of the articles found either new variables or new relationships among known variables, and another 20% either provided one sentence about implications for design or gave very general and vague recommendations for planning and design (e.g., users need support for discovering).[31] Articles also reported on new models that were created through the empirical study (12%), claimed that the study pointed to an area that requires additional investigation (10%), and provided specific design recommendations (7%). Five percent of the articles claimed that their results could be generalized.

While not rigorous as a generalizable study, these numbers show the spirit of in-context research: Contribution to practice is low on the list of priorities. It is possible that some in-context researchers believe that since the results of their studies cannot be generalized, they can never be applicable to practice. Consequently, they may think it is better to focus on conceptual and methodological matters. This explanation does not account for the relatively large proportion of articles that lack any mention of contribution, however. The typical character of in-context research may explain why many studies are unable to offer any contribution, and in particular, a contribution to practice.

In summary, the concept *in-context* is frequently understood as a tag for studies that focus on a particular user group. *Context* itself is commonly defined ad hoc as everything that is not the object of study (Dervin 1997, 14), and as such, it is rarely investigated.[32] Most often, when the context is explicitly addressed, it is described briefly, usually without consideration of whether the elements described relate in some way to seeking behavior.[33] In addition, the selection of groups to study is only occasionally guided by a comprehensive research agenda; more often it is driven by the interests of funding sources or solely by the personal interests and beliefs of the researcher.

Researchers are always guided by their personal interests and beliefs. Yet it is reasonable to claim that a problem-based field should also include a consideration of how the work contributes to addressing the problem at hand. This, unfortunately, is not evident in a considerable portion of in-context research.

7.3   Generalizations Derived from In-Context Studies

Can findings from an in-context study be generalized? It is accepted, as I stated at the beginning of this chapter, that findings of an in-context research project are valid only for the study's setting and participants. This limitation does not necessarily reduce the value of in-context research and its ability to present significant contributions: The new research strands in HIB that have emanated from in-context research, such as Chatman's (1987) concept of *avoiding information* and the introduction of the affective aspects of information-seeking by Kuhlthau and Nahl (2007) (see chapter 3), are examples of important contributions. Moreover, in-context studies—both individual ones and in aggregate—have the potential to arrive at certain forms of generalizations that are relevant to research beyond the specific groups and context of the study. There are at least three such forms:

- Expanding the population to which the study results are relevant
- Developing new methods and techniques for in-context research
- Finding *dimensions* or *categories* of elements that are relevant to all in-context studies.

7.3.1   Expanding the Population

Numerous researchers have tested the validity of their study's findings on additional actors, aiming at some level of generalization. Such a test is usually carried out through a survey that is based on a researcher's previous findings and is administered to a sample of the population of interest.[34] This instrument facilitates statistical analyses, which in turn validate generalization. While this method is relatively simple to apply, it is also somewhat risky because the survey may not produce the desired results.[35]

A safer approach, albeit much more resource-demanding, is a gradual generalization through a series of coordinated qualitative studies. One way to accomplish this task is by using the method of controlled comparisons. A researcher studies a group of actors in a certain context and uncovers patterns in their information behavior. Next she selects for a second study a group that is similar to the first one but different in some identifiable attribute—such as a slight change in the context or in the activities. When the two studies are completed, she compares their results to identify common-alities and differences. The outcome is a description of the behavior of the actors in the two groups that is based on common patterns, with an identification of the dif-ferences. This process continues to include additional groups, one after the other—a process that expands the population whose information behavior is analyzed.

In a study about collaborative information retrieval (e.g., Bruce et al. 2003; Poltrock et al. 2003), the researchers followed this procedure and investigated three teams of engineers in the following order: (1) the software design team, (2) the hardware design team, and (3) the customer services team. An example may explain the process described above. In the observation of the software team, the researchers found that the software program manager, who was not involved directly in the details of the design but participated in some of the team meetings, sometimes presented the team with an information problem. No such event occurred at the meetings of the hardware design team, and the customer services team rarely had a team meeting. That is, on the surface, there were no apparent parallels to the types of information problems raised in team meetings among the other teams.

When investigating the manner in which information problems were collabora-tively generated and identified, the researchers realized that for the software team some of the information problems were not generated by the team itself but rather were raised by the manager. That is, the problems were brought in from an external source. This discovery made the researchers recognize that the other teams also received information problems from external sources: the hardware team from the factory representative, and the customer services team from the customers.[36] Thus, the researchers concluded that all the actors they studied had to solve information prob-lems brought by external sources, but each type of engineer received these problems from a different type of source.[37] In other words, one of the constraints under which the engineers operated was that information problems were delivered to them from external sources.

Following the process of controlled comparisons can expand the population for which the findings are valid, but it is not likely to generate general models for several reasons: (a) It would take a monumental, and probably impossible, amount of research to cover all possible populations in all possible contexts; (b) the more diversity is introduced, the more abstract the model becomes and the "final" model is likely to be abstract to a level that would render it useless; and most importantly, (c) since context has been shown to shape HIB, it is not useful to arrive at universal generalizations and thus eliminate its presence, particularly not through a series of in-context studies. Nevertheless, researchers can still expand the groups of actors and the context to a level they desire.

This inductive process is useful for the design of context-specific systems—those designed for a certain community of actors (see section 1.1.1.1). The engineers in the collaborative information-retrieval project worked in very large corporations, but the model can be expanded to include engineers in additional kinds of settings and of other types—such as safety or quality-control engineers. This expansion may lead to a set of requirements for the design of an information system for engineers with modules to fit a particular type of engineer and possibly a specific context. Such a process could also contribute to another aspect of generalization. Because it would require the employment of various methods and techniques, it could support developments in research methods. In addition, a study that aggregates the results of a series of studies is likely to arrive at dimensions or categories of elements that are relevant to in-context research in general.

In summary, composing a survey instrument based on the results of a single in-context study and administering it to a relatively large population—thus testing the validity of expanding the population—is the simplest method to arrive at generalizations. Yet this method is somewhat of a gamble since the survey results may indicate that the planned expansion is not valid. A safer way to arrive at a larger population is the controlled comparison method, which is much more complicated and labor intensive. Researchers who desire to expand a study's finding may use one of these methods or a combination of both.

7.3.2 Developments in Research Methods

Qualitative studies in general have the potential to contribute to the methods and techniques employed in in-context research. Because the object of study, rather than the method, is the center of qualitative inquiry, it is not uncommon for researchers to encounter situations for which they need to create new methods or techniques to arrive at their research goals. In-context research projects study HIB in a variety of contexts, each of which may present its own challenges to carrying on the project. Researchers may need, for example, to devise a technique to tackle data that are difficult to access or to create a new way to analyze data when, say, the analysis that was derived from the selected conceptual approach could not offer substantial results. Qualitative studies in in-context research promise to contribute to the enrichment of the repertoire of methods and techniques that can be employed in in-context studies.

By and large, though, this promise has not been fulfilled. Although at times reported studies had required creative solutions to challenges in the application of their research designs, these innovations are usually buried in the research reports. Most often these new methods are considered a byproduct of the study—rather than being findings that are discussed independently—and therefore only researchers who read the study's report benefit from their novelty.[38] Moreover, it is not clear if all such improvements are reported. If placed in a methodological context, these methods would be of use to in-context researchers with diverse interests.

Suggestions for conceptual and methodological improvements are more common in the in-context research literature than the depiction of new methods and techniques. Typically, a researcher identifies a conceptual framework in another field—such as ecological psychology, decision theory, or the concept of the *third place*—and applies it to an in-context study. If the study is productive, the researcher concludes that the conceptual framework has been proven to be constructive to all in-context studies.

This conclusion is reasonable: If a methodological approach provided insights in one study, it is likely to provide similar outcomes across contexts. However, the introduction of such approaches requires systematic use and presentation in order for them to make a mark. Such systematic application has not been the case in in-context research, as the growth in new methodological and conceptual approaches has been unplanned and haphazard. This situation is clearly demonstrated by the fact that the number of in-context researchers who suggest such approaches is much larger than the number of those who consistently and repeatedly apply them. That is, most of the suggested approaches are short-lived, and neither their originators nor their colleagues have found them useful enough to apply them in additional studies. It is also possible that the drive to bring something new to the research landscape motivates some researchers to explore approaches that have not been applied before, whether or not the scholars are committed to them in their own research (see the discussion in section 6.4).

In summary, while the results of an in-context study cannot be generalized beyond the investigated conditions, this limitation is not a flaw. In fact, in-context studies focus on unique and specific cases, which afford them in-depth investigations, and this focus is their strength. At the same time, it is possible to find robust methods and methodologies through these studies that will help advance in-context research in general. It is advantageous to the field to recognize this possibility and for researchers in the field to increase their participation in systematic methodological investigations and presentations.

7.3.3   General Dimensions

Even though specific findings of in-context studies cannot be generalized to other contexts, categories of these findings might be useful for in-context research in general. Consider the collaborative information-retrieval project previously discussed. Suppose the statement "Engineers receive information problems from outside sources" proved to hold for additional communities of their colleagues. Since it describes the way engineers work, the statement cannot be transferred automatically to other professionals or other types of communities. Moving the statement to a higher level of abstraction, however, creates the category "sources for information problems," which can be relevant to any context because information problems always have an originating source. Although it cannot be assumed that "sources for information problems" shapes the behavior of actors in other contexts, it is important to consider this category because it was found to be a constraint that shaped the information behavior of three communities of actors.

Identifying a category is just the beginning of a process. To verify its contribution to in-context research, scholars may check whether other studies found elements of this category to be behavior shaping, or they may examine its application in their future research.[39] If it is found to be relevant in a variety of studies, a category may be established and become a dimension in HIB research.

One may claim that *dimensions* are actually *variables* and that the latter have been investigated in in-context research from its inception. Indeed, on the surface, dimensions and variables seem to be one and the same. Yet they are different by their very nature. A variable is identified to test how different values that it receives affect other variables. The variable *age*, for instance, can be identified to study its effect on the variable *searching success*. On the other hand, a dimension is created to guide research by pointing to issues that are relevant to the study of a phenomenon. The concept *dimension* is also more abstract than that of *variable*. Consider the concept *social network*. As a variable, one may test the effect of different types of social networks on specific elements of seeking behavior: One can examine, for instance, how the size of a network is associated with the speed of utilizing it to receive information. As a dimension, *social network* directs a researcher to investigate social networks in HIB studies and to uncover their attributes in the context of the studied phenomenon, rather than specifying which of its aspects or attributes should be examined. Most of the efforts to identify dimensions in in-context research have focused on looking for the dimensions of the system's context, while attempts at generalizations in seeking behavior itself have centered on the search for general variables.[40]

When examining dimensions in in-context research, it is common to distinguish between information behavior in the workplace and that in everyday life because the dimensions of the first are more visible than those of the latter. A workplace is usually part of an organization with its own policies and routines—and those are explicit and relatively easy to identify. Although routines and policies shape everyday behavior as well, it is more complex to determine them because many of them might be implicit.[41]

Nevertheless, Courtright (2007) reviewed in-context studies and gleaned several general dimensions that are relevant to both workplace and everyday life: social dimensions (e.g., social networks, social norms, and workplace requirements for collaboration); rules; resources; culture; and task (in a workplace) or problem situation (in everyday life). She found that each dimension was investigated in a number of studies, which is an indication that some conversion is beginning to occur.

When investigating a dimension, a researcher has to decide which of its aspects or attributes to study. To return to the previous example, how should one study a *social network*? Should one examine the strength of ties (e.g., Pettigrew 1999), the stability of the network, its acceptability, or its size? There is no one answer, nor is it desirable to define general aspects. These aspects are particular to the goal of a study, to its methodological approach, and to the studied phenomenon. That is, while a dimension may be established as almost universal, the aspects to be investigated are determined by the researcher according to the particular study.

The dimension *task* provides an example of how the relations between a dimension and its aspects play out.[42] Task is a common dimension for analysis in in-context research (Byström 2007),[43] and is usually viewed as a container of variables.[44] Researchers have defined these variables to examine the effect of the task variables on searching variables. The most commonly used variable is *task complexity*, which has been studied and analyzed by various researchers (e.g., Byström and Hansen 2002; Vakkari 1999). The purpose of task-complexity studies has been to investigate how the level of complexity affects searching behavior.[45] Other variables have been recognized as well, such as task support and prior knowledge relating to the task (Solomon 2002) and task stages and their timeframe (Xie 2009), but they have not been investigated (to my knowledge). Identifying these particular variables was unsystematic, based on either research in other fields or a single research project in HIB, or defined with the help of a researcher's intuition.

Borlund (2000, 2003a, 2003b, 2009; Borlund and Ingwersen 1997), on the other hand, viewed a task in its entirety, and recognized that it shaped information-retrieval behavior. Her goal was not to analyze tasks but rather to find ways to introduce them to experiments into information retrieval and evaluation. One of her suggestions was that participants in an experiment be given a description of a task as a context for the made-up requests they are asked to search, and that these tasks be typical to those carried out by the participants in their own lives. This way, participants who are university students, for example, would be given queries that are relevant to student life.

In between these two approaches is the framework of cognitive work analysis that perceives *task* as a dimension, rather than as a container of variables or a solid entity that remains unanalyzed. It names the aspects of a task that should be examined when one wishes to understand an investigated task in a way that is relevant to information interactions. These aspects were derived systematically from theoretical constructs and empirical research, and are based on an abstraction hierarchy (see section 12.1). Viewing the task as an activity, the framework suggests that when studying information interaction in context, one investigates the task's goals, priorities, general functions, the processes and resources required to accomplish the task's goals, and the decisions that need to be made. In an in-context study that is guided by this framework, researchers analyze each task according to these aspects.[46]

This example demonstrates the value of dimensions to in-context research. It may serve as a container for variables, but more importantly, it is a guide for research design. While a dimension is deemed relevant to all contexts, it can still be tailored to the requirements of individual studies, as the unique conditions of each study determine the specific aspects to be selected and analyzed.

7.3.4 Generalizations Derived from In-Context Studies: Conclusions

In-context research focuses on studying unique and special cases of particular user groups, each in a certain context. Should its ability to offer findings that are relevant beyond the case under study be of concern? Some may claim that this is an important issue because only results that can be generalized are of value, and therefore outcomes of in-context studies are of no significance until they have been generalized. Yet not many in-context researchers are likely to subscribe to this view. They realize that context shapes information behavior and that to *understand* this behavior requires a consideration of the context. For this reason, they are interested in particular conditions. This focus does not mean that an in-context researcher should not consider contributions that are relevant beyond the specific conditions in his study. For a field to develop, it is necessary for investigations to contribute to the field itself, not only to the understanding of the particular studied phenomena. That is, having studies with broader implications is beneficial to the well-being of the field. In addition to generalizing in-context study results by surveying additional populations, researchers can best contribute to the field through discussions about new methods and techniques they employed and by uncovering general dimensions that are relevant to in-context research in general.

7.4   In-Context Research: Conclusions

In-context research is growing on both the empirical and the conceptual levels as well as with respect to methodological investigations. In the conceptual arena, several scholars have suggested that a context's boundaries are fluid and its elements are constantly changing. Such a construal of the concept, however, makes it almost impossible to conduct empirical studies that lead to implications for practice because some stable core elements are required for the design of information systems and services. Indeed, most empirical in-context research has assumed, if implicitly at times, that the context they investigated was stable and well defined. However, while contributing to the description of the HIB behavior of certain user groups, most in-context empirical studies failed to provide guidance for the design and management of information systems and services.

To improve the applicability of their studies to practice requires in-context researchers to do the following:

• Focus on activities rather than on the person. While the personal attributes of an actor and her psychological state shape her HIB to a certain degree, her information problems are motivated by activities in which she is involved—rather than merely by personal and situational factors—and thus strongly shape HIB. When a person is leisurely looking for a good movie to rent, she is likely to exhibit information behavior that is dissimilar to her behavior when she is looking for legal information on the job. It is useful, therefore, to study the context of an actor's activities, rather than that of the actor as a person.

• Investigate the context. Most in-context researchers consider a study of a certain group of people as an in-context study. At times they only name the group—e.g., graduate students, nurses, immigrants—and at other times they describe the context, most often fairly briefly. While usually interesting, most of these descriptions do not point to the relations between the context they describe and the information behavior of their actors. Therefore, they are not likely to contribute to the *understanding* of the group's behavior—which is the goal of in-context studies. In addition to providing understanding, an investigation of the context may lead to the construction of a formative model because it describes the constraints under which the actor operates (see section 10.1.1)—the type of model that is essential as a guide to the design of systems and services.

In-context empirical researchers have not followed this direction in their research. As a result, very few studies have provided insights that are relevant to the design and management of information systems and services. Chapters 11 and 12 introduce an approach that guides investigations of actor activities and their context: the cognitive work analysis conceptual framework.

At the same time, conceptual in-context research is alive and active, if in limited quarters. In addition to conceptual discussions, empirical studies have brought to light new concepts, variables, and research methods—despite the unique and special nature of each study. Indeed, a growing number of researchers recognize the importance of the conceptual and methodological contribution that individual studies can offer, instead of lamenting their lack of generalizability. However, the task of bringing convergence to these diverse and disconnected contributions still lies ahead for the in-context research community.

8 Theoretical Traditions in Human Information Behavior

Theoretical traditions play an important role in empirical research, whether or not a researcher recognizes them, and human information behavior is no exception. Each method used in an empirical study has roots in methodological and theoretical traditions. The method *micromoment timeline interview* (Dervin 1992), for example, is derived from the sense-making methodology (see section 3.2.1), which is grounded in a number of theoretical traditions. Research in every field, discipline, and science is directed by such foundations, which together embody its theoretical traditions.[1]

Research in human information behavior (HIB) has been guided by a range of theoretical traditions in the social sciences and the humanities and has explicitly addressed some of them, mostly in theoretical writings with a few applications to empirical research. This chapter examines on a general level how theoretical traditions have been viewed and used in HIB research; it does not provide a survey of these theoretical traditions or describe individual ones. Since the discussion requires a mention of some elementary philosophical concepts, the chapter begins with a simplified presentation of some basic issues.

8.1 Some Basic Issues

A theoretical tradition—such as positivism, phenomenology, or constructivism—is based on certain *epistemological* and *ontological* foundations. An epistemological stance has distinctive answers to questions such as: What is knowledge? How is knowledge acquired? How do we know what we know? Why do we know what we know? Benton and Craib (2001) explained that an epistemological stance implies a set of "criteria by which to distinguish genuine knowledge from mere belief, prejudice or faith" (181).

An ontological stance reflects a position about "what kinds of things or substances there are in the world" (Benton and Craib 2001, 183). Each stance offers its own answers to questions such as: What is existence? What is a physical object? What does it mean to say that an object exists?

For the analysis of philosophical issues in HIB, the discussion here distinguishes between the empiricist epistemological stance and the set of all the other stances that are not empiricist, and between the realist ontological stance and the nonrealist one. For an individual researcher, both epistemological and ontological stances are born from her worldview and her understanding of the place of research in the world.[2] Thus, while a phenomenon can be studied from both realist and nonrealist stances or from empiricist and nonempiricist stances, and while a theoretical tradition may be based on more than one specific epistemological or ontological stance,[3] researchers preserve their stance across their work unless their worldview has changed.[4] This consistency does not imply that researchers always adhere to one theoretical tradition; in fact, it is not uncommon among HIB researchers who apply theoretical traditions to harness more than one, even in one study. These researchers, however, usually select epistemologies or ontologies that are compatible.

8.1.1   The Empiricist Stance

The empiricist stance was originally developed for the natural sciences, in which it is still the dominant approach.[5] Benton and Craib (2001) explained:

[T]he empiricist view of science can be characterized in terms of seven basic doctrines:

1. The individual human mind starts out as a "blank sheet." We acquire our knowledge from our sensory experience of the world and our interaction with it.

2. Any genuine knowledge claim is testable by experience (observation or experiment).

3. This rules out knowledge claims about beings or entities which cannot be observed.

4. Scientific laws are statements about general, recurring patterns of experience.

5. To explain a phenomenon scientifically is to show that it is an instance of a scientific law. ...

6. If explaining a phenomenon is a matter of showing that it is an example or "instance" of a general law, then knowing the law should enable us to predict future occurrences of phenomena of that type. The logic of prediction and explanation is the same. ...

7. Scientific objectivity rests on a clear separation of (testable) factual statements from (subjective) value judgments. (14)[6]

Most central to the discussion in this chapter are doctrines 2, 3, and 7. That is, researchers in this tradition claim that a statement constitutes knowledge, rather than a belief, only if it can be tested empirically and proven or disproven. Because testing requires observable entities, knowledge can be arrived at only from entities that can be observed. In addition, when created through testing, scientific knowledge is objective and free of value judgments. The most well-known empiricist approach in the social science is *positivism*, which claims that "Scientific method, as presented by the empiricists, can and should be extended to the study of human mental and social life, to establish these disciplines as social *sciences*" (Benton and Craib 2001, 23).[7]

The stances of nonempiricists are diverse and nuanced. Rationalism, for instance, maintains that knowledge can be established through the use of human reason, and relativism argues that there are no context-free criteria that can guide a judgment between different points of view. While the differences among these epistemological stances are significant, this chapter ignores them for the sake of clarity. With these complex issues, simplifying is likely to lead to misrepresentations. The purpose of the chapter is to examine the patterns in which HIB researchers attend to theoretical traditions, and yet a reliable explanation of them all would require a book of its own. Some of these nonempiricist theoretical traditions have been elucidated in the HIB literature (e.g., Benoit 2007; Budd 2005; Hjørland 2004, 2005a; B. Jones 2008; Leckie, Given, and Buschman 2010); Radford and Radford 2005; Sundin and Johannisson 2005; Talja, Tuominen, and Savolainen 2005; Vickery 1997; Wang 1999; Wikgren 2005; T. D. Wilson 2003).

8.1.2 The Realist Stance

Realists hold the position that reality has an existence independent of how people know it and how they perceive it. More precisely, a realist has the "view that (some of) the things about which we have beliefs are independent of those beliefs and are, in principle, knowable" (Benton and Craib 2001, 184).[8] This view is easy to accept in the natural sciences, as is concisely reflected in Gertrude Stein's sentence, "A rose is a rose is a rose." The objects of study in the social sciences, however, are humans and groups of humans, which have certain abilities to intervene in the world. Therefore, a realist HIB researcher studies not only reality, independent of participants' knowledge and perception, but also the participants' perception of reality (see the discussion in section 7.1.3). Two researchers who study the human perception of a phenomenon can hold opposite ontological stances: One maintains that these perceptions are reality in its totality (the nonrealist), and the other (the realist) claims that they are views of reality—as well as being part of it—and that reality itself is independent of the participants' perceptions of it.[9]

Most popular among the nonempiricist and nonrealist researchers in HIB are the interpretive stances, such as phenomenology, constructivism, and hermeneutics—that is, those that concentrate on the interpretation of human actions and cultural products and claim that all knowledge is a matter of interpretation. Positivism, on the other hand, requires realism. If there is no objective reality that is independent of humans', how can a researcher be objective? In fact, at times *realism* and *positivism* are mistakenly used interchangeably.[10]

8.2 Patterns in Reliance on Theoretical Traditions

The most prominent shift in HIB research has been the gradual move from a focus on fixed attributes—such as *the experience of an actor* or *the physical environment*—to the inclusion of dynamic and process-related phenomena as objects of study. This shift was accompanied by a growing acceptance of interpretive approaches in a predominantly positivist research field. Yet HIB is taking its very first steps in the philosophical and methodological world and is very far from reaching the initial stages of maturity. Among the many challenges the field faces are the HIB researchers' disinclination to consider methodological issues and the inconsistency with which these issues are addressed when they are considered.

8.2.1 Researchers' Attention to Methodological Issues

HIB researchers in the first generation applied the "scientific method," that is, positivism. This preference is not surprising because most often researchers in the United States were scientists or engineers in their organizations and so they applied the methodological approach common to the natural sciences. Social science itself had just begun to accept other theoretical traditions into its empirical research at that time, and it was too early for these to migrate into HIB work.

A clear example of the adherence to positivism was provided by Bawden (2008), when he summarized Bertram Brookes's philosophical writings about the science of information:

[S]uch a science would be based on several foundational principles:

• its main role would be "the exploration and organization of Popper's World III of objective knowledge";

• it would be scientific, in that all the data studied would be "publicly observable and the whole approach objective";

• it would require a recognition that information and knowledge were not physical, but "extra-physical entities which exist only in cognitive (mental or information) spaces";

• quantitative analysis would be paramount, using techniques from the physical sciences, adapted to cognitive spaces. (418)

Bawden also noted that "Brookes' series of papers has been highly influential and widely cited, and continues to be cited to the present day" (418).

Positivism is still strong today, and relatively few HIB researchers consider alternative theoretical traditions. The majority follows the "scientific method," or ignores the issue altogether and continues "the way we have been doing research," following the methods demonstrated by their mentors and other researchers. As a result, a significant portion of HIB research is positivist.[11] At the same time, though, positivism has become much less appreciated by social scientists, and therefore very few researchers see themselves as positivists.[12]

Positivism in HIB research is manifested not only by the disinterest in theoretical traditions (Hjørland 2004) but also by the explicit adherence of some researchers to the empiricist doctrines listed above from Benton and Craib (2001). Positivist arguments can be found in various articles. Järvelin and Ingwersen (2004), for instance, argued, "Theoretical understanding must be grounded on observables. Otherwise it turns into speculation." Ford (2004) stated, "An essential defining criterion of *research* is that it should produce evidence that is open to, and bears, scrutiny. Implicit in the concepts evidence and scrutiny is the notion of objectivity" (1169).[13] Similarly, Järvelin and Wilson (2003) required models to have explanatory power, that is, "the ability to explain and predict phenomena" (see Benton and Craib's doctrines 6 and 7 above). A testimony to the deep diffusion of a positivist theoretical tradition can be found in data analyses and in the presentation of results. Statements about a study's limitations are an example. Although every study has limitations, most quantitative-study reports do not include a "limitations" section, while most of the qualitative ones do spell out their limitations. Determining what is a "limitation" seems to follow informal, yet well-established standards. For instance, most, if not all, qualitative-study reports have followed these standards and caution that their findings cannot be generalized. Yet these standards are not all-encompassing and they ignore other issues that can be considered limitations. For instance, "providing no contribution to theory development" is a limitation, but researchers do not point to it (to my knowledge). The widely held focus on generalization has been induced by the prevailing positivist approach that requires generalizability but releases studies from other duties such as generating new theories.

On a more general level, it seems that most HIB researchers strive toward objective results. Statements of facts in a research's findings are rarely qualified with the researcher's point of view or her theoretical approach. This "objectivity" is attained through experiments and through quantitative analyses of well-defined, observable variables. In addition, most HIB studies limit their investigations to the observable and avoid the development of findings through rational means.[14]

A simple example may elucidate this point. In a study of sanitary workers for the City of Seattle who used mobile computers (Fidel et al. 2007), my colleagues and I thought that interacting with the system was somewhat complicated and far from intuitive. Nevertheless, all workers could interact with the system with a reasonable level of proficiency. One of our findings at that point was that the workers had received some type of training, even though we had not observed the training directly nor heard about it through interviews.[15] This type of finding would probably not be considered a genuine knowledge claim by many HIB researchers because it was not based on observables.

Centering on the observable sometimes leads to false knowledge claims, according to positivist criteria. One example is the use of questionnaires to establish facts. Researchers ask respondents to answer questions that are objective in the researchers' eye,[16] and then present the results as facts about reality, rather than as the participants' *perception* of reality. As a hypothetical example, a questionnaire might ask study participants about their searching behavior, with questions about objective issues such as the level of their experience, the frequency of their web searches, and the number of searches they conduct simultaneously. Researchers would then compile the results and present them as facts, that is, as genuine knowledge claims. On a closer examination, however, it is clear that at least two of the questions are not objective according to positivist criteria—those about the level of experience and the number of simultaneous searches. Answers to the former present the participants' perception of the level of their experience, which may be viewed differently by others. Answers to the question of simultaneous searches clearly depend on the participant's understanding of the concept *search*, which may be different from that of the researchers. According to positivist criteria, the objective level of experience needs to be determined through observables. In the experience case, this determination can be accomplished by means such as a test administered to all participants to determine their individual levels of experience.

Despite the dominance of positivism, which is partly generated by a lack of knowledge and recognition of theoretical traditions, interest in theoretical traditions is rising among HIB researchers (Cronin and Meho 2009). HIB research literature shows that a few researchers have selected a set of theoretical traditions as their guide, the majority of which are interpretive.[17] Most active in analyzing these traditions are researchers in the European Nordic countries.[18] Among them, some have limited their research to the theoretical and philosophical levels, while others have been engaged in empirical research as well. Their work has been influential to some extent, and their approaches have not only been accepted but have been followed by other researchers, particularly in the area of in-context research.

In summary, while most HIB researchers have, with or without intent, followed the positivist theoretical tradition, new voices have championed interpretive approaches. At the same time, the number of discussions and debates about methodologies and about theoretical developments has been on the decline (Kim and Jeong 2006; Vakkari 2008). It is hoped that the attention to new theoretical traditions will encourage other researchers to increase their knowledge about them and their engagement with them.

8.2.2 Misconceptions and Contradictions

Two trends are typical among the researchers who are cognizant of the contribution of theoretical traditions to HIB research. Some researchers write about certain theoretical traditions and may also be engaged in empirical research that is guided by them, while others are avid empirical researchers who thread methodological assertions into their research reports or their reflections on their empirical work. While the former are usually highly familiar with the theoretical traditions they discuss and their historical and philosophical roots, the latter are usually less proficient. This relative lack of knowledge may lead them to include some misconceptions or contradictions in their view of the theoretical traditions they select to employ or discuss.

For example, although positivism is dominant in HIB research, researchers may have misconceptions about its doctrines. T. D. Wilson (2003), for instance, explained the reasons for rejecting positivism when he discussed the need for a theoretical tradition unique to HIB.[19] After examining papers that were prepared for a conference, he concluded that their shortcomings were rooted in positivism, which emphasizes quantitative analyses and provides very little understanding of information behavior, context, or the factors that affect information behavior. These shortcomings, however, are not those of positivism but probably of the papers he examined. While a positivist study requires quantitative analysis and an interpretive study requires a qualitative component, quantitative and qualitative analyses can both be employed with the positivist theoretical tradition and in other theoretical traditions as well. The difference is in the role the results play in knowledge claims. A positivist study, for example, may conduct a qualitative investigation to generate hypotheses, rather than knowledge claims. Similarly, a nonpositivist one may carry out a quantitative analysis to guide the development of the study's sample, rather than generate knowledge claims. The other shortcoming Wilson pointed to—that of providing little understanding of behavior and its context—is not a flaw of positivism, but rather of the research project being examined regardless of the theoretical tradition that guided it.[20]

Another type of misconception is the unwarranted claim about the employment of a theoretical tradition. The simplest way to make this claim is by stating its use, ignoring other methodological considerations distinctive to the theoretical tradition. A typical example is a hypothetical researcher who declares that her study is guided by the systems approach because she is designing it with a holistic view, but then ignores the fundamental requirements of the approach, such as giving a boundary definition for the studied system and examining the interactions among its elements (see section 1.2). While her approach is holistic, her study is not guided by the systems approach.

Contradictions may also surface when a researcher applies two theoretical traditions that rest on opposing philosophical foundations. Wilson's criticism of positivism can serve as an example. Analyzing models in HIB research, T. D. Wilson (1999) explained that one of the reasons for the field's failure to build a cumulative body of research is that, in "the positivist [theoretical tradition], quantitative research methods were adopted that were inappropriate to the study of human behavior" (250).[21] Later in the article he claimed that a model he proposed in the past was limited because "it provides no suggestion of causative factors in information behavior and, consequently, it does not directly suggest hypotheses to be tested" (251–252). Hypotheses are tested, however, to fulfill the conditions required by positivism for genuine knowledge claims. That is, Wilson rejected positivism but at the same time employed one of its doctrines: Any genuine knowledge claim is testable by experience (observation or experiment).

In an earlier essay, T. D. Wilson (1994) noted that "his view of information needs and information-seeking behavior is phenomenological in character" (32). Yet at the beginning of the article he expressed a positivist approach when he reported that he had used the term *information-seeking behavior* "to identify those aspects of information related activity that *did* appear to be identifiable, observable, and, hence, researchable" (16). That is, only identifiable and observable aspects can lead to genuine knowledge claims. This understanding is incompatible with a phenomenological approach. The term *phenomenology* has received several meanings, such as a philosophy, an ontology, an interpretive theory, and a research method framework. Wilson understood it to be a philosophical framework according to which "we need to focus upon human experience of the world, rather than on the world itself and, indeed that the 'real world' should be 'bracketed,' that is, put aside from consideration while we focus on the individual experiences" (Wilson 2003, 447). This latter statement confirms that phenomenology, in his view, is nonrealist, whereas the positivism he earlier espoused is realist.

Without discussing the various flavors of phenomenology, it is clear that it is in conflict with positivism. Budd (2005), for example, asserted that "Across all conceptions of phenomenology there is a clear and explicit recognition that experience is richer than what our physical senses can apprehend" (45). Patton (2002) elucidated that, for the phenomenologist, "There is no separate (or objective) reality for people. There is only what they know their experience is and means" (106). That is, positivism and phenomenology have opposite ontological stances on reality and therefore cannot reside within the same worldview.

On an abstract level, scholars believe either in the positivist approach or in a non-positivist one; this belief is fundamental and therefore one cannot shift back and forth between approaches. Similarly, researchers either believe that there is a reality independent of us and that some of it is knowable, or they do not—that is, they are realists or nonrealists—and this belief cannot regularly shift from one stance to the other. Nevertheless, researchers at times employ simultaneously theories from incompatible theoretical traditions.

It seems that the main source for these misconceptions and contradictions is the researchers' notion about the role of a theoretical tradition. All researchers ally themselves with a set of theoretical traditions, whether or not they are cognizant of this alliance. Yet most empirical HIB researchers ignore the role of these traditions in their work. Nevertheless, theoretical traditions can creep in at times, unbeknownst to the researcher. If a researcher selects a conceptual construct to guide his research project, for example, the construct is embedded in a theoretical tradition, and therefore selecting a conceptual construct also means (perhaps unknowingly) choosing a tradition to guide the project.

Researchers often see constructs as helpful tools they can use in a project, rather than as a part of their own conceptual makeup. Some even have developed a research agenda in which they try various conceptual constructs one after the other. Misconceptions and contradictions may occur when a theoretical tradition that a researcher claims to apply does not fit the worldview that guides the project or program.[22] This problem might arise when a researcher has not articulated to himself his worldview, or when he is not familiar with the philosophical roots of the theoretical tradition he is employing.[23] It is not uncommon in such situations for researchers to select trendy theoretical traditions for their investigations.[24] A basic understanding of one's own worldview and the philosophical foundations of individual conceptual constructs is a promising path for avoiding misconceptions and contradictions.

Characterizing one's own worldview in philosophical terms and studying theoretical traditions require a large investment of time and intellectual effort. Is it necessary to invest so much energy just to avoid a few possible misconceptions and contradictions? Are there any other benefits?

8.3   The Role of Theoretical Traditions

Understanding one's own worldview and theoretical traditions offers benefits to both the HIB research community and to the individual researcher. On the community level, discussions about the definitions of basic concepts could be placed in a constructive perspective; an infrastructure for cumulative research and for convergence would be present; and theoretical growth would be supported, as would the distinction between the central and the peripheral. Individual researchers would get support when facing challenging situations and would increase their understanding of research in other theoretical traditions, which in turn would make their communication with other researchers more effective.

Discussions about the definitions of concepts that are basic to information science in general and to HIB in particular—such as *information* and *information need*—were at their peak at the junction between the two generations of research but are not very common today. Scholars seem to have concluded that these discussions did not reach a resolution, and therefore they might as well continue their work and avoid the issue. Indeed, HIB research saw great development and growth without a definitional consensus. It is not clear, moreover, whether a resolution is desirable. Different theoretical traditions may lead to diverse definitions, and unless one advocates a single tradition for HIB, this diversity enriches the research scene. An example of the differences between positivist and interpretive definitions is given in table 8.1.

Table 8.1
An example of two definitional approaches (May 2009)

	Positivist	Interpretive
Information	A real entity that exists independently of human's interaction with it	Something that is created as humans interact with each other and with the world
Information need	A real entity that exists in an actor's mind	An actor's realization that she misses something that is required to move from one situation to another

Consider the definitions of the concept *information* (e.g., Buckland 1991; Bates 2005). In section 1.1.2, I introduced my own interpretation of the concept that was guided by the systems approach[25]—in particular, the requirement that information is for decision making. Others have defined *information* in various other ways—as whatever reduces uncertainty or changes an actor's state of knowledge, or as a social construct, as two examples. All these definitions are "legitimate" and there is no need to find the "best" one. What is missing, however, is an explicit explanation of which theoretical tradition induced each one of them. Knowing the roots of these definitions would demonstrate that there is no one "right" definition, and would afford their harmonious coexistence.[26] A researcher can then select the definition that fits her worldview, while also benefiting from the scholarly work of researchers with other worldviews. A purely cognitive approach, for instance, is incompatible with systems thinking because the cognitive approach is not holistic. As a result, I have not considered, for instance, Belkin's ASK model (see section 3.3.2) as a framework in any of my studies. Nevertheless, the model highlighted the requirement that information systems must support users not only in the retrieval of information but also in crystallizing the information problem—a notion that is relevant (and important) beyond the specific model.

One may claim that accepting a diversity of theoretical traditions would stand in the way of creating a cumulative body of research and that this would be disadvantageous to HIB research, which is already highly divergent. A theoretical tradition, however, is a progeny of a worldview. Therefore, to develop a single theoretical tradition for HIB calls for all scholars to share a similar worldview, which is an unreasonable requirement. One unique theoretical tradition for HIB can be suggested only if one incorrectly views theoretical traditions as "neutral" providers of productive tools for research, rather than as embodiments of worldviews. With this approach, scholars can extract from each theoretical tradition the tools that are useful to HIB and put them together to form "the HIB theoretical tradition."

This pragmatic view has been expressed by various scholars. Wilson (2003), for example, recommended phenomenology as a theoretical tradition for HIB because of the "tools" it provides. Similarly, Bates (2005) built her view of information on the "productive metatheory" of evolutionary psychology. Hjørland (2005b) expressed the most pragmatic view (coming from a pragmatist stance) when he required that theoretical traditions be introduced only if their usefulness is demonstrated:

It is important to emphasize that knowledge about different positions in the philosophy of science is not an aim in itself. If a position has no potential to contribute to the further development of [library and information science] it is principally of no interest to us. … If a new position should be introduced into LIS, it should be demonstrated what new arguments this position is capable of contributing compared with arguments that have already been put forward. Also, I claim that if researcher X is influenced by a particular position, then this should somehow be visible in X's publications. If a position makes no visible difference in research output, then this position cannot be said to be important. (156)

It seems, therefore, that having multiple theoretical traditions in HIB is unavoidable. Zwadlo (1997) drew a more sweeping conclusion. Reviewing a few proposals advanced by various library and information science (LIS) scholars who were seeking *the* theoretical tradition for HIB, he argued that the scholars had been promoting theoretical traditions of their choice, but there was no logical way to choose among these competing traditions. Therefore, he maintained, LIS did not have, and did not need, its own philosophy. Bates (2005) also advocated a plurality of theoretical traditions and "argued that the several metatheories driving research in information seeking each have much of value to offer, and should not be placed in a life or death struggle for dominance in our thinking and research."

One may claim that this diversity of theoretical traditions would prevent the convergence of HIB research. However, the opposite might materialize if HIB researchers understood the various theoretical traditions and their roots. Then, the diversity of traditions could support convergence because scholars would understand the positions of their colleagues and could relate them to their own positions. In fact, the theoretical traditions that HIB researchers follow could serve as the infrastructure for developing a cumulative body of research and bringing a measure of convergence to it. In addition, one may suggest that the various interpretations of basic concepts and the motivation among HIB researchers to introduce new approaches to research and new concepts or phenomena are significant barriers to a cumulative research body (see section 6.4). An open and explicit guidance by theoretical traditions could reduce fragmentation by providing foci around which studies would converge. This way, a new concept or research approach could be connected to existing ones through the theoretical tradition involved. The "Related Literature" section in a research report would address not only the literature on the study's topic, but also the tradition employed through an analysis of other studies guided by it, or of the use of closely related theoretical traditions. Such analysis would point to the multidimensional place of the new study among previous ones. This way, the theoretical traditions could create a network in which research projects would be the nodes.

Generally speaking, knowledge and understanding of theoretical traditions would support the conceptual growth of the field. This growth could happen in several ways. For example, conceptual constructs that have already been created could be associated with one another through their theoretical traditions, whether similar or different. This association could create a map of HIB constructs that are currently isolated and scattered. The map, in turn, may show current trends and at the same time point to gaps in need of development. Further, researchers who develop new constructs inductively from field studies would be able to place them in one or more theoretical traditions, which in turn will enrich the constructs, since a tradition's foundations might bring new insights and place the constructs in a broad context.

Consider, for example, the concept *information grounds*, that is, "environment[s] temporarily created when people come together for a singular purpose but from whose behavior emerges a social atmosphere that fosters the spontaneous and serendipitous sharing of information" (Pettigrew 1999, 811). Writing later as Karen Fisher (2005), she explained that she drew upon social constructivism to develop the information grounds theory. This alliance immediately points to the social and cultural forces that shape information grounds and the language used to produce this social atmosphere.[27] Investigations in these directions would enrich the theory.

Related to this support, theoretical traditions could help researchers determine what is central to HIB and what is peripheral. For instance, holistic traditions would advocate an important position for context in HIB studies, while reductionist ones would focus on well-defined, clearly isolated aspects of behavior, such as cognitive styles and gender. Clearly, this would not bring about a common notion of what is central to HIB. The differences among the notions and their roots, however, would be understood rather than viewed as idiosyncratic.

The distinction between the important and the marginal would support individual researchers as well when they contemplate what phenomenon to study and what research questions to formulate.[28] Similarly, finding one's own worldview and the compatible theoretical tradition is essential to the development of a sound and consistent research agenda because stable philosophical foundations, rather than trendy research approaches, would guide its development. In addition, having a philosophical self-identity makes it possible to position oneself in relation to other scholars. This awareness, in turn, can improve a researcher's understanding of her colleagues, which would increase the efficacy of interaction with them. As a result, she might gain new insights through learning from others' work by, say, translating new ideas to her own stance, including those ideas that would seem unacceptable at first sight. Further, exploring the fundamentals and nuances of a theoretical tradition would lead to a comprehensive yet fine-grained view of the specific field of study. Such a view would create a structure to support researchers when they encounter challenging situations. This structure would point to possible directions in which solutions can be found.[29]

In summary, attention to theoretical traditions and self-awareness of those that are compatible with one's own worldview would support a systematic and stable development of a rich and diverse conceptual body in HIB.

8.4   Theoretical Traditions in Human Information Behavior: Conclusions

Theoretical traditions from the natural sciences, social sciences, and the humanities have influenced HIB research. Some scholars claim that this plurality stands in the way of developing a cumulative body of research. In fact, it has the potential to create a kernel around which HIB research can converge. Moreover, it is inevitable. Convergence can take place only when HIB researchers are knowledgeable about theoretical traditions and find their own approach. Today, as several scholars have pointed out, most HIB researchers pay no attention to philosophical and theoretical foundations (e.g., Budd 2005; Vakkari 2008). Scholars' disinterest in theoretical traditions is a significant barrier to bringing some convergence to HIB research.

Given the benefits that a community aware of theoretical traditions could offer, why has the situation not changed? Why is the number of researchers who anchor their work in philosophical foundations relatively small? One may claim that the field is still young and has not established itself on the conceptual level. The ever-increasing number of theoretical traditions in the social sciences and the humanities may also be a reason that HIB researchers avoid them altogether instead of constantly keeping abreast of new developments. In addition, because of its short history, information science has not created a culture in which philosophical foundations are of interest. These factors are indeed constraints to the growth of interest in theoretical traditions among HIB researchers.

Another reason for this disinterest is the reward system applied in the academic world, particularly in North America. This domain has turned into a market in which scholars compete for research support and recognition, with productivity used as the basic criteria for promotion and other rewards. The value of scholarly work is measured quantitatively, which encourages an emphasis on the quantity of scholarly output.[30] In the United States, public universities have been thrown into the free market because state support of higher education is on a steady decline. As a result, scholars have the additional responsibility of bringing money to their institutions. Under these conditions, professors are primarily concerned with writing research grants and papers. Given this drive to produce, it is difficult to contemplate and reflect on philosophical issues because this exercise requires much time and does not bring immediate results. Being proficient in the theoretical traditions of HIB would not increase the number of papers one could write during a given period of time—in fact, it may reduce it—and it is not likely to increase one's chances of successfully competing for a research grant.

To encourage appreciation for philosophical understanding and in-depth conceptual work requires a transformation of the reward system so that a professor's intellectual work is recognized according to its quality and contribution to society, whether through direct or indirect means. While achieving such a system is a worthy goal, its attainment is a long-term project. In the meantime, academic institutions can raise interest in philosophical foundations among future HIB researchers through their doctoral programs, which should include at least one required course in the philosophy of social science. Doctoral studies are the formative years of new researchers, and the best time to develop a scholarly identity. In fact, the responsibility of doctoral students is to develop their individual expertise and approach to scholarship. Being exposed to the various theoretical traditions in social science would support this development and might even generate an interest in them in their future work.

That is, instilling appreciation for theoretical traditions in future researchers is the most promising way for HIB to cope with the lack of interest in philosophical issues among researchers at this time. Such an appreciation may further the conceptual growth of HIB as well as its convergence.

IV Human Information Behavior and Systems Design

Research projects in human information behavior (HIB) have often claimed to offer contributions to HIB research, to practice, or to both areas. Contributions to research typically occur in the following forms:

• developing conceptual constructs that would guide research
• checking how such constructs from other fields can be employed in HIB research
• discovering the factors (or variables) that need to be considered in HIB research.

Studies intending to contribute to HIB practice try to help improve information behavior. They may focus on various goals, such as

• improving the context in which people operate through organizational and social changes
• improving training
• improving the design of systems and services that support and enable HIB.

This part of the book addresses the ways HIB research can contribute to the design of information systems. This discussion leads to the introduction of cognitive work analysis. While the focus here is on computer-based systems, the principles discussed are applicable to any type of information system.

9   Interlude: Models and Their Contribution to Design

Every design is informed by some representation of a section of reality. That is, the design of all artifacts, whether a chair, a bridge, an airplane, or an information system, is informed by some kind of model. The models can be presented in various forms, such as blueprints, pictures, or narrative descriptions. In addition to their form of presentation, models can be classified by other categories. Some of these classifications can help uncover which models are most beneficial for design.

9.1   A Typology of Models

Models have been classified in various ways—by their form, for instance, as abstract, conceptual, graphical, and mathematical models; or whether they are domain-specific or universal models. One typology that is relevant to design was presented by Vicente (1999, 6–8), and was based on Rasmussen's (1977) work. It categorized models according to what they represent: how things are, how they should be, or how they could be (i.e., what the possibilities are):

Descriptive models describe actual behavior.

Normative models prescribe what behavior should be.[1]

Formative models describe requirements that must be satisfied so that behavior takes place in a new, desired way.

To demonstrate the differences among these types of models, consider the following scenario. Mary is visiting Monterey, CA, and staying in the Casa Munras Hotel (bottom left in figure 9.1).[2] It is a hot day, and she wants to go to the beach. But this is her first visit, and she needs to ask the concierge, John, how to get to the beach (top right in figure 9.1). John can help her in three ways (among others):

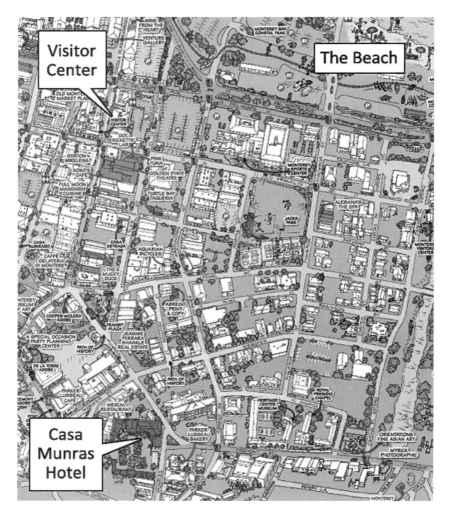

Figure 9.1
A section of a Monterey, California, tourist map. *Source*: http://mappery.com

a. He may give her directions by describing the route that people usually take. That is, John could present Mary with a *descriptive model*.

b. He may give her directions that he thinks are the best. Or, he may give directions to the most scenic or sun-sheltered routes. That is, John could present a *normative model*.

c. He may give Mary a map. Looking at the map, Mary can see the possible ways to get to the beach, and choose one of them. In this case, John would present a *formative model*, showing Mary the routes she can take—the possible ways to get to the beach.

Getting directions (whether descriptive or normative) requires Mary to invest very little cognitive effort: John has already discovered the route most people take, or the best ones, and she just needs to follow his directions. Using a map, on the other hand, would require that she make decisions in order to select the desirable route. A map, however, would give Mary much more flexibility. She could deviate from her planned route if she spotted a place of interest that is not on the route, and then find a new way to get to the beach, one that would not require a return to the original plan. This flexibility is not available with directions, as every deviation entails backtracking to the original route. With a map, Mary can see the possible routes to the beach and may decide to change her route daily to see more of the city's views. Having all possible routes in front of her, she can choose the daily one according to the weather: going along the water on very hot days and through covered streets when it rains. Moreover, if one day Mary decides to go to the Visitors' Center, she would not need any new directions; she can figure out the route herself. In fact, with the help of a map she can get to any destination within the city limits from any site she is visiting. Therefore, getting directions is helpful for visitors who stay in a place for a short time or for those who prefer to relax without having to make any decisions. Other visitors are likely to find a map more useful.

This example shows that each model a tourist receives of the road from a hotel to another destination would shape the day the tourist would design.

9.2 Types of Models and Their Contribution to Design

To examine the contribution of models to design, it is useful to expand the concept *model* to include other constructs which, according to their creators, inform design, regardless of their form, such as information-seeking behavior (ISB) research reports. Thus, the term *model* is construed here as any construct that is a representation of reality and that has been created to inform the design of information systems.

Using the typology above, an ISB model that is handed to a designer of a new system can (1) describe how seeking is being carried out currently, (2) describe how seeking behavior should be, or (3) present a "map" of the "seeking behavior terrain" and ask the designer to create the best system possible, given the constraints of the terrain and current technology.

In what way can each of these three types guide the design of information systems?

9.2.1 Descriptive Models

Descriptive models are very useful when one wants to examine how people look for information. Indeed, most ISB studies are descriptive: They report how people behave when they seek information. The strength of descriptive empirical studies, and in particular naturalistic field studies, lies in their potential for providing a solid basis for the development of theories and models. Chatman (2000), Kuhlthau (2004), and Nahl (2007) have formed outstanding examples out of this potential. At the same time, they do not provide a sufficient base for the design of information systems because they describe *current* behavior. Descriptive models cannot predict the new behavior that will replace the current behavior when a newly designed system is put into operation. But this new behavior is the one according to which the new system should be designed.[3]

This problem with descriptive models is manifested in various ways. Most important is the fact that seeking behavior is tied to existing technology, and therefore using a descriptive model as a base for the design of new systems is not useful for two reasons. First, part of seeking behavior is determined by the limitations of the current system—for which users find workarounds to get desired results. As Vicente (1999) explained: "Analyses of current practice lead to design ideas for supporting this practice" (100). Recording observed behavior, researchers may recommend that a workaround behavior be supported by the new system, which is clearly undesirable. Second, the value of a new system lies in whether it offers new and better possibilities. An analysis of current behavior alone cannot point to new possibilities of any value because they do not exist in the current configuration. The best such analysis can do is to point to problems in the current user-system interaction, and this feature is indeed one of its strengths. But the solutions to these problems cannot be generated only from the description of current seeking behavior.[4] Other types of analyses are required for that purpose.

9.2.2 Normative Models

It seems sensible to assume that normative models of searching behavior are ideal for guiding design because they prescribe the "right" behavior, and thus that systems should be designed to support and encourage this type of behavior.[5] One of the weaknesses of norms, though, is that they are based on rational behavior. To employ a normative model in support of systems design entails the assumption that people behave rationally (according to some universal standards) when they use systems. Yet research has shown that this ideal behavior is frequently not the case. Chatman's (1987) participants, for example, avoided information that could have helped them solve vital life problems, and high school students searching the web employed only the browsing strategy, which was inefficient and frustrating to them (Fidel et al. 1999). The validity of the rationality assumption is the main shortcoming of the normative model as a prescription for design.

Normative models might not be useful for the design of information systems, in particular for information retrieval (IR) systems, for several other reasons. Information-seeking processes, and information retrieval processes in particular, are complex and dynamic. In contrast, establishing norms requires some level of reduction or averaging, which limits the usefulness of these models in representing complexity. As a result, normative models can provide only a reduced representation of the search process or one that is highly abstract and thus not useful for design.[6] The dynamic nature of a search is caused by the unanticipated developments along the way. Normative models can prescribe behavior only in cases of anticipated situations because norms can be established only on known circumstances. Therefore, they cannot represent the dynamic side of a search.

Consider Taylor's (1968) normative model that represents which questions librarians should use to interview a user to understand her query and in what order they should use them (see section 3.3.1). The order of the questions is a central norm because each question is informed by the previous one, beginning with the determination of the subject of the query and concluding with the anticipated answers. Theoretically, a machine could be designed to help users crystallize their queries by presenting appropriate questions in the right order, following Taylor's model,[7] assuming that users crystallize their queries rationally, following the stages in the model. Yet such a machine would leave unhappy the users who need help the most. A user who has ready responses to the questions posed during the interaction, and in the right order, probably can formulate the query on his own. The user needing help is the one who knows only, say, what answer she anticipates (the last question), but cannot be specific about the subject (the first question). Our machine, alas, cannot help her because, following Taylor's order, it needs to have the subject of the query recorded before any other interaction can take place.[8]

Normative models guide the design of a system that supports the "best" way to perform a search, but, at the same time, they make other approaches impossible to employ. Therefore, while design based on normative models may help users to avoid mistakes in searching, it restricts a searcher from employing creative ways of searching that at times might be more productive than the normative way. Moreover, because the way to search is prescribed a priori with such systems, searchers cannot improve their searching skills or learn how to search. This limitation will reduce their capability to resolve unanticipated developments in the search process, which, in turn, would affect the quality of the results.

Detailed normative models, of the type that is necessary to guide design, inevitably are dependent on the retrieval technology used. For instance, the "right" way to search with current web search engines is different from the "right" way to search retrieval systems with relevance feedback.[9] Therefore, when a search engine designer wishes to add a relevance feedback device to his web-based product, a model that prescribes how to search the old system is not likely to be useful.

In summary, neither the descriptive model nor the normative model is useful for guiding the design of information systems by itself because of its dependence on the existing technology and its limitations in preparing a system for unanticipated and complex situations. While descriptive models offer understanding of current behavior, which is useful for design, normative models can be useful only for the design of simple systems with a limited set of capabilities.

Before we leave these models, we should make one further observation. Both types of models represent procedures, or specific activities. HIB studies, for example, describe procedures such as how people analyze their information problem, select information sources, exchange information, search the web, and evaluate search results. Procedures are dynamic, however, and can change with even small changes in circumstances and with slight modifications in the technology. Paradoxically, design that is based on the description of current procedures will inevitably result in new and different procedures. But these procedures will not be supported by the new system, which was designed around the old procedures. As a result, the new system is likely to become outdated shortly after its implementation.

One of the ways to resolve this situation is to consider *categories* of procedures, which are more stable than the procedures themselves, and can be selected so that they are independent of technology. For instance, instead of investigating the specific interaction between a searcher and a search engine, step by step, we may want to identify the search strategies that have been employed (e.g., browsing, analytical search).[10] Vicente (1999)—based on Rasmussen (1981)—provided a useful definition for a strategy: "a category of cognitive task procedures that transform an initial state of knowledge into a final state of knowledge" (220). Whereas the interactions with a search engine, as well as its procedures and activities, are likely to change when a new search engine is installed, the strategies will stay the same because they are independent of the technology,[11] even though they may require new procedures for their application in a new system (hopefully simpler and more productive ones). The procedures people follow when they browse library shelves are dissimilar to those employed in web browsing, but mentally, people use the same strategy. Looking at categories, an information system would be designed to support browsing, and each new version would make available procedures that users' circumstances dictate and technology affords. Descriptive models alone cannot support this approach to design.

9.2.3   Formative Models

In contrast to descriptive and normative models, formative models offer the foresight required for future design because they represent the possible ways in which information-seeking behavior could take place, whether or not they occur currently. Moreover, they can lead directly to the formation of design requirements.

9.2.3.1   Constraints-Based Formative Models

One may claim that while, in theory, the idea of formative models and their contribution to design makes sense, such models are not likely to be practical. How can researchers predict all possibilities or know what seeking behavior may occur in the future when a new system is in place? As stated, this task is indeed impossible.

To demonstrate how a formative model can be constructed without enumerating all the possibilities, but representing them nonetheless, we return to Mary who is visiting Monterey, using the map John gave her.

With a map—which is a formative model of the city—Mary is free to design a route from every place in the city to another, because the map lays out all the possible routes. How can Mary make out all the possible routes? Obviously, the clear marking of the streets presents the standard (or normative) routes to her destination. But the map also suggests other possibilities, such as cutting across a parking lot or a small park. An even more detailed map, one that marks the entrances to buildings, for instance, could have suggested the possibility of shortcuts that would eliminate the necessity of going around a block by entering a building, say, through the front entrance and exiting through the back door.

In fact, any area that is not blocked for passage can be a segment in the route from the hotel to the beach. The best way to present all the possible segments is by presenting what is blocking the way, that is, by presenting what limits movement—i.e., the constraints. Mary can then choose the route that fits her agenda for the day from among all the possible routes, whether standard or "deviant."[12]

We can consider a city map, then, as a layout of the constraints associated with moving around the city. In other words, a map shows the possible routes from one location to another by displaying the constraints to these routes. With this approach to the construction of a formative model, the possibilities are represented by laying out what is *not* possible. That is, to model what *could be* requires first the identification of what *could not be*. This approach to design is called *constraints-based design*.

In ISB, a formative model can be constructed by representing the constraints on information seeking.[13] While taking the approach of cognitive work analysis (CWA) leads to the creation of a constraint-based model, there are very few formative models in the field of HIB.[14] One example is a study conducted by Martin Rose (2006) which investigated the "information activities" of passenger information officers (PIOs), that is, staff that provided information to passengers at the command and control center of a rail network. Through observations and interviews he uncovered both the constraints (e.g., dynamic environment, time pressure, information shortage, and pervasive uncertainty) and categories of information activities (e.g., monitoring network status, investigating service disruptions, and relaying information to operational staff). His analysis then produced a set of requirements that specified what activities the system should support. The requirements included: "Allow communication tasks related to different audiences or different channels to be separately allocated to different PIOs," and "allow PIOs to freely allocate and reallocate communication tasks between each other as situations change, without losing any of the work completed" (Rose 2006).

An earlier constraints-based approach was developed by Mick, Lindsey, and Callahan (1980), who were concerned about the gap between information behavior studies and the design of information systems. To build up the approach, they had created a conceptual framework that guided a questionnaire-based study of scientists and engineers in a corporate environment. The framework addressed the environmental, organizational, role, and task constraints. The resulting model, which was adequate to guide system design, was validated through various tests.

Not all constraints on seeking behavior are relevant to the design of information systems. For the purpose of system design, only those constraints that shape seeking behavior are pertinent. There is no magic formula that can be used to distinguish such constraints from the irrelevant ones, and in fact, the role that constraints play may change from one context to another. Therefore, the discrimination between important constraints and insignificant ones is best achieved through an in-depth study of the seeking behavior of the actors for which the system is designed and their environment. From a practical aspect, formative models should represent only stable constraints. For example, the seeking behavior of the PIOs in Rose's (2006) study might have been affected by the character and temperament of their manager. Yet managers come and go, particularly in this era of frequent reorganizations. If one considers this constraint as a basis for system requirements, a new information system would have to be designed for each incoming manager, which is impractical. That is, according to this approach, a formative model represents *stable* and *behavior-shaping* constraints. Stable constraints are called *invariants*.

Constraints-based design is a relatively new approach in the world of design, and documents describing the process of translating constraints into requirements are hard to come by. This scarcity is not surprising because, in addition to being new, the translation process itself is complex, due to the complexity inherent to real life, which requires the design of real-life information systems to consider a complex network of constraints.[15] A simple example from my own experience may suggest how such a translation can be prepared. In a study of engineers searching the web for their daily, job-related work (Fidel and Efthimiadis 1998), we observed that our participants planned their searches, and even displayed help screens to guide them in this process. In addition, they were disappointed that they were unable to predict the results. These observations highlighted one of the constraints we had identified earlier in the study: the type of education and training engineers received which had shaped their professional thinking. These observations validated our commonsense assumption that engineers plan before they act, that they are methodical and analytical in their work and prefer to understand what effects their moves and actions would have. This constraint then gave birth to the requirement that the system support planning web searches and predicting results. It also pointed to other requirements that were not based on observations, such as supporting systematic and structured ways of searching, and increasing the visibility of the retrieval mechanism. In time, and with technological developments, engineers may create new ways to plan their searches and to predict the results, but the nature of their education and work, which has trained them to be methodical and analytical, is not likely to go through radical changes in the near future.

Being stable and shaping behavior are not inherent attributes of certain constraints. Each context has its own set of such constraints, and a constraint that is stable and behavior-shaping in one context may not be so in another. It is the role of the HIB researcher to find such constraints in the context under study. This goal is usually achieved through naturalistic field studies that aim at describing *both* the current behavior (a descriptive model) and the constraints that shape it (a formative model).

9.2.3.2   The Advantages of Constraints-Based Design

The formative model overcomes several shortcomings of both the descriptive and normative models. By definition the formative model provides a full representation of possible behaviors, whereas descriptive models represent only current possibilities and normative models must rely on simplified and reduced representations. Uncovering the possibilities also reveals ways of seeking that are not currently employed, some of which might be productive and enjoyable. Because it represents constraints rather than current procedures, a constraint-based design is not guided by workarounds or current practice that may change with the new system. It also does not have to be based on any universal assumptions about the way users behave—e.g., people behave rationally—thus avoiding erroneous assumptions. A system that is designed to support possible behaviors has many advantages; most notably, the changed behavior that the new system brings about will be supported without the need to know ahead of the design the specific shape it will take. The system will also help a user stay on track despite unanticipated circumstances because it can support the behavior that new circumstances require. This way, a formative model can lead to the design of adaptive systems.

One may claim that a design guided only by stable constraints is likely to limit the possibilities for the user, resulting in a static system. Such limits will indeed be the case if the dynamic constraints are completely ignored. Constraints-based design, however, can provide affordances to behaviors that are shaped by changing constraints even when it is guided by stable constraints. An example may illustrate how formative models can guide the design of adaptive systems. The mCity project (e.g., Fidel et al. 2007) investigated the use of mobile technology to support field work in the Drainage and Wastewater Department of the City of Seattle. Workers in the department, who were responsible for keeping the city's drainage system in working order and responding to breakdowns, received their work orders for the day on a hand-held computer the size of an average book, which they could carry and use at any time and in any place. Some difficulties occurred on days when work orders were given for several sites in different locations. The following are some of the stable, behavior-shaping constraints we found that are relevant to these difficulties:

• Workers aim at an efficient and effective use of their time, and thus prefer to sequence work locations according to the physical proximity of the relevant sites.

• The first or the last location for the day should be close to their base.

• Around lunch time they need to be near an enclosed space in which they are allowed to eat despite their often dirty uniforms.

• At some point they may discover that they need to postpone work in some locations because of unanticipated complications in previous locations or because they need to get additional equipment when they discover new problems in the site.

These constraints point to a requirement: The system should facilitate visible and flexible work-order scheduling. Because of its size, the hand-held screen could only display information about one location at a time. Without being able to see all the work orders on one screen, workers had a hard time scheduling their site visits or rescheduling them when necessary. There are at least two approaches to resolving this difficulty. Given the technological constraints (e.g., the small screen) and ignoring the particular conditions in the field, the department's work flow could be modified so that the back-office schedulers, who assign the work orders to a team and work with large screens, arrange the work orders in a sequence that fits these constraints.[16] In this case, field workers could safely follow the sequence assigned to them. This solution is not ideal because workers have the same difficulties as before when facing unanticipated complications that require rescheduling; that is, workers would not be able to benefit from the information in the system when facing unanticipated situations, or when a completely new situation arises.

A different approach—and one that affords behaviors that are shaped by dynamic constraints—is to provide various facilities that make it possible for the workers to easily schedule and reschedule the work orders for which they are responsible. This capability could be implemented in various ways, such as by providing easy communication channels with the schedulers, adding access to paper printouts (e.g., of addresses and maps) while in the field,[17] or providing easy access to various types of information to support decisions. When such facilities, and possibly others, are provided, workers can consider the situational factors they face (i.e., the dynamic constraints), select a facility, and use it in a way that best supports making a decision in specific work situations. That is, the system makes it possible for the workers to adapt to changing, situational circumstances or to unanticipated ones. In such cases, the workers "finish the design" (Vicente 1999).

An example from the BookHouse system for fiction retrieval in schools and public libraries may illustrate adaption to changing, situational circumstances. Annelise Mark Pejtersen (1984, 1989, 1992) created a constraints-based model of fiction searching behavior through the analysis of over 100 user-librarian conversations. She then developed a fiction retrieval system based on the requirements that had been derived from the analysis. A searcher could choose the strategy to employ (and easily shift from one to another);[18] when employing the analytical strategy, for example, she could retrieve books according to various facets, such as author, title, graphics on the book cover, names of the central characters, the setting of the plot, the genre, and the nature of the experience. When a book is selected, the information that is displayed on the screen includes all the facets. For example, in addition to finding a list of the character's names, a searcher may discover that the selected book has icebergs and whales on the cover, that the story took place in the 1980s, and that it is a novel with happy ending.

One of the strategies a user of the BookHouse system could employ is the similarity strategy, according to which she enters a book title as an example of the kind of book she desires and asks the system to find similar books. The system then displays 10 books through which she can browse and hopefully find one that she likes.[19] This is the straightforward use of the similarity strategy. But the system also afforded productive searching when unanticipated situations arose. If while browsing the 10 books, the user found another book she had read that would be a better example of the kind of book she wanted, she could enter this book as an example, which would generate a new search using the similarity strategy. Or, while scanning the facets for a book, the user might realize that she liked the example book because it was an animal story from the 1980s that was both exciting and sad—a desire she could not articulate before. She could then directly click on these terms on the book display and retrieve the books satisfying these requirements. Thus, while the similarity strategy is based on a stable constraint (a user can find a "good" book only with the use of an example), the system enables searching under dynamic constraints. In this case the system adapted to an unanticipated situation when the reader finished its design by using it in a new way.

Constraint-based systems are thus designed to adapt to actors in the sphere of stable constraints (invariants), and to make it possible for actors to adapt in the sphere of situational constraints.[20] Formative models are not always required for system design, but they are necessary for the design of complex and dynamic systems—that is, for the design of information systems.

9.3   Models and Their Contribution to Design: Conclusions

What a model represents also determines how it can contribute to design and to what degree. By and large, there is no evidence that ISB researchers have considered this factor or how their models could contribute to design. Is it possible, then, for ISB models to inform the design of information systems? If it were possible, would the current IR researchers' common approach to design be open to being informed by them? These questions are discussed in the next chapter.

10 Human Information Behavior and Information Retrieval: Is Collaboration Possible?

Scholars in human information behavior (HIB) are actively continuing to construct the field's theoretical and conceptual foundations (e.g., Godbold 2006; Niedźwiedzka 2003; Pharo 2004). Not all studies in HIB, however, aim at developing conceptual constructs. Pettigrew and McKechnie (2001), for example, found that only 3% of the 1,160 journal articles they examined were theoretical in nature, and only 34% mentioned a conceptual construct. That is, most empirical studies investigate information behavior without a specific theoretical or conceptual backing, and without claiming to contribute to the construction of a theory or concept. How might the contribution of such studies be recognized?

In addition to the conceptual arena, there are other areas in which a study can play a role: It can improve our understanding of the studied phenomenon, discover new insights that can guide future research, offer new research methods that might be effective in future research, or provide implications for the design of information systems. Indeed, Julien and Duggan (2000) found that 45% of the articles published in HIB between 1984 and 1998 were concerned with systems design and use.[1]

This chapter focuses on the contributions of HIB research to the design of information retrieval (IR) systems, and on the degree to which research in information retrieval informs HIB studies.[2]

10.1 "Implications for Design"

It is not uncommon for research articles in HIB to include the phrase "implications for design," whether in a one-sentence statement (e.g., "These findings have implications for the design of information systems"),[3] or as a section's heading.[4] Yet the claim that a study's results contribute to design is not always warranted; in fact, quite often it is indefensible. Saracevic (2007b) reflected that such statements had been used much like a mantra: Researchers included them in their articles, presumably to increase the value of their studies, whether or not design could actually benefit from the study's results. This state of affairs is not unique to HIB. Dourish (2006), for instance, described the problem in the area of human-computer interaction (HCI):

> It has often been noted, not without irony, that the canonical paper reporting ethnographic field results in an HCI context will close with a section entitled "Implications for Design." The section may be long or short, comprising discursive prose or brief, bulleted items, but nonetheless figures as a staple feature of ethnographic reports. (541)

Dourish also laid out some social and political forces that have motivated the persistence of the problem, such as power relations between disciplines and the marginalization of theory. Some of his analyses are relevant to HIB as well, but the design arena is more complex in HIB than in HCI. Research to inform design in HCI focuses on the interaction between humans and machines. Computer-based information systems, by their very nature, cannot independently change themselves, and their behavior can be controlled to a large degree, altering only when they are redesigned. HIB, on the other hand, studies human interaction with *information*—a thing (entity, property, activity, etc.) that is multifaceted and somewhat amorphous. In addition, while HCI equates the concept *system* with computer-based systems, HIB perceives the concept more broadly to include humans as well. Because the design processes for computer-based and human systems are different from one another, it is important to distinguish between "implications for design" aimed at each type of system.

The design of human systems to support information retrieval began when libraries commenced user services. Since then, library personnel have planned services and programs to help patrons find information—that is, they have designed human-based information systems. Most studies for this purpose have also been carried out by practicing librarians in order to improve their services, most often with no aspiration to contribute to the profession at large. Such studies are sparse in academic HIB research. Moreover, it is a common notion among librarians that results of academic research have very little value to user services in libraries. There are exceptions to this view, however. One example of a relevant academic study is the INISS (Information Needs in Local Authority Social Services Departments in England) Project, carried out by Tom Wilson and his colleagues (Streatfield and Wilson 1982; Wilson and Streatfield 1977; Wilson, Streatfield, and Mullings 1979). Based on structured observations, semi-structured questionnaires, and 151 interviews in four local authority departments, they determined what type of information services would be most valuable to each community of actors. The team recommended, for instance, that subject specialists in areas related to social services would greatly benefit from a "properly staffed and organized research library" (Wilson et al. 1979, 133), while social workers would benefit most from a directory of formal and informal experts. The INISS team applied their recommendations experimentally in seven departments.

In comparison to computer-based systems, human-based information systems are more pliable in design. Whereas the design of both human systems and computer-based systems is subject to many constraints, the range of possibilities for design is much greater in human systems than in computer-based ones because people and organizations can make decisions and change to adapt to new circumstances. The greater challenge, therefore, is to explore how HIB studies could contribute to the design of computer-based information systems.

One way to uncover possible contributions is to examine the effects that studies in HIB and in information retrieval (IR) can have on one another. This interaction is the focus of this chapter. A strong motivation for this examination is the fact that, to date, the only HIB-style studies that have directly contributed to system design were those carried out by IR researchers themselves (e.g., Jansen and McNeese 2005; Ju and Gluck 2005; Tombros, Ruthven, and Jose 2005).

The gap between studies in information seeking in HIB and the design of information systems[5] in IR has been lamented by many HIB scholars. Saracevic (1999), for example, concluded an article about information science with the following warning:

I am afraid that the greatest danger facing information science is losing the sight of users, of human beings. By concentrating on or chasing the systems, I am afraid that more often than not we have lost that sight. But I am also convinced that the greatest payoff for information science will come if and when it successfully integrates systems and user research and applications. Society needs such a science and such a profession. (1062)

Despite Saracevic's warning, very few useful ideas have emerged that could have led to shrinking the gap. Some have questioned if it was even possible to build a bridge between the two fields. Those scholars who believe that the gap can be reduced put the responsibility on HIB's shoulders: They have suggested that HIB studies take a different course, quite often without specifying which one (e.g., Saracevic 2007b). Järvelin and Ingwersen (2004), for example, charted this course for HIB studies:

Studies in information-seeking rarely include information (retrieval) system design features in their study settings. We mean features that the information (retrieval) system designers find relevant and deal with. In such a situation the research results cannot communicate to systems design, because the worlds do not touch. In principle, of course, it may also be the case that information retrieval system designers are busy with the wrong variables or features.

Very little effort to bridge the gap has been required of IR researchers. In fact, it is not clear how many IR scholars believe that HIB studies can help them develop better systems—even though the statement above recognizes that IR researchers might sometimes consider the wrong variables. Most IR researchers seem to doubt that any contributions by potential users, for whom the systems are designed, could be valuable. At the same time, all parties agree that some level of understanding of how people look for information is relevant to systems design. To date, most design requirements were developed by IR scholars based on their thoughts of how people search (or by reflecting on how they themselves search), rather than on systematic studies of the search process. Clearly, better systems can be developed if the requirements are based on attributes that have been validated by studies, rather than on an IR researcher's opinion.

Several issues play a role in maintaining the HIB-IR gap. Among them are the types of models HIB and IR studies create; the communication between HIB and IR researchers; the differences between the fields; and the ability of IR research to incorporate results from HIB studies. What follows is a discussion of these issues.

10.1.1   Types of Models in Human Information Behavior and in Information Retrieval

Most HIB models are action models (see section 3.3.1). Action models describe current activities, that is, they are descriptive.[6] Element models, which represent variables that affect information-seeking behavior (see section 3.3.2), have the potential to be formative models. The HIB element models discussed in chapter 3, however, cannot support constraints-based design, as described in chapter 9, either because they are too general or because not all the constraints they represent shape human information behavior.

Leckie and Pettigrew's (1997) model of professionals' seeking behavior represented a number of dimensions of constraints, including work roles, tasks, characteristics of information needs, sources of information, and awareness of information. The distinguishing point of the model is the claim that there are relationships among the dimensions, but the nature of the relationships remains unexplained. Therefore, as a formative model it is too general.

Belkin's (1980) and Ingwersen's (1999) models, while valuable to research, raise another barrier for their usefulness to constraints-based design: They consider actors and systems as equal partners in human information interaction, and both models are symmetrical in representing the two collaborators. As Järvelin and Ingwersen (2004) stated explicitly above:

Studies in information seeking rarely include information (retrieval) system design features in their study settings. We mean features that the information (retrieval) system designers find relevant and deal with.

In other words, studies of information-seeking behavior should be partly guided by design constraints.[7] This approach to human-based design has various flaws, among them the fact that it considers the system and the design as a given, that is, as a constraint. This view is clearly reflected in the graphic presentations of both models. How can a new system be designed with the requirement that the current system is a given and cannot be changed? This requirement seems particularly extreme when, according to Ingwersen's model, the designer's cognitive and emotional states are constraints that should inform the requirements for the new system.

Considering the information system and the actor as equal partners not only prevents constraints-based design but is also system-centric. With such equality, both systems and actors have to change their behavior to adapt to a new design. Due to both the limited ability of current information systems to adapt and the great adaptive capabilities that humans possess, designers are motivated to consider systems' capabilities first, which is a system-centric approach to design. Actors and information systems, however, are not equal partners: The role of an IR system is to support the actor's seeking behavior, whereas the role of the actor's seeking behavior is not to support the system but to support his own decision-making.

While HIB researchers have been constructing descriptive models, IR researchers have been employing normative models that they themselves have constructed.[8] The first and most basic norms are the requirements that (1) retrieval should include *all* relevant documents (recall), and (2) retrieval should include *only* relevant documents (precision). Obviously, these requirements are unattainable, but measuring recall and precision allows IR researchers to evaluate how close they are to achieving this ideal retrieval.

IR models have the same drawbacks of any other normative model. Most importantly, they assume that people behave rationally. For instance, IR models are built on the assumption that actors always want to get all the relevant documents and no irrelevant ones, which would seem to be rational behavior. Yet research in information-seeking has demonstrated that this assumption has no standing in reality. Studies (e.g., Heisig, et al. 2010) have shown that it is not unusual for an actor to seek just a couple of documents, rather than all the relevant ones, or to consider it beneficial to examine documents that are not "relevant."

In addition, these models cannot guide the design of systems that cater to the complexity of the search process. Topicality is the main, and often the only, criteria for retrieval, although in recent years other factors have been considered in the design of models and algorithms for IR systems. The reductionist nature of IR models does not account for the dynamic nature of a search. Although interactive IR systems seem dynamic, they are not so by design. They enable the *searcher* to be dynamic, leading the interaction with the system, but the system responds to actors' queries in the same way for each iteration in the interaction.[9]

The averaging, or reductions, that is required to create norms usually results in relatively simple models. IR models are no exception. Ingwersen and Järvelin (2005) bring some examples of norms for best-match models: The distinction between relevant and nonrelevant documents should be flexible and graded;[10] documents that are most relevant should be listed first; users should have full control of the size of the result list; search keys should be weighted; and user interface should be simple and given through natural language queries (119). These normative requirements are simple because they are commonsensical and no study was required to uncover them. At the same time, they also illustrate the pitfalls in the commonsensical approach: It may lead to erroneous assumptions. The last norm above is an example.

The assumption that searching with natural language is better for users than using a structured, artificial language may seem obvious to IR researchers. In fact, this norm is commonly accepted among researchers in systems design in general. But scholars experienced in research about retrieval languages and seeking behavior may not accept it readily. They may ask, "Better for what?" For the users' ability to express their requests? For the users' general satisfaction? For precision and recall? For the users' chance of solving their information problems completely? No matter which option is selected, none is obvious, and none is supported by empirical evidence that demonstrates the advantages of interaction in natural language. Moreover, there are quite a few commonsensical arguments to support a contradictory norm. For example:

• Having to express their request in a structured language motivates actors to reflect on their information problem and thus understand it better.

• With the use of natural language, most algorithms are likely to retrieve documents that are relevant to terms that are in the query but that, taken alone, are not relevant to the request. Such terms include those that express relationships or are required for a sentence to be coherent, as in "the *relation* between television viewing and violence in children" or "the *conflict* between Israel and its neighbors."

IR models are also tied to the technology in current use, which is typical of both normative models and system-centric approaches. They take technology as a given, rather than provide insight that can lead to the development of new technologies that could improve information retrieval. This dependence on technology not only limits the possibilities that IR researchers may consider for retrieval mechanisms, it may also bar them from recognizing possibilities that can be supported by existing technology.

An example of such a possibility that has not been captured by academic IR research-ers is the integration of information about users' behavior into retrieval procedure as is practiced in the design of commercial web search engines. Here designers have incorporated into their retrieval algorithms data that is mined from the huge databases of recorded user behavior they have accumulated to add recommender features to their system.[11]

Some IR scholars engage users in the evaluation of systems they have designed, often under experimental conditions. Typically, a researcher develops a new facility or modifies an existing one, and then tests it, with user participation, to find out if the new system performs better than the old one. Systems are evaluated using some variation of the classic recall and precision measurements and at times additional criteria, such as user satisfaction, time to complete a search, and number of errors. There are some exceptions, though. Tombros et al. (2005), all computer scientists, conducted an experiment to elicit criteria that participants used to evaluate web pages when they conducted searches for simulated tasks. The outcome of this project was a set of criteria to support decisions about the utility of web pages for different types of tasks, criteria that can be used in the design of web-based information systems. Though descriptive, studies taking this approach or a similar one are still very rare among IR scholars.

The research method employed in IR also contributes to the simplicity inherent to its models. IR developments are based only on experiments, and experiments require variables with low complexity, as Robertson (2008), a leading IR researcher, explained:

Any laboratory experiment is an abstraction, based on a set of choices: choices to represent certain aspects of the real world (directly or indirectly) and to ignore others. Choices are made deliberately for the end in view—to isolate certain variables in order to be able to understand them. But choices are also made perforce—because certain aspects of the real world are highly resistant to abstraction. This factor introduces inevitable biases in what is studied: some groups of variables are more amenable than others to abstraction into a laboratory setting. From this point of view, the most important grouping of variables in the IR field is of those that directly concern users and those that do not. On the whole, user variables are resistant to abstraction. (452)

The contribution of experiments should not be discounted, however. They are necessary for the design of IR systems and for the development of models and methods. The advantages of a quantitative laboratory experiment are its relative sim-plicity and the researcher's control of variables.

Some areas of research may require the inclusion of human participants in experi-ments, such as studies in interactive IR or usability tests. To increase the external validity of experiments, IR researchers try at times to create experimental conditions that are closer to real life by including potential users as participants or by other means, such as providing the participants with a description of a simulated task as a starting point for their searches, rather than with a topic (Borlund 2009). The effectiveness of a laboratory experiment is partly due to the artificial conditions under which it takes place, which facilitate researcher control. Attempts to create conditions that are closer to real life do not necessarily increase the pertinence of the results to real life. In fact, the closer we bring an experiment to mimicking real life, the weaker its power to generalize becomes because real life is always contextual. Researchers can make experiments relevant to real life, however, when they select to test the "right" variables—those that shape the search and its process in real life. Such a choice is likely to increase the contribution of the new system to improving IR and at the same time would keep the simplicity required for normative models.

The difference between the type of model that is created in HIB research (descriptive) and those on which IR researchers rely (normative) plays a part in maintaining the gap between the two areas. At the same time it demonstrates the importance of collaboration because neither of the two models, each on its own, can guide the design of information systems that are responsive to complex and dynamic search processes.

10.2   Barriers and Challenges to Information Retrieval and Human Information Behavior Collaboration

As an HII researcher with some understanding of IR, I have personally experienced the importance and appropriateness of some HIB findings to the models and processes used in IR design. Participating in a panel at a 1998 conference of ACM's Special Interest Group on Information Retrieval (which is dedicated to IR research), I presented the results of a study (Fidel and Efthimiadis 1998) about how engineers use the web and offered a few resulting system requirements. One of them was based on engineers' tendency to plan their searches and their frustration with not being able to do so in web searches, which led me to suggest that the system should provide support for this activity. During the question period I was hit by insulting dismissal of my ideas, with comments such as "Just tell us exactly what you want, and we will build it," and "Why don't you build a system yourself?" Trying to improve my reputation, I suggested in a private conversation that one way to support this activity is to provide a planning set on which engineers can test their search plan. This, however, worsened the situation. I learned later that having a "planning set" was not compatible with ranked search results, which is a central procedure in current IR retrieval.[12]

This experience led me to think that HIB researchers would not be able to suggest requirements that are compatible with IR design processes because doing so requires a level of understanding of these processes that is beyond the interest of most HIB researchers. Similarly, IR designers would have to acquire a level of understanding of HIB research that is beyond their professional expertise, and which may require them to introduce major changes to their models.

Most IR researchers have the improvement of retrieval and user satisfaction as motivating forces for their work. Indeed, IR systems are used widely, as demonstrated by the heavy use of search engines. Similarly, most researchers in information seeking are inspired by the desire to support the user and improve the effectiveness of the seeking process on various levels, such as the cognitive, affective, and decision-making levels. Yet research approaches and practices in these fields reside at two opposing poles. This polarity manifests itself in various points of difference, such as the focus of the research, the variety of questions covered, the level of generalizability, and the typical research methods employed. Some of these points are presented in table 10.1.

Most of the attributes on which IR and HIB differ are inherent to their fields. Bridging the gap seems a monumental task. Nevertheless, the recognition that collaboration would benefit both fields is on the rise, if slowly.

Establishing productive communication with IR researchers has been a concern of HIB scholars, several of whom have suggested ways to remedy the situation. Kuhlthau (2005), for example, stated that in order to facilitate collaboration, "There is a need for a broad view of library and information science incorporating concepts of [information retrieval and information systems] into a unified whole." Bowler and Large (2008) do not address the gap directly but suggest that a design-based methodology that is employed in the education discipline might be relevant to library and information science (LIS), for this methodology integrates research, design, and practice into one process.

HIB researchers' interest in contributions to IR remains unreciprocated, however. At the same time that HIB researchers are suggesting implications for design, there are very few researchers in IR who are concerned with the lack of collaboration with HIB, or who believe they can benefit from its research. Järvelin and Ingwersen (2004), for instance, claimed that collaboration may occur if studies in information-seeking behavior included the design features of retrieval systems. Otherwise, "the research results cannot communicate to systems design, because the worlds do not touch" (Järvelin and Ingwersen 2004). This lack of communication had already been

Table 10.1
Differences between HIB and IR research practice

HIB research	IR research
Focuses on actors in the information-seeking process	Focuses on the system's success in retrieving information in response to actors' queries (system performance)
Considers both computer-based and human-based information systems (e.g., libraries, information desks)	Considers only computer-based systems
May encompass multiple elements involved in the process, from the cognitive to the contextual	Core research focuses on developing principles, models, and methods to construct and test retrieval algorithms with enhanced performance
Is evaluated by the contributions of the new insights it produces	Is evaluated by the performance power of the resulting algorithms, as usually measured by precision and recall and their derivatives
Interested in both generalizable results and contextual findings	Aims at developing general-context systems that successfully retrieve information to satisfy anyone and in any situation[a]
Evaluates the current system first (computer- or human-based), and then turns to designing a new or improved system	Designs systems first, and then evaluates them
Stimulated by theories in the social sciences	Affected by computational theories
Active in creating conceptual constructs	Limited activity in creating conceptual constructs
Most studies are carried out in naturalistic settings	All studies are lab experiments
Includes both qualitative and quantitative studies, with the former creating the larger portion of the research body. As a result, there is no concern about whether the concepts involved are quantifiable	Is mainly quantitative, and therefore requires that concepts involved be quantifiable. Qualitative studies, though few, are usually carried out to develop a certain system component (e.g., help facility, menu display) or to provide subjective evaluations of a system's performance
Is often holistic	Is reductionist
Constructs primarily descriptive models	Bases design on normative models

a. It is not surprising that the models that bind HIB and IR (e.g., Belkin's and Ingwersen's) are cognitive; cognitive processes and attributes are considered generalizable to all humans, regardless of context and situation.

recognized before the era of online information systems. In summarizing research in the information needs and uses of scientists, Lin and Garvey (1972) concluded:

There seems to be a tremendous communication gap between researchers and designers of scientific information systems. The researchers, on the one hand, discuss and single out the crucial elements of exchange and feedback between an information system and the scientists and technologists ... the designers, on the other hand, seem to invest almost all of their efforts in the technical soundness of the innovative information system. Given the present state of lack of communication, we may predict that cooperations [sic] between researchers ... and the developer and administrators of innovations ... will continue to be few. Unless the funding agencies and policy-makers of innovations are made aware of the fact that the feedback [from users] component must be an integral part of any innovation in the information system, we may further predict that many innovations will falls far short of the use envisioned by scientists and technologists. (32)

There are at least two strong reasons for this attitude among IR researchers: (1) Most findings from information-seeking studies could not support design, and (2) IR researchers do not *have* to consider results of studies in seeking behavior, even when they are relevant to IR design.

10.2.1 The Relevance of Human Information Behavior Research to Information Retrieval

Being descriptive, HIB models have a limited ability to guide design (see section 9.2.1). Moreover, researchers often simply convert their finding directly into design requirements in statements such as: "I found that people do X; therefore, the system should support doing X." A few examples may demonstrate this attitude. T. D. Wilson (1999) offered his model (see section 3.3.3) as a source for design requirements, stating that IR systems should be designed to reduce the users' risk of failure and increase their sense of self-efficacy.[13] Huang and Soergel (2006) were more specific in the requirements they proposed. In their user study they identified four types of evidence-based topical relevance: (1) direct evidence that explicitly gives an answer to a user's question; (2) indirect evidence that lets a user infer an answer to the question; (3) contextual evidence that provides peripheral or background information surrounding an answer; and (4) comparative evidence that provides a basis for interpretation or inspires some answer through perceived similarity to the question. To achieve an "ideal" system, they require that it automatically search from different angles and provide a list of results organized by type of relevance.[14]

These requirements, however, imply almost impossible missions and put heavy responsibility on the shoulders of IR researchers, most of whom conduct research in computer science departments and are experts in developing principles and methods for retrieval algorithms, rather than in translating emotional and general behavior into specific systems requirements. Therefore, from the designer's point of view, such requirements are not relevant to design.

Yet some HIB researchers have extracted and developed requirements from their study findings. Vakkari (1999), for instance, analyzed several features of work tasks and related them to types of information people seek and use in their tasks, which pointed to patterns of search strategies for obtaining information and relevance assessments typical of the task's features. These he offered to IR researchers to inform their design. Ross J. Todd's studies provide another example (Todd 2005). The cognitive model he has constructed identified five classes of information intents that actors have when they look for information. Each intent was described by the way actors plan to use the information received, such as to build an expanded and more complex picture of what they already know, or to see existing ideas and how these ideas are related. The system requirements that Todd presented were based on the typical behavior for each intent and suggested that IR systems make it possible for actors to search for documents that contain facts, opinions, argument, or explanation, in addition to the topic. Although these requirements are in a form that may inform design, there might be difficulties in implementing them because they are situational and subjective. What may seem a document of facts to one person, for instance, may not be that for another person or to the same person at another time.[15] Therefore, within the current approach to IR research, the requirements cannot be translated to design directly without developing "objective" methods to identify these attributes.

10.2.2 Information Retrieval Researchers' Interest in Human Information Behavior

Unlike the complex attributes that were discovered in HIB research, IR researchers have created simple models of users to guide their design. Simplicity allows for the construction of algorithms, which are formal constructs. This simplicity is also reflected in IR experiments, even when they attempt to address users' concerns. In a study that "simulated real users" (Keskustalo, Järvelin, and Pirkola 2008), for instance, the central user variable was the level of patience the user had when interacting with a system with relevance feedback. This feature would puzzle HIB researchers, especially researchers of information-seeking behavior, who would question the need to improve systems in order to address the user's patience. "Level of patience" has not been found to shape searching behavior, in contrast to other attributes that do play a role in shaping this behavior—such as familiarity with the search topic, the purpose of the search, and the importance of the information problem to the task at hand.

Not only are findings of HIB research not relevant to IR researchers, IR user models do not require empirical studies in order to be substantiated because the features on which they are constructed are commonsensical and obvious.[16] There is no reason to prove, for example, that actors would usually be better off if they saw relevant documents before irrelevant ones or that a simple interface is likely to support user-system interaction better than one that is difficult to use. But even if some IR researchers were interested in the findings of HIB studies, they do not *have* to consider them as design requirements.

IR researchers are in a privileged position in comparison to HIB scholars, primarily because of their disciplinary affiliations—the former to science and engineering, and the latter to social science. Various scholars have observed similar disparity in other fields. Lucy Suchman, an anthropologist who has participated in research and development projects in the information systems industry for over two decades, and whose work has had a significant impact on research in human-computer interaction, reflected that

A crucial assumption underwriting [the boundaries drawn between professional technology design and sites of technology-in-use] is the premise that technical expertise is not only a necessary, but is *the* sufficient form of knowledge for the production of new technologies. (Suchman 2002, 141)

Similarly, Dourish (2006), a computer scientist by training, drew attention to

[the] differential between engineering sciences and social sciences in terms of academic and funding structures; a brief perusal of the relative size of research grants will demonstrate that amply.... At a large scale it creates a status hierarchy in which engineering demands tend to override social ones. (544)

These roles in society are reflected in the relationship between IR and HIB research.[17] While some HIB researchers feel that showing how their studies may support design is necessary to establish the importance of their contribution, IR researchers are free to ignore this body of research, and when needed, conduct their own user studies, even though their expertise and experience in this area are limited.[18] Moreover, when steps to encourage collaboration are considered, it has been the responsibility of the HIB community either to create avenues to facilitate it (e.g., Kuhlthau 2005) or to change its ways (Järvelin and Ingwersen 2004).

The recommendation to HIB scholars is rather demanding: include systems in your research. This step requires researchers to study and understand information systems and their design. On the other hand, as Järvelin and Ingwersen (2004) forgivingly mention in the passage quoted earlier, "In principle" (which may not be the case in reality?) "it may also be the case" that IR designers consider "the wrong variables or features" (quite an ambiguous qualifier; "wrong" according to what standard?). Other IR researchers have claimed that studies in information-seeking behavior do not investigate features that are relevant to them. What are these relevant features? IR researchers have never explicitly laid them out. The IR community has not articulated, to itself or to others, the range of requirements they can consider in their design. How can HIB studies then be guided to address features that are relevant for IR design?

Given the barriers and challenges to collaboration between the two fields, is it possible for IR and HIB researchers to collaborate at all?

10.3   Could Information Retrieval and Human Information Behavior Researchers Collaborate?

Collaboration between the two groups of researchers would be highly beneficial to all involved and, most importantly, to users of IR systems. Indeed, the importance of this collaboration had already been recognized several years before online communication became available (Paisley 1968, 23–24). With such collaboration, IR systems would support searching behavior that is typical of users, and HIB research would make a direct contribution to the improvement of the seeking process. In spite the barriers and challenges, there is no reason to conclude that such collaboration is intrinsically unattainable.

10.3.1   Collaborations in Other Fields

Both IR and HIB research communities can be encouraged by developments in three cognate fields: human-computer interaction (HCI), computer-supported cooperative work (CSCW), and information systems. These three fields focus on the design of computer-based systems to support human activities, and the integration of findings from naturalistic studies into design occupies a valued position in their discussions and practice.

As an anthropologist working in the information systems industry, Suchman's (1987) conceptual work has had a noticeable impact on the HCI research community. By studying the actual use of systems, she learned that context is a major force in shaping the interaction between humans and computers. This observation led her to develop a new approach to design based on the concept of *situated actions*—actions taken in the context of particular, concrete circumstances (Suchman 1987, viii). That is, for a system to be useful, its design should be based on the contextual features of its users, rather than being limited to general-context features. Through her research,

Suchman came to the conclusions that action is situated in its circumstance, that understanding the interaction of people and environment is important for understanding human action, and that the view of *situated actions* recognizes the existence of rules and structures—they are not given, but rather are the products of actions and situations. Based on her experience with design teams in industry, she explained why industry prefers to design general-context systems, rather than context-specific ones:

A recurring question for me as a participant in discussions on design … is, "Who is doing what to whom here?" Within the prevailing discourses, anonymous and unlocatable designers, with a license afforded by their professional training, problematize the world in such a way as to make themselves indispensable to it and then discuss their obligation to intervene, in order to deliver technological solutions to equally decontextualized and consequently unlocatable "users." This stance of *design from nowhere* is closely tied to the goal of constructing technical systems as commodities that can be stabilized and cut loose from the sites of their production long enough to be exported en masse to the sites of their use. (Suchman 2002, 140)[19]

Today, context-specific design is accepted by researchers in both HCI and CSCW, although it is not yet a leading approach.

Like Suchman, Nardi (1993) explained that an understanding of human action that does not consider its surrounding environment is limited. To support useful systems, Nardi—and others as well, e.g., Bødker (1991) and Sachs (1995)—advocated using activity theory to study actors in their context (Kaptelinin and Nardi 2006). Activity theory is a framework based on the view that consciousness is shaped by our activity with other people and the artifacts with which we interact, rather than being confined inside our heads. With roots in the Soviet psychologist Vygotsky's work, activity theory was founded by Alexei N. Leont'ev and Sergei Rubinshtein, who sought to understand human activities as complex, socially situated phenomena in order to go beyond the theoretical traditions of psychoanalysis and behaviorism.[20] Nardi (2008) explained that "Activity theory works well with design because activity theorists have always tested their theories in practical ways and believe that application is an outcome of theory, not a separate activity." The framework has various interpretations and has been adapted by different fields, such as education and organizational design.[21] Various design studies have employed activity theory, such as Bardram (2000) and Mwanza (2001). In the area of information systems, Mursu et al. (2007) expanded on activity theory and proposed criteria that are required of models which inform the design of information systems.[22]

Whatever approach is employed to investigate actors in context, it always requires a study in naturalistic settings. Since context is social and dynamic, laboratory simulations are not likely to be productive for design because they create a new and artificial context: a laboratory with simulated context. Moreover, qualitative methods are required at least when first exploring actors in their context. Such methods are foreign to many researchers in the design of computer-based systems, most of whom are computer scientists. Therefore, integrating qualitative methods with design work requires circumstances that facilitate it. Dourish (2006) pointed out that the contextual approach did not grow within HCI but was imported: "a number of social scientists who made use of ethnographic approaches turned their attention to questions of interest to the HCI community and found positive reception for aspects of their work."[23] As contextual design and the associated research methods are percolating into HCI research, contextual HCI researchers still see the need to explain the contributions that their approach offers.

10.3.2   Contextual Research in Information Retrieval

Unlike work in HCI, IR research has remained mostly immune to contextual design. A shift from the design of general-context systems is present, though, in a new area: contextual information retrieval systems (Crestani and Ruthven 2007). Researchers in this area have integrated data about subject domains, types of task, and relevance judgments of actors in the same context to improve retrieval. Designing a system for one subject domain, for example, has been raised as an option because it makes it possible to support retrieval based on the characteristics of the domain. Adding an ontology based on the typical tasks carried out by a group of users in the domain (e.g., physicians, nurses, health administrators) makes it possible to tailor the retrieval to the specific needs of a user at a particular time.

The contextual approach in IR, however, is different from that in other fields. Its definitions of context, as well as its boundaries and themes, can be created automatically or can be created by experimentation with a few actors or with various degrees of researcher control. For instance, Campbell et al. (2007) defined "contextually related documents" as a relation between two documents in which either one cited the other or the two were cited together in a third document. After building an algorithm that captured these relations and employing them in retrieval, they tested the usefulness of the approach in a field experiment with six participants.[24] Most other considerations of context address the semantic context, which relates to the subject of the request (e.g., Hideo and Joemon 2006; Groth and Lannerö 2006). Hernandez et al. (2007) defined the context as "[t]he themes of the user's information need and the specific data the user is looking for to achieve the task that has motivated his search" (143), and developed an algorithm to build an ontology that would support the identification of these elements. Even though their approach touched upon the task that had generated the information problem, they considered only its semantic properties.

To be applicable to real life, however, context must be defined in naturalistic conditions where people actually look for information, rather than in laboratory experiments. Yet contextual IR researchers have not turned to the findings of naturalistic studies but have determined instead the features they would consider, most often guided by previous research. As a result, a context that is taken into account in design may have only one or two dimensions, or no representation of its typical attributes at all.

Another spot in which HIB and IR meet tangentially is in the relation between information retrieval and the actor's task. The concept *task* has been developed by "soft" IR researchers—those who do not create computational models and algorithms.[25] Vakkari (1999, 2003) argued that tasks need to be considered because they are the source of information problems:[26] Actors look for information when they cannot solve a problematic situation in the task because their knowledge is insufficient for them to proceed (Vakkari 1999, 824). Taking a cognitive, decontextual approach, IR researchers have been considering task complexity—according to the actor's perception—as a central element in task performance and one that is likely to have impact on seeking behavior. For empirical studies, the definition of *complexity* was determined by the operationalization of various variables associated with the idea that the level of complexity was reflected by the level to which the actor knew a priori what the task entailed. To date, research in this direction has produced conceptual contributions (e.g., Byström and Järvelin 1995; Li 2009), but no implications for design.

The concept *task* has also contributed to the evaluation and testing of interactive IR systems. Pia Borlund's studies (Borlund and Ingwersen 1997; Borlund 2009) aimed at improving current evaluation methods by developing a test that is as close as possible to real life with regard to cognitive activities. She achieved this goal in various ways. In a classic IR evaluation, subjects are given topics for which they perform searches, and the retrieval results are then evaluated by measuring precision and recall based on a dichotomous relevance judgment. Borlund's new method created a context for the test questions by representing them as simulated information needs, adding explanations about the topic of the need, and representing a simulated work task that generated the need. As part of the method, subjects searched for the simulated needs as well as for their own needs. They could then rank relevance on three levels and evaluate the usefulness of the documents (situational relevance); in addition, a panel of judges provided an evaluation of the documents' topicality. One part of the method, the use of simulated tasks in test requests, has already been used in various

IR experiments.[27] Like task complexity, this method using simulated tasks has not contributed directly to design, even though it is a contribution to testing and evaluation of IR systems.

Why is IR research relatively slow to accept contextual design, while other fields that design computer-based systems have been making meaningful progress? There are probably several reasons for this distinction. One possible explanation is the heightened complexity that IR researchers need to tackle. In addition to the interaction between a user and a machine, they need to address the interaction with information. The higher the level of complexity, the more difficult it is to boil it down to a set of variables that can be tested in experiments, which are required for the design of any computer-based system.

10.3.3   What Is Required for Collaboration to Take Place?

During the last five decades, HIB and IR became independent fields due to the types of studies their researchers have carried out. The call for collaboration between the fields is not new; it has been advocated by several researchers (e.g., Bates 1989; Belkin, Seeger, and Wersig 1983; Ellis 1989; Marchionini 1995). Yet collaboration is not a universal goal. While some researchers are attracted to the new possibilities that would be created through collaboration, others prefer to continue their research only within their own field and contribute to their field's growth.

There are at least two approaches that would enhance collaboration: direct collaboration between HIB and IR researchers, and the participation of an intermediary who bridges the gap between the fields.

10.3.3.1   *Direct Collaboration*

In principle, teams that bring together researchers from IR and HIB have the potential to advance methods and designs for retrieval systems that are guided by findings from information-seeking research. This collaboration would benefit HIB researchers because it would guide the conduct of studies that can lead to realistic recommendations for design. IR researchers would gain as well because their design would likely increase its effectiveness. Collaborative teams still face the barriers that separate the fields—such as the focus on process versus retrieval performance, the holistic versus the reductionist approach, and the models created and used: descriptive versus normative. This collaboration is likely to be productive, therefore, only if each team member thoroughly understands the nature of the research in the collaborating field and the culture associated with it, even though she has no interest in conducting research in that field. To gain a thorough understanding of the nature of research in a very different field entails special training, an aptitude for figuring out and intuitively understanding approaches in the other field, and much good will. A combination of such attributes is very rare among researchers in general, as well as in both IR and HIB. This rarity has probably prevented the formation of stable and established collaborating teams.

In spite of these impediments, a few researchers have joined their counterparts to demonstrate how HIB investigations can inform IR research.

Ingwersen and Järvelin (2005) provided the most comprehensive approach to bridging the gap. Based on the empirical literature in both IR and HIB and on Ingwersen's previous models (see section 3.3.2), they developed a descriptive model from a cognitive viewpoint that placed actors at the center. On one side of the model were actors and their organizational, social, and cultural context; on the other side was the retrieval system with its interface, information objects, and information technology (engines, logic, and algorithms). Actors were of different types, such as authors of information objects, designers of retrieval systems, and information seekers. Each type of actor has her own type of interaction with the elements of the system.

Analyzing these relationships, Ingwersen and Järvelin (2005) developed five general dimensions of variables that are relevant to IR: (1) the organizational task, (2) the actor, (3) the document, (4) the interaction with what the algorithms provide, and (5) the interaction with what the access mechanism provides. They also specified the variables in each dimension. The actor dimension, for instance, brought forward variables such as the actor's declarative knowledge and procedural skills, the actor's perception of the work tasks, and the actor's emotions. Given these variables, Ingwersen and Järvelin proposed a research program based on studying various combinations of variables, such as information objects, information technology, and actors; or interface, actors, and socio-organizational contexts. For each combination they list the studies that should be carried out, pointing out which should be the independent variables and which the dependent ones.

This research program is comprehensive and detailed, and it requires researchers in one field to understand research in the other. For example, the contribution of HIB scholars to collaboration, Ingwersen and Järvelin (2005, 350) asserted, can be materialized "[b]y explicitly studying IR system features and the contribution their components deliver in the overall retrieval effectiveness." For the IR community they suggested research questions that would facilitate the building of test collections for specific domains, such as:

What kinds of work tasks are typical of Domain X?

What kinds of search tasks do these tasks typically generate?

What kinds of documents or other knowledge sources tend to be relevant to these search tasks?

How many documents would actors in the domain expect to retrieve in a collection and how many [would] they want to see? (362)[28]

These examples clearly point to the additional expertise that researchers will have to acquire for a bridge to be built: HIB researchers would have to be able to understand features of IR systems and their contribution to performance;[29] and IR researchers who specialize in quantitative research that is conducted in laboratories with a high level of control would need to be able to harness the complexity of real life to reach crisp results when answering the research questions above. It is thus not clear whether researchers would be prepared to participate in the proposed research program.

Nicholas Belkin and his colleagues took a more concrete approach. They have transferred attributes of information behavior directly into design requirements and specifications (Belkin, Marchetti, and Cool 1993; Belkin et al. 1995). These attributes were derived from a model they had developed of information-seeking strategies (ISS), which defined *strategies* as the behaviors in which people engage when searching for information.[30] They decided to focus on strategies because they represent the concept of *interaction*, which they considered central to IR. The model, which was based on informal analysis of empirical studies, presented four mutually exclusive dimensions (or facets) of strategies, each including a continuum of strategies. For each dimension they listed the two extreme strategies. The dimensions are method of interaction (from scanning to searching); goal of interaction (from learning to selecting); mode of retrieval (from recognition to specification); and resources considered (from information to metainformation).

In one study they addressed the design of an interface to support user interaction (Belkin, Marchetti, and Cool 1993). For each strategy in their model they employed cognitive task analysis[31]—analyzing a strategy according to how they thought it was accomplished—to identify the problems that might be encountered when using it. One problem they identified in browsing (i.e., scanning), for instance, was "lack of knowledge of structure," and a problem in learning was "identifying appropriate resources" (330). They then translated these problems into specifications for the functionality that would support the resolution of these problems. Thus, the first problem could be solved by "structured display of resources, with explanation of the link type," and the second by "display of resources available to user, direct user choice based on content description" (330). The team then selected the tools and approaches that would make it possible to implement the desired interface, and implemented the first out of three stages.

In another study, design specifications were derived more systematically (Belkin et al. 1995). This time, each strategy was defined by its four dimensions. This way, *scanning*, for instance, was not a complete description of a strategy. To be complete, one strategy had to include the other dimensions: the goal, the mode of interaction, and the resources considered. To identify all 16 possible strategies, they created all the possible combinations of the eight extreme "strategies" (according to the definition in the first study). One strategy, for example, combined the original "strategies" of *scanning*, *selecting*, *recognition*, and *information*. This strategy pertains to the case when a user wants to find an item of information she knows exists and will be able to recognize when she sees it, but she cannot specify it by searchable characteristics.

To select the tools that could support carrying out the 16 strategies, Belkin et al. (1995) viewed each strategy as a dialog between the user and the computer. This approach made it possible for them to formally describe the dialogs, using a tool they had developed for analyzing conversations. To program the system to support the interaction process, they used "scripts," techniques used in artificial intelligence.[32] Belkin and his colleagues created a script for each strategy, based on the most effective way to execute it according to their view.[33] Integrating the tool for analyzing dialogs into the scripts, they experimentally implemented some examples in an existing system. If developed, their system would conduct dialogs with users that would support their interaction and suggest useful procedures.

Since the time that the projects' reports were written, no prototype has been completed, and no testing was ever conducted to assess the system's effectiveness. Building a prototype may prove to be a treacherous process since a comprehensive analysis of all possible strategies and their possible "best practices," which would generate a very large set of uncoordinated possibilities, may lead to inconsistencies in the design requirements. Belkin et al.'s projects are unique, however, because they investigated design possibilities to support the search *process*, rather than being limited to retrieval, which has been the typical approach in IR research.

In summary, while Ingwersen, Järvelin, and Belkin and colleagues have carried out productive projects, collaborations between HIB and IR researchers to advance the design of retrieval systems based on findings from research on information-seeking behavior are very rare. The effectiveness of these researchers' approaches is not known yet, but one hopes it will be tested in the future. To collaborate, these researchers overcame one significant obstacle: the need for each collaborating researcher to acquire a substantive understanding of approaches and methods of research employed by the other field. It is not likely that many other researchers would be ready for this task. An intermediary who knows the research traditions in both fields, and communicates comfortably with all researchers, could remove this obstacle.

10.3.3.2   An Intermediary to Bridge the Gap

The many differences between the attributes inherent to HIB and IR, as well as the barriers and challenges to collaboration between the fields, suggest that the intervention of an intermediary—a system planner—who belongs to neither HIB nor IR might facilitate cross fertilization. Like a designer, the intermediary could translate the requirements generated by HIB projects into specifications that would nourish IR research, through negotiations with researchers on the parallel edges of the gap. Researchers and practitioners in the area of design are promising candidates for the task of a system planner because their expertise includes experience in representing complex and multifaceted realities in formal structures. To create requirements or specifications for usable artifacts, designers must understand both realities and structures. The system planner who bridges HIB and IR may not have the knowledge to develop IR models and algorithms but can understand how they are developed and what assumptions and principles guide their construction. Similarly, he may not be able to design and carry out an in-depth and holistic study of information behavior, but he can see and understand the major themes that have emerged and the complexity that has been uncovered.

The system planner is much like an architect who designs a bridge (or any other structure): She gives the requirements to the civil engineers who will actually build the bridge. To develop these requirements, she consults with experts and studies reports that inform her about the role the bridge will play in the area's economy, voters' opinions about it, the projected traffic density, and the aesthetic demands of all stakeholders, among other issues. The architect relies on studies conducted by experts to understand the economic effects of the bridge, for instance, rather than conducting a study on her own, and she knows what studies would be relevant to the bridge's design.[34] Similarly, she has a good understanding of material sciences, so she knows what requirements will be useful to the engineer, but she does not develop new materials or make final decisions about which ones would be best to use.[35]

The system planner has the skills and creativity to build a bridge between the two camps: to inform HIB researchers what type of results are likely to be relevant to design, and to help IR researchers make their processes more compatible with central issues in HIB. The intermediation can take place on both the practical and the research levels. On the practical level, the development of a context-specific system can be informed by a study of the HIB of its potential users. Possible examples include a system that provides economic information to citizens to support their private financial planning, a retrieval system for fiction to serve actors in public libraries and schools, and a system to serve women with breast cancer during their treatment periods.

The role of the system planner is not limited to informing practicing designers. Nourished by conceptual constructs in the areas of design, HIB, and IR, and with the support of experience in practice, research in planning may develop new constructs specific to the intermediation. They may find which types of methodologies in HIB, and even which types of research questions, are promising in guiding the design of IR systems. They may possibly define new retrieval mechanisms that are more compatible with findings in HIB research than the current algorithms.

One may claim that the role of a system planner requires much knowledge and effort but is not as highly esteemed as that of an IR researcher/designer or a HIB researcher. As a system planner, one may claim, one is caught in between the specialties, serving them both without an independent identity. Moreover, the value of this role may not be recognized by those who think that IR and HIB cannot enrich one another. Nevertheless, even if it is not esteemed, the role is important and rewarding. Given the shortcomings of current retrieval systems and their low level of compatibility with actual or desired information-seeking (or any other mode of HII), one can recognize the importance of the system planner's role. In addition, this role is not limited to the IR component of system design. The knowledge garnered by an intermediary about information seeking can guide the design of other system components, such as interface and content, and the relationships among them. Moreover, the role of a system planner can be greatly satisfying because it requires a high level of imagination and creativity—skills that are bound to bring fulfillment when used. As Dourish (2006, 556) observed: "the gap is where all the interesting stuff happens."

10.4 A Paradigm Shift

Ingwersen and Järvelin (2005) hinted at the need for a paradigm shift in IR when they claimed, "it is more important to look into different actor types, their *current* task knowledge, and their information behavior in a systematic and controlled way. *Request and task modeling* is more central to IR than general user modeling" (336). Their research program implies that systems would be designed to specialize in providing information to actors conducting specific tasks in a specific domain (see their research questions in section 10.3.3.1). Their approach is a radical departure from the dominant view in IR research, which has focused exclusively on general-context systems.

A paradigm shift (in the Kuhnian sense) in both fields would provide the base for constructing a solid bridge, whether through direct collaboration or with the help of a system planner. The current paradigm in IR research is based on comparing user queries with documents' representations and then evaluating the resulting retrieval. Researchers have constantly aimed at improving retrieval results and evaluation methods and have taken various approaches to achieve these goals. This approach to design casts searchers as somewhat passive partners who are largely dependent on the system's ability to retrieve relevant documents. Since searchers do not understand what effect their query formulations will have on the retrieved results, they can participate in improving the results only in systems with relevance feedback.[36] One way IR researchers can improve the usefulness of IR systems for real-life users is to aim at providing support to the search *process* and to consider designing systems for local contexts instead of focusing exclusively on general contexts.[37]

The need to support the search process has been voiced by various HIB scholars (e.g., Bates 1989; Schamber 1994), but no research has been carried out in this direction. Designing systems that support people's activities, rather than focusing only on high retrieval performance, would produce systems with useful retrieval performance and with increased user satisfaction. Browsing the web is an example that demonstrates how process support may improve search results. The web facilitates browsing; one can go from one site to another with just one click. However, the web does not *support* browsing.[38] Searchers get lost in cyberspace, and it may take much browsing (and time) before they find useful information. A search engine (i.e., an IR system) can improve retrieval and user satisfaction with aids for browsing that will keep searchers from getting lost, and help them zoom in on documents of value. The current IR paradigm, however, would not consider developing such facilities because it requires a new approach. Principles, methods, and algorithms to keep searchers on track, for example, would be different in nature from those comparing the representations of queries and documents. In addition, performance evaluation would entail the development of a new set of measurements, or may even require qualitative evaluations. Examples of other activities in the search process that can be supported are shifting from one strategy to another (e.g., from browsing to the analytical strategy), planning a search, evaluating retrieved documents, and query formulation.

Designing such facilities may help the design of context-specific systems. Instead of designing a system for each attribute of a context—e.g., complex task, expert users, high-pace workplace, and subject domain—systems can be composed of the facilities that support the seeking behavior of each community of actors. For example, users new to the web (e.g., elementary school students, older adults who now have to use the web to manage their daily life) may require facilities that support browsing, help in query formulation, and aid in shifting strategies. They may not require a facility to support planning a search. Engineers, on the other hand, would benefit from planning support, but may not require help in query formulation. Combining such facilities with domain-based retrieval may produce IR systems that are tailored to their community of actors and thus are more powerful than general-context systems.[39]

To identify the activities that can be supported by IR systems, designers should be able to turn to HIB research, which both discovers these activities and provides insight into the ways actors carry them out. For that purpose, HIB researchers who are interested in the benefits of collaboration with IR need to shift their approach as well. To bridge the gap with IR research, HIB scholars need to develop theories and constructs that are relevant to information systems. Chatman's theories (Chatman 2000) and Dervin's methodology (Dervin 1992) have been two great contributions to basic research and have shaped some branches of HIB research, but they are not relevant to system design. Information systems are not relevant to actors who avoid information, and IR systems cannot help an actor facing a situational gap in sense-making that is created by multiple dimensions.[40]

In addition, for HIB empirical studies to be used in IR, they need to have results that are relevant to design. It is not difficult to find examples of results that are not up to the task, even when they provide contributions to HIB in general. Typical study findings include statements such as: There is no difference between men and women in the level of uncertainty they feel during a search; information systems are not the first place to which people turn when they look for information; [members of a specified profession and position] seek and accumulate information that is not only related, but may be unrelated, to their role in the organization. In addition, there is a trend in HIB research to study the information behavior of "exotic" groups and situations (see section 7.2.2) most of which require information but not a special information system.[41] Some hypothetical examples are studies of the information behavior of mothers playing with their toddlers in a public park, security guards on their breaks, and students in a modern art class with a female teacher.

Part of the research tradition in HIB is the high importance that is bestowed on the Sisyphean task of uncovering all the procedures employed in information-seeking processes. Discovering a new procedure is considered a meaningful contribution to the field. While this task is relevant to the work of many HIB researchers, it is not relevant to design. Each procedure that has been discovered thus far was shaped by the specific view of the researcher who brought it to light.[42] As a result, the sets of procedures are not compatible with one another. A design that is guided by current studies and that considers the various procedures (which is almost impossible) would create a system that is a discordant patchwork. Therefore, instead of finding new procedures in each study, HIB research would be more relevant to design if it focused on investigating categories of procedures. Once these categories are established, researchers could investigate the features of each category and its manifestation in a manner that is relevant to design.[43]

In conclusion, a paradigm shift in both IR and HIB that led each field to consider the other would have an enormous impact not only on research in both fields, but on the effectiveness of IR systems. If good will existed in both camps, such a radical transition would be possible.

11   Cognitive Work Analysis: Dimensions for Analysis

Cognitive work analysis (Vicente 1999) is a work-centered conceptual framework developed by Rasmussen, Pejtersen, and Goodstein (1994) at Risø National Laboratory in Denmark.[1] Its purpose is to guide an analysis of cognitive work that leads to design requirements. The framework is motivated by the assumption that designing a system that can effectively support actors in their work requires an in-depth understanding of the work that actors do and the work's environment. Cognitive work analysis (CWA) considers as "cognitive work" any activity that requires decision making. Thus, the academic activities of elementary school students, patients' management of their medical treatment, and engineers' design of artifacts are all examples of cognitive work. Being a work-centered approach, CWA focuses on the cognitive work itself, regardless of the specific individuals who carry it out.

CWA is a context-centered approach (see section 4.4) that focuses on the context of the work under investigation. As a result, it is useful for the design of systems in their context, rather than for the design of general-context systems. In this framework the context is the set of constraints that shape actor behavior. That is, CWA provides an *ecological approach* to the study of human information interaction (HII) because it centers on explicit analysis of the constraints that the work ecology impresses upon actors (see section 1.1.3). For the purpose of information system design, such an approach is more promising than the user-centered (or human-centered) approach because information problems are spawned from activities in which a person is involved—whether the activities are cognitive or physical—rather than from innate cognitive or other personal attributes. In addition, human cognitive activities themselves—that is, cognitive work—are shaped by the context in which they take place. Therefore, to understand cognitive work requires an understanding of its context (see the discussion in section 7.1.2).

In addition to being context-centered, the major advantage of CWA over other design approaches is its facility in preserving real-life complexity in design requirements. Harnessing complexity in design increases the ability of systems to adapt themselves to the actors' real world and reduces the level of adjustment required from the system's users. The approach is promising for the design of information systems because HII is a highly complex process with cognitive, social, organizational, political, and physical aspects.

My motivation to study CWA and apply it in my research stems from my belief that

• Human information interaction is a highly complex phenomenon and thus its study requires complex approaches. Reductionist approaches lead to incomplete analyses of the phenomenon.

• Information systems cannot be effective if they are designed without understanding how they will fit into work processes.

• Context shapes HII patterns to a large degree. Therefore, the search for general, context-free HII patterns to guide design is limited in its potential to support the design of effective systems. It might be best to limit generalizations about HII to local contexts, and generalize the approaches and methods of analysis that can be used across contexts.

The CWA framework's main theoretical roots lie in the systems approach (see section 1.2) and in Gibson's ecological psychology (e.g., Gibson 1979). It resulted from the generalization of experiences from field studies that led to the design of support systems for a variety of modern work domains such as process plants, hospitals, and libraries. Developed since the 1960s (Rasmussen 1986), CWA belongs to a set of approaches that together constitute cognitive systems engineering. As Hollnagel and Woods (2005) explained: "The focus of [cognitive systems engineering] is how humans can cope with and master the complexity of processes and technological environments, initially in work contexts but increasingly also in every other aspect of daily life" (1). In the tradition of systems thinking, CWA is employed to improve the effectiveness of a workplace and the satisfaction of the actors involved.

Using this framework in the study of HII, one analyzes cognitive work to inform the design of systems—whether intellectual or computerized—that support HII. CWA's approach to the design of information systems is different from the common one. Under current views of best practice, a designer builds a prototype based on her assumptions about the needs of potential users—assumptions that are sometimes based on some analysis of actor behavior. The designer then tests and evaluates the prototype—typically through experiments with the participation of potential users or other types of subjects—and modifies the design to arrive at the version that is ready for implementation. CWA, on the other hand, first analyzes and evaluates the system already in place and its context—a system which may be formal or informal, digital or physical—and then develops design requirements (e.g., Sanderson 1998; Sanderson et al. 1999). The framework also guides designers who build systems based on CWA-induced requirements when they test prototypes and evaluate the new systems.

The range of CWA applications is diverse. Naikar (2006) summarized several cases in which CWA had been applied at the Australian Department of Defense—for example, in the analysis of training needs, the evaluation of alternative design proposals for the acquisition of a new system, the development of team design for a new and complex system, and the development of training strategies to manage human error for a certain aircraft (423). The majority of CWA applications, however, have focused on the analysis, design, and evaluation of interfaces for complex socio-technical systems.[2] Examples of such interfaces include a display of an aircraft's status during flight (Dinadis and Vicente 1999), sensors that provide information about functions in complex and dynamic systems such as pasteurization process control (Reising and Sanderson 2002), support systems for operators of petrochemical refineries (Jamieson and Vicente 2001), a nuclear power plant feedwater subsystem (Dinadis and Vicente 1996), support for monitoring patients in the operating theater (Sanderson et al. 2004; Watson, Russell, and Sanderson 2000), and clinical displays (Effken et al. 2001). A collection of articles about applications of CWA (Bisantz and Burns 2009) presents a variety of additional applications. In contrast, only a few HIB studies have attended to the study of context at all, whether employing CWA or any other approach.[3]

In the examples above, researchers applied the framework to the design of a system interface and considered system contents and functionality as given. In the area of information science, CWA has been applied not only to the design and evaluation of information system interfaces, but also to the design and evaluation of their content and functionality. For example, it guided the development of BookHouse, the first retrieval system for fiction (Pejtersen 1989, 1992; Rasmussen et al. 1994). Based on the analysis of reference interviews in public and school libraries, Pejtersen developed this fiction retrieval system, with a graphical user interface, in which users can look for books by a variety of attributes such as the subject, historical period, mood, and cover design. It serves children and adults, as well as library catalogers. The system also caters to various strategies: Users can just browse without any particular attribute in mind, look for a specific book, or look for books that are similar to one they liked (see section 9.2.3.2 for more details about BookHouse).

Later, CWA was used to analyze data collected in a study of high school students searching the web (Fidel et al. 1999; Pejtersen and Fidel 1998). In this study, the framework proved to be very powerful in helping to uncover the problems that students experienced when using the web to search for information, and offered recommendations for design that could alleviate such problems. In the next study, Pejtersen and her colleagues completed the COLLATE project that supported multi-institutional collaboration in indexing and retrieval among the national film archives of Germany, Austria, and the Czech Republic (e.g., Albrechtsen, Pejtersen, and Cleal 2002; Hertzum et al. 2002). The most recent application of CWA in the context of HII took place at the Drainage and Wastewater Division of the City of Seattle (the mCity project; see section 9.2.3.2). Field workers in the department use computerized handhelds to receive work orders, to access information that is relevant to their specific job, and to report about their work (e.g., Scholl et al. 2007). The analysis generated many requirements for system and organizational improvements.

CWA proposes dimensions for the analysis of cognitive work, and provides analytical tools to harness complexity. This chapter describes the CWA dimensions and the next chapter presents its analytical tools. The last chapter analyzes CWA's contribution to design-oriented research in HII.

11.1   The Dimensions for Analysis

Cognitive work analysis considers people who interact with information—that is, "actors" who are involved in their work-related activities—rather than "users" of systems. Although CWA can be applied to the analysis of all kinds of cognitive work, the discussion of CWA in this book centers on cognitive work in the workplace because almost all CWA-based studies to date were conducted in this context; as a result, the application of CWA to the workplace is more developed than its application in other contexts. Focusing on information behavior on the job, CWA views human information interaction in the context of work activities. It assumes that, in order to design systems that work harmoniously with humans, one has to understand

• The work actors do
• Their information behavior
• The context in which they work
• The reasons for their actions.

Therefore, CWA focuses *simultaneously* on the task actors perform, the environment in which it is carried out, and the perceptual and cognitive attributes of the people who carry out the task.

11.2   The Onion Model

A graphic presentation of the framework's dimensions is given in figure 11.1. In this presentation, each category of attributes listed above is designated with a circle and is considered a dimension for analysis. Thus, each dimension is a host for constraints, attributes, factors, or variables—depending on the purpose and method of a study. For example, an analysis carried out with the goal of developing design requirements investigates the *constraints* in each dimension. An analysis for the purpose of determining detailed specifications may identify *variables* in each dimension, as might be the case when attempting to determine the desired structure for navigation (the dependent variable) that is most effective for actors in each category of membership in an organization (the independent variable).

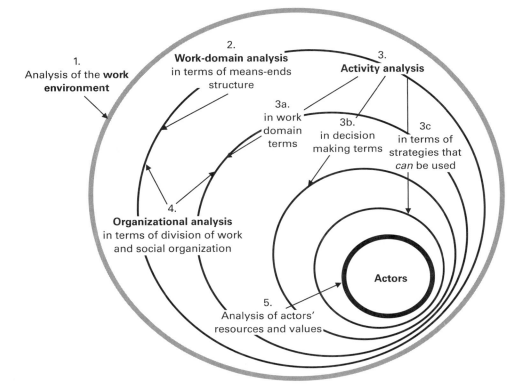

Figure 11.1
CWA's dimensions of analysis.

1. *The work environment* indicates the need to investigate the environment in which the workplace operates. Before embarking on the analysis of this dimension, researchers view the workplace as a system and define its boundaries. Such a system might be, for instance, a whole organization, a unit within an organization, or all that is involved in performing a function, such as teaching in an elementary school or administering a nonprofit organization. Because elements in a system are identified by their functions (see section 1.2), it is often challenging to define a system's boundary. In complex systems the functional structure is usually obscure to those who are unfamiliar with a particular workplace.[4] Therefore, a certain level of familiarity with the workplace is required to draw the boundary that will be most relevant to the desired analysis. At the same time, paradoxically, becoming familiar with a system requires that researchers first know the system they are investigating, which, in turn, means that they must know its boundary.

This conundrum is not a no-win situation, however. A system's definition, and thus its boundary, is an intellectual and abstract construct, rather than a physical reality. That is, a system's boundary is not set in concrete. Researchers draw the boundary of a system to the best of their knowledge before they begin an investigation. If needed, the boundary can be modified during the investigation as researchers gain increased understanding of the system and its activities. Similarly, elements in the environment—that is, the given constraints that shape the system's behavior—are discovered as a study progresses.

An example may illustrate the nature of the challenges that can be experienced when defining a system boundary. In our mCity study of fieldworkers who use mobile handhelds (e.g., Fidel et al. 2007), the system's boundary became stable only after we were a year into the project. The decision on whether crew chiefs were in the system or in the environment is an example of the challenges we faced. Because our aim was to center the system on the fieldworkers, it was easy to decide that managers on all levels were elements in the environment. Crew chiefs were not managers and were very central to the teams' work, but they did not work in the field; they distributed work orders they had received from the schedulers among workers, were available for consultations and advice, and synchronized the individual handhelds with the backend system at the end of the day. However, there were also reasons to include the crew chiefs in the system. For instance, they were closely involved with the details of the fieldwork, and their status was temporary because the position was rotated among the fieldworkers, and crew chiefs returned to the field once their term was over. Our research team had deliberated about the place of the crew chiefs within the system for several months. Eventually we decided to include them in the system's environment because their daily work was different from that of the fieldworkers.[5]

2. *The work domain analysis* indicates the need to investigate the workplace system itself. This analysis is guided by an abstraction hierarchy (see means-ends analysis in section 12.1) and focuses on uncovering the goals of the system and its constraints, the functions and activities in the system, and the resources the system uses to do its work.

3. *Activity analysis*

3a. *Activity analysis in work domain terms*, or *task analysis*, indicates the need to look at specific tasks and to analyze each one of them according to the same facets employed in *work domain analysis*: goals, constraints, functions, activities, and resources. In the context of CWA, *task* is defined as "[a]ctions that can or should be performed by one or more actors to achieve a particular goal" (Vicente 1999, 9).

3b. *Activity analysis in decision-making terms*, or *decision analysis*, indicates the need to provide a specific analysis of individual decisions. Complex decision-making processes are mapped onto the decision ladder (see section 4.3) to uncover the stages in the decision process. The decision itself is analyzed with an abstraction hierarchy in a way that is similar to the techniques used in the *work domain analysis* and *task analysis* dimensions.

3c. *Analysis in terms of strategies that can be used*, or *strategies analysis*, indicates the need to examine which strategies are *possible* for each task and decision. This examination is based on the findings in the other dimensions, such as task constraints, actor resources, and the criteria actors use in strategy selection (see the example in section 5.4.2).

4. *Organizational analysis* indicates the need to study the organizational, social, and political elements that shape how activities are carried out in the local workplace system—that is, in the work domain. Examples of such elements include management style, organizational culture, social conventions, and criteria for work distribution.

5. *The actors' resources and values analysis* indicates the need to identify characteristics of each community of actors. It addresses experience and expertise, priorities, preferences, and values, among other attributes. Because CWA's purpose is to present design requirements for certain work carried out in a particular work domain, it focuses on a prototypical actor rather than on individual actors and their demographic and cognitive characteristics. A *prototypical actor* is one who is the best example of actors in his group (Lakoff 1987, 41). The image of a prototypical actor crystallizes during

the analysis along all the CWA dimensions. CWA recognizes that not all actors are prototypical, and that their individual attributes and histories might affect their interaction with information. However, because the goal of CWA is to design information systems for distinct work domains and tasks, regardless of the individuals who are carrying out a task at a certain point in time, it considers the prototypical attributes as most important.

The decision as to which prototypical attributes to analyze may change from one work domain to another. In the study of web-searching behavior of high school students (Fidel et al. 1999), for example, we analyzed the following:

• The students' education
• Their experience with computers and with retrieving information from the web
• Their knowledge in the subject domain
• Their educational plans for the future
• Their preferences with regard to searching the web
• The priority criteria they used to select a search strategy
• The performance criteria they employed
• The level of their motivation to expand their knowledge
• Their opinion about their own situation, abilities, and preferences.

To take another example, when analyzing attributes for engineers, we may find some new attributes to be relevant, while some that we observed for the students— such as their educational plans for the future and the level of their motivation to expand their knowledge—will play no role. Nevertheless, several attributes are common to most domains, such as the level of expertise and experience with the subject domain, experience and expertise with information systems and technology, preferences, values, structure of the subject domain, and type of training required to carry out the task. Future research on the application of CWA to the design of information systems could develop a core set of attributes that are relevant to most studies.

To further explain the dimensions for analysis, table 11.1 provides examples of issues to investigate in each dimension, and table 11.2 offers a small sample of study results for each dimension.

11.2.1 An Example

A sample of study results is presented here as an example of elements in each dimension. The sample is taken from our study of high school students' web searching for homework assignments (Fidel et al. 1999). Our team studied students in a public

Table 11.1
Examples of issues to investigate in each dimension

Dimensions	Examples of issues to investigate
1. Work environment analysis	What elements outside the workplace affect its work? What are the boundaries for the work environment?
2. Work domain analysis	What are the goals, priorities, and constraints of the work domain? What are its functions and physical processes? What tools are employed?
3a. Task analysis	What are the current tasks? What are the goals of the actors' activities? Constraints? The functions involved? The technology used?
3b. Decision analysis	What decisions are made? What information is required? What information sources are useful? What information is used? What information is created? What information is shared? Among whom? What information is disseminated?
3c. Strategies analysis	What strategies are possible (e.g., browsing, the analytical strategy)? What strategies do the actors prefer? How do the actors select the strategies to be used? What criteria do they use?
4. Organizational analysis	How is work divided among teams? What criteria are used? What is the nature of the organization? What are the organizational values? How is work divided among team members? What is the informal structure of the organization?
5. Analysis of actors' resources and values	What is the formal training of the actors? Area of expertise? Experience with the subject domain and the work domain? Personal priorities? Personal values?

school in Seattle working on their assignments for a horticulture class. The teacher explained each assignment in class, and the librarian added tips about how to find information. The students then went to a computer room in the library to spend the rest of the class time doing their homework. Table 11.2 offers a few examples of the study's findings. The work domain is the horticulture class.

11.3 Applying the Onion Model

Although the dimensions are laid out in a certain order, employing them in actual projects follows no fixed sequence. Due to the interdependence among the dimensions, a researcher moves from one dimension to another in an iterative process. The path of this movement is determined by the particular research problem at hand and by pragmatic considerations, such as the level of access a researcher has to the study participants and constraints on a study's budget.

Table 11.2
A sample of study results in each dimension

Dimensions	Examples of study results
1. Work environment analysis	The state of the current technology; graduation requirements; the availability of teachers with horticulture expertise to teach the class; school policies regarding instruction and computer use; quality control of teaching materials in horticulture
2. Work domain analysis	*Goals*: Teach students about plants outside the curriculum, information about horticulture available on the web, and how to search the web
	Constraints: The teacher did not have expertise in horticulture; the teacher was highly motivated to support students in their studies; students took the class to fulfill science course requirement but were not interested in the subject; students have almost no prior knowledge in the topic
	General functions: Teaching; finding information (information retrieval)
	Processes: Explain the task required by the assignment; give instructions on navigation and troubleshooting; circulate among students in the computer room
	Physical resources: Internet; the web; computers; networks; classroom; library; teacher; librarian
3a. Task analysis	For students:
	Goal: To get the teacher off their back; to have fun; to conserve intellectual efforts
	Constraints: The requirements of the assignments; the amount of help the teacher and librarian could offer during the search; experience in web searching
	General functions: Information retrieval (IR); asking for help
	Processes: Go to the computer room; find an available computer; key in a word in the search box; click on links; read the results; consult with other students; ask for the teacher's or the librarian's help
	Physical resources: Internet; the web; computers; teacher; librarian; other students

Table 11.2

(continued)

Dimensions	Examples of study results
3b. Decision analysis	Students' decisions for the task of IR: What is required by the assignment? What information do I need? How shall I plan the search? Which text on the screen can answer the questions in the assignment? Which sections of the results to copy into the assignment form? To whom to turn for help?
3c. Strategies analysis	Browsing was the only viable strategy; criterion for strategy selection: find the information without much effort
4. Organizational analysis	*Role allocation*: Students searched and gave tips to one another; the teacher explained the assignment, gave tips on how to search, and gave help during the search about both content of the assignment and how to search; the librarian gave tips in class on how to search and gave help during the search about both searching and the assignment
	Management style and collaboration: Very little organization of tasks; very little organization of collaboration among students and among teacher, librarian, and students; both teacher and librarian encouraged collaboration of any kind
5. Analysis of actors' resources and values	*Students' resources*: Educational background: grade 11 and 12 (age 17–18); about half were college bound; varied computer experience; varied experience in web surfing; little experience in information retrieval; no knowledge in the subject domain
	Students' personal preferences: To surf the web; to find information fast; to have all topics in one place; to have pictures and graphics (and would like more); to have updated information; to be able to access sites from all around the world; to have access to different kinds of materials

In the context of HII, the CWA dimensions represent the constraints on information interaction, starting with the external environment of the work domain and leading to the individual resources and values of the actors. Each dimension represents the constraints for the one nested in it. Thus, the work environment shapes how a workplace operates, and this mode of operation shapes the tasks that actors perform. The tasks, in turn, shape the decisions that actors make, and these decisions influence the actors' interaction with information, that is, the strategies they select. In addition, the actors' characteristics have an effect on their behavior, as does the social organization of the workplace. In general, the lower the layer, the greater the role actors play and the greater the independence they can show. A design engineer, for example, is usually the only one to select strategies for a web search; she can exercise more independence in strategy selection than in selecting the goals of a task, for instance. That is, the *actors' resources and values* dimension has the most diverse types of constraints, while at the same time it affords the actors the highest levels of participation and independence.

CWA assumes that while one can *describe* information interaction without taking these constraints into account, the best way to *analyze* information interaction is through an in-depth analysis of these constraints. Work analysis is, therefore, an analysis of the constraints that shape information interaction. Ordinarily, analyzing the constraints is a daunting task because it is difficult to decide which constraints to include in an analysis and what to leave out for each dimension. CWA assumes that within this richness and complexity there are "basic sources of regularity that underlie the responses of the work domain to human actions" (Vicente 1999). Work analysis focuses on these "basic sources of regularity," which are the constraints that shape actor behavior. These stable and behavior-shaping constraints are called *invariants* (see section 9.2.3.1). Concentrating on the analysis of invariants does not ignore or reduce the complexity in the environment since invariants can be highly complex. It merely focuses our attention on the elements in each dimension that have significant effect on information behavior.

The concept of *invariants* has also been transferred to the constraints-based design of information systems (see section 9.2.3.2). Such systems are designed to adapt to the actors' work in the realm of the invariants. At the same time, CWA recognizes that situational and individual factors influence information behavior. But designers cannot predict all the possible ways in which a system can support the work of all actors in all possible situations. As a result, a system that adapts to all possible situational and individual factors is unattainable. Actors have to adapt themselves to the system when a situation deviates from that predicted by the invariants; that is, actors will have to behave adaptively as well. It is the task of the designer to build systems that support actors when they adapt to the system's behavior. The goal is to design an information system that is adaptive to the actors' work in the realm of stable, behavior-shaping constraints, while at the same time enabling actors to adapt when situational and unpredictable factors arise.

CWA assumes a predictive power that is not deterministic because it recognizes the complexity in the studied phenomena. The constraints in each dimension create the *conditions* for actor behavior, but, as a general rule, uncovering them does not guarantee that a certain behavior will occur. Consider, for example, the decision about which strategy to employ (see section 5.4.2). Table 5.2 shows that browsing is useful for actors who have little experience and expertise in the subject domain and in searching, and are not pressed by time. However, one cannot predict that all people with few resources and more time will browse, not even that most of them will do so. For example, a student who has these attributes may find it important to impress his friends with his searching abilities and thus may try the analytical strategy when his friends are watching him. Even though the student is experiencing all the conditions that recommend the browsing strategy, other considerations have moved him to choose another one. Thus, even if the conditions for a certain behavior are in place, other considerations and situational conditions may result in a different behavior (see also section 4.4).

The CWA dimensions may support other types of research in HII, even though they were developed to guide design-oriented research. The dimensions can guide researchers who are studying information-seeking behavior in order to improve their understanding of the phenomena or to develop theories, for example. Investigating this behavior, both empirically and theoretically, researchers can review the dimensions and the constraints that have been uncovered in CWA-guided empirical studies of information seeking. This review will offer a range of elements that are likely to shape the particular behavior the researchers are investigating. For instance, the dimensions suggest that a researcher who studies search strategies can increase her understanding of this behavior if she considers the decisions the actors implement along with the strategies and the tasks that generated these decisions. Minimally, CWA provides a general structure for any type of HII study by pointing to the dimensions of elements that shape HII behavior.

11.4   Evaluation

Commonly, evaluation in the design of information systems is carried out *after* the initial design has produced at least a prototype, and its purpose is to evaluate the performance of the new system. Design that is guided by CWA, in contrast, begins with the evaluation of the *existing* system. Its purpose is to evaluate the match between the existing system and the constraints-induced behavior that was uncovered through work analysis. A CWA evaluation is directed by the dimensions, and the basis for its process is provided by the findings of the work analysis. Consequently, the evaluation leads directly to specific design requirements for a new system or to recommendations for system improvement. For retrieval systems, the evaluation seeks to determine if the system supports the *search process*, given the constraints in each dimension and the behavior they shape. That is, for each constraints-induced searching behavior in a dimension, the evaluator asks: Does the system match the behavior?

An example from the study we have previously discussed (Fidel et al. 1999) may demonstrate this procedure. For the dimension *strategy analysis*, we investigated the strategies the students could employ and the ones they actually used. The analysis showed that, given the students' resources, *browsing* was the most useful strategy for them, which they indeed used almost exclusively (see section 5.4.2 for a discussion of this case). To evaluate the web with regard to search strategies, we asked: Given the work that these students do and its context, does the web support strategy selection, strategy implementation, and strategy shifts?

Web design matched strategy selection by providing the functionality for employing the *browsing* strategy.[6] There was no support, however, for the selection process itself because the web provided no information about the other strategies that were available. Technically, it was easy to implement the browsing strategy; students had to enter a term into the search box (which was easy to find) and continue by clicking on links (which were easy to locate). But the strategic and analytical facets of strategy implementation received no support. Several obstacles reduced the effectiveness of browsing. Students had difficulty selecting the correct link when the link did not provide enough information for them to understand what the site's topic was or to decide whether the site was on the subject of their search. In addition, the web did not match two constraints: the method the students used to employ the strategy and their preference for assessing a site's relevance by its graphics.

When browsing, students selected a "home base" from which they followed a chain of links, planning to return to the base and try another chain if the first was not productive. But the web had no facility to support the students when they were ready to return to their base. When they could not get back to the base, they got lost and had to start a new search. The lack of support in assessing the relevance of a site was another obstacle to browsing. Given the relatively large number of sites one examines during browsing, it is reasonable to require that a site's relevance could be assessed in a glance. The students employed the graphics on a site to determine its subject and its nature, whether academic, commercial, or just fun. Although this strategy provided for faster browsing than one that was guided by reading the text on home pages, the graphics on web sites often do not convey the site's attributes, and some sites do not even have graphics.

The web supported shifting from any strategy to the browsing strategy, for at any point of a search, one could begin clicking through a chain links. Any other shifts required new searches. Thus, when a student realized during browsing that the *analytical* strategy would increase the focus of her search—and she had an idea how to implement it—she had to start a new search. This situation presented a dilemma: Should she begin a new search and lose the possibly useful sites she had collected during browsing, or should she continue to browse even though a strategy shift might increase the effectiveness of her search?

In addition to demonstrating the evaluation procedure, this example shows the requirements that can be derived from evaluations. Some examples of requirements for web design, including both interface and functionality, that could support the students' searching follow:[7]

• Provide information about the strategies that are available

• Make a link's presentation informative about the site to which it links and its relation to the search query

• Provide for a fast and easy return to a "home base"

• Create and display graphic presentations of metadata elements[8]

• Support shifts between strategies.[9]

This approach to system evaluation is essentially different from that information retrieval (IR) researchers commonly employ to evaluate retrieval systems. The most significant variance is in the purpose for which an evaluation is conducted. IR experiments are focused on comparing and ranking retrieval systems according to their performance. This comparison is sometimes made to identify the "best" systems among a set of systems, and at other times to compare two or more systems that are the same except for one component: the one that is being tested. The best design for the component is the design employed in the winning system. In contrast, an evaluation guided by the CWA dimensions assesses any component of a system that is found pertinent by comparing it to the constraints on the system users and the resulting behavior—rather than a comparison to other systems—to determine whether and how its usefulness can be enhanced.

This difference in purpose is also reflected in the nature of the criteria employed for the evaluation. IR researchers have aimed at the smallest number of measurements for a system's performance. While precision and recall are still in use, there have been attempts to find a single performance measurement with very little success.[10] Using the CWA's dimensions, on the other hand, an evaluator is free to employ all the evaluation criteria he judges pertinent for the new design.

Most importantly, IR evaluations look at *system performance* and do not lead directly to design requirements. Evaluations guided by the CWA dimensions look at the support a system offers to the *search process* and lead directly to design requirements.

11.5   The Dimensions for Analysis: Conclusions

The dimensions of CWA define the context of HII behavior and provide a framework for its analysis. CWA focuses, then, on the analysis of the constraints in a local context, that is, the elements that both limit and enable work and HII behavior (i.e., the elements that shape them). CWA offers dimensions for analysis but no specific constraints, variables, or factors that warrant investigation. The analysis is carried out to *identify* and study the constraints for a given context, assuming that each context presents its own constraints.

CWA has several distinct attributes that are useful for the study of human information interaction and for the design of information systems. Most importantly, it provides a holistic approach that makes it possible to account for several dimensions simultaneously. In addition, the framework and the structure of the dimensions facilitate an in-depth examination of the various dimensions of a context. A study of a local context is, therefore, a multidisciplinary examination with the purpose of understanding the interaction between people and information in that context. These two attributes make the framework a powerful guide for the evaluation and design of information systems for the context under investigation because, in reality, all dimensions—personal, social, and organizational—play a role simultaneously and interdependently.

The dimensional structure allows each researcher to employ his favorite epistemological approach. While the framework is based on a set of conceptual and epistemological constructs, it provides a structure for the analysis of information interaction, rather than subscribing to specific theories or models. As Sanderson (2003) explained, "the scientific foundations of CWA are various—a 'conceptual marketplace' as Rasmussen described it—because they have been appropriated to fulfill a practical need." One can employ a wide variety of theories, methods, or tools that may be deemed helpful for the analysis of a specific situation. This flexibility turns the focus of an investigation to the phenomenon under study, rather than to testing and verifying models and theories or to the employment of a particular methodology. At the same time, CWA has built-in mechanisms to carry out rigorous and systematic research. It provides several templates to support both analysis and modeling, in addition to the dimensions for analysis. One of these templates is an abstraction hierarchy: the means-end analysis, which I will discuss in the next chapter.

Human information interaction is a complex phenomenon reflecting the variability inherent to human cognitive processes and the highly complex contexts in which humans operate in the modern world. The CWA dimensions (see figure 11.1) provide a first step for dealing with this complexity. They parcel out the investigated phenomenon but preserve the relationships among the resulting parts. They indicate that some attributes are organizational, some are determined by the work and subject domains, and others are cultural or individual. Each dimension, however, is complex as well. How can these complexities be made compliant with the requirements of the design process?

To harness complexity, CWA provides analytical tools for each dimension:

The analysis of *actors' resources and values*—which identifies characteristics of the community of actors under study—is carried out according to a stable set of attributes: the expertise, priorities, preferences, and values of the actors. Empirical research has demonstrated that these attributes shape actor behavior. Each community of actors may be characterized by additional traits that a researcher uncovers during a study. Thus, the analytical tool for this innermost dimension is the set of stable attributes.

The complexity associated with *strategies analysis*—which examines which strategies are *possible* for each task and decision—is highly related, on the other hand, to the definition of the term *strategy*. Scholars have coined various definitions for the term, most of which are on a concrete level of specific cognitive and physical actions (see section 5.1). Such interpretations of the term make strategy analysis highly difficult, if not impossible, because it requires the identification of all potential strategies, which are countless. CWA provides a definition that facilitates strategy analysis—an analysis that leads to the formation of design requirements. *Strategy* is defined as a *category* of "cognitive task procedures that transform an initial state of knowledge into a final state of knowledge" (Vicente 1999, 220), rather than as the specific actions that are taken for this transformation (see section 5.4). This construal has made it possible to empirically identify five strategies in decision making: the browsing, analytical, empirical, known-site, and similarity strategies. The analyses of the other CWA dimensions reveal the constraints that shape searching behavior and these in turn identify the possible strategies (see section 5.4.2 for an example). In addition, a researcher observes actor actions and maps them to the set of five strategies and thus understands how each strategy is materialized.[1]

Decision analysis is guided by a specific analytical tool to analyze individual decisions. Complex decision-making processes are challenging to analyze because they do not progress in an orderly manner and sometimes it may even be difficult to understand the problem that the decision is supposed to resolve. To arrive at a description of the process that lends itself to analysis, CWA researchers map the observed activities to the decision ladder (see section 4.3), which is specifically tailored for this purpose. This tool outlines the stages of a rational, ideal decision-making process. It identifies each information-processing event that leads to a new state of knowledge, and arranges them in a rational order, beginning with becoming alert to the situation and ending with the actual execution of the decision. Once a decision is mapped, it is ready for analysis.

The dimensions *decision analysis*, *task analysis*, and *work environment* are all analyzed with an abstraction-hierarchy tool that provides a *means-ends analysis* (MEA). MEA may prove useful in analyses relating to other dimensions as well. When it is employed, each unit under investigation is considered a system. Thus, a work domain is a system, a task is a subsystem of the work domain, and a decision is a subsystem of the task.

12.1   Means-Ends Analysis: An Abstraction Hierarchy

Means-ends analysis, as an abstraction hierarchy, is guided by a template in which the top level is the most abstract facet of the analysis and the one at the base is the most concrete. In MEA, the top level represents the goals and constraints of the system,[2] while the bottom level addresses the physical resources that are used by the system (see table 12.1). One level down from *goals and constraints* is a more concrete concept: the priorities of the system, that is, the ways that the goals can be materialized given the constraints. The next levels get gradually more concrete down to the last level, which is the most concrete.

This abstraction hierarchy provides an analytical tool to thoroughly investigate the system under study and its subsystems. Returning again to our example of the high

Table 12.1

The means-ends analysis abstraction hierarchy

Goals/constraints	What are the ultimate goals and purposes? What affects the system but cannot be changed?
Priorities	What can *actually* be attained to achieve the goals, given the constraints?
Functions	What is done in general terms?
Processes	What actual activities take place?
Resources	What is being used to perform the activities?

school students and their homework (Fidel et al. 1999) may help to illustrate the abstraction hierarchy. Recapping the general situation, we found that the teacher was assigned to teach the class even though he was not an expert on the subject; similarly, most of the students were not interested in horticulture and took the class only to fulfill the science requirements for graduation. The students had very little experience in using computers and no experience in web searching—some had practiced web surfing and some had learned word processing. In class, the teacher explained the assignment, gave some searching tips, and invited the librarian to add instructions about searching. They all then went to the library where the computers were located. The students searched the web, with the teacher and librarian available for help. The teacher had very little knowledge or experience in web searching, and the librarian, while being more knowledgeable and experienced, felt she needed additional training.

Some of the elements in the MEA of the task of teaching horticulture are presented in table 12.2.[3]

While each level in the template has its own degree of abstraction, researchers are free to choose the amount of detail that fits their study for each level. The amount of detail depends on the study objectives and on the reality that is being investigated and uncovered. In addition to facilitating an in-depth study of a phenomenon, MEA is a tool to construct explanations for the study findings. The creation of such explanations is supported by the means-ends relationships between each two adjacent levels.

The abstraction hierarchy shows the *means* to carry out each level and the *ends* that it produces. That is why it is labeled a template of means-ends analysis. Consider the function *teaching* in the analysis of the teaching horticulture task (table 12.2). The processes listed in the level below (e.g., explaining the searching task, explaining navigation principles, and providing a few relevant URLs) explain how the teacher and the librarian taught (i.e., carried out the function "teaching")—that is, the means

Table 12.2

An example of task analysis: teaching horticulture

Goals/constraints	*Goals*: To have the students know about: (a) plants outside the curriculum, (b) information on horticulture available on the web, and (c) how to search the web
	Constraints: The students' interest in the subject; their experience in web searching; graduation requirements; the teacher's and the librarian's work load; the web-searching experience of the teacher and the librarian; the state of the technology
Priorities	Integrating web searching into the curriculum; involving the librarian in class sessions
Functions	Preparing class sessions; teaching
Processes	*For teaching*: Explaining the searching task; explaining navigation principles; providing a few relevant URLs; troubleshooting during students' searching
Resources	Internet connection; computers; the web; the library; the teacher; the librarian

by which they gave instructions. At the same time, the function *teaching* led the teacher to a certain end (the priorities), such as integrating web searching into the curriculum. Similarly, the results of the processes in which the teacher and the librarian were involved (i.e., their ends)—such as troubleshooting during students' searching—were their way to teach (the function). The resources—such as the Internet connection, the computers, and the web—were the means by which they carried out the processes. Generally speaking, each level represents the means for carrying out the level above it, and the ends of the level below it.

Another way to formulate this relationship is to observe that each level explains the level below it—that is, *why* the level is in place—and shows *how* the level above it is carried out. This means-ends chain connects the top and the bottom levels. Consider an MEA template that is based on the librarian as a resource (table 12.3). A consecutive chain of *why* questions leads from the librarian (at the bottm level) to the teacher's goals (at the top level), as demonstrated in table 12.4.

At the same time, beginning with the top level, asking a chain of *how* questions leads us to the resources, as demonstrated in table 12.5.

This example shows that the MEA template is not only an effective tool for uncovering elements in the work domain, task, or decision systems, but can also explain actor behavior. It helps to lay out how actors are engaged to achieve their goals, and why they use certain tools. In addition, MEA supports predictions of the consequences of changes in any element in the template. Suppose there was no librarian in the

Table 12.3

A very short example of means-ends analysis based on the librarian as a resource

Goals/constraints	How to search the web
Priorities	Integrating web searching into the curriculum; involving the librarian in class sessions
Functions	Teaching
Processes	Explaining navigation principles; troubleshooting
Resources	The librarian

Table 12.4

A chain of *why* questions leading from the concrete to the abstract

Resources	The librarian
Why question	*Why have the librarian?*
Processes	(For the purpose of) explaining navigation principle; troubleshooting
Why question	*Why explain?*
Functions	(For the purpose of) teaching
Why question	*Why teach?*
Priorities	(For the purpose of) integrating web searching into the curriculum
Why question	*Why this integration?*
Goals/constraints	(For the purpose of teaching the students) how to search the web

Table 12.5

A chain of *how* questions leading from the abstract to the concrete

Goals/constraints	How to search the web
How question	*How did the student know how to search the web?*
Priorities	(By) involving the librarian in class sessions
How question	*How was the librarian involved?*
Functions	(By) teaching
How question	*How did she teach?*
Processes	(By) explaining navigation principles; troubleshooting
How question	*How did she explain principles and troubleshooting?*
Resources	(By using) Internet connection; computers; the web; the librarian

Table 12.6
The template that facilitates means-ends analysis

Goals/constraints	What				
	↓	Why			
Priorities	How	↑			
		What			
		↓	Why		
Functions		How	↑		
			What		
			↓	Why	
Processes			How	↑	
				What	
				↓	Why
Resources				How	↑
					What

school: How would that affect the teacher's task? Students would not understand navigation principles and teaching would not be complete. As a result, integrating web searching into the curriculum would be incomplete, which in turn would prevent students from knowing how to search the web. Alternately, suppose the teacher had much experience and expertise in web searching. This additional competency would eliminate his priority to involve the librarian in teaching students how to search the web; in fact, he may not need the help of the librarian at all.

Table 12.6 provides a general presentation of the means-ends relationships.

The five levels of abstraction presented here have proven highly effective for the analysis of actors and their information-seeking behavior. Projects to analyze actor behavior of another kind may suggest other levels. Vicente (1999), for instance, used similar but different types of levels when he analyzed the work domain of process control: functional purpose, abstract function, generalized function, physical function, and physical form (173). That is, the selection of the levels and their number depends on the researcher and the purpose of the study. Nevertheless, the levels presented here, or approximations to them, have been used in most CWA studies.

12.1.1 Harnessing Complexity: Conclusions

The means-ends analysis template facilitates the building of formative models that support the design of effective information systems. This facilitation is made possible by several central attributes of the template:

Preserving complexity The MEA preserves complexity because each level provides a different description of the system *as a whole*, rather than breaking it into isolated parts. That is, it analyzes the system as a whole but from different views. In addition, it provides a good mechanism for coping with complexity because each upper level provides the context for the lower one. That is, it reflects how constraints in one level affect the level below. Another mechanism to preserve complexity is afforded by the structure of the abstraction hierarchy in which *goals* are at the most abstract level. A complex system is likely to have more than one goal, which adds to the complexity of the analysis. However, because *goals* are at the top of the hierarchy, researchers can investigate the goals one at a time.

Returning to our horticulture teaching scenario, suppose another goal in the teaching task was to help students receive good grades on nationwide examinations. This goal would bring up a new set of constraints, such as the questions in the specific examinations, the standards for grading, and the preparation students receive from other sources. If the teacher's task were analyzed more completely, all goals and the related constraints would have been included in the first level. Yet in the analysis of the task—that is, in the process of identifying the chain of means and ends—each goal could be analyzed separately. Some constraints, priorities, and functions would be common to all goals, and others would be unique.

Providing explanations   MEA explicitly uncovers the relationship between the levels—relationships that provide the basis for an explanation of the observed behavior. Moving up the hierarchy provides an understanding of the system and moving down provides an understanding of how the system works to achieve its goals.

Supporting crisp definitions of objects of study   When investigating complex systems, it is difficult to establish clear definitions of systems and subsystems. MEA supports the creation of a system definition (see section 1.2) by providing a template to (a) define the system boundary (the first level), and (b) build a general inventory of system elements and some of their relationships.

12.2   Challenges to the Application of CWA

Because of its built-in flexibility, cognitive work analysis provides no recipes for its deployment. While other research frameworks often instruct researchers about what methods to use and what questions to ask (e.g., Ingwersen and Järvelin 2005; Sonnenwald 1999), CWA does not subscribe to a set of methods or research questions. It offers a general approach, and requires the individual researcher to select the appropriate methods and the specific questions to ask, based on the phenomenon that is being investigated and the researcher's view. Therefore, employing the framework entails more effort on the part of the researcher than other approaches and adds to the complexity of a research project.

Moreover, CWA itself is a complex framework and requires investment in practicing its application and in adapting it to a new problem. Even though the CWA dimensions and the analytical tools are highly structured, applying them is complex. While the CWA structure can preserve the complexity inherent to the studied phenomenon, it is the task of researchers to fit the complex reality they are investigating into the structure. This process is not straightforward and requires interpretation, deliberations, and iterations. Using CWA necessitates a departure from focusing on descriptions of behaviors, which is the dominant approach in information behavior studies. Looking on objects of study with new lenses engages scholars in added deliberations as well. While experience with CWA decreases the effort involved in fitting reality into the framework's structure, applying CWA is still complex and is likely to attract scholars who enjoy the challenge of complexity.

CWA has been criticized by both scholars and designers. Some scholars maintain that CWA cannot be part of scholarly research because the findings of a study guided by this approach cannot be generalized. The requirement for generalizability is important in the positivist theoretical tradition, although it is ignored by most scholars who subscribe to interpretive traditions. In a similar vein, some scholars claim that CWA has not contributed to scholarly research because it is a practical method with no scholarly implications.[4]

The issue of generalizability is not unique to CWA but is present in all other in-context studies (see section 7.3). There are, however, methods to derive some level of generalization from in-context studies. In particular, CWA provides a framework for building generalization, which is carried out in an incremental process. The findings of a study in system A can be extended to system B if the constraints in each dimension are the same. Clearly, this exact situation is unlikely to occur, but an extension can also be carried out when the constraints are similar. In this case, generalizing to system B involves a comparison between the elements in each dimension and identifying commonalities and differences. The subsequent generalization includes the common elements, but also the findings of differences and their reasons.[5] In a study of collaborative information retrieval (e.g., Poltrock et al. 2003), for example, our team found that the information behavior of two teams—one in the software industry and the other in the hardware industry—had the same threads but differed in intensity. Employing CWA, we identified the reasons for this difference.[6]

The criticism that CWA has no place in the corridors of scholarship is obviously influenced by subjective opinions because there are no agreed-upon standards for what constitutes scholarly work. Yet this issue brings to light a basic methodological characteristic of CWA: It has been developed, and is still being developed, through a cross-fertilization of empirical and conceptual research. The best way to further develop CWA is through empirical study of actors in local contexts, and the best support to applying CWA in empirical research is an understanding of its conceptual underpinning. Thus, every study employing the CWA framework has both practical and conceptual implications.

Designers who consider applying CWA in their design work are thwarted by the resources that are required to conduct a CWA investigation. They also find CWA's lack of a method for deriving a system's requirements from the results of the analysis a major drawback. A CWA study is resource-demanding because it calls for an in-depth understanding of the constraints and processes in a work domain. As a result, a typical study involves an extensive field study in addition to the laboratory experimentation that is needed for the design itself. Investment in CWA investigation is highly beneficial for the long term because a CWA study is independent of the technology used at the time of the study and because it investigates invariants—that is, relatively stable constraints. The findings of such a study would, therefore, be relevant long-term and remain applicable with changes in technology. Most approaches to the design of information systems require many fewer resources but are vulnerable to such change, with the result that the design becomes obsolete in a relatively short time. In the long run, applying CWA might possibly be less expensive than the use of other approaches. However, in the dynamic, competitive, and profit-driven economy of today, most investments are short term,[7] and this window reduces the likelihood of applying CWA.[8] Given this reality, a future, useful development to enhance CWA might be the creation of tools that would reduce the resources required in its application without losing much of its power.

Another project for future CWA development is the building of a systematic method to derive requirements from CWA analyses. In HIB, for instance, each study that generated requirements employed its own method, but these methods have not been documented. Generally speaking, a method to derive requirements is shaped by the type of work domain under study and by the researcher's worldview, experience, and expertise. Therefore, it is unlikely that a single, "best" CWA method will be found because the framework can be used in almost every work domain and can be guided by any epistemological view that accepts realism. To arrive at a starting point for developing a method for constructing requirements for a particular type of work domain necessitates a body of studies that have derived requirements for the domain and an investigation of the methods they used. An example of such a domain is the area of ecological interface design (EID). A few researchers (e.g., Bisantz and Burns 2009; Burns and Hajdukiewicz 2004; Jenkins et al. 2009) crafted procedures for the application of CWA to interface design for process control systems—procedures that include requirements building as well. These procedures were based on many studies and much experience in developing such interfaces. For other areas, CWA provides a structure that supports deriving requirements from a study's findings. It is possible, but not certain, that methods and procedures for specific domains will be developed in the future.

To conclude, applying CWA introduces various challenges. Some are inherent to the framework—such as its openness to various epistemologies and its complexity—and others can be addressed with future research and development—such as the lack of a set method to derive design requirements.

12.3   Cognitive Work Analysis: Conclusions

Cognitive work analysis is an ecological approach to creating constraints-based formative models of human information interaction in a work domain (see section 9.2.3). As such, the CWA framework offers a bridge between the study of HII and the design of information systems. In addition, it addresses various challenges to systems design.

A CWA project can provide applications beyond systems design and can support the improvement of several other elements in the work domain, in addition to the design of a new system. Since the analysis is of the work and the work domain—rather than being limited to actor behavior—a detailed understanding of both has the potential to point to improvements in other dimensions of the work domain. In the mCity project (see section 9.2.3.2), for example, we found that certain changes in the training of workers, the workflow, and the management style would produce more effective use of technology and would increase work efficiency. In addition, CWA's dimensions and analytical tools provide a solid and stable structure for conceptual investigations. Since the tools and dimensions were developed and tested through empirical research, they can guide conceptual research that is relevant to practice.

In summary, CWA contributes to the study of HII in context in various ways. While it does not identify the specific context-related variables that affect human information interaction for all actors, it delineates the dimensions that together shape and contribute to this interaction. Moreover, these dimensions have been developed through many empirical studies of human interaction with systems in the workplace, and can be used to analyze this interaction and aid in the design of information systems. Through its dimensions, analytical tools, and formative approach, CWA has proven highly effective in investigating the complex and dynamic nature of the context and the phenomena that HII research addresses. While to date only a few information retrieval systems have been designed based on this approach, these systems have proven highly effective and have impacted future designs. Because CWA has been developed through empirical research, future research in HII will not only result in requirements for the design of additional information systems—it will also further refine the general application of CWA to their design.

V An Ecological Approach to Information Behavior: Conclusions

The ecological approach focuses on the environment[1]—that is, it gives primary importance to the context in which information interaction is situated. As Vicente (1999)
writes, it "suggests that … analysis should begin with, and be driven by, an explicit
analysis of the constraints that the environment imposes on action" (55). The ecological approach addresses cognitive constraints as well, yet it is different from the *user-
centered* approach. This difference stems from the origins of the approaches: The
ecological approach is based on the systems approach, while the user-centered approach
originated from basic research in psychology.

Vicente (1990) explained that, in contrast to the user-centered approach, the
primary emphasis of the ecological approach is the system. The reasoning for this
approach is that

Knowledge of the entire system cannot be built up solely from knowledge of the parts. Emergent
properties exist as a function of system structure, and understanding of these properties is only
possible by knowing how the parts are organized. As a result, from the systems perspective the
human is viewed as one of many system elements, not as a privileged entity. (493)

Because the human element has a great impact on system performance, Vicente added,
properties of human cognition, perception, and action receive much attention. Focusing primarily on the actor, however, steers attention away from the global factors that
impact the actor's information interaction.

The ecological approach directs researchers of sociotechnical systems to study the
specific (that which pertains to a community of actors), rather than the *general* (that
which applies to all humans).[2] It gives primacy to the study of the environment, but
since no environment can be recognized in the case of a system that has no boundaries, any community of actors that is selected for an ecological study has to be defined
and bounded. In fact, of course, if there are no boundaries, there is no system by definition. General studies carry their own value and contributions but they cannot
be ecological. Similarly, a single ecological study cannot be general.[3] Therefore, a

discussion about ecological research is inherently about studies of context-specific systems. Focusing on the local allows for in-depth investigations and a thorough understanding of the phenomenon under study.

The goal of many scholarly fields is to improve the quality of life in some aspect. The goal of human information interaction (HII) is to better the conditions that facilitate interaction with information. How far is the HII scholarly community from achieving this goal? It is too early to investigate the impact that various HII areas have on information interaction—primarily because many of them are at early stages of development. The earliest HII area, and one that is fully centered on HII, is human information behavior (HIB). Its research began in the early 1960s, and it has been drawing an increasing number of scholars. Today, HIB is a well-established and active area within information science. Nevertheless, its contribution to improving support for information interaction has been very limited, focusing only on human-based systems, even though several of its scholars have emphasized the value of producing research results that are relevant to practice.

The critical review of HIB research presented in this book has pointed to the achievements of this area and also to its limitations. The review led to the suggestion that using the conceptual framework of cognitive work analysis (CWA) has the potential to enhance the impact of HIB research on both theoretical and practical developments. One of the advantages of CWA as a conceptual framework for HIB research is its ecological approach. An ecological approach leads to a holistic view of the phenomenon under study, which is required in order to understand the complexity inherent to information interaction of any kind. A holistic view is especially necessary for research that aims at enhancing practice because information practice cannot avoid complexity, while research for other purposes may employ a reductionist approach and still be effective.

In addition to being an ecological approach, CWA has other unique attributes that have the potential to enhance the contributions of research, such as its analytical approach to dealing with complexity and the framework of dimensions that guides research. Therefore, when considering the contributions of CWA to the study of information interaction, it is helpful to identify those contributions that can be offered by any ecological approach and those that are distinctive to CWA. Similarly, it is useful to make a distinction between contributions that are relevant only to HIB and those that might bring benefit to other areas in HII as well.

What, then, is the contribution of the ecological approach in general, and that of CWA in particular, to our understanding of information interaction in HII in general, and specifically in HIB? How can this approach enhance the impact of HII research? The following chapter is an examination of this question.

13 Enhancing the Impact of Research in Human Information Interaction

Research in human information interaction (HII) has the potential to improve both its conceptual basis and the practice of information interaction in various ways. Clearly, materializing this potential requires that research in a particular area be conducive to theoretical developments and relevant to the design of systems that support information interaction—whether human or computer-based. Yet these requirements are not sufficient; realizing this potential also necessitates a conceptual basis that is continuous—rather than a fragmented puzzle of conceptual constructs—and research strands that touch one another—rather than strands in isolation. That is, it requires a research area with some level of convergence. Cognitive work analysis (CWA) can contribute to both design and research convergence.

13.1 Implications for Design

Investigating environment constraints is not foreign to research in human-technology interaction. Scientists in human factors (e.g., Vicente 1999) and human-computer interaction (e.g., Gay and Hembrooke 2004; Nardi and O'Day 2000) have systematically studied the environments in which interaction with technology takes place. They have recognized that studying the constraints under which human interaction occurs provides for a deeper understanding of human behavior during this interaction, which in turn leads to an enhanced design.

As Vicente (1990) put it, "Design is fundamentally concerned with constraints" (493). With an ecological approach, the design of information systems gives priority to environmental constraints whether organizational, social, or cognitive. The advantage of placing primary emphasis on investigating the environment is twofold.

First, a system is designed to support the activities of actors, whether in a local community or the whole human race. Since it is not realistic to design a host of systems each supporting one individual, it is more useful to consider design requirements that benefit a community as a whole, rather than its individual members—that is, to pursue design that is based on the constraints that are typical of the community. The source of typical constraints is the system in which the members operate—that is, the environment of their activities.[1] Within the system in which actors are situated, their activities and behavior serve the goals of the system, rather than their individual goals. As examples, an academic researcher's interaction with information serves the goals of the academic institution of which she is a part and of other organizations such as the scholarly community, while a homemaker's interaction with information about everyday life serves the goals of the family, whether the immediate or extended one. The typical constraints of academic researchers would include the structure of academic institutions, access to funding, and publishing rules and convention, among other constraints.

Actors in a community may share cognitive attributes as well. For example, academic researchers are likely to possess well-developed analytical skills and an inclination to investigate the unknown. Though some researchers might be guided primarily by their intuition, all researchers must have some level of analytical skills to perform their work to their satisfaction and to that of others. The requirement for such skills stems from the nature of the work researchers do—that is, from their environment—and therefore having these skills is typical of researchers.[2] But researchers are not likely to share a common cognitive style or personality. Both cognitive style and personality shape a researcher's interaction with information to a degree, but designing a separate system for each cognitive style and personality combination is not a viable proposition.[3] Therefore, a design that is based only on typical cognitive attributes of researchers, with no consideration of the environment that requires these attributes, is not likely to produce a system that serves researchers in the best way possible.

In general, the design of a system for a community of actors, rather than for a single member, would be most beneficial if it is based primarily on environmental constraints.

Second, one of the goals of an information system is "To provide a good fit between the support provided by the information system and the work demands" (Vicente 1999, 47). Consider, for example, a researcher searching a library catalog who types in keywords and receives a message that the collection includes no documents for the request. In this case, however, there actually are such documents, but the query she typed included two typos. Automatically assuming that all online systems check for spelling errors, she does not check her spelling or consider the possibility that her search failed because of typos. As a result, she concludes that no items are available on the subject. This example is a case in which the user's mental model of how the system operates does not fit reality. The role of an information system is to secure a fit between reality and the user's mental model.[4] For a system to play this role, its designer needs to understand the reality in which actors operate, that is, the environment of the actor's interaction with information. A design that is based only on cognitive constraints, such as a user's mental model, is limited in its ability to secure a fit between a user's cognitive perceptions and reality.

Some of the HII fields have successfully based their systems design on cognitive constraints. For instance, human-computer interaction (HCI), which has based most of its interface-design research on cognitive research, is a flourishing field with many applications for practice. This success is not surprising because a system interface closely relates to cognitive characteristics such as perception and comprehension. Nevertheless, interface design that is based only on cognitive constraints can be improved when environmental ones are considered as well. The case of the academic researcher and her library catalog is an example of the contribution of environmental constraints to interface design. A researcher's work often requires much information that can be retrieved from a variety of sources. As a result, most researchers build their mental model of a search system on their experience in searching a variety of systems, most of which protect against typos. It is natural that they would assume that the online catalog in their library operates the same way. Were a catalog designer aware of this experience and its influence on actors—rather than focusing only on the academic mental model—the catalog could have been designed to alert its users to the the real-life possibility that a typo may have occurred.

While cognitive constraints play an important role in interface design, there is no evidence that such constraints affect the design of other aspects of an information system, such as its content and functionality. At the same time, it is clear that content and functionality are both shaped primarily by environmental constraints. Environmental constraints of an information system's content include the information that is obtainable at the time of the design, the subject matter that the system is to cover, and the external policy that directs the flow of information into a system. Similarly, the design of system functionality must consider the technology available at that time, the requirements of the task for which information is sought, and the budget, among other environmental constraints. On the other hand, decisions about the display of information are based on the cognitive attributes of actors to insure that they understand the information on the screen in the most effective way.

As an ecological approach, the conceptual framework of cognitive work analysis (CWA) views information interaction as an element in a system, rather than focusing on the individual actor. It goes further, identifying the dimensions of the elements in

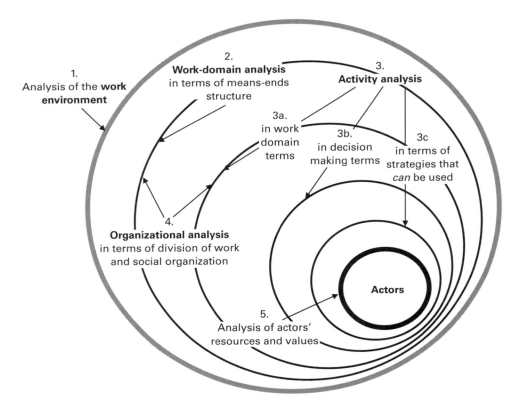

Figure 13.1
CWA's dimensions of analysis.

the environment of the interaction. Thus, the seven CWA dimensions in the onion model are of the environmental constraints that have been shown to shape interaction with information (see figure 13.1).[5] The elements in each dimension are uncovered for each particular community in a work domain, although some elements in a dimension are common to all communities in the domain, such as management style in an organization.

CWA views the interaction itself as a nucleus and analyzes its environment. Centering the analysis on a process leads to the design of information systems that support the *process* of interaction, which results in the design of systems that are more robust than systems that are designed only to achieve interaction *outcome* of high quality. Systems that are developed in the area of information retrieval (IR) illustrate this point. It has always been assumed that high-quality retrieved sets—that is, the outcomes of the process of information retrieval—are those that include a maximum number of relevant items and a minimum of irrelevant ones. But these criteria for quality may not apply to all individual searches. Actors who interact with an IR system when they are still crystallizing their request might find it beneficial to examine irrelevant items, and actors with limited time may appreciate just a few items on the subject.

A well-supported process is likely to produce a better outcome than a process with less support. Systems that support the interaction itself support users directly in their actions and empower them to conduct an interaction that will lead to the desired outcome for the particular search.[6] A system that supports the process of information retrieval—for instance, by increasing the effectiveness and efficiency of browsing or providing a mechanism to support query formulation—provides the flexibility needed for a user to conduct the search process that will retrieve sets that fit the desired criteria for the particular search. This flexibility is afforded by system features that support searching, from which the user can select the most helpful ones for a particular search. That is, systems that are designed to support the process of interaction with information can adapt themselves to changing requirements on the interaction outcome, and thus are flexible enough to afford users to interact with information through a process that is directed by the desired outcome.

CWA analyzes the environmental constraints to create a formative model of the interaction and its environment. A formative model describes requirements that must be satisfied so that behavior takes place in a new, desired way. It represents "what could be." The models created by CWA are constraints-based models: They describe the limitations on the interaction instead of describing how the interaction takes place or prescribing how it should take place. Basing the design of a new system on a description of the interaction that occurred through the old one restricts the new design from considering new ways of interaction. On the other hand, describing the constraints—that is, describing what could not be—leaves the field of possibilities open. Designers are not bound to consider only current modes of interaction and can envision all future modes within the boundaries created by the constraints.

In summary, with its ecological approach, CWA tailors design requirements for the community of future system users, and leads to the design of systems that secure a fit between a user's cognitive perceptions and reality. CWA-based design brings about systems that support the *process* of interaction, and thus allows the user the opportunity to conduct an interaction process that can lead to the outcome that is best for the situation. Additionally, the constraints-based model that is the outcome of the application of CWA is highly relevant for design because it lays out future possibilities for information interaction.

13.2   Research Convergence

In addition to creating requirements for the design of context-specific information systems,[7] CWA can enhance HII research and theoretical developments. Research in human information behavior (HIB) has suffered from persistent fragmentation, due to various conditions. For instance, the lack of a single fundamental theory may encourage researchers to hastily create new conceptual constructs to fill the void. An appreciation of the new and disregard for the old may lead to the same effect, as would the need to be original or the reluctance to invest the effort required to build on the work of others. Such conditions are created by the informal culture among scholars in a research area, which is created and sustained in turn by social and economic conditions in its environment, and cannot be altered without major changes. Nevertheless, it is constructive to consider mechanisms that may support convergence once a research area is ready for change.

CWA has the potential to connect various elements that have been fragmented in HIB research and in other HII areas. It can establish relations between

• theory and practice
• various areas of research expertise
• seemingly diverse areas of research
• various theoretical traditions and conceptual constructs.

Additionally, it can guide decisions about which variables to study.

Theory versus practice
HIB research is motivated by the wish to support information professionals as they assist users. Currently, however, a gap exists between scholarly research and applied information work, with most HIB research projects being inspired by considerations other than issues that challenge information work. Not surprisingly, research results seldom contribute to the work of information professionals. Maintaining cross-fertilization between theory and practice is particularly important in a domain that is based on a problem, rather than on disciplinary traditions, because the main purpose of problem-based domains is to address a situation that exists in real life, that is, in practice. One may even claim that, with no connections to practice, such a domain misses its reason for being and is likely to become marginal. Practice and theory nourish one another when practice formulates the phenomena to be investigated, and theory guides research that can bring improvements to practice. Information science—of which HIB is a part—is a problem-based field with a gap between theory and prac-

tice. While the gap has been lamented by both practitioners and scholars, it is not uncommon in information science to view the theoretical and applied components of the field as two separate conceptual branches (e.g., Bates 1999; Saracevic 1999).

The disconnect between theory and practice has also had an adverse effect on HIB research. Being removed from practice, scholars at times "discover" new insights that are rather commonsensical, sometimes through resource-demanding studies. Familiarity with practice can help researchers to distinguish between issues that require systematic research and those that are obvious to practitioners through their experience and do not warrant empirical research.[8]

The development and application of CWA have taken place where theory and practice assisted and relied on one another. CWA was first developed through a series of applied projects based on theoretical foundations, and has continued to be refined— and its application diversified—by researchers engaged in the design of context-specific systems. Though developed through practice, CWA is a conceptual framework rather than a collection of useful practices, and its continuous development is in the conceptual sphere rather than the practical one. At the same time, the approach is designed to guide investigations that generate findings that are directly relevant to practice. Applying CWA in HIB, for example, results in requirements for the design of an information system for the actors and work domain under study. That is, while being a conceptual construct, CWA is constantly being developed by practice—both of practitioners and researchers—and in return produces findings that enhance practice. Applying this conceptual framework, one is constantly moving between the practical and the conceptual.

Bridging research expertise
An HII research area may be fragmented because its community is composed of specialists in diverse fields, each developing within the bounds of their discipline. This fragmentation is in conflict with the very nature of HII, which investigates the interaction between distinct forces—humans and information—and therefore requires expertise in multiple disciplines.[9] It is not uncommon for fields in HII to focus on one force and neglect the other—an approach that excludes multidisciplinary collaboration. HIB and information retrieval (IR) are clear examples of this approach, the first focusing on the human side and the second on technological mechanisms to manipulate information in order to improve the interaction's outcome.

An ecological approach offers multidisciplinary collaboration because it investigates the environment, rather than limiting its focus to the examined phenomenon. Consider a hypothetical ecological study in personal information management (PIM) that investigates the record-keeping behavior of stay-at-home parents. The study explores not only their behavior but also the decisions they make, the tasks for which they keep records, the goals of the tasks, the value system under which they act, the family as an institution, and the image of the stay-at-home parents' role in their culture, among other environmental elements that shape PIM behavior. An in-depth understanding of this PIM behavior and its environment may require expertise in areas such as information behavior, cognitive science, decision making, computer technology, sociology, and cultural studies. In other words, it encourages a multidisciplinary collaboration.

Clearly, multidisciplinary collaborations have the potential to bridge interdisciplinary gaps, and they do not necessarily require an ecological approach. However, not all collaborations of this type lead to decreasing the gap among the various areas of expertise involved. A multidisciplinary project may assign each specialist a discrete part of the investigation without establishing connections among the project's parts. An ecological approach, while being only one of the approaches that can serve as a conduit for multidisciplinary collaborations, *invites* such collaborations because of its very nature. A common practice in many disciplines is to investigate a phenomenon from a single disciplinary aspect. Yet the phenomenon's environment is almost always composed of several types of elements and therefore calls for investigations from several disciplinary angles. Moreover, some integration of the various areas of expertise is likely to occur because scholars are investigating the *same* phenomenon with a variety of disciplinary lenses.

My research experience has convinced me that collaboration in CWA-guided HIB research helps build strong connections among various areas of expertise. Using my expertise in HIB, I have collaborated with experts from diverse fields. In a project that investigated work teams when they collaborated in information retrieval, for instance, I worked together with experts in HCI, in IR, and in computer-supported cooperative work. In addition to our enriching one another's knowledge of the other fields, the project had a strong technological component that was closely integrated with information behavior. Similarly, in a project that examined the information behavior of sanitation field workers in the City of Seattle (Fidel et al., 2007), our team incorporated expertise in management of information systems, knowledge management, and information ethics. The project's outcomes were many. In addition to linking organizational and social conditions with information behavior, the team expanded the CWA dimensions by developing a detailed structure for the organizational analysis dimension (see figure 13.1).

In conclusion, applying an ecological approach is likely to lead to some level of disciplinary convergence in HII research projects.

Seemingly diverse areas of research

HIB scholarship that considers the context in which information behavior takes place makes a clear distinction between behavior at the workplace and that outside it, in everyday life. Most HIB scholars focus their theoretical and applied investigations on one setting or the other, and models of information behavior in context never mix the type of context.[10]

It is reasonable to assume that the information behavior in each of the two types of contexts is distinct because of the basic differences between the two. One basic divide is created by the rules and conventions actors follow. On the job, they are influenced by the workplace as an organization and by professional standards, while in everyday life actors conform to social and cultural conventions. As a result of the rules/conventions divide, most workplace studies focus on the tasks and professional responsibilities of the actors, while everyday studies highlight social and cultural aspects of life.

Why should workplace studies ignore social and cultural aspects, and why should everyday-life studies ignore the nature of the tasks performed and the responsibilities of the actors involved? The HIB literature presents no answer to these questions. This divide leads scholars to neglect aspects that are not obvious but might play a nontrivial role in shaping information behavior. Yet research in in-context HIB has focused on different aspects for each type of context.[11] While the specific social and cultural rules and conventions in everyday life are induced by society and those on the job primarily by the workplace organization, rules and convention play a role in both types of context. Therefore, models of information behavior that are not limited to one type of context—unless they represent a specific community of actors in a local context— are more powerful than models bounded by a type of context. Free of context type, such models represent relevant aspects of contextual information behavior whether or not an aspect is immediately visible.

CWA is an example of a conceptual framework that can guide research in any type of context. While its dimensions presented in figure 13.1 are clearly relevant to the analysis of cognitive work in the workplace, they are also clearly relevant to other types of context, as we have seen in Pejtersen's design of the BookHouse fiction-retrieval system previously described. Also consider again record keeping by stay-at-home parents. The work domain in this case would be the family, as a family can be considered a work domain when analyzing the decisions that family members make with regard to their lives. The environment of the work domain includes the economic, social, legal, and cultural conditions in the community to which the family belongs.[12] Means-ends analysis addresses the complexity of the family as a work domain, because families have goals, constraints, priorities, processes, and resources. These might be implicit, and it is the task of the researcher to make them explicit and record them for analysis. A study of other activities by stay-at-home parents, such as managing health treatments, involvement in the schools or charities, and neighborhood activism, would each define its own work domain.

In summary, a model or a conceptual framework that includes *dimensions* of elements of information behavior in context may be relevant both to the workplace and to the everyday contexts and thus would enrich both areas of study. CWA is an example of such a framework and it has been proven productive in studies of both contexts.

Theoretical traditions and conceptual constructs
Although many HIB researchers do not subscribe explicitly to a particular theoretical tradition or conceptual construct, a host of traditions and constructs inhabit this research area. Some are relatively central, with more than a few researchers applying them (e.g., positivism), while others are promoted or applied, knowingly or unknowingly, by only a few scholars. This diversity leads at times to contradictory conclusions, which may ignite fruitful discussions that lead to new developments in HIB. Conceptual and theoretical discussions are not common in HIB and, usually, contradictions remain just that—contradictions. A necessary condition for productive discussions to take place is for researchers to explicitly situate themselves in the theoretical tradition's landscape and present their approach when they report on their projects.

The relation between the cognitive and the affective in information behavior is one example of contradicting conclusions. Nahl (2007) claimed that the cognitive and affective aspects are interdependent, and has substantiated this claim by uncovering the way they mutually affect one another. In a similar vein, Kuhlthau (2004) coined the "uncertainty principle," which asserts that a state of uncertainty creates certain emotions. Savolainen (1995), on the other hand, arrived at a contradictory conclusion: Not only are the cognitive and the affective independent from one another, but they are opposites. He argued: "A cognitive orientation emphasizes an analytic and systematic approach to problems whereas the affective orientation refers to its exact opposite: an emotionally laden and rather unpredictable reaction to issues at hand" (265). This contradiction stems from conflicts among the theoretical traditions that guided each of the researchers.[13]

Based on its own theoretical foundations, CWA does not seek to resolve philosophical contradictions. On the contrary, it accommodates investigations from all points of view. Applying CWA may provide a tool for researchers from incompatible theoretical traditions to come together. CWA facilitates such gatherings by being local, realist, and rational. Researchers from different traditions may bring different methodologies to a study, which are likely to direct them to disparate investigations within a CWA dimension, each looking for its own type of finding. But they are likely to agree on answers to highly specific questions about the actors and the work domain—such as, What are the goals of the organization? What are the resources used to accomplish a task?

Consider a hypothetical study about the information behavior of secret service agents who infiltrate street gangs, in which Nina and Paul collaborate as principle investigators. Nina and Paul subscribe to different theoretical traditions: Nina's tradition led her to conclude that the cognitive and affective aspects of information behavior depend on one another, and Paul's tradition guided him to claim they are independent. Applying the CWA framework, they discover that the agents displayed a strong relation between emotions and cognitive actions (among many other findings). They agree on this finding, even though it contradicts Paul's claim, because they extracted it not only from interviews—which checked the agents' perception of their behavior—but also from direct observation—which presented the actual behavior.

To further confirm the finding, they compare it with findings in other dimensions in the onion model. This comparison reveals a clear inconsistency because the nature of the agents' work requires them to ignore emotional influences. The agents are under constant pressure, face a highly dynamic environment, and make instantaneous decisions about life and death. Generally speaking, it is unlikely that such intense characteristics of the work domain coexist with a strong connection between the cognitive and affective aspects of the agents' decision making and information behavior. Yet this coexistence may occur when agents' resources and values do not fit the work domain, for example in the case of actors who feel anxious when facing uncertainty and thus are not good candidates for this job. The inconsistency is likely to persist if the agents are willing to accept great suffering on their job (because they have to constantly fight their emotions), if the organization is completely ineffective (because the agents succumb to their emotions when they are required to make purely rational decisions), or both. These conditions were not seen in Nina and Paul's study, and they reexamine the findings to either resolve the inconsistency or explain it. Suppose a reexamination reveals that while they are on the job the agents' cognition and emotion are actually independent. Should Nina abandon her theoretical tradition of choice? Not necessarily. She may consider the agents as an extreme group with regard to cognitive/affective relations and might conclude that it is an exception to the rule.

In summary, research guided by CWA is open to all research traditions. When applying it, researchers with incompatible views can agree on particular findings because the framework addresses only a particular community of actors and a local work domain, it constantly checks findings against a particular reality, and it provides a conceptual structure for spotting inconsistencies.

Which variables to study?

A continual challenge to HIB scholarship is the selection of variables for investigation (see section 6.3). A set of variables that makes a major contribution to shaping information behavior and a set of variables that define information behavior are still waiting to be discovered. While a set of the latter is relatively manageable (e.g., information sources used, strategies applied, search formulation, relevance judgment), the number of variables that may shape information behavior is enormous and ranges from social to organizational to demographic to cognitive variables. HIB scholars have applied various approaches in their attempts to find central variables—such as trial-and-error testing of variables that researchers assumed were likely to shape behavior, applying qualitative methods in naturalist settings to uncover variables, and recruiting theoretical traditions to the cause. Despite these efforts, no consolidated list of variables has emerged. Instead, the list of variables is growing steadily as many research projects bring new ones to light. The indecision about which variables are most likely to shape behavior makes it difficult for HIB research to grow through accumulation of study results, and insights gained in studies often go unused.

CWA sheds a new light on the variables issue. One of its basic ideas is that we are not likely to achieve a universal list of influential variables, and the task of making such a list should not be attempted because variables are unique to each domain. Indeed, the term *variable* is not in the CWA vocabulary because CWA does not aim at testing relationships among elements in a system, but rather at investigating the elements themselves. Instead, CWA provides the dimensions to which influential variables belong—dimensions that are common to all contexts. CWA can also guide researchers who are searching for variables. For them, the onion model (figure 13.1) can serve as a framework that points to the categories of variables that have been proven to shape information behavior. At the same time, the framework identifies the types of variables that are not likely to meaningfully shape behavior by excluding their dimension. In addition, it presents the shaping relations among the dimensions as each one is shaped by the one in which it is nested. Applying a framework of categories can increase convergence in research, as each study can be placed in one or more dimension, thus bringing together investigations of variables in the same dimension.

13.3 Enhancing the Impact of Research in Human Information Interaction: Conclusions

Research projects that are guided by CWA produce requirements for the design of context-specific information systems that harmoniously integrate into cognitive work, whether in the workplace or in everyday life. This integration is made possible by giving priority to the analysis of the cognitive work that an information system is designed to support. Design is directed by an in-depth understanding of the work, and as a result creates a system that is integrated into cognitive work.[14] In addition, the analytical tools CWA provides can be used to increase the convergence of research in HII.

As an ecological approach, CWA is context-centered, rather than user-centered. While user-centered approaches—particularly the cognitivist approach—may lead to the design of general-context systems, a context-centered approach leads to the design of context-specific information systems, that is, systems that are designed for a *particular* community of actors. In the context of CWA, actors in a community share a work domain and a set of tasks, as well as formal and informal characteristics of the work domain's organization. Focusing on a particular information interaction facilitates a depth of understanding of the interaction and its environment that cannot be achieved when looking for universal understanding of the process. In addition to the depth afforded by analyzing the particular, such an analysis can direct the design of systems that closely fit the actions of the actors for which it is designed. As a result, ecological design crafts information systems that are more useful to the local actors than a general-context system would be. Moreover, due to its ecological approach, basic principles, and structure of analysis, CWA addresses several common challenges to design and reduces their effects.

Norman (1988) and Vicente (1999) delineated the challenges a designer faces in any design project, and those that are specific to the design of computer-based systems. In the context of HII some of these challenges can be formulated as follows:

- The system needs to serve people with many different backgrounds, priorities, and value systems. How can one system serve them all?
- How can the design fit the dynamics of the interaction with information?
- What part of the design should be automated, and what part should be left to the actor?
- Can a designer know how users will behave when a new system is in place?

These issues emanate from stable constraints in the design environment, and therefore are inherent to the design process and cannot be resolved or completely eradicated. Nevertheless, scholars have been applying various strategies to tackle them or work around them. Researchers in the area of user modeling, for instance, have been attempting to deal with the variability among users. They aim at finding methods that would make it possible for a machine to identify a specific individual and to adapt to his personal traits. On the other hand, most in-context HIB studies ignore individual variability altogether as well as the dynamic nature of work. CWA attends to some of these challenges as well.

These challenges are particularly acute in the design of general-context systems because their designers must consider a massive number of factors that relate to priorities, values, and cultures around the world, in addition to those that shape the dynamics of information interaction. At the same time, designers face constraints on the design process imposed by time and economics and have to consider the limitations of the technology. Having to consider a large number and diverse types of constraints, a designer constantly faces tradeoff situations in which the potential users, the technology, and the goals for the design play a part.

Various problems occur when these challenges are not resolved. For instance, actors may not use the system, or may try to avoid it as much as possible, or may use the system in an ineffective way. These behaviors could lead to the discontinuation of the system and decrease the quality of work and of its products as well. Engaging in workarounds is a typical problem, as well as preferring an easy way rather than what is necessary. The most important problem is actors' dissatisfaction with work and with their interaction with information. Designing context-specific systems reduces the impact of the challenges listed above.

The system needs to serve people with many different backgrounds, priorities, and value systems. How can one system serve them all?
To address this issue, CWA takes a very different approach from user modeling and other approaches that aim at incorporating this variability into design—it focuses on

the *work* actors do rather than on individual actors and their traits. As a result, a system is designed to support a certain type of work regardless of the individuals who perform it. But CWA does not ignore the workers; it investigates the resources and values of the community of actors who perform the work—that is, that of the prototypical actor. This development of a prototype is based on the observation that actors who do the same work and share a context have common attributes that make it possible for them to perform the work in a manner that is satisfactory to them and that contributes to the effectiveness of the work domain.

At the same time, it is reasonable to assert that personal traits, such as cognitive and learning styles, contribute to the shaping of an actor's interaction with information. Yet empirical research has demonstrated that contextual elements play a major role in shaping actor behavior. This observation is not meant to suggest that personal traits should be completely ignored but—following the ecological approach—to emphasize that, for effective design, contextual constraints take precedence.[15] With the recent rapid growth of the global economy, the question of how to cater to actors in different cultures has become of special interest. CWA addresses this issue directly. For work domains in which culture shapes actor behavior, the culture is a stable constraint in the work domain environment; thus, an analysis of the environment reveals the cultural elements that shape behavior, which in turn lead to culture-sensitive design requirements.

How can the design fit the dynamics of the interaction with information?
Most information interaction takes place in dynamic work domains. This condition is particularly the case in current workplaces, where the intensity of work is constantly accelerating and information technology is developing rapidly, with a somewhat unpredictable trajectory. How can the design fit the dynamics of the modern workplace and its environment? This question raises a crucial issue because the recurrent reorganizations in workplaces frequently alter actors' work. It is not uncommon for a new technology to arrive before the design of a system for the previous technology is completed, which causes technology-based design to address a "moving target." CWA attends to this issue by virtue of being an ecological approach. Investigating the relationships between actors and their environment is independent of the technology used. Even when one investigates the technology as an element in the actors' environment, the approach is independent of the technology. The purpose is to understand how the current technology shapes actor behavior in order to separate technology-induced behavior from that induced by steady elements in the context. Regardless of technology, CWA-based design rests on the analysis of *stable* constraints. Its purpose

is for the system to adapt to stable aspects of the work and to make it possible for actors to "finish the design" for the dynamic aspects.[16] That is, a CWA-based design creates systems that can withstand dynamic developments until they change the stable constraints.

What part of the design should be automated, and what part should be left to the actor?
With the progress in the level of support an information system can offer, a new question has arisen: Which functions should be automated and which should be left for the user to make (e.g., Bates 1990)?[17] An example may highlight this issue. In their series of studies of an online library catalog with relevance feedback functionality, Robertson and Hancock-Beaulieu (1992) found that their design was not completely satisfactory to their study participants. Relevance feedback is a mechanism to improve the results of a search in systems with ranked output.[18] In a relevance feedback system, users mark relevant items in the result of a search, and the system automatically generates other terms that can be integrated into an improved query. Once these terms are generated, a system may be designed to apply them automatically without user input, or it may present the terms to users so that they can select the terms they prefer to include in the next version of their query. Robertson and Hancock-Beaulieu designed their catalog with automatic feedback and found that study participants wanted more control over the search process and were discontented with automatic feedback.

This example is typical of common design procedures: First build a prototype and then test it to detect problems, fix them, and then test again until the prototype is satisfactory. A CWA-based design may go through the same cycle, but the cycle is likely to be much shorter because the initial design is already based on an in-depth understanding of the actors' constraints as well as their resources and values. For instance, if the online catalog in Robertson and Hancock-Beaulieu's (1992) study were designed in line with CWA, researchers would have known the level of control users desired before they designed the prototype. More generally, decisions about which of a system's functions should be automated are best based on knowing actors' resources, values, and the constraints on their behavior. CWA provides a framework that guides the study of these elements.

Can a designer know how users will behave when a new system is in place?
As a rule, systems are designed to improve a situation. They may be planned to improve the conditions under which users operate, the quality of the product, or the rate of production, among other elements. To design an effective system, one that improves the situation, designers predict how users will interact with the new system

to support design decisions. When a new system is based on the behavior of users interacting with the old system, it is very difficult to predict how the users will behave with the new system. One of the reasons for this difficulty is that users adapt their behavior to the technology they use. Therefore, it is not productive to base the design for a new system on their interactions with the old one. This creates a problematic situation because researchers who investigate user behavior can study only current behavior and cannot predict future behavior with a new system.

CWA provides an approach that facilitates the prediction of future behavior in several ways. The focus on *stable* constraints that shape actor behavior guarantees that these constraints will remain the same when new technology is introduced. Therefore, a new system is unlikely to affect the behavior that is shaped by these constraints. Moreover, the framework guides an in-depth analysis of the actors and their work domain—an analysis that also *explains* their behavior. The explanations that are derived from the analysis can point to changes in actor behavior once resources have changed. Thus, CWA predictions of future behavior are highly probable because they are independent of the technology used, they focus on constraints, they are detailed, and they provide explanations of behavior. Moreover, CWA does not claim to predict actual future behaviors but rather predicts the *conditions* that generate certain behaviors.

The merits of the ecological approach increase with technological developments. The more sophisticated the technology, the larger is the range of its functionality. This in turn makes it more practical to design information systems that are tailored to a community of actors—that is, to the design of context-specific systems. A context-specific system is clearly more robust than a general-context system because it includes features specific to the needs of the community of actors in addition to general-context ones. The design of context-specific systems invites an ecological approach.

Since the dominant tendency of designing general-context systems rather than context-specific ones is motivated by industry, their design is driven by profit and competition instead of human needs. Most HII researchers accept this tendency and believe that context-specific systems are low on the cost-benefit scale partly because a context-specific-system approach would require the design of many more systems than would a general-context approach. This argument has no grounds, however. When pulled together, the resources that have been invested in producing the many general-context information systems that compete with one another—such as web search engines—could support the design of a large number of context-specific systems. Not only is the design of multiple and competing general-context system a waste of resources, the systems produced are not as helpful to their users as they could have been. Nevertheless, even though context-specific systems are likely to be of great benefit to their users, they are not likely to be produced by for-profit industry because their customer pool is relatively small.

Another contribution of the ecological approach to the design of context-specific systems is its focus on environmental constraints. Typically, design is based on the information interaction that takes place with the aid of an information system that is to be replaced. In contrast, design requirements that are based on constraints—that is, on what cannot be done—provide designers with a range of future possibilities that are independent of the current interaction and technology.

Applying CWA to the design of information systems seems like a daunting undertaking, as CWA projects are resource demanding and require skill, expertise, and patience. Yet CWA-based design is a long-term investment because it creates stable systems that constantly evolve and thus withstand unpredictable changes. Most important, a CWA system adapts to actors' cognitive work and therefore minimizes the need for actors to adapt to it, increases the effectiveness of an information system and of the actor's work, and makes interacting with information pleasant, satisfying, and rewarding.

Glossary

Note: Terms that appear in boldface within a definition are also defined in the glossary.

Abstraction hierarchy A hierarchy in which the classes are derived from a parent class that is more abstract in nature than the class. In this case, going down the hierarchy ladder leads to class members that are increasingly concrete.

Actor A person who is engaged in an activity when both the person and the activity are the focus of an investigation.

The analytical strategy The *explicit consideration* of attributes of the **information problem** and of the search system when looking for information.

The browsing strategy Intuitive scanning in which leads are followed by association *without much planning ahead* when looking for information.

Cognitive style A term used in cognitive psychology to describe the way individuals perceive, process, and remember information, or their preferred approach to using such information to solve problems.

Cognitive work analysis A conceptual framework that guides the analysis of cognitive work. In this context, *cognitive work* designates any activities that require decision making. The framework is ecological in its nature.

Community of actors A group of **actors** who operate in the same type of environment, carrying out the same type of tasks.

Constraints Elements that are outside a system but interact with the system's elements in a way that impacts the system's goals. For the systems analyst, constraints are the element that are given and cannot be altered. Constraints limit the possibilities for action but also enable it.

A context-specific information system A system that is designed for a particular **community of actors**.

Decision making A decision-making process is required when a person wants to move from state A to state B without knowing intuitively and immediately how to go about it.

Descriptive models   **Models** that describe actual behavior.

The ecological approach   An approach to research that starts with an investigation of an environment's **constraints** and gives them priority. Using the research vocabulary of human information behavior, an ecological approach focuses on and gives priority to the investigation of context in which the behavior takes place.

The empirical strategy   Based on an **actor**'s previous experience, the use of *rules and tactics that were successful in the past* when looking for information.

Encountering information   The act of "bumping" into information *that was not sought at the time* but that can solve a particular **information problem** that presented itself in the past or is scheduled to be solved in the future.

Environment   *See* **System's environment**

Formative models   **Models** that describe what could be. They describe requirements that must be satisfied so that behavior takes place in a new, desired way.

A general-context information system   A system that is designed for all to use, with no specific **community of actors** in mind.

Human information behavior   An area of research in library and information science that focuses on **human information interaction**. It is the area that lies in the intersection of library and information science and human information interaction. No agreed-upon definition for this area exists as yet.

Human information interaction   An area of research that investigates how humans interact with information. It is a multidisciplinary umbrella with manifestations in various fields. For example, it is manifested as **human information behavior** in library and information science, and as human-computer interaction in computer science.

In-context research   Research that investigates a particular **community of actors**.

Information need   A basic concept in **human information behavior** with no agreed-upon definition. Definitions based on a cognitive approach maintain that it is the result of some gap in understanding the world, whereas a pragmatic approach may define it as the motivation that leads **actors** to seek information.

Information problem   A problem that is created when a decision cannot be made because of lack of relevant information.

Information retrieval (IR)   An area related to building and investigating retrieval models and mechanisms for computer-based systems that retrieve information in response to user requests.

Information searching behavior   *See* **Information-seeking behavior**

Information seeking   The act of *purposely* looking for information to support actual **decision making** or to resolve an **information problem**.

Information-seeking behavior   An area of research in **human information behavior** that studies how people look for information.

The known-site strategy   Going *directly* to the place where the information is located when looking for information.

Means-ends hierarchy   A hierarchy in which elements in each class represent the means for materializing elements in the parent class and in which elements in each class represent the purposes (ends) for the elements in its child class.

Mental model   A representation of the surrounding world, including the relationships between its various parts and a person's intuitive perception about her own acts and their consequences. In the context of information systems, a mental model is "a model of the system the user builds in his or her head" (Borgman 1984a, 37).

Model   A representation of a segment of reality.

Normative models   **Models** that prescribe what behavior should be.

Prescriptive models   *See* **Normative models**

Problem solving   *See* **Decision making**

Search strategy   "A category of cognitive task procedures that transform an initial state of knowledge into a final state of knowledge" (Vicente 1999, 220). Strategies are applied when people look for information to solve a problem.

The similarity strategy   Finding information based on a previous *example* that is similar to the current need when looking for information.

Surfing   The act of browsing through a source of information just to see what it contains, *without reference to a particular decision or* information problem.

System-centered approach   An approach that centers on a system's attributes. Some scholars expand the definition to include other requirements (e.g., Dervin and Nilan 1986).

System's environment   The set of a system's **constraints**.

A theoretical tradition   A tradition that is based on certain epistemological and ontological foundations.

User-centered approach   An approach that centers on the individual attributes of users. Some scholars expand the definition to include other requirements (e.g., Dervin and Nilan 1986).

Work-centered approach   An approach that centers on prototypical **actors** (rather than on individuals), their work-induced attributes, and the attributes of the work they carry out and its environment. The work-centered approach is **ecological** in nature.

Abbreviations

ARIST	*Annual Review of Information Science and Technology*
ASK	anomalous state of knowledge
CSCW	computer-supported cooperative work
CSE	cognitive systems engineering
CWA	cognitive work analysis
ELIS	everyday-life information-seeking
HCI	human-computer interaction
HIB	human information behavior
HII	human information interaction
ICT	information and communication technology
IR	information retrieval
ISB	Information-seeking behavior
ISIC	Information-seeking in context
LIS	library and information science
MEA	means-ends analysis
MIS	management of information systems
OPAC	online public access catalogs
PIM	personal information management
PIO	passenger information officers

Notes

Preface

1. The negative and the positive poles of a magnet are an example of interdependent opposites because there cannot be a negative pole if a positive pole is absent. Magnets also induce movement by moving objects toward or away from them.

2. Although the number of women in these professions is growing steadily, there is no equal gender distribution at present.

Part I

1. The field *information science* emerged from *library and information science* and is loosely defined as the research areas that are addressed in information schools in the United States.

Chapter 1

1. Benton and Craib (2001) explained that the lack of agreed-upon definitions of basic concepts is typical to the social sciences.

2. An expanded discussion on the definition of *information interaction* is part of the introduction to chapter 2.

3. At times, the term *user* is also employed in instances where the interaction between actors and systems is the focus of the discussion.

4. The concepts *environment* and *task* have had many interpretations and therefore require definitions themselves. The concept *environment* is defined in section 1.2.2, but for the moment I will define it as the context in which a task is performed. The concept *task* is discussed in several chapters and is defined here as an activity undertaken with explicit goals. In chapter 11, *task* is defined within the framework of cognitive work analysis as an activity that (1) has certain goals, constraints, and priorities; (2) involves specific functions and actions; and (3) utilizes particular resources.

5. The term *context* has generated several definitions and vigorous discussions. These are reviewed in section 7.1.

6. This statement depends, of course, on the definition of *environment* and what is considered to be included in it. For the sake of demonstration I leave the concept undefined. A definition and a discussion are offered in section 1.2.2.

7. See review articles on the topic such as Capurro and Hjørland (2003), Cornelius (2002), and Furner (2010).

8. My construal is also informed by Faibisoff and Ely (1976, 3).

9. This requirement was first introduced by several researchers in response to Shannon and Weaver's (1949) model, which offered a measurement for the amount of information but did not address the semantic aspect of information. Also, their view was that whether or not a string of symbols (a message) is considered information is an individual decision. There cannot be universal agreement about whether a certain message is information because, while it may be information to one person, it may be just a message to another.

10. For the discussions in this book, we can consider *decision making* and *problem solving* interchangeable.

11. The term *ecological design* is also used to designate design that aims at preserving the ecology, such as green architecture and sustainable agriculture.

12. *Metadisciplinary* might be a more accurate characterization.

13. I use the terms *systems approach* and *systems thinking* interchangeably.

14. The systems approach is particularly suitable for studying complex phenomena. Simple ones may be understood straightforwardly without the analysis required by this approach.

15. This statement may not be accepted by scholars who reject the notion that information is for decision making.

16. This is a very fundamental understanding of a *system* in systems thinking, and a most difficult one for novices to internalize.

17. A system's boundary may shift during an investigation as the researcher increases her understanding of the studied phenomenon. Creating and revising the boundary is a challenging task because of the complexity involved.

18. Clearly, the design of general-context systems requires some assumptions about their potential users. Trivially, designers assume that users have access to the system, can read and write in the "spoken language" used in the system, and can make at least simple deductions. That is, design is not completely free of context, but the context for which it is designed is general.

19. Some might be off-the-shelf systems.

Chapter 2

1. Tom Wilson and Reijo Savolainen have debated the meaning of the term in HIB, in relation to the term *practice* (Behaviour/practice debate 2009).

2. Savolainen (2007) provided an analysis of the development of the phrase "information behavior" and the approaches it represents.

3. See section 5.4.1.1 for a discussion of the browsing strategy.

4. See a short overview in Erdelez (2005).

5. A few researchers have investigated some aspects of it. Heinström (2006), for example, studied the psychological factors supporting this form of acquiring information.

6. The term "document" is loosely construed as anything that contains information (my apologies to document scholars).

7. *Information science* is used to denote the extension of LIS, which includes approaches and research areas from other fields, as reflected by the research activities in information schools today.

8. See Borlund (2009) for a historical review of the development of testing the performance of information systems.

9. Although they are still the basis for all performance measurement used today, recall and precision have experienced waves of criticism: "The issue of the choice of measures and their analysis was then and remains now a common concern of researchers in the [IR] field—a theme which generates a significant and probably increasing number of new papers every year" (Robertson 2008, 7).

10. Systems that facilitate relevance feedback allow users to mark relevant documents in a retrieved set. The system then uses this information to reformulate the query, whether automatically or with the user's intervention, with the aim of achieving better retrieval results.

11. Measuring with an open scale is usually called *magnitude estimation*.

12. While the studies are carried out in a particular context, the characteristics of the context itself are rarely investigated.

13. Julien and Duggan (2000) reviewed the HIB literature published between 1984 and 1998 and found that 38% of the actor communities studied were students and scholars.

14. See section 1.2.4 for a definition of such systems.

15. It should be noted that recent research has increasingly used subjective measurements such as the participants' level of satisfaction with various attributes of the system.

16. These are expanded upon and discussed in section 10.1.

17. A *community of actors* is a group of actors who operate in a certain type of environment, carrying out the same type of task. See section 1.1.1.1 for an explanation of the concept.

18. Remember: constraints limit action as well as *enable* it. See section 1.2.2.1.

19. These circumstances are not completely imaginary. Many studies in HII claim general, context-free validity, while employing samples drawn from students in the same class, carrying out one and the same task.

20. In the 1970s filtering and routing were developed with special-purpose parallel processors and other systems for intelligence and diplomatic applications where electronic text was available. No other information agency used computers for this purpose at that time.

21. Chatman's studies are discussed in section 3.1.1.

22. See section 1.1.2.

23. In spite of its importance to information seeking and retrieval, the process of determining the subject of a document is still a mystery.

Part II

1. See W. Jones (2008).

2. However, the participants in a sizeable number of the experiments were students, and so the ability to generalize is questionable.

Chapter 3

1. As Pettigrew and McKechnie (2001) explained their method for detecting a theory: "Consider a 'theory' as identified if the author(s) describes it as such in the article … or uses such key terms as 'conceptual' … 'framework,' 'grounded,' or 'underpinnings' to describe an idea/view or approach as such" (65).

2. See Chatman (2000) for her description of her intellectual journey.

3. This question does not mean to imply that researchers always have to assess participants' experience. Recognizing its effect, they may choose to focus on the other aspects of information seeking, such as the cognitive or the social, while disregarding experience or controlling for it.

4. See section 5.4.1.1 for a discussion about browsing.

5. Sonnenwald (2005) defined the concept in the third proposition: "Within a context and situation is an 'information horizon' in which we can act. When an individual decides to seek information, there is an information horizon in which they may seek information. An information horizon may consist of a variety of information resources and relationships among these resources" (193).

6. This reformulation is not precise since it changes "may do" to "have the tendency to do," which might not have been Sonnenwald's intent. However, if the "may do" infers not a tendency but rather "may or may not," the value of this proposition is not clear, as humans by their very nature tend to perceive, reflect, and evaluate changes around them.

7. See section 8.1.1 for a very short discussion of positivism.

8. See section 8.1.2 for a discussion on the realist stance.

9. In this spirit, the model employs the term *message* to designate information retrieved (Soergel 1985, 15).

10. Wilson (1999) attempted to integrate several models to create a unified one without success. He was able, however, to combine Kuhlthau's ISP and a new model of Ellis's activities type (which he ordered in a sequence). This resulted in a universal model that included four general stages in a successive order, each reflecting a change in the level of uncertainty: problem identification, problem definition, problem resolution, and solution statement.

11. See section 4.1 for a description of Taylor's model of the stages in need development.

12. See chapter 9 for a discussion about the use of models in systems design.

13. A general-context system is designed with no particular community of actors in mind. See section 1.2.4 for an explanation of the concept.

14. An increasing number of cognitive researchers, however, no longer accept this assumption. In their view, cognition is also shaped by social and situational conditions.

15. For a self-description of his intellectual journey, see Wilson (2005).

16. Fisher, Erdelez, and McKechnie's (2005) book on theories of information behavior described 72 conceptual constructs (not all of them are theories as the title suggests), most developed in the last three decades.

Chapter 4

1. It should be noted that, while this statement is theoretically sound, there is still no empirical evidence to substantiate it.

2. The concept of *seeking* is defined here by the statement: When people seek information, they *purposely* look for information to support actual decision-making or to resolve an information problem (section 2.1.1.1). Of course, as we've noted, people may acquire information without searching for it (encountering information) or without having a decision to make (surfing).

3. Context has not been considered by most of the definitions that included elements from Taylor's model, primarily because the model is purely cognitive. Once information need is associated with the search process, contextual elements can be introduced.

4. Throughout this book I have made my best effort to avoid using *information need*. *Information problem* has been my favorite substitute because it is compatible with the notion that information is for problem-solving, which is derived from my understanding of the concept *information* (see section 1.1.2).

5. See table 8.1 for positivist and interpretive definitions of *information need*.

6. On a general level, their analysis showed that scholars' approaches have indeed been shaped by theoretical traditions (see chapter 8). Nevertheless, the HIB literature demonstrates that most scholars were not aware of the traditions they tacitly followed.

7. See my discussion of *task* in section 7.3.3.

8. There are other interpretations of these terms. This variation is sometimes a source of misunderstandings among researchers.

9. Faibisoff and Ely (1976) began their discussion with the statement: "Words and phrases often interfere with understanding" (3), which is a succinct summary of the relations among the three concepts.

10. As is explained in section 4.3, employing the decision ladder to analyze information needs with a thorough understanding of the decision-making context, a researcher may arrive at a relatively clear understanding of what information may solve the actor's problem.

11. In my definition, *information* is a string of symbols that (1) has meaning; (2) is communicated; (3) has an effect; and (4) is for decision-making (see section 1.1.2).

12. A reminder: *problem solving* and *decision making* are used interchangeably.

13. In fact, we identified a couple of instances in which the actors began *planning* without identifying the decision to be made. In one instance this behavior resulted in an iterative process between *planning* and *observation*.

14. One possible exception is Westbrook's (2009) study of domestic violence survivors. Guided by the person-in-situation model, she defined needs as "using 'practically effective information' in order to make progress towards moving from one situation to the next situation" (101). If we accept the view that decisions are made when an actor wishes to move from state A to state B, her definition might be construed as relating information need to decision making.

Chapter 5

1. Some researchers believe that an information need is constantly changing during the search process. This view is reasonable from a cognitive point of view because the actor's state of knowledge is constantly changing during the search process. Yet it might not be accepted by researchers who see the context as shaping a need and enabling it to emerge, because they usually perceive context as stable during the search process. They may also claim that a change in the state of knowledge does not necessarily alter the information need. In addition, there is no empirical evidence that information needs actually change through the process (to my knowledge). Results

of studies about changes in relevance criteria (which represent aspects of a need) are contradictory (see section 2.1.1.2).

2. Whether or not strategies are observable depends on the definition of *strategy*, as will become clear later in this chapter.

3. Best-match systems retrieve documents by matching the terms in a query directly with the terms in the text and selecting only the documents that provide an exact match with the query. For instance, a query of the form X and Y will retrieve only documents that include both X and Y, all of which are assumed to be relevant to the same degree.

4. Ranked-output systems employ an algorithm to match a query with documents and recognize gradations in the level of relevance. The list of retrieved documents is arranged according to their relevance, most often beginning with the most relevant.

5. See a more detailed description in section 10.3.3.1.

6. The authors view search strategies "as types of user interaction within the IR system," which may explain the selection of these specific dimensions.

7. Note that these are attributes of a set of strategies, rather than definitions of individual strategies. That is, there is no one analytical strategy, for example; rather, there are several that possess attributes that categorize them as analytical. Most researchers nevertheless use the terms *analytical* and *browsing* as names of two specific strategies, even when they report that these are based on Marchionini's hierarchy.

8. Thatcher (2008) analyzed several studies about search strategies and employed Marchionini's (1995) hierarchy to demonstrate the various levels in which they were created, from *moves* to *strategies*.

9. This approach may be termed *variable-centered* because the research question is of the type, How does variable X affect the defined search strategies? rather than, What variables affect strategy A?

10. According to the terminology presented in chapter 2, however, both Bates's and Toms's definitions of *browsing* actually define *surfing*, because they both assume that the activity takes place without any information need.

11. "Mental model" is understood here to mean an explanation of someone's thought process about how something works in the real world.

12. The terms *searching* and *information retrieval* (as an activity) are used interchangeably.

13. This list of strategies is open; future studies may discover additional ones.

14. Iris Xie has conducted several studies on strategy shifts (e.g., Xie 2007, 2008).

15. This definition of *browsing* is not that of a strategy, as Bates defines that term, because it focuses on procedures rather than on a plan. That is, browsing is more concrete than a strategy is. It is possible that Bates does not consider browsing a strategy. According to the terminology

used in this book, Bates's use of *browsing* is similar to my use of *surfing* (see section 2.1.1.1), which is a mode of acquiring information.

16. The dimensions are: (1) the level of scanning activity; (2) the specificity of the information provided by the source; (3) the definiteness or specificity of the patron's goal; and (4) the specificity of the object sought (Chang 2005, 71).

17. Bates (2007) maintains that browsing is built into humans and is intuitive, and therefore requires no training. This statement might be reasonable if browsing is considered to be affected only by purely cognitive elements, and mainly by curiosity. Training is reasonable, however, when contextual elements are brought into the mix, and when browsing is goal directed, rather than motivated by sheer curiosity. Learning ways to shorten the path to the needed information can make browsing more efficient, and possibly increase its effectiveness as well.

18. More accurately, a web directory supports browsing, much like the arrangement of books on a library's shelves. However, it seems that the use of directories is not common in web searching, and most web directories need to be improved before they can be of useful support for browsing.

19. In this chapter I use *information need* in the intuitive sense.

20. The need for training may seem obvious because applying the analytical strategy requires an understanding of the system's capability, whether it is the method for arranging books on the shelves or the capabilities of a search engine.

21. I actually got this rule from a 10-year-old girl.

22. The similarity strategy is employed when an actor is unable to articulate the specific attributes of the desired documents. When search engines retrieve additional documents on a topic or by an author, they are not employing the similarity strategy because both topic and author can be expressed explicitly.

23. A workaround way to employ the similarity strategy when looking for books is to enter a bookseller's site and act as if you want to buy the book you're using as an example. You can then continue to the checkout until the stage at which similar books are offered for sale. There are no studies on whether the strategy is ever employed this way, or how effective it might be.

24. This analysis was first done by Annelise Mark Pejtersen.

25. This procedure is also called "hub and spokes."

26. It is beyond the scope of this discussion to bring examples of how this support could be implemented or to evaluate the mechanisms that exist today. Fidel et al. (1999) discussed some possibilities.

27. For example, a couple of the engineers we observed attached database software to their bookmarks to facilitate searching their list.

28. Unlike *information need*, which is an abstract concept that can possess a commonsense meaning, *search strategy* relates to concrete procedures and has no commonsensical meaning.

Part III

1. British researchers named both the area and its empirical research *user studies*.

Chapter 6

1. Later studies have found that humans are a major information source for actors in a large variety of contexts and situations.

2. The AACR provides rules for cataloging a variety items. It is employed in libraries around the globe and is now in its revised second edition (Gorman et al. 1998).

3. Before electronic access was available to all, and for free, librarians had access to online bibliographic databases and could retrieve articles for their users. Interaction with the databases was much less flexible than it is today, and libraries were charged, partially by connect time. Therefore, searching required training and experience. Those who performed such searches were called online searchers.

4. Recall that Flowers (1965) found this was not the case for physicists and chemists.

5. The phrase *second-generation scholars* points to a community of researchers, not to the individuals in it. It denotes researchers who have conducted their studies after the transition of HIB from the first generation to the second.

6. My intent is not to claim that only cognitive HIB researchers are concerned with the level of generalization produced by their studies. Generalizability is still considered a highly desirable attribute of research results. Unfortunately, it is not uncommon for research reports to assume generalizability when it is not warranted. Apparently, in their wish to improve the perceived value of their study, researchers are at times somewhat careless in determining the appropriate level of generalizability.

7. This fact does not reduce their value. Taylor's (1968) model has been the foundation of several later models, and Krikelas's (1983) was a blueprint for later conceptions of the search process.

8. Much like the decision about whether a document is relevant or not.

9. Most researchers noted in addition that eventually these conceptual developments will improve information systems and services without explaining how that would materialize.

10. While *neuroticism* may appear to be a rather clinical term, it represents traits that are quite normal. "High level" is characterized by feeling anxiety, having a tendency to worry, and being upset in stressful situations. "Low level" implies emotional stability, calmness, confidence, and stress resistance (Hyldegård 2009). A testimony to the trait's normalcy is the fact that Hyldegård

found that most of the participants in her study—all master's students about to complete their education—had a high level of *neuroticism*.

11. Yet it is not uncommon for scholars who present a new view of the process to show the weak points of the previous descriptions.

12. Models that are shaped by the evidence collected in an empirical study are also influenced by the conceptual models and viewpoints of their creators.

13. In some studies the conditions are so restricted—and, thus, far removed from real-life situations—that their findings may have value only if they can be applied to other, more relaxed conditions, which is almost always not the case.

14. Such incorporation is likely to happen when readers do not extend careful and critical consideration to the details of the research method employed.

15. This is a good example of overextended generalization. It is possible that the speed in which requests are answered is part of the technical center policy, rather than a variable that characterized HIB. There are other examples of such irrelevant results. A few studies, for example, aimed at finding difficulties students encounter when searching the web and used their university web site as the search system in the experiment. The results showed that most of the "problems" the students had were caused by the poor design of the web site.

16. For my dissertation research, I collected variables that had been considered in the online searching literature and found over 300 of them (Fidel and Soergel 1983).

17. This change has not been adopted by all HIB researchers; a number of them are still using the first-generation method today.

18. It is not uncommon in these studies to collect data through interviews. The question is: If the researcher had no a priori conception, where did the interview questions come from? How did she decide what questions to ask? (An exception is an interview that asks the participant to describe actions, thoughts, or feelings that took place in the past, rather than more specific questions. Such questions do not entail preconceptions.)

19. *Corpora* in the information science context refers to stable bodies of given items that can be used in laboratory testing under various conditions. This phrase might not be acceptable today because users are no longer considered a random collection of bodies that can be used to test systems.

20. This issue is discussed in greater details in section 8.3.

21. Indeed, it is becoming more common to employ the term *human-centered*. In fact, with the growth in objects of study, methods, and approaches, the designation of the population studied can be further refined. A study of people using a system investigates *users*; a study of people active in a context focuses on *actors*; and a study of general patterns in HII—such as triggers for looking for information or deciding when there is enough information—examines *people* or *individuals*. (See also section 1.1.1.)

22. T. D. Wilson's (1981) article is also considered as a turning point to the user-centered approach.

23. Obviously, this construal of *user-centered* was created from a certain epistemological view—a view that is not shared by all user-centered researchers. Nevertheless, each researcher can probably find a few elements that fit her view.

Chapter 7

1. As in other social sciences, central concepts in LIS are challenging to define and stimulate protracted discussions among researchers, who are guided by their personal conceptual viewpoint, if often implicitly. At the same time, research in which these concepts play a significant role is progressing, often without considering the debates. Other examples from LIS are the concepts *information* and *information need* (see sections 1.1.2 and 4.1).

2. Chapter 8 includes a discussion about coherent accumulation of research results.

3. See Courtright's (2007) review article in *ARIST*. Also, Agarwal, Xu, and Poo (2009) applied a framework from sociology to define the boundaries of context in HIB research.

4. It is not surprising that these researchers perceived an information system to last for a long while, rather than evolving constantly: The role of researchers was done once they had found the specifications for the best system for a certain context. Given the state of information technology at that time, many of the studies were conducted in physical libraries, which were difficult to modify and improve frequently.

5. One exception to this statement is Dervin's (1992) sense-making methodology (see section 3.2.1).

6. Situational view is sometimes confused with Suchman's (1987) concept of *situated actions*, which she defined as "actions taken in the context of particular, concrete circumstances" (viii). Her concept is closer to *actions in context* than to *actions in a situation*.

7. See the discussion about invariants in section 9.2.3.1.

8. This is a normative statement. The ad hoc approach is useful only when nothing is known about the target community. Nevertheless, it is sometimes applied under other circumstances.

9. Most research reports include the "The Setting" section in the "Research Methods" part of the report. In an exploratory study to discover the context, this section should be included in the "Findings" section, and yet this practice is usually ignored.

10. See also the discussion in section 1.2.1.1.

11. Baker created the model for a specific situation and named it "Conceptual model for discussions of end-of-life issues." I treat it as a more general model only to show the difference between the two views.

12. This example is not meant to imply that designers should ignore the source of a condition. In this example it may be the case that only the family can provide the needed information. A designer, then, may consider resolving the issue by suggesting procedures for the family to provide consistent information in spite of their lack of communication and coordination. Or, in the extreme, she may decide to get involved and help to resolve the family's problems.

13. This view, focusing on activities, is often called the *work-centered* approach (see chapter 11).

14. Taylor's (1991) *Information Use Environment* is an example of a realist view of context.

15. These are not accurate labels, but they crudely relate to the realist ontology and the constructivist theoretical tradition. See section 8.1 for a more complete discussion of these concepts.

16. See Talja, Keso, and Pietiläinen (1999) for an example of a constructivist view on context.

17. Were each person to view the world in a very individual way, there would be chaos all around us. There are several scholars within this school of thought who explain that a personal view is shaped by social interactions and norms and that these functions facilitate some common threads among the individual's views.

18. The study of the context of activities also includes an investigation of the person's perception of the context.

19. This statement may seem unsubstantiated because a number of empirical researchers actually claim to follow certain theoretical traditions. Not infrequently, however, contradictions exist between a study's methodology and the declared tradition (See section 8.2.2).

20. See section 1.2.2 for a discussion of environment.

21. Time of day may be relevant to other elements in the system, such as the physical setting or energy consumption.

22. Although this assertion is conceptually sound, the definition of a system's boundary may evolve as the system is being investigated and its environment may evolve along with it (see section 1.2.2).

23. Even in cases in which the researcher defines a context before a study begins—based on a conceptual construct or on previous research—she rediscovers it when she applies it to the object of study.

24. Specific recommendations for system and service design are not typical of in-context studies. The nature of the recommendations here, however, is typical of studies that offer some discrete implications for design: They are general and often commonsensical.

25. Courtright (2007, 286) offered citations for several studies as examples.

26. There are some notable exceptions. Some conceptual frameworks that have been used in HIB research, such as cognitive work analysis and activity theory, guide the researcher to focus on the context of HIB activities.

27. These constraints are made-up examples.

28. Some of these studies emanate from the researcher's personal interests; often they are themselves members of the group they studied.

29. Similarly, Vakkari (2008) found that 56% of the papers presented at the ISIC conference in 2008 did not identify special contributions.

30. The constructs were Arendt's (1958) tripartite division of human activities, self-determination theory, Taylor's (1991) information use environment, social representation methodology, activity theory, and decision theory.

31. The total percent is higher than 100% because several articles offered more than one type of contribution.

32. Kari and Savolainen (2007) defined *context* explicitly in this way: "Context is all those things which are not an inherent part of information phenomena, but which nevertheless bear some relation to these" (48). The main challenge in this definition, on both the individual and general levels, is the determination of what is inherent to information phenomena and what just "bear[s] some relation to these." Is technology, for instance, inherent? (Systems thinkers would explain that what is inherent to a system is determined by the researcher's definition of the system, which is constructed according to the researcher's goals.)

33. A hypothetical study of the searching behavior of adults who are novices to web searching, for instance, may offer statistics about the library in which their activities take place—such as the year it was established, the size of the collection, and the number of programs it provides—without presenting the relations between these statistics and the novice adults.

34. Such a survey can be carried out for the sole purpose of validating the findings of the qualitative inquiry, in which case the population is limited to the community and context that are under study.

35. A failure to validate the expansion does not necessarily imply that such an expansion is generally impossible; it proves that the specific set of results that was tested is not valid in relation to the set of actors selected. Because findings of indicative qualitative studies are influenced by the researcher's approach, it is possible that another study of the same user group would bring other results that *can* be validated. It is also possible that another set of actors may validate the results of the original study.

36. Note that the statement "receives information problems from outside sources" is more general and abstract than "the manager sometimes presented the team with an information problem." When a statement is valid for more than one community, it is likely to be more abstract than the originating statements for the individual communities. The more communities that are included, the more abstract the statements about the actors' information behavior are likely to become.

37. This description is an extreme oversimplification of a complex phenomenon, and it is made here only for the purpose of demonstration.

38. A few studies that have been carried out for the purpose of testing a method are the exception (e.g., Foster, Urquhart, and Turner 2008).

39. In the case of the source of information problems, one may recall, for example, Gross's (1995) work on imposed queries—those that originated from people other than the searcher himself.

40. Slightly different is a study carried out by Kari and Savolainen (2007) that identified four dimensions in the *relations* between information seeking and context.

41. Clearly, a workplace also has implicit policies and routines and may have an informal structure, but the presence of a formal structure provides a starting point for the analysis of the work context.

42. Most in-context researchers who investigated this dimension examined it in the workplace. Everyday life, however, has its own tasks—and in the same sense that this concept materializes itself in workplace studies—but this dimension is usually ignored in everyday-life studies.

43. Byström (2007) also explains that, like *context*, the concept *task* has several interpretations and conceptions.

44. Vakkari (2003) describes the viewpoint on *task* in various fields cognate to information science.

45. Because each researcher selected his own definition for *complexity*, the levels of complexity were measured differently in the studies of diverse researchers.

46. Note that, unlike variables, aspects of dimensions do not require operationalization. In fact, they cannot be operationalized. Variables are operationalized for the purpose of measuring them. How would one operationalize the aspect *task's goal*, for example, or *task's priorities and activities*? The purpose of a CWA study is to understand these aspects—e.g., What *are* the goals, the priorities, and the activities?—not to measure them.

Chapter 8

1. The concept *theoretical tradition* is often called *metatheory*. The latter term, however, has had various interpretations and is not used here for simplicity's sake.

2. This statement is colored by my worldview, and others may maintain that different aspects define a scholar's epistemological and ontological stance. Bates (2003), for example, explained that this is a matter of cognitive styles that "are developed and sharpened through decades of study and intellectual development in individuals and in whole intellectual communities and disciplines."

3. The systems approach is an example here because, while it is based on a realist stance, it can be applied with an empiricist or nonempiricist stance.

4. This seems reasonable when one examines the positions of each stance (see next sections). For example, a researcher cannot maintain simultaneously that research can be objective and

that it is always value laden. Similarly, one cannot claim that reality has an existence independent of us and at the same time that reality is what we perceive it to be. (See a display of the contrasts among three theoretical traditions in Pickard and Dixon 2004.)

5. This observation should be used carefully. There is a tendency among those who are not well versed in theoretical traditions to make no distinction between the statements "conducting empirical research" and "having an empiricist stance." As we have seen in previous chapters, empirical research can be conducted from various epistemological stances.

6. Benton and Craib (2001) presented an "ideal-typical" version of empiricist philosophy and noted that there are many different versions of empiricism.

7. For the rest of the discussion, *positivism* and *empiricism* are used interchangeably because *empiricism* is discussed here only in the context of social science.

8. Some definitions of this stance do not require that reality be knowable. In this chapter I follow Benton and Craib's definition.

9. That is, realists understand that human actions are shaped by their perception of reality but maintain that other parts of reality—those that might not be perceived by humans in a certain situation—can shape humans' activities as well.

10. Furthermore, *realism* does not entail *positivism*. Some interpretive views maintain that reality has an existence that is independent of how people know it and how they perceive it, but argue that we do not have a *direct* access to it.

11. Claiming that one's work is not affected by any theoretical tradition is a positivist stance, as empiricism maintains that scientific research can be objective, that is, not affected by the researcher's stance.

12. This is mostly due to lack of knowledge about the various theoretical traditions, as well as the similarity between the concepts of *scientific method* and *positivism*.

13. Ford (2004) continued: "*Objectivity* is defined here in the sense of judgment and acceptance according to standards agreed [upon] by scrutinizers other than the person conducting the research—typically standards agreed [upon] within a research community." It is not clear, however, what constitutes a "research community," or whether each research community has its own standards of objectivity.

14. One may claim that researchers do deviate from the observable when they explain the results of a quantitative study. These explanations, however, are often speculations rather than rational inferences from the findings.

15. At that point we could not determine if or how they were trained or to what degree (which we found out later), but it was clear that some type of training, formal or informal, was in place.

16. There is a trend, particularly among researchers who focus on searching digital systems, to explicitly divide a questionnaire into a subjective part (in which participants respond to questions

about their thoughts, opinions, and feelings) and an objective one. The subjective part is considered to represent participants' perceptions, while the objective one is considered to supply objective facts about reality.

17. Looking for citations of French theorists—most of whom are interpretive—in information science journal articles, Cronin and Meho (2009) found that only 1.2% of the articles included such citations. With information science ranked 24th, general arts and humanities had 10.4%, geography 4%, and law 1.6% citations of these theorists.

18. An exception that stands out is Brenda Dervin in the United States. She was guided by various interpretive theoretical traditions when she developed the sense-making methodology.

19. Other researchers have maintained that HIB requires its own theoretical tradition (e.g., B. Jones 2008; Budd 2001). This assumes that HIB should be guided by one tradition that is unique to it, rather than encouraging pluralism among researchers where each selects the theoretical tradition to employ according to his worldview. A similar view was expressed in the area of management information systems (MIS) (Benbasat and Zmud 1999).

20. In fact, most in-context studies, regardless of the methodology they employed, have provided very little understanding of their context because they did not actually investigate it (see section 7.4).

21. Wilson (2003, 447) also regarded positivism as less "sophisticated" than other approaches.

22. A hypothetical researcher might, for example, declare that he is a phenomenologist because he examines the experiences actors go through which create their reality. He defines the experiences, however, by analyzing the number of errors actors made while searching and analyzing their types of errors through an analysis of search logs. Such analysis cannot provide an understanding of the actors' experience because it does not reflect the actors' constructed reality.

23. This condition is prevalent among HIB researchers but it is not noticeable because researchers often avoid referring to the theoretical tradition guiding their work. This reticence is not surprising because many HIB researchers consider their findings to be objective—that is, they believe a researcher's worldview and the philosophical roots of a theoretical tradition play no role in their work.

24. Phenomenology is an example of such a "faddish" theoretical tradition. Without diminishing its value for HIB, Bawden (2006), for example, noted that it achieved a "fad" status, and Vakkari (1997) claimed that it had been used as a buzzword. The call for papers for ISIC 2010 (2009) also points to trendy theoretical traditions; it states: "particular theoretical frameworks that are currently of interest include (but are not restricted to) social network theory, actor network theory, cultural-historical activity theory, genre theory, etc."

25. This is not to claim that all definitions of *information* guided by the approach would be the same.

26. Some scholars maintain that information science should have its own, all-encompassing definition (e.g., Bates 2005).

27. These are some of the central elements of constructivism, broadly presented.

28. Quite a few HIB studies seem to be guided by the researcher's momentary interest, rather than by the mindful selection of important topics. Researchers guided by theoretical traditions would be more likely to be consistent in their selections.

29. Quite often when I encounter a problem in a research project I ask, Did I select the "right" system for the purpose of the project? (See section 1.2.) Reflecting on this issue usually helps me find a solution.

30. This system also automatically reduces the chances for faculty of marginalized groups to succeed, especially when their area of interest is outside the mainstream, such as ethnic or women's studies. There are only a few venues of scholarly publications that will accept their papers, and once they are published, the pool of scholars who might cite their work is relatively small.

Chapter 9

1. Normative models are also called *prescriptive models*.

2. The map was found in http://mappery.com, May 25, 2009.

3. Descriptive models can be useful, however, when an information system is upgraded without introducing major changes in its functionality and interface.

4. Vicente (1999, 98–100) discussed a few examples of research methodologies, such as ethnomethodology and activity theory, that are aimed at building descriptive models and the problems they have created when employed to inform design.

5. Models of searching behavior that serve as a guide for systems design should be differentiated from models of the system to be designed. Design requirements are derived from models of behavior. Once established, requirements create a model of the system. This model *is* normative because it determines how the system should be designed.

6. The six stages in the Big Six approach (Eisenberg and Berkowitz 1990) are an example of an abstract model.

7. Although not popular, the idea that IR systems could help users to crystallize their requests is not unconventional. Soergel (1997–98) stated that information systems should support users throughout the HIB process and gave examples of the tools necessary for this purpose. Belkin's (1980) *ASK* model suggested an approach to the design of IR systems that can perform this function. On the design side, Oddy (1977) built an experimental system in which users can retrieve information by interacting with sample documents without entering a query—an interaction that had the potential to support the process of crystallizing a request.

8. While inadequate for the design of IR systems, both the Big Six (Eisenberg and Berkowitz 1990) and Taylor's (1968) model have been highly successful when employed in human systems

(for which they were intended). This success is not surprising because humans can see the con-crete manifestations of abstract concepts and therefore be guided by Big Six.

9. Systems that facilitate relevance feedback allow users to mark relevant documents in a retrieved set. The system then uses this information to reformulate the query, whether automatically or with the user's intervention, with the aim of achieving better retrieval results.

10. See chapter 5 for a discussion about strategies.

11. Search strategies may evolve over time, and partly with the aid of new technology. Yet this process is gradual and evolutionary, rather than following fast quantum steps. This characteristic makes strategies amenable to consideration in design.

12. This is an example of the dialectical nature of constraints. Were there no buildings or other physical constraints blocking her way, Mary would not have been able to plan her route. She would have only one reasonable option: moving in a straight line.

13. Representing constraints may not be a straightforward task. For the design of general-context systems, finding all the constraints that limit seeking activities in general is as monumental a task as enumerating the behavior possibilities (unless the model is based on all the cognitive constraints that have been discovered thus far). Therefore, this approach to design is more useful when designing context-specific systems, in which case the constraints are relatively ready to be uncovered, than when designing general-context systems. This topic is further discussed in chapter 7.

14. The best example is the model created for the design of BookHouse (Pejtersen 1984), which guided the design of a retrieval system for fiction in public and school libraries—the only model that was created by an in-depth study of seeking behavior and that led to the design of an opera-tional information system.

15. An example of the use of constraints to produce requirements for a system to support col-laborative indexing in national movie archives is presented in Albrechtsen, Pejtersen, and Cleal (2002).

16. This option is the one that the city selected. To support the schedulers, the city installed large plasma screens in the schedulers' office that can display detailed interactive maps.

17. To my knowledge, technology to produce paper-based documents with a mobile hand-held is not in wide use yet. This example demonstrates that when the behavior possibilities are not tied to current technology, constraints-based requirements may also inform technological devel-opments. Instead of developing new technologies because they are "cool," possible, or potentially profitable, such requirements point to technological developments that will satisfy human needs. Moreover, once such technology is developed, its developers do not need to convince customers that it would improve their lives: It can be put to useful application right away.

18. See section 5.4.1 for a discussion of the five search strategies.

19. If no book was found, another set would be displayed.

20. The desire of actors to adapt to their situation by having more possibilities and control has been uncovered in several studies. Xie (2006), for example, found that participants in her study wanted to have more advanced features to customize the way they search, access, view, and disseminate information, when interacting with a digital library.

Chapter 10

1. They used the concept *design* to include systems and services (e.g., programs in libraries, help at an information desk). They also found that an article concerned with design is more likely to consider users from a cognitive point of view than from other views.

2. In this section, *research in information retrieval* is construed as *academic IR research*, which is different from IR research conducted by vendors of search engines, whether of general-context systems or ones dedicated to a specific user population.

3. A typical example is the concluding paragraph in Gwizdka's (2009) article: "Our findings have implications for the design of search interfaces. They suggest benefits of providing result overviews. They also suggest the importance of considering cognitive abilities in the design of search results presentation and interaction."

4. McKechnie et al. (2008) found that of the articles published in the ISIC proceedings during 1996–2006, most (59%) included implications for practice (including systems design). Of these, however, only 43% explained the implications explicitly. The other 57% provided vague, general, or unclear descriptions of them. See also the discussion in section 7.2.3.

5. For the rest of this chapter, the term *system* means *computer-based system* unless otherwise indicated.

6. See chapter 9 for a description and discussion of the types of models: descriptive, normative, and formative.

7. This attitude is not foreign to designers of search engines. For instance, Daniel Russell, senior research scientist for search quality and user happiness at Google, lamented people's poorly developed search skills. He explained that successful searches require a set of skills and an understanding of the interface one is using (Howard 2010). In other words, users have to adapt to the search system if they wish to be happy with the search and the quality of the results.

8. This is not surprising because design is a normative process. Every system is supposed to support something and achieve a certain level of performance. These establish the norms according to which a design should take place.

9. Well-developed and mature systems with user-controlled relevance feedback may be considered dynamic because they are sensitive to changes in the user's perception of the information problem.

10. The idea that the relevance scale should not be dichotomous was developed during studies of searching behavior (see section 2.1.2.1) unlike the other norms, which lack an empirical basis.

11. The databases and the algorithms that exploit them are trade secrets and have not been published, and thus are unavailable to outside researchers. Academic IR researchers may want to consider how to make use of data about users' searching in the development of IR algorithms.

12. Although I was disconcerted by these reactions, I should have expected them, if not in form at least in content. The requirement to consider search planning is foreign to the dominant IR research paradigm because there is no reason to assume that a "good" plan is likely to increase either ranked precision or ranked recall. Most IR researchers are reluctant to explore other research paradigms, for such an act may risk their standing in their research community.

13. He added that it is the role of the designer to decide by what means to satisfy the requirement, and that better systems were likely to result if the designer understood these concepts.

14. Since they recognized the limitations of current IR systems, they explained that the requirements are for systems with intellectual indexing and reasoning power.

15. Consider an article about intelligent design (also called *creationism*, the theory that God created nature, set in opposition to the theory of evolution). While its author would claim that it presents facts, most scientists would classify this as an opinion piece.

16. What is commonsensical and obvious is shaped by a researcher's epistemological stance. For a positivist, nothing is obvious. Scholars who have an interpretive bent may agree to accept certain statements without empirical evidence.

17. This trend is not surprising. To keep the economy going in a profit-based system, the most valued research is that which is likely to contribute to the well-being and development of industry. The citizens' role is to be customers.

18. Based on past investigations, it is safe to assume that many IR researchers believe that no education or expertise is required to conduct a seeking behavior study.

19. This understanding is not uncommon among IR researchers. On the several occasions when I have advocated the design of context-specific IR systems, IR colleagues responded that this line of research is not feasible because industry would not be interested in producing such systems. Clearly, they may invest the same amount of resources (and possibly fewer) in the design of general-context systems as in the design of context-specific ones, but they can then sell the product to a number of users that is greater by several orders of magnitude than those who will buy a context-specific product.

20. It is beyond the scope of this book to explain activity theory, which is rich and complex.

21. HIB research has recently started to pay attention to the framework, although T. D. Wilson (2008) noted that research in the Soviet Union has applied the theory to LIS since the 1970s. For example, an issue of *Information Research*—12(3), April 2007—was dedicated to activity theory. See also D. K. Allen et al. (2008) for a study guided by activity theory.

22. Some of the criteria follow: The starting point must be work activity as a systemic entity; technology, including computer-based technology, must be seen as a tool to facilitate work,

embedded in the work system; work systems need to be studied in their organizational context; the analytical model must be applicable to both descriptive studies and practical development (Mursu et al. 2007).

23. Dourish also explained that the term *ethnography* has been used incorrectly, and in various ways, in HCI. The concept *ethnography* represents immersive participation of the researcher in the life of the study participants, and understanding their perspectives and experiences. Most HCI researchers consider it a "toolbox of methods for extracting data from settings" (Dourish 2006, 543).

24. The usefulness of citations to retrieval had been recognized by Eugene Garfield, who produced the first Science Citation Index in 1960. Today, citation indexes cover almost 9,000 journals worldwide.

25. Kalvero Järvelin is an exception. He and his colleagues have developed algorithms and also conducted field studies.

26. See my discussion about the relations between *task* and *information need* in section 4.1.1.

27. This approach to testing also allows the introduction of some elements of context. Borlund (2009) recommended that the simulated task be crafted so that subjects can relate to the task, envision themselves executing it, and find it interesting. These conditions require that subjects have a similar context and that the simulated task be relevant to that context. As a consequence, the generalizability of the results is reduced because they were obtained in a specific context with a certain type of participants.

28. These questions are based on very strong assumptions that have no empirical evidence, and some fly in the face of evidence from a number of studies. One such assumption is that the domain in which an actor works determines the number of documents he expects to retrieve and the number he expects to see. In addition, it is not clear what is included in a "domain."

29. This contribution sometimes may not be clear even to the IR researcher.

30. See chapter 5 for a discussion about search strategies and their definitions and in particular section 5.1.2 for an expanded description of Belkin et al.'s work.

31. Cognitive task analysis is the analysis of how a task is accomplished, including a detailed description of manual and mental activities, task complexity, environmental conditions, problems, and any other unique cognitive factors associated with the task.

32. To describe it in an overly simplified manner, a script lays out the events of a particular process and their sequences (e.g., serving sliced watermelon)—much like a script for a movie.

33. They also commented that each strategy may have more than one script. That is, there is not always a single best way to execute a strategy.

34. This analogy helps explain the importance of formative models for design. An architect is not likely to use the description of the old bridge and its traffic patterns (a descriptive model) as

a basis for the design of a new bridge. She is also not likely to find the details of an ideal bridge (a normative model) helpful because, even though standards exist for safety and legal purposes, bridges come in different shapes, structures, and forms. She bases her design on the physical, economic, social, and political conditions, among others—that is, on the constraints that shape the requirements for a new bridge.

35. It would be fitting to name the system planner an architect of some sort—such as "retrieval-systems architect" or "HII architect." This term, however, is used in related fields and has assumed other meanings—as in "information architecture" or "computer architecture." Using it, therefore, may introduce confusion.

36. Even then, their ability to steer retrieval to a useful direction is very limited.

37. There are a few exceptions in research outside the IR field. Johnson, Griffiths, and Hartley (2003), for example, developed some evaluation measurements that reflected the success of the system in supporting the search process.

38. A reminder: browsing is a mode of information-seeking, that is, of a purposeful search.

39. One may claim that this approach is not feasible because the number of IR systems that would be required might be too high for production. This situation could be accomplished, though, by replacing the hundreds of general-context search engines with a hundred others, each for a particular actor community. Such an approach would require coordination among producers of search engines—a step that is unthinkable in a competitive market.

Yet commercial vendors of information systems already employ this approach; they frequently "customize" a system by integrating general-context systems to create a context-specific one that satisfies the need of a client.

40. Generally speaking, situational features cannot guide design, as one cannot design a system for each possible situation. Design can be based on *patterns* of activities because they are more stable than situations.

41. See chapters 6 and 7 for a more detailed discussion about the types of HIB studies.

42. The concept *search strategies* is a good example of one with a large diversity of definitions and procedures as a consequence (see section 5.1).

43. This approach would create groups of researchers investigating connected topics, and thus increase the direct contribution of the work of one scholar to that of another. This would also help to reduce the fragmentation in HIB research.

Chapter 11

1. Chapters 11 and 12 are an expanded version of Fidel and Pejtersen (2004).

2. Vicente (1999) defines a sociotechnical system as "A system composed of technical, psychological, and social elements" (9).

3. For instance, the leading group of HIB researchers—the American Society for Information Science and Technology's Special Interest Group on Information Needs, Seeking and Use (SIG/USE)—centers on "encourag[ing] research about cognitive and affective information behavior" (Fulton 2010), with no explicit recognition of other aspects of information behavior.

4. The onion model presents the context for information-interaction activities. Its context is functional rather than structural. When the work domain is analyzed, the main issues are related to the functions of the domain not to its organizational structure (although very often knowledge of the organizational structure is necessary to understand the function of the domain).

5. Had we studied the work before the mobile technology was introduced, we probably would have included the crew chiefs in the system. When work orders and end-of-the-day reports had been submitted on paper, crew chiefs had time to visit workers in the field and thus became involved in the fieldwork itself. With the introduction of the mobile technology, their time was consumed by handling the technology, and they had no time left for field visits.

6. Given appropriate support, students could have employed other strategies as well—and sometimes they actually tried to do so. These strategies are not discussed here for the sake of brevity.

7. These requirements may not be specific enough for a designer. An understanding of how students would take advantage of seeing the search as a whole, for instance, and of how graphics can represent the content of a site is necessary to achieve requirements that can be translated into design specifications.

8. For example, index a web site about roses with an image of a rose, one about a rock band with an image of a band, and one about the band's music with an image of a CD.

9. Several of these requirements may not fit the current role distribution among all who are involved in web design, such as the providers of the browser, search engine, or web site. Satisfying the requirements may entail a revised distribution.

10. In the last decade some IR empirical studies have looked at other evaluation criteria. These criteria were considered subjective (e.g., how satisfied the users were, how difficult it was to search), and data were collected through questionnaires and/or interviews.

Chapter 12

1. The list of five strategies is used in a way similar to that of the decision ladder (see section 4.3).

2. These goals and constraints define the boundary of the system, which is itself an abstract construct.

3. This is a very simple example that may not require MEA. It is raised here in this oversimplified form to demonstrate the attributes of the analysis. An example of a realistic, and thus much more complex, analysis can be found at Jenkins et al. (2009, 88–89).

4. It is possible that this view is supported also by CWA's inability to generalize.

5. This approach to generalization is preferred to the common methods that consider only common attributes. Noting differences preserves some of the complexity involved. In HIB research, for example, studies that have generalized across contexts based on common attributes have most often produced findings that were commonsensical.

6. I am not aware of any other HIB study that attempted to systematically generalize across context.

7. Norman (1988, 143) explains that in addition to the time pressure, the competition among producers compels designers to make a product different from the others on the market. Therefore, if a perfect product is on the market, all the other products of its kind would be designed somewhat differently—that is, they would be inferior.

8. Indeed, in the United States, CWA has been used primarily in the military context.

Part V

1. A reminder: the environment of a system is composed of the system's constraints (see section 1.2).

2. Sociotechnical systems are "composed of technical, psychological, and social elements" (Vicente 1999, 9).

3. Note that a study of a bounded and defined system does not have to be ecological. In fact, most in-context studies have focused on actor communities and have taken approaches other than the ecological.

Chapter 13

1. The system in which the actors are placed is defined by each design project. In the workplace, for example, it is likely to be the organization for which the actors work, whereas in everyday life the system may be determined by a task and the social structure or culture.

2. Note that the source of this cognitive feature is in the environment of the researcher's work.

3. In addition, there is evidence that environmental constraints contribute a great deal more to shaping behavior than cognitive ones (see section 6.2.1), which means that the practical argument for emphasizing environmental constraints is not the only argument for ecological design.

4. Indeed, to overcome this particular roadblock, some online catalogs display a suggestion for users to check for typos next to the "no items available" message.

5. Note that the dimension *actor's resources and values* is also viewed as an environmental constraint to the interaction.

6. Current search systems provide better outcome to users who know how to manipulate them than to other searchers.

7. CWA leads to the development of the *requirements* for a system that fits a community of actors. Context-specific systems, however, are not necessarily designed from scratch. They can be composed, partially or wholly, of a network of existing software or by customizing a general-context system.

8. This is not to claim that *all* that is obvious to practitioners should be free of systematic investigations. However, simple observations—such as that people evaluate the information they retrieve—are not the most useful subjects for empirical research.

9. Human-computer interaction (HCI) is an example of a field that is progressing toward a multidisciplinary approach, if slowly. This trend was initiated by a few researchers from human sciences who joined HCI—an area that focuses primarily on technology and is peopled mainly by experts in computer science.

10. The division of type of context does not exist in universal models and studies, which aim at findings that are valid to all actors, regardless of their context.

11. One example of this imposed division between the types of context is Savolainen's (1995) model of information seeking in everyday life. Though it was developed and tested on theoretical and empirical foundations that are specific to everyday life, in my opinion the model can be applied to actors in the workplace as well.

12. The nature of this community, whether the extended family, a tribe, or a social strata, can be determined only during the investigation, unless a researcher focuses the study on a certain community. Generally speaking, it would be reasonable to focus on a community because of its influence on its individuals. Thus, the record keeping of a stay-at-home parent in one social stratum is likely to be dissimilar to that of a stay-at-home parent in a far removed stratum.

13. The researchers explained the traditions that influenced their work. It is beyond the scope of this chapter to elaborate on them.

14. CWA analyzes the interaction with information itself, and design also considers the technology available, as it must.

15. Indeed, a first step in adding personal traits to a CWA-based design has already materialized. When Torenvliet, Jamieson, and Vicente (2000) tested various demographic and cognitive characteristics of operators of a special type of control panel situation, they found that among the traits they examined, a holistic cognitive style would benefit most from ecological interface design.

16. As a result, CWA does not consider technology as a stable constraint in areas with rapid technological developments.

17. This question becomes central when artificial intelligence techniques are employed in the design of information systems.

18. That is, systems that organize the display of the results of a search according to the level of relevance of the retrieved items.

References

Ackerman, M. S. 1994. Augmenting the organizational memory: A field study of Answer Garden. In J. Smith, F. Smith, and T. W. Malone, eds., *Proceedings of the ACM Conference on Computer Supported Cooperative Work (CSCW'94)*, 243–252. New York: ACM.

Adomi, E. E. 2002. Patterns of the use of information for decision making by administrative staff of a university in Nigeria. *Library Management* 23(6/7): 330–337.

Agarwal, N. K., Xu, Y. C., and Poo, D. C. C. 2009. Delineating the boundary of "context" in information behavior: Towards a contextual identity framework. In A. Grove, ed., *Proceedings of the ASIS&T Annual Meeting*, 2009. http://asis.org/Conferences/AM09/open-proceedings/open-page.html

Agosto, D. E., and Hughes-Hassell, S. 2005. People, places, and questions: An investigation of the everyday life information-seeking behaviors of urban young adults. *Library and Information Science Research* 27(2): 141–163.

Akers, S. G. 1931. To what extent do the students of the liberal-arts colleges use the bibliographic items given on the catalogue card? *Library Quarterly* 1(4): 394–408.

Albrechtsen, H., Pejtersen, A. M., and Cleal, B. 2002. Empirical work analysis of collaborative film indexing. In H. Bruce, R. Fidel, P. Ingwersen, and P. Vakkari, eds., *Emerging frameworks and methods: Proceedings of the Fourth International Conference on Conceptions of Library and Information Science (CoLIS 4)*, 85–107. Greenwood Village, CO: Libraries Unlimited.

Allard, S., Levine, K. J., and Tenopir, C. 2009. Design engineers and technical professionals at work: Observing information usage in the workplace. *Journal of the American Society for Information Science and Technology* 60(3): 443–454.

Allen, B. 1991a. Cognitive research in information science: Implications for design. *Annual Review of Library and Information Science* 26: 3–37.

Allen, B. 1991b. Topic knowledge and online catalog search formulation. *Library Quarterly* 61(2): 188–213.

Allen, D. K., Wilson, T. D., Norman, A. W. T., and Knight, C. 2008. Information on the move: The use of mobile information systems by UK police forces. *Information Research* 13(4), paper 378. Retrieved from http://InformationR.net/ir/13-4/paper378.html

Allen, T. J. 1969. Information needs and uses. *Annual Review of Information Science and Technology* 4: 3–29.

Allen, T. 1977. *Managing the flow of technology: Technology transfer and the dissemination of technological information within the R&D organization.* Cambridge, MA: MIT Press.

Althaus, S. L., and Tewksbury, D. 2002. Agenda setting and the "new" news: Patterns of issue importance among readers of the paper and online versions of the *New York Times. Communication Research* 29(2): 180–207.

Arendt, H. 1958. *The human condition.* Chicago: University of Chicago Press.

Argote, L., McEvily, B., and Reagans, R. 2003. Managing knowledge in organizations: An integrative framework and review of emerging themes. *Management Science* 49(4): 571–582.

Auster, E., and Choo, C. W. 1994. How senior managers acquire and use information in environmental scanning. *Information Processing and Management* 30(5): 607–618.

Ayers, F. H., German, J., Loukes, N., and Searle, R. H. 1968. Author versus title: A comparative survey of the accuracy of the information which the user brings to the library catalogue. *Journal of Documentation* 24(4): 266–272.

Baker, L. M. 1994. The information needs and information-seeking pattern of women coping with and adjusting to multiple sclerosis. Doctoral dissertation. University of Western Ontario, London, Canada.

Baker, L. M. 2004a. Information needs at the end of life: A content analysis of one person's story. *Journal of the Medical Library Association* 92: 78–82.

Baker, L. M. 2004b. The information needs of female police officers involved in undercover prostitution work. *Information Research* 10(1), paper 209. Retrieved from http://InformationR.net/ir/10-1/paper209.html

Bánáthy, B. H. 1997. *A taste of systemics.* Retrieved August 3, 2009, from http://www.newciv.org/ISSS_Primer/asem04bb.html

Bardram, J. 2000. Temporal coordination: On time and collaborative activities at a surgical department. *Computer Supported Cooperative Work* 9(2): 157–187.

Barry, C. L., and Schamber, L. 1998. User criteria for relevance evaluation: A cross-situational comparison. *Information Processing and Management* 34(2): 219–236.

Barzilai-Nahon, K. 2008a. Gatekeeping revisited: A critical review. *Annual Review of Library and Information Science* 43: 433–478.

Barzilai-Nahon, K. 2008b. Toward a theory of network gatekeeping: A framework for exploring information control. *Journal of the American Society for Information Science and Technology* 59 (9): 1–20.

Bates, M. J. 1979a. Information search tactics. *Journal of the American Society for Information Science American Society for Information Science* 30: 205–214.

Bates, M. J. 1979b. Idea tactics. *Journal of the American Society for Information Science* 30: 280–289.

Bates, M. J. 1981. Search techniques. *Annual Review of Information Science and Technology* 16: 139–169.

Bates, M. J. 1986. Subject access in online catalogs: A design model. *Journal of the American Society for Information Science* 37(6): 357–376.

Bates, M. J. 1989. The design of browsing and berrypicking techniques for the online search interface. *Journal of the American Society for Information Science* 13(5): 407–424.

Bates, M. J. 1990. Where should the person stop and the information search interface start? *Information Processing and Management* 26: 575–591.

Bates, M. J. 1999. The invisible substrata of information science. *Journal of the American Society for Information Science* 50(12): 1043–1050.

Bates, M. J. 2003. Toward an integrated model of information seeking and searching. *New Review of Information Behaviour Research* 3: 1–16. Retrieved September 14, 2009, from http://www.gseis.ucla.edu/faculty/bates/articles/info_SeekSearch-i-030329.html

Bates, M. J. 2005. Information and knowledge: An evolutionary framework for information science. *Information Research* 10(4), paper 239. Retrieved from http://InformationR.net/ir/10-4/paper239.html

Bates, M. J. 2007. What is browsing—really? A model drawing from behavioural science research. *Information Research* 12 (4), paper 330. Retrieved from http://InformationR.net/ir/12-4/paper330.html

Bawden, D. 2006. A three-decade perspective on Tom Wilson's "On user studies and information needs." *Journal of Documentation* 62(6): 671–679.

Bawden, D. 2008. Smoother pebbles and the shoulders of giants: The developing foundations of information science. *Journal of Information Science* 34(4): 415–426.

The behaviour/practice debate: A discussion prompted by Tom Wilson's review of Reijo Savolainen's *Everyday information practices: A social phenomenological perspective.* 2009. *Information Research* 14 (2), paper 403. Retrieved May 25, 2009, from http://InformationR.net/ir/14-2/paper403.html

Belkin, N. J. 1978. Information concepts for information science. *Journal of Documentation* 34(1): 55–85.

Belkin, N. J. 1980. Anomalous states of knowledge as a basis for information retrieval. *Canadian Journal of Information Science* 5: 133–143.

Belkin, N. J. 2005. Anomalous state of knowledge. In K. E. Fisher, S. Erdelez, and E. F. McKechnie, eds., Theories of information behavior, 44–48. Medford, NJ: Information Today.

Belkin, N. J., Cool, C., Stein, A., and Thiel, U. 1995. Cases, scripts, and information-seeking strategies: On the design of interactive information retrieval systems. *Expert Systems with Applications* 9(3): 379–395.

Belkin, N. J., Marchetti, P. G., and Cool, C. 1993. BRAQUE: Design of an interface to support user interaction in information retrieval. *Information Processing and Management* 29(3): 325–344.

Belkin, N. J., Seeger, H., and Wersig, G. 1983. Distributed expert problem treatment as a model for information system analysis and design. *Journal of Information Science* 5(5): 153–167.

Benbasat, I., and Zmud, R. W. 1999. Empirical research in information systems: The practice of relevance. *Management Information Systems Quarterly* 23(1): 3–16.

Benoit, G. 2007. Critical theory and the legitimation of LIS. *Information Research* 12(4), paper colis30. Retrieved from http://InformationR.net/ir/12-4/colis30.html

Benton, T., and Craib, I. 2001. *Philosophy of social science: The philosophical foundation of social thought.* New York: Palgrave.

Berends, H. 2005. Explore knowledge sharing: Moves, problem solving and justification. *Knowledge Management Research and Practice* 3: 97–105.

Berryman, J. M. 2006. What defines "enough" information? How policy workers make judgments and decisions during information seeking: Preliminary results from an exploratory study. *Information Research* 11 (4), paper 266. Retrieved from http://InformationR.net/ir/11-4/paper266.html

von Bertalanffy, L. 1968. *General system theory: Foundations, development, applications.* New York: G. Braziller.

Biradar, B. S., and Vijayalaxmi, I. 1997. Patterns of information use by Indian neurological scientists: A bibliometric study. *Annals of Library Science and Documentation* 44(4): 143–151.

Bisantz, A. M., and Burns, C. M. 2009. *Applications of cognitive work analysis.* Boca Raton, FL: CRC Press.

Blackshaw, L., and Fischhoff, B. 1988. Decision making in online searching. *Journal of the American Society for Information Science* 39(6): 369–389.

Bødker, S. 1991. Activity theory as a challenge to systems design. In H.-E. Nissen, H. K. Klein, and R. Hirscheim, eds., Information systems research: Contemporary approaches and emergent traditions, 551–564. Amsterdam: Elsevier.

Borgman, C. L. 1984a. Psychological research in human-computer interaction. *Annual Review of Information Science and Technology* 19: 33–64.

Borgman, C. L. 1984b. The user's mental model of an information retrieval system: Effects on performance. Doctoral dissertation. Stanford, CA: Stanford University.

Borlund, P. 2000. Experimental components for the evaluation of interactive information retrieval systems. *Journal of Documentation* 56(1): 71–90.

Borlund, P. 2003a. The concept of relevance in IR. *Journal of the American Society for Information Science and Technology* 54(10): 913–925.

Borlund, P. 2003b. The IIR evaluation model: A framework for evaluation of interactive information retrieval systems. *Information Research* 8(3), paper no. 152. Retrieved from http://informationr.net/ir/8-3/paper152.html

Borlund, P. 2009. User-centred evaluation of information retrieval systems. In A. Göker and J. Davies, eds., Information retrieval: Searching in the 21st century, 21–37. London: Wiley.

Borlund, P., and Ingwersen, P. 1997. The development of a method for the evaluation of interactive information retrieval systems. *Journal of Documentation* 53(3): 225–250.

Bowler, L., and Large, A. 2008. Design-based research for LIS. *Library and Information Science Research* 30(1): 39–46.

Brittain, J. M. 1970. *Information and its uses: A review with a special reference to the social sciences*. Bath, UK: Bath University Press.

Bruce, C. 1997. *The seven faces of information literacy*. Adelaide, Australia: Auslib Press.

Bruce, H. 1994. A cognitive view of the situational dynamism of user-centered relevance estimation. *Journal of the American Society for Information Science* 43(3): 142–148.

Bruce, H. 2005. Personal anticipated information need. *Information Research* 10(3), paper 232. Retrieved from http://InformationR.net/ir/10-3/paper232.html

Bruce, H., Fidel, R., Pejtersen, A. M., Dumais, S., Grudin, J., and Poltrock, S. 2003. A comparison of the collaborative information retrieval behaviour of two design teams. *New Review of Information Behaviour Research: Studies of Information Seeking in Context* 4(1): 139–153.

Buckland, M. K. 1991. Information as thing. *Journal of the American Society for Information Science* 42(5): 351–360.

Budd, J. M. 2001. *Knowledge and knowing in LIS: A philosophical framework*. Lanham, MA: Scarecrow.

Budd, J. M. 2005. Phenomenology and information science. *Journal of Documentation* 61(1): 44–59.

Burns, C. M., and Hajdukiewicz, J. R. 2004. *Ecological interface design*. New York: CRC Press.

Byström, K. 2007. Approaches to "task" in contemporary information studies. *Information Research* 12 (4), paper colis26. Retrieved from http://informationr.net/ir/12-4/colis/colis26.html

Byström, K., and P. Hansen. 2002. Work tasks as units for analysis in information seeking and retrieval studies. In H. Bruce, R. Fidel, P. Ingwersen, and P. Vakkari, eds., Emerging frameworks and methods: Proceedings of the Fourth International Conference on Conceptions of Library and Information Science (CoLIS 4), 239–251. Greenwood Village, CO: Libraries Unlimited.

Byström, K., and Järvelin, K. 1995. Task complexity affects information seeking and use. *Information Processing and Management* 31(2): 191–213.

Campbell, D. R., Culley, S. J., McMahon, C. A., and Sellini, F. 2007. An approach for the capture of context-dependent document relationships extracted from Bayesian analysis of users' interactions with information. *Information Retrieval* 10: 115–141.

Capurro, R., and Hjørland, B. 2003. The concept of information. *Annual Review of Information Science and Technology* 37: 343–411.

Card, S. K., Mackinlay, J. D., and Shneiderman, B., eds. 1999. Readings in information visualization: Using vision to think. San Francisco: Morgan.

Case, D. O. 2007. *Looking for information: A survey of research on information seeking, needs, and behavior.* 2d ed. Boston: Elsevier.

Chang, S. J. L. 2005. Chang's browsing. In K. E. Fisher, S. Erdelez, and E. F. McKechnie, eds., Theories of information behavior, 69–74. Medford, NJ: Information Today.

Chang, S. J., and Rice, R. E. 1993. Browsing: A multidimensional framework. *Annual Review of Information Science and Technology* 28: 231–276.

Chatman, E. A. 1986. Diffusion theory: A review and test of a conceptual model in information diffusion. *Journal of the American Society for Information Science* 37(6): 265–283.

Chatman, E. A. 1987. The information world of low-skilled workers. *Library and Information Science Research* 9: 265–283.

Chatman, E. A. 1992. *The information world of retired women.* Westport, CT: Greenwood Press.

Chatman, E. A. 1996. The impoverished life-world of outsiders. *Journal of the American Society for Information Science* 47(3): 193–206.

Chatman, E. A. 1999. A theory of life in the round. *Journal of the American Society for Information Science* 50(3): 207–217.

Chatman, E. A. 2000. Framing social life in theory and research. *New Review of Information Behaviour Research* 1: 3–17.

Chen, C. C., and Hernon, P. 1982. *Information seeking: Assessing and anticipating user needs.* New York: Neal-Schuman.

Chen, S. Y., and Ford, N. 1998. Modelling user navigation behaviours in a hypermedia based learning system: An individual differences approach. *Knowledge Organization* 25(3): 67–78.

Chen, S. Y., Magoulas, G. D., and Dimakopoulos, D. 2005. A flexible interface design for web directories to accommodate different cognitive styles. *Journal of the American Society for Information Science and Technology* 56(1): 70–83.

Chervany, N. L., and Dickson, G.W. 1978. On the validity of the analytical-heuristic instrument utilized in "The Minnesota Experiments": A reply. *Management Science* 24(10): 1091–1092. (Cited in Huber 1983.)

Choo, C. W., and Auster, E. 1993. Environmental scanning: Acquisition and use of information by managers. *Annual Review of Information Science and Technology* 28: 279–314.

Churchman, C. W. 1971. *The design of inquiring systems: Basic concepts of systems and organization.* New York: Basic Books.

Churchman, C. W. 1979a. *The systems approach.* New York: Dell.

Churchman, C. W. 1979b. *The systems approach and its enemies.* New York: Basic Books.

Cleverdon, C. W. 1962. *Report on the testing and analysis of an investigation into the comparative efficiency of indexing systems.* Cranfield, UK: College of Aeronautics.

Cleverdon, C. W. 1967. The Cranfield test on index language devices. *Aslib Proceedings* 19(6): 173–194.

Cleverdon, C. W., Mills, J., and Keen, E. M. 1966. Factors determining the performance of indexing systems. 2 vols. Cranfield, UK: College of Aeronautics.

Cochrane, P. A., and Markey, K. 1983. Catalog use studies since the introduction of online interactive catalogs: Impact on design for subject access. *Library and Information Science Research* 5(4): 337–363.

Cole, C. 1999. Activity of understanding a problem during interaction with "enabling" information retrieval system: Modeling information flow. *Journal of the American Society for Information Science* 50(6): 544–552.

Cole, C. 2011. A theory of information need for information retrieval that connects information to knowledge. *Journal of the American Society for Information Science American Society for Information Science* 62 (7):1231–1236.

Cook, S. N., and Brown, J. S. 1999. Bridging epistemologies: The generative dance between organizational knowledge and organizational knowing. *Organization Science* 10(4): 381–400.

Cornelius, I. V. 2002. Theorizing information for information science. *Annual Review of Information Science and Technology* 36: 393–425.

Courtright, C. 2004. Health information-seeking among Latino newcomers: An exploratory study. *Information Research* 10(2), paper 224. Retrieved from http://InformationR.net/ir/10-2/paper224.html

Courtright, C. 2007. Context in information behavior. *Annual Review of Information Science and Technology* 41: 273–306.

Crane, D. 1971. Information needs and uses. *Annual Review of Information Science and Technology* 6: 3–39.

Crane, D. 1972. *Invisible colleges: Diffusion of knowledge in scientific communities*. Chicago: University of Chicago.

Crawford, S. 1978. Information needs and uses. *Annual Review of Information Science and Technology* 13: 61–81.

Crestani, F., and Ruthven, I. 2007. Introduction to special issue on contextual information retrieval systems. *Information Retrieval* 10(2): 111–113.

Cronin, B. 2008. The sociological turn in information science. *Journal of Information Science* 34(4): 465–475.

Cronin, B., and Meho, L. I. 2009. Receiving the French: A bibliometric snapshot of the impact of "French theory" on information studies. *Journal of Information Science* 35(4): 398–413.

Cushing, A. 2010. "I just want more information about who I am": The search experience of sperm-donor offspring, searching for information about their donors and genetic heritage. *Information Research* 15(2), paper 428. Retrieved from http://InformationR.net/ir/15-2/paper428.html

Davidson, D. 1977. The effect of individual differences of cognitive styles on judgments of document relevance. *Journal of the American Society for Information Science* 28(5): 273–284.

Derr, R. L. 1984. Information seeking expressions of users. *Journal of the American Society for Information Science* 35: 124–128.

Dervin, B. 1976. The everyday information needs of the average citizen: A taxonomy of analysis. In M. Kochen and J. C. Donohue, eds., Information for the community, 19–38. Chicago: American Library Association.

Dervin, B. 1980. Communication gaps and inequities: Moving towards reconceptualization. *Progress in Communication Sciences* 2: 73–112.

Dervin, B. 1992. From the mind's eye of the user: The sense-making qualitative-quantitative methodology. In J. D. Galzier and R. R. Powell, eds., Qualitative research in information management. Englewood, CO: Libraries Unlimited.

Dervin, B. 1997. Given a context by any other name: Methodological tools for taming the unruly beast. In P. Vakkari, R. Savolainen, and B. Dervin, eds., *Information seeking in context: Proceedings of the International Conference on Research in Information Needs, Seeking, and Use in Different Contexts*, 13–38. London: Taylor Graham.

Dervin, B. 2006. Being user-oriented: Convergences, divergences, and the potentials for systematic dialogue between disciplines and between researchers, designers, and providers. From a panel discussion at the 2006 Annual Meeting of the American Society for Information Science and Technology. Retrieved on January 10, 2011 from http://imlsproject.comm.ohio-state.edu/imls_papers/asist06_panel_full_proposal.pdf

Dervin, B., and Naumer, C. M. 2009. Sense-making. In M. Bates and M. N. Maack, eds., Encyclopedia of library and information sciences. 3rd ed. New York: Taylor and Francis.

Dervin, B., and Nilan, M. 1986. Information needs and uses. *Annual Review of Information Science and Technology* 21: 3–33.

Dimitroff, A. 1992. Mental models theory and search outcome in bibliographic retrieval systems. *Library and Information Science Research* 14(2): 141–156.

Dinadis, N., and Vicente, K. J. 1996. Ecological interface design for a power plant feedwater subsystem. *IEEE Transactions on Nuclear Science* 43(1, pt. 2): 266–277.

Dinadis, N., and Vicente, K. J. 1999. Designing functional visualizations for aircraft systems status displays. *International Journal of Aviation Psychology* 9(3): 241–269.

Dourish, P. 2004. What we talk about when we talk about context. *Personal and Ubiquitous Computing* 8(1): 19–30.

Dourish, P. 2006. Implications for design. In R. Grinter, T. Rodden, P. Aoki, E. Cutrell, R. Jeffries, and G. Olson, eds., *Proceedings of the SIGCHI Conference on Human Factors in Computing Systems (CHI 2006)*, 541–550. New York: ACM.

Dresang, E. 1999. *Radical change: Books for youth in a digital age.* New York: H. W. Wilson.

Dunne, J. E. 2002. Information seeking and use by battered women: A "person-in-progressive-situations" approach. *Library and Information Science Research* 24(4): 343–355.

Effken, J., Loeb, R., Johnson, K., Johnson, S., and Reyna, V. 2001. Using cognitive work analysis to design clinical displays. In V. Patel, R. Rogers, and R. Haux, eds., *MEDINFO 2001: Proceedings of the 10th World Congress on Medical Informatics*, 127–131. Amsterdam: IOS Press.

Eisenberg, M. B. 1988. Measuring relevance measurements. *Information Processing and Management* 24(4): 373–389.

Eisenberg, M. B., and Berkowitz, R. E. 1990. *Information problem-solving: The Big Six skills approach to library and information skills instructions.* Norwood, NJ: Ablex.

Ellis, D. 1989. A behavioral approach to information retrieval system design. *Journal of Documentation* 45: 171–212.

Ellis, D. 1993. Modeling the information seeking patterns of academic researchers: A grounded theory approach. *Library Quarterly* 63(4): 469–486.

Endres-Niggemeyer, B. 2000. SimSum: An empirically founded simulation of summarizing. *Information Processing and Management* 36(4): 659–682.

Endres-Niggemeyer, B., Maier, E., and Sigel, A. 1995. How to implement a naturalistic model of abstracting: Four core working steps of an expert abstractor. *Information Processing and Management* 31(5): 631–674.

Erdelez, S. 2005. Information encountering. In K. E. Fisher, S. Erdelez, and E. F. McKechnie, eds., Theories of information behavior, 179–184. Medford, NJ: Information Today.

Eriksson-Backa, K. 2008. Access to health information: Perceptions of barriers among elderly in a language minority. *Information Research* 13(4), paper 368. Retrieved from http://InformationR .net/ir/13-4/paper368.html

Faibisoff, S. G., and Ely, D. P 1976. Information and information needs. *Information Reports and Bibliographies* 5(5): 2–16.

Fenichel, C. H. 1980. The process of searching online bibliographic databases: A review of research. *Library Research* 2(2): 107–127.

Fenichel, C. H. 1981. Online searching: Measures that discriminate among users with different types of experience. *Journal of the American Society for Information Science* 31(1): 23–32.

Fidel, R., and Crandall, M. 1997. Users' perception of the performance of a filtering system. In N. J. Belkin, ed., *Proceedings of the 20th annual International ACM/SIGIR Conference on Research and Development in Information Retrieval*, 198–205. New York: ACM Press.

Fidel, R., Davies, R. K., Douglass, M. H., Holder, J. K., Hopkins, C. J., Kushner, J., Miyagishima, B. K., and Toney, C. D. 1999. A visit to the information mall: Web searching behavior of high school students. *Journal of the American Society for Information Science* 50: 24–37.

Fidel, R., and Efthimiadis, E. 1998. Content organization and retrieval project—Phase I: A work-centered examination of web searching behavior of Boeing engineers. Final report for The Boeing Company.

Fidel, R., and Green, M. 2004. The many faces of accessibility: Engineers' perception of information sources. *Information Processing and Management* 40: 563–581.

Fidel, R., and A. M. Pejtersen. 2004. From information behaviour research to the design of information systems: The cognitive work analysis framework. *Information Research* 10(1), paper 210. Retrieved from http://InformationR.net/ir/10-1/paper210.html

Fidel, R., Pejtersen, A. M., Cleal, B., and Bruce, H. 2004. A multidimensional approach to the study of human-information interaction: A case study of collaborative information retrieval. *Journal of the American Society for Information Science* 55(11): 939–953.

Fidel, R., Scholl, H. J., Liu, S., and Unsworth, K. 2007. Mobile government fieldwork: A preliminary study of technological, organizational, and social challenges. International Conference on Digital Government Research (DGO 2007), Philadelphia, PA.

Fidel, R., and Soergel, D. 1983. Factors affecting online bibliographic retrieval: A conceptual framework for research. *Journal of the American Society for Information Science* 34(3): 163–180.

Fikar, C. R., and Keith, L. 2004. Information needs of gay, lesbian, bisexual, and transgendered health care professionals: Results of an Internet survey. *Journal of the Medical Library Association* 92(1): 56–65.

Fishenden, R. M. 1965. Information use studies. Part 1: Past results and future needs. *Journal of Documentation* 21:163–168. (Cited in T. D. Wilson 1994.)

Fisher, K. E. 2005. Information grounds. In K. E. Fisher, S. Erdelez, and E. F. McKechnie, eds., Theories of information behavior, 185–190. Medford, NJ: Information Today.

Fisher, K. E., Durrance, J. C., and Hinton, M. B. 2004. Information grounds and the use of need-based services by immigrants in Queens, New York: A context-based, outcome evaluation approach. *Journal of the American Society for Information Science and Technology* 55(8): 754–766.

Fisher, K. E., Erdelez, S., and McKechnie, E. F., eds. 2005. Theories of information behavior. Medford, NJ: Information Today.

Fisher, K. E., and Julien, H. 2009. Information behavior. *Annual Review of Information Science and Technology* 43: 317–358.

Fisher, K. E., E. Marcoux, L. S. Miller, A. Sánchez, and E. Ramirez Cunningham. 2004. Information behaviour of migrant Hispanic farm workers and their families in the Pacific Northwest. *Information Research* 10(1), paper 199. Retrieved from http://InformationR.net/ir/10-1/paper199.html

Fisher, K. E., C. M. Naumer, J. C. Durrance, L. Stromski, and T. Christiansen. 2005. Something old, something new: Preliminary findings from an exploratory study about people's information habits and information grounds. *Information Research* 10(2), paper 223. Retrieved from http://InformationR.net/ir/10-2/paper223.html

Flowers, B. H. 1965. Survey of information needs of physicists and chemists. *Journal of Documentation* 21(2): 83–112.

Ford, N. J. 1980. Relating "information needs" to learner characteristics in higher education. *Journal of Documentation* 36: 99–114.

Ford, N. J. 2004. Creativity and convergence in information science research: The roles of objectivity and subjectivity, constraint, and control. *Journal of the American Society for Information Science and Technology* 55(13): 1169–1182.

Ford, N., and Chen, S. Y. 2002. Individual difference, hypermedia navigation, and learning: An empirical study. *Journal of Educational Multimedia and Hypermedia* 9(4): 281–311.

Ford, N., Eaglestone, B., and Madden, A. 2009. Web searching by the "general public": An individual differences perspective. *Journal of Documentation* 65(4): 632–667.

Ford, N., Wilson, T. D., Foster, A., Ellis, D., and Spink, A. 2002. Information seeking and mediated searching. Part 4: Cognitive styles in information seeking. *Journal of the American Society for Information Science and Technology* 53(9): 728–735.

Ford, N., Wood, F., and Walsh, C. 1994. Cognitive styles and searching. *Online and CDROM Review* 18(2): 79–86.

Foster, A., C. Urquhart, and J. Turner. 2008. Validating coding for a theoretical model of information behaviour. *Information Research* 13(4), paper 358. Retrieved from http://InformationR.net/ir/13-4/paper358.html

Foster, J. 2006. Collaborative information seeking and retrieval. *Annual Review of Information Science and Technology* 40: 329–356.

Froehlich, T. J. 1994. Relevance reconsidered—Towards an agenda for the 21st century: Introduction to special topic issue on relevance research. *Journal of the American Society for Information Science* 45(3): 124–133.

Fulton, C. 2010. Celebrating SIG/USE and information behavior research. *Bulletin of the American Society for Information Science and Technology* 36(3). Retrieved June 23, 2011 from http://www.asis.org/Bulletin/Feb-10/FebMar10_Fulton.pdf

Furner, J. 2010. Philosophy and information studies. *Annual Review of Information Science and Technology* 44: 161–200.

Garvey, W. D. 1979. *Communication, the essence of science: Facilitating information exchange among librarians, scientists, engineers, and students.* New York: Pergamon.

Gay, G., and Hembrooke, H. 2004. *Activity-centered design: An ecological approach to designing smart tools and usable systems.* Cambridge, MA: MIT Press.

George, C., A. Bright, T. Hurlbert, E. C. Linke, G. St. Clair, and J. Stein. 2006. Scholarly use of information: Graduate students' information seeking behaviour. *Information Research* 11(4), paper 272. Retrieved from http://InformationR.net/ir/11-4/paper272.html

Gibson, J. J. 1979. *The ecological approach to visual perception.* Boston: Houghton-Mifflin.

Given, L. M. 2002. Discursive constructions in the university context: Social positioning theory and mature undergraduates' information behaviours. *New Review of Information Behaviour Research: Studies of Information Seeking in Context* 3: 127–141.

Godbold, N. 2006. Beyond information seeking: Towards a general model of information behaviour. *Information Research* 11(4), paper 269. Retrieved from http://InformationR.net/ir/11-4/paper269.html

Gorman, M., and P. W. Winkler, and the Joint Steering Committee for Revision of AACR. 1998. *Anglo-American cataloguing rules.* 2nd ed. Chicago: American Library Association.

Granovetter, M. S. 1973. The strength of weak ties. *American Journal of Sociology* 78: 1360–1380. (Cited in Courtright 2007.)

Gross, M. 1995. The imposed query. *RQ* 35: 236–243.

Gross, M. 2001. Imposed information seeking in public libraries and school library media centres: A common behaviour? *Information Research* 6(2). Retrieved from http://InformationR.net/ir/6-2/paper100.html

Gross, M. 2005. The imposed query. In K. E. Fisher, S. Erdelez, and E. F. McKechnie, eds., Theories of information behavior, 164–168. Medford, NJ: Information Today.

Groth, K., and Lannerö, P. 2006. Context browser: Ontology-based navigation in information spaces. In I. Ruthven, P. Borlund, P. Ingwersen, N. Belkin, A. Tombros, and P. Vakkari, eds., *Proceedings of the First International Conference on Information Interaction in Context*, 75–78. New York: ACM.

Gull, C. D. 1956. Seven years of work on the organization of materials in special library. *American Documentation* 7: 320–329.

Gwizdka, J. 2009. What a difference a tag cloud makes: Effects of tasks and cognitive abilities on search results interface use. *Information Research* 14(4), paper 414. Retrieved from http://InformationR.net/ir/14-4/paper414.html

Hartel, J. 2006. Information activities and resources in an episode of gourmet cooking. *Information Research* 12(1), paper 281. Retrieved from http://InformationR.net/ir/12-1/paper282.html

Heinström, J. 2003. Five personality dimensions and their influence on information behaviour. *Information Research* 9(1), paper 165. Retrieved from http://InformationR.net/ir/9-1/paper165.html

Heinström, J. 2006. Psychological factors behind incidental information acquisition. *Library and Information Science Research* 28(4): 579–594.

Heisig, P., Caldwell, N. H. M., Grebici, K., and Clarkson, P. J. 2010. Exploring knowledge and information needs in engineering from the past and for the future: Results from a survey. Design Studies 31(5): 499–532.

Hendriks, P. 1999. Why share knowledge? The influence of ICT on the motivation for knowledge sharing. *Knowledge and Process Management* 6(2): 91–100.

Hepworth, M. 2004. A framework for understanding user requirements for an information service: Defining the needs of informal careers. *Journal of the American Society for Information Science and Technology* 55(8): 695–708.

Hernandez, N., Mothe, J., Chrisment, C., and Egret, D. 2007. Modeling context through domain ontologies. *Information Retrieval* 10: 143–172.

Herner, S., and Herner, M. 1967. Information needs and uses in science and technology. *Annual Review of Information Science and Technology* 2: 1–34.

Hersberger, J. 2001. Everyday information needs and information sources of homeless parents. *New Review of Information Behaviour Research* 2: 119–134.

Hersberger, J. A., A. L. Murray, and S. M. Sokoloff. 2006. The information use environment of abused and neglected children. *Information Research* 12(1), paper 277. Retrieved from http://InformationR.net/ir/12-1/paper277.html

Herschel, R. T., Nemati, H., and Steiger, D. 2001. Tacit to explicit knowledge conversion: Knowledge exchange protocols. *Journal of Knowledge Management* 5(1): 107–116.

Hertzum, M., Pejtersen, A. M., Cleal, B., and Albrechtsen, H. 2002. An analysis of collaboration in three film archives: A case for collaboratories. In H. Bruce et al., eds., *Emerging frameworks and methods: Proceedings of the Fourth International Conference on Conceptions of Library and Information Science*, 69–84. Greenwood Village, CO: Libraries Unlimited.

Hideo, J., and Joemon, M. J. 2006. Slicing and dicing the information space using local contexts. In I. Ruthven, ed., *Proceedings of the First International Conference on Information Interaction in Context*, 66–74. New York: ACM.

Hirsh, S. G. 1999. Children's relevance criteria and information seeking on electronic resources. *Journal of the American Society for Information Science* 37: 25–36.

Hjørland, B. 2004. Arguments for philosophical realism in library and information science. *Library Trends* 52(3): 488–506.

Hjørland, B. 2005a. Empiricism, rationalism and positivism in library and information science. *Journal of Documentation* 61(1): 13–155.

Hjørland, B. 2005b. Comments on the articles and proposals for future work. *Journal of Documentation* 61(1): 156–163.

Hjørland, B. 2010. The foundation of the concept relevance. *Journal of the American Society for Information Science and Technology* 61(2): 217–237.

Hollnagel, E., and Woods, D. D. 2005. *Joint cognitive systems: Foundations of cognitive systems engineering*. New York: Taylor and Francis.

Howard, J. 2010. Conference explores how to find—and make findable—information in a digital sea. *Chronicle of Higher Education*, September 29. Retrieved June 28, 2011 from http://chronicle.com/article/Conference-Explores-How-to/124665/

Huang, X., and D. Soergel. 2006. An evidence perspective on topical relevance types and its implications for exploratory and task-based retrieval. *Information Research* 12(1), paper 281. Retrieved from http://InformationR.net/ir/12-1/paper281.html

Huber, G. P. 1983. Cognitive styles as a basis for MIS and DSS designs: Much ado about nothing? *Management Science* 29(5): 567–579.

Hurd, J. M. 1992. Interdisciplinary research in the sciences: Implications to library organization. *College and Research Libraries* 53(4): 283–297.

Hyldegård, J. 2006. Collaborative information behavior: Exploring Kuhlthau's Information Search Process model in a group-based educational setting. *Information Processing and Management* 42: 276–298.

Hyldegård, J. 2009. Beyond the search process: Exploring group members' information behavior in context. *Information Processing and Management* 45: 142–158.

Iivonen, M., and White, M. D. 2001. The choice of initial Web search strategies: A comparison between Finnish and American searchers. *Journal of Documentation* 57(4): 465–491.

Ingwersen, P. 1986. Cognitive analysis and the role of intermediary in information retrieval. In R. David, ed., Intelligent information systems, 206–237. Chichester, West Sussex: Ellis Horwood.

Ingwersen, P. 1996. Cognitive perspectives of information retrieval interaction: Elements of a cognitive theory. *Journal of Documentation* 52(1): 3–50.

Ingwersen, P. 1999. Cognitive information retrieval. *Annual Review of Information Science and Technology* 34: 3–51.

Ingwersen, P., and Järvelin, K. 2005. *The turn: Integration of information seeking and retrieval in context*. Dordrecht: Springer.

ISIC. 2009. Call for papers. Retrieved November 1, 2009 from http://www.um.es/isic2010/papers .php

Jacobsen, T. L., and Fusani, D. 1992. Computer, system, and subject knowledge in novice searching of a full-text, multifile database. *Library and Information Science Research* 14(1): 97–106.

Jamieson, G. A., and Vicente, K. J. 2001. Ecological interface design for petrochemical applications: Supporting operator adaptation, continuous learning, and distributed, collaborative work. *Computers and Chemical Engineering* 25(7–8): 1055–1074.

Janes, J. W. 1994. Other people's judgments: A comparison of users' and others' judgments of document relevance, topicality, and utility. *Journal of the American Society for Information Science* 45(3): 160–171.

Jansen, B. J., and McNeese, M. D. 2005. Evaluating effectiveness of and patterns of interactions with automated searching assistance. *Journal of the American Society for Information Science and Technology* 56(14): 1480–1503.

Järvelin, K., and P. Ingwersen. 2004. Information seeking research needs extension towards tasks and technology. *Information Research* 10(1), paper 212. Retrieved from http://informationr.net/ ir/10-1/infres101.html

Järvelin, K., and Kekäläinen, J. 2000. IR evaluation methods for retrieving highly relevant documents. In N. J. Belkin, P. Ingwersen, and M.-K. Leong, eds., *Proceedings of the 23rd ACM Sigir Conference on Research and Development of Information Retrieval. Athens, Greece, 2000,* 41–48. New York: ACM Press.

Järvelin, K., and Vakkari, P. 1990. Content analysis of research articles in library and information science. *Library and Information Science Research* 12: 395–421.

Järvelin, K., and Vakkari, P. 1993. The evolution of library and information science 1965–1985: A content analysis of journal articles. *Information Processing and Management* 29(1): 129–144.

Järvelin, K., and T. D. Wilson. 2003. On conceptual models for information seeking and retrieval research. *Information Research* 9(1), paper 163. Retrieved from http://InformationR.net/ir/9-1/paper163.html

Jenkins, D. P., Stanton, N. A., Salmon, P. M., and Walker, G. H. 2009. *Cognitive work analysis: Coping with complexity*. Burlington, VT: Ashgate.

Johnson, F. C., J. R. Griffiths, and R. J. Hartley. 2003 Task dimensions of user evaluations of information retrieval systems. *Information Research* 8(4), paper no. 157. Retrieved from http://informationr.net/ir/8-4/paper157.html

Jones, B. 2008. Reductionism and library and information science philosophy. *Journal of Documentation* 64(4): 482–495.

Jones, W. 2008. *Keeping found things found: The study and practice of personal information management*. Boston: Elsevier.

Jones, W. 2010. No knowledge but through information. *First Monday* 15(9). Retrieved September 6, 2010, from http://www.uic.edu/htbin/cgiwrap/bin/ojs/index.php/fm/article/viewArticle/3062/2600

Jones, W., Pirolli, P., Card, S. K., Fidel, R., Gershon, N., Morville, P., Nardi, B., and Russell, D. M. 2006. "It's about the information stupid!": Why we need a separate field of human-information interaction. *CHI '06: CHI '06 extended abstracts on human factors in computing systems*. Retrieved July 10, 2011, from http://portal.acm.org/citation.cfm?id=1125451.1125469&coll=DL&dl=GUIDE&CFID=34210393&CFTOKEN=75586447

Ju, B., and Gluck, M. 2005. User-process model approach to improve user interface usability. *Journal of the American Society for Information Science and Technology* 56(10): 1098–1112.

Julien, H., and Duggan, L. 2000. A longitudinal analysis of the information needs and uses literature. *Library and Information Science Research* 22(3): 291–309.

Kaptelinin, V., and Nardi, B. 2006. *Acting with technology: Activity theory and interaction design*. Cambridge, MA: MIT Press.

Kari, J. 1998. Paranormal information seeking in everyday life: The paranormal in information action. *Information Research* 4(2). Retrieved from http://informationr.net/ir/4-2/isic/kari.html

Kari, J. 2007. Conceptualizing the personal outcomes of information. *Information Research* 12(2). Retrieved from http://informationr.net/ir/12-2/paper292.html

Kari, J., and Savolainen, R. 2007. Relationships between information seeking and context: A qualitative study of Internet searching and the goals of personal development. *Library and Information Science Research* 29(1): 47–69.

Katter, R. V. 1968. The influence of scale form on relevance judgment. *Information Storage and Retrieval* 4(1): 1–11.

Katz, R., Tushman, M., and Allen, T. J. 1995. The influence of supervisory promotion and network location on subordinate careers in a dual ladder. *Management Science* 41(5): 848–863.

Katzer, J., and Fletcher, P. T. 1992. The information environment of managers. *Annual Review of Information Science and Technology* 27: 227–263.

Katzer, J., and Snyder, H. 1990. Towards a more realistic assessment of information retrieval performance. *Proceedings of the American Society for Information Science* 27: 80–85.

Kenney, L. 1966. The implications of the needs of users for the design of a catalogue: A survey at the International Labour Office. *Journal of Documentation* 22(3): 195–202.

Kent, A., Berry, M. M., Luehrs, F. U., and Perry, J. W. 1955. Machine literature searching. VIII: Operational criteria for designing information retrieval systems. *American Documentation* 6(2): 93–101.

Keskustalo, H., Järvelin, K., and Pirkola, A. 2008. Evaluating the effectiveness of relevance feedback based on a user simulation model: Effects of a user scenario on cumulated gain value. *Information Retrieval* 11: 209–228.

Khalil, O. E. M., and Elkordy, M. M. 2005. EIS information: Use and quality determinants. *Information Resources Management Journal* 18(2): 68–93.

Kidd, J. S. 1976. Determining information needs of civic organizations and voluntary groups. In M. Kochen and J. C. Donohue, eds., Information for the community, 39–54. Chicago: American Library Association.

Kim, S., and Oh, S. 2009. Users' relevance criteria for evaluating answers in a social Q&A site. *Journal of the American Society for Information Science and Technology* 60(4): 716–727.

Kim, S. J., and Jeong, D. Y. 2006. An analysis of the development and use of theory in library and information science research articles. *Library and Information Science Research* 28(4): 548–562.

King, D. W., and Tenopir, C. 1999. Using and reading scholarly literature. *Annual Review of Information Science and Technology* 34: 423–477.

Kirk, J. 2002. Theorizing information use: Managers and their work. Doctoral dissertation. University of Technology, Sydney, Australia.

Kling, R. 2009. About social informatics. Retrieved January 26, 2009, from http://rkcsi.indiana.edu/index.php/about-social-informatics

Komlodi, A., Marchionini, G., and Soergel, D. 2007. Search history support for finding and using information: User interface design recommendations from a user study. *Information Processing and Management* 43(1): 10–29.

Koshman, S. 2006. Visualization-based information retrieval on the Web. *Library and Information Science Research* 28(2): 192–207.

Krikelas, J. 1983. Information-seeking behavior: Patterns and concepts. *Drexel Library Quarterly* 19: 5–20.

Kuhlthau, C. C. 1991. Inside the search process: Information seeking from the users' perspective. *Journal of the American Society for Information Science* 42(5): 361–371.

Kuhlthau, C. C. 1997. The influence of uncertainty on the information seeking behavior of a securities analyst. In P. Vakkari, R. Savolainen, and B. Dervin, eds., *Information seeking in context: Proceedings of the International Conference on Research in Information Needs, Seeking, and Use in Different Contexts*, 268–274. London: Taylor Graham.

Kuhlthau, C. C. 2004. Seeking meaning: A process approach to library and information services. 2d ed. Westport, CT: Libraries Unlimited.

Kuhlthau, C. C. 2005. Towards collaboration between information seeking and information retrieval. *Information Research* 10(2), paper 225. Retrieved from http://InformationR.net/ir/10-2/paper225.html

Lakoff, G. 1987. *Women, fire, and dangerous things: What categories reveal about the mind.* Chicago: University of Chicago Press.

Lamb, R., King, J. L., and Kling, R. 2003. Informational environments: Organizational contexts of online information use. *Journal of the American Society for Information Science and Technology* 54(2): 97–114.

Leckie, G., Given, L. M., and Buschman, J. E., eds. 2010. Critical theory for library and information science: Exploring the social from across the disciplines. Santa Barbara, CA: Libraries Unlimited.

Leckie, G. J., and Pettigrew, K. E. 1997. A general model of the information seeking of professionals: Role theory through the back door? In P. Vakkari, R. Savolainen, and B. Dervin, eds., *Information seeking in context: Proceedings of the International Conference on Research in Information Needs, Seeking, and Use in Different Contexts*, 99–110. London: Taylor Graham.

Leckie, G. J., Pettigrew, K. E., and Sylvain, C. 1996. Modeling the information seeking of professionals: A general model derived from research on engineers, health care professionals, and lawyers. *Library Quarterly* 66(2): 161–193.

Lee, H., Belkin, N. J., and Krovitz, B. 2006. Rutgers information retrieval evaluation project on IR performance on different precision levels. *Journal of the Korean Society for Information Management* 23(2): 97–111.

Lesk, M. E., and Salton, G. 1968. Relevance assessments and retrieval system evaluation. *Information Storage and Retrieval* 4(3): 343–359.

Levinthal, D.A., and March, J. G. 1993. The myopia of learning. *Strategic Management Journal* 14 (Special issue on organizations, decision making): 95–112.

Lewin, K. 1951. *Field theory in social science: Selected theoretical papers.* New York: Harper.

Li, Y. 2009. Exploring the relationships between work task and search task in information search. *Journal of the American Society for Information Science and Technology* 60(2): 275–291.

Limberg, L. 1997. Information use for learning purposes. In P. Vakkari, R. Savolainen, and B. Dervin, eds., *Information seeking in context: Proceedings of the International Conference on Research in Information Needs, Seeking, and Use in Different Contexts*, 275–289. London: Taylor Graham.

Limberg, L. 1999. Experiencing information seeking and learning. *Information Research* 5(1). Retrieved June 6, 2008, from http://informationr.net/ir/5-1/paper68.html

Lin, N., and Garvey, W. D. 1972. Information needs and uses. *Annual Review of Library and Information Science* 7: 5–37.

Line, M. B. 1971. The information uses and needs of social scientists: An overview of INFROSS. *Aslib Proceedings* 23: 412–434.

Lipetz, B. 1970. Information needs and uses. *Annual Review of Information Science and Technology* 5: 3–32.

Logan, E. 1990. Cognitive styles and online behavior of novice searchers. *Information Processing and Management* 26(4): 503–510.

Long, N. 1976. Information referral services: A short history and some recommendations. In M. Kochen and J. C. Donohue, eds., Information for the community, 55–73. Chicago: American Library Association.

Mackay, D. M. 1960. What makes a question. *The Listener* 63: 789–790. (Cited by Taylor 1968.)

Marchionini, G. 1989. Making the transition from print to electronic encyclopaedias: Adaptation of mental models. *International Journal of Man-Machine Studies* 30(6): 591–618.

Marchionini, G. 1995. *Information seeking in electronic environments*. Cambridge: Cambridge University Press.

Marchionini, G., and Komlodi, A. 1998. Design of interfaces for information seeking. *Annual Review of Information Science and Technology* 33: 89–130.

Marshall, L. 1997. Facilitating knowledge management and knowledge sharing: New opportunities for information processionals. *Online* 21(5): 92–98.

Martzoukou, K. 2008. Students' attitudes towards Web search engines: Increasing appreciation of sophisticated search strategies. *Libri* 58(3): 182–201.

May, J. E. 2009. Private email communication. May 16.

McGrath, J. E., and Argote, L. 2001. Group processes in organizational contexts. In M. A. Hogg and R. S. Tindale, eds., Blackwell handbook of social psychology, vol. 3: Group processes, 603–627. Oxford, UK: Blackwell.

McKechnie, L. (E. F.), Julien, H., Genuis, S. K., and Oliphant, T. 2008.Communicating research findings to library and information science practitioners: A study of ISIC papers from 1996 to

200. *Information Research* 13(4), paper 375. Retrieved from http://InformationR.net/ir/13-4/paper375.html

McKenzie, P. J. 2006. The seeking of baby-feeding information by Canadian women pregnant with twins. *Midwifery* 22(3): 218–227.

Meadow, C. T., Boyce, B. R., and Kraft, D. H. 2000. *Text information retrieval systems*. 2d ed. San Diego, CA: Academic Press.

Meho, L. I., and Haas, S. W. 2001. Information-seeking behavior and use of social science faculty studying stateless nations: A case study. *Library and Information Science Research* 23(1): 5–25.

Menzel, H. 1966. Information needs and uses in science and technology. *Annual Review of Information Science and Technology* 1: 41–69.

Metoyer-Duran, C. 1993. *Gatekeepers in ethnolinguistic communities*. Norwood, NJ: Ablex.

Meyers, E. M., L. P. Nathan, and M. L. Saxton. 2006. Barriers to information seeking in school libraries: Conflicts in perceptions and practice. *Information Research* 12(2), paper 295. Retrieved from http://InformationR.net/ir/12-2/paper295.html

Mick, C. K., Lindsey, G. N., and Callahan, D. 1980. Towards usable user studies. *Journal of the American Society for Information Science* 31(5): 347–356.

Mizzaro, S. 1997. Relevance: The whole history. *Journal of the American Society for Information Science* 48(9): 810–832.

Moores, C. S. 1950. Coding, information retrieval, and the rapid selector. *American Documentation* 1(4): 225–229.

Mote, L. J. B. 1962. Reasons for the variations in the information needs of scientists. *Journal of Documentation* 18(4): 169–175.

Mursu, Á., I. Luukkonen, M. Toivanen, and M. Korpela. 2007. Activity theory in information systems research and practice: Theoretical underpinnings for an information systems development model. *Information Research* 12(3), paper 311. Retrieved from http://InformationR.net/ir/12-3/paper311.html

Mutshewa, A. 2010. The use of information by environmental planners: A qualitative study using grounded theory methodology. *Information Processing and Management* 46(2): 212–232.

Mwanza, D. 2001. Where theory meets practice: A case for an activity theory based methodology to guide computer system design. In M. Hirose, ed., *Proceedings of INTERACT'2001*. Oxford, UK: IOS Press.

Nahl, D. 2007. The centrality of the affective in information behavior. In D. Nahl and D. Bilal, eds., Information and emotion: The emergent affective paradigm in information behavior research and theory, 3–37. Medford, NJ: Information Today.

Naikar, N. 2006. Beyond interface design: Further applications of cognitive work analysis. *International Journal of Industrial Ergonomics* 36(5): 423–438.

Nardi, B. 1993. *A small matter of programming: Perspectives on end user computing.* Cambridge, MA: MIT Press.

Nardi, B. 2008. Home page. Retrieved July 22, 2009, from http://darrouzet-nardi.net/bonnie/index.html

Nardi, B. A., and O'Day, V. L. 2000. *Information ecologies.* Cambridge, MA: MIT Press.

Naumer, C. M., and Fisher, K. E. 2009. Information needs: Conceptual and empirical developments. In M. Bates and M. N. Maack, eds., Encyclopedia of library and information sciences. 3rd ed. New York: Taylor and Francis.

Nicholas, D., Huntington, P., Jamali, H. R., Rowlands, I., and Fieldhouse, M. 2009. Student digital information-seeking behaviour in context. *Journal of Documentation* 65(1): 106–132.

Nicholas, D., Huntington, P., Williams, P., and Gunter, B. 2003. Health information and health benefit: A case study of digital interactive television information users. *New Review of Information Behaviour Research* 4(1): 177–194.

Nicolaisen, J. 2009. Compromised need and the label effect: An examination of claims and evidence. *Journal of the American Society for Information Science and Technology* 60(10): 2004–2009.

Niedźwiedzka, B. 2003. A proposed general model of information behaviour. *Information Research* 9(1), paper 164. Retrieved from http://InformationR.net/ir/9-1/paper164.html

Nilsen, K. 1998. Social science research in Canada and government information policy: The Statistics Canada example. *Library and Information Science Research* 20(3): 211–234.

Nolin, J. 2007. "What's in a turn?" *Information Research* 12(4), paper colis11. Retrieved from http://InformationR.net/ir/12-4/colis/colis11.html

Norman, A. D. 1988. *The design of everyday things.* New York: Basic Books.

O'Connor, J. 1967. Relevance disagreements and unclear request forms. *American Documentation* 18(3): 165–177.

Oddy, R. N. 1977. Information retrieval through man-machine dialogue. *Journal of Documentation* 33: 1–14.

Oldenburg, R. 1989. *The great good place: Cafes, coffee shops, community centers, beauty parlors, general stores, bars, hangouts, and how they get you through the day.* New York: Paragon House.

Paisley, W. J. 1968. Information needs and uses. *Annual Review of Information Science and Technology* 3: 1–30.

Palmquist, R. A., and Kim, K. S. 2000. Cognitive style and on-line database search experience as predictors of Web search performance. *Journal of the American Society for Information Science* 51(6): 558–566.

Park, O. N. 2008. Current practice in classification system design: An empirical investigation of classification system design team practice. Doctoral dissertation. University of Washington, Seattle.

Park, T. K. 1994. Toward a theory of user-based relevance: A call for a new paradigm of inquiry. *Journal of the American Society for Information Science* 45(3): 135–141.

Patton, M. Q. 2002. *Qualitative research and evaluation methods*. 3rd ed. Thousand Oaks, CA: Sage.

Pejtersen, A. M. 1979. Investigation of search strategies in fiction based on an analysis of 134 user-librarian conversations. In T. Henriksen, ed., *IRFIS 3: Proceedings of the Third International Research Forum in Information Science*, 107–132. Oslo, Norway: Staten Biblioteks- och Informasjons Høgskole.

Pejtersen, A. M. 1984. Design of a computer-aided user-system dialogue based on an analysis of users' search behavior. *Social Science Information Studies* 4: 167–183.

Pejtersen, A. M. 1989. The BOOK House: Modeling user needs and search strategies as a basis for system design. Risø Report M-2794. Roskilde: Risø National Laboratory.

Pejtersen, A. M. 1992. The BookHouse: An icon based database system for fiction retrieval in public libraries. In B. Cronin, ed., The marketing of library and information services, 2: 572–591. London: Aslib.

Pejtersen, A. M., and Fidel, R. 1998. *A framework for work-centered evaluation and design: A case study of IR on the Web*. Grenoble, France: Report for MIRA.

Pettigrew, K. E. 1999. Waiting for chiropody: Contextual results from an ethnographic study of the information behavior among attendees at community clinics. *Information Processing and Management* 35: 801–817.

Pettigrew, K. E. 2000. Lay information provision in community settings: How community health nurses disseminate human services information to the elderly. *Library Quarterly* 70(1): 47–85.

Pettigrew, K. E., Fidel, R., and Bruce, H. 2001. Conceptual frameworks in information behavior. *Annual Review of Information Science and Technology* 35: 43–78.

Pettigrew, K. E., and McKechnie, E. F. 2001. The use of theory in information science research. *Journal of the American Society for Information Science and Technology* 52(1): 62–73.

Phares, E. J. 1991. Introduction to psychology. 3rd ed. New York: Harper Collins. (Cited in Heinström 2003.)

Pharo, N. 2004. A new model of information behaviour based on the Search Situation Transition schema. *Information Research* 10(1), paper 203. Retrieved from http://InformationR.net/ir/10-1/paper203.html

Pickard, A., and Dixon, P. 2004. The applicability of constructivist user studies: How can constructivist inquiry inform service providers and systems designers? *Information Research* 9(3), paper 175. Retrieved from http://InformationR.net/ir/9-3/paper175.html

Pipek, V., Hinrichs, J., and Wulf, V. 2003. Sharing expertise: Challenges for technical support. In M. Ackerman, V. Pipek, and V. Wulf, eds., Beyond knowledge management: Sharing expertise. Cambridge, MA: MIT Press.

Poltrock, S., Grudin, J., Dumais, S., Fidel, R., Bruce, H., and Pejtersen, A. M. 2003. Information seeking and sharing in design teams. In M. Pendergast, K. Schmidt, C. Simone, and M. Tremain, eds., *Proceedings of the 2003 International ACM SIGGROUP Conference on Supporting Group Work, Sanibel Island, Florida,* 239–247. New York: ACM.

Prigoda, E., and McKenzie, P. J. 2007. Purls of wisdom: A collectivist study of human information behaviour in a public library knitting group. *Journal of Documentation* 63(1): 90–114.

Radford, G. P., and Radford, M. L. 2005. Structuralism, post-structuralism, and the library: De Saussure and Foucault. *Journal of Documentation* 61(1): 60–78.

Ramirez, A., Jr., Walther, J. B., Burgoon, J. K., and Sunnafrank, M. 2002. Information-seeking strategies, uncertainty, and computer mediated communication: Toward a conceptual model. *Human Communication Research* 28(2): 213–228.

Ranganathan, S. R. 1957. *The five laws of library science.* London: Blunt.

Rasmussen, J. 1977. Risk management in a dynamic society: A modeling problem. *Safety Science* 27: 183–213. (Cited by Vicente 1999.)

Rasmussen, J. 1981. Models of mental strategies in process plant diagnosis. In J. Rasmussen and W. B. Rouse, eds., Human detection and diagnosis of system failures, 241–258. New York: Plenum. (Cited by Vicente 1999.)

Rasmussen, J. 1986. *Information processing and human-machine interaction: An approach to cognitive engineering.* New York: North Holland.

Rasmussen, J., Pejtersen, A. M., and Goodstein, L. P. 1994. *Cognitive systems engineering.* New York: Wiley.

Reising, D. V. C., and Sanderson, P. M. 2002. Work domain analysis and sensors. II: Pasteurizer II case study. *International Journal of Human-Computer Studies* 56(6): 597–637.

Reitz, J. M. 2007. *Online dictionary for library and information science.* Westport, CT: Libraries Unlimited. Retrieved May 9, 2008 from http://lu.com/odlis/index.cfm

Resnick, P., and Varian, H. R. 1997. Recommender systems. *Communications of the ACM* 40(3): 56–58.

Rice, R. E., McCreadie, M., and Chang, S. L. 2001. *Accessing and browsing information and communication.* Cambridge, MA: MIT Press.

Rieger, J. H., and Anderson, R. C. 1968. Information sources and need hierarchies of an adult population in five Michigan counties. *Adult Education Journal* 18: 155–175. (Cited in Faibisoff and Ely 1976.)

Robertson, S. 2008. On the history of evaluation in IR. *Journal of Information Science* 34(4): 439–456.

Robertson, S. E., and Hancock-Beaulieu, M. M. 1992. On the evaluation of IR systems. *Information Processing and Management* 28(4): 457–466.

Robinson, M. R. 2010. An empirical analysis of engineers' information behavior. *Journal of the American Society for Information Science and Technology* 61(4): 640–658.

Rose, M. 2006. The information activity of rail passenger information staff: A foundation for information system requirements. *Information Research* 12(1), paper 275. Retrieved from http://InformationR.net/ir/12-1/paper275.html

Ross, C. S. 1999. Finding without seeking: The information encounter in the context of reading for pleasure. *Information Processing and Management* 35(6): 783–799.

Rothbauer, P. 2004. "People aren't afraid anymore, but it's hard to find books": Reading practices that inform the personal and social identities of self-identified lesbian and queer young women. *Canadian Journal of Information and Library Science* 28(3): 52–74.

Rouet, J. F. 2003. What was I looking for? The influence of task specificity and prior knowledge on students' search strategies in hypertext. *Interacting with Computers* 15: 409–428.

Sachs, P. 1995. Transforming work: Collaboration, learning, and design. *Communications of the ACM* 38(9): 36–44.

Sanderson, P. 1998. Cognitive work analysis and the analysis, design, and evaluation of human-computer interactive systems. In P. Calder and B. Thomas, eds., *Proceedings of the 1998 Australasian Computer Human Interaction Conference*, 220–227. Los Alamitos, CA: IEEE.

Sanderson, P. M. 2003. Cognitive work analysis. In J. M. Carroll, ed., HCI models, theories, and frameworks: Toward a multidisciplinary science, 225–264. New York: Morgan-Kaufmann.

Sanderson, P., Crawford, J., Savill, A., Watson, M., and Russell, W. J. 2004. Visual and auditory attention in patient monitoring: A formative analysis. *Cognition Technology and Work* 6(3): 172–185.

Sanderson, P., Naikar, N., Lintern, G., and Goss, S. 1999. Use of cognitive work analysis across the system life cycle: From requirements to decommissioning. In *Proceedings of 43rd Annual Meeting of the Human Factors and Ergonomics Society*, 318–322. Santa Monica, CA: Human Factors and Ergonomics Society.

Saracevic, T. 1975. Relevance: A review of and a framework for the thinking on the notion of information science. *Journal of the American Society for Information Science* 26(6): 321–343.

Saracevic, T. 1999. Information science. *Journal of the American Society for Information Science* 50(12): 1051–1063.

Saracevic, T. 2007a. Relevance: A review of the literature and a framework for thinking on the notion in information science. Part II: Nature and manifestations of relevance. *Journal of the American Society for Information Science and Technology* 58(13): 1915–1933.

Saracevic, T. 2007b. Relevance: A review of the literature and a framework for thinking on the notion in information science. Part III: Behavior and effects of relevance. *Journal of the American Society for Information Science and Technology* 58(13): 2126–2144.

Sauperl, A. 2002. *Subject determination during the cataloging process*. Lanham, MD: Scarecrow Press.

Savolainen, R. 1995. Everyday life information seeking: Approaching information seeking in the context of "way of life." *Library and Information Science Research* 17(3): 259–294.

Savolainen, R. 2006. Spatial factors as contextual qualifiers of information seeking. *Information Research* 11(4), paper 261. Retrieved from http://InformationR.net/ir/11-4/paper261.html

Savolainen, R. 2007. Information behavior and information practice: Reviewing the "umbrella concepts" of information-seeking studies. *Library Quarterly* 77(2): 109–132.

Schamber, L. 1991. User's criteria for evaluation in multimedia environment. *Proceedings of the American Society for Information Science* 28: 126–133.

Schamber, L. 1994. Relevance and information behavior. *Annual Review of Information Science and Technology* 29: 3–48.

Schamber, L., Eisenberg, M. B., and Nilan, M. C. 1990. A re-examination of relevance: Towards a dynamic, situational definition. *Information Processing and Management* 26(60): 755–776.

Scholl, J. H., Liu, S., Fidel, R., and Unsworth, K. 2007. Choices and challenges in e-government field force automation project: Insights from case studies. In T. Janowski and T. A. Pardo, eds., *ICEGOV: Proceedings of the First International Conference on Theory and Practice of Electronic Governance, Macau, China, December 2007*, 408–416. New York: ACM.

Shannon, C. E., and Weaver, W. 1949. *The mathematical theory of communication*. Urbana: University of Illinois Press.

Shoham, S., and S. K. Strauss. 2008. Immigrants' information needs: Their role in the absorption process. *Information Research* 13(4), paper 359. Retrieved from http://InformationR.net/ir/13-4/paper359.html

Smithson, S. 1994. Information retrieval evaluation in practice: A case study approach. *Information Processing and Management* 30: 205–221.

Soergel, D. 1985. *Organizing information: Principles of data base and retrieval systems*. Orlando, FL: Academic Press.

Soergel, D. 1997–98. An information science manifesto. *Bulletin of the American Society for Information Science* 24 (2). Retrieved from http://www.asis.org/Bulletin/Dec-97/Soergel.htm.

Solomon, P. 2002. Discovering information in context. *Annual Review of Information Science and Technology* 36: 229–264.

Sonnenwald, D. H. 1999. Evolving perspectives of human information behaviour: Contexts, situations, social network and information horizons. In T. D. Wilson and D. K. Allen, eds., *Exploring the contexts of information behaviour: Proceedings of the Second International Conference on Research in Information Need, Seeking, and Use in Different Contexts*, 176–190. London: Taylor Graham.

Sonnenwald, D. H. 2005. Information horizons. In K. E. Fisher, S. Erdelez, and E. F. McKechnie, eds., Theories of information behavior, 191–197. Medford, NJ: Information Today.

Spink, A., and Cole, C. 2006. Human information behavior: Integrating diverse approaches and information use. *Journal of the American Society for Information Science and Technology* 57(1): 25–35.

Spink, A., and Park, M. 2005. Information and non-information multitasking interplay. *Journal of Documentation* 6(14): 548–554.

Starbuck, W. H. 1992. Learning by knowledge-intensive firms. *Journal of Management Studies* 29(7): 713–740.

Steinerova, J., and Susol, J. 2007. Users' information behavior—A gender perspective. *Information Research* 12(3), paper 320. Retrieved from http://InformationR.net/ir/12-3/paper320.html

Streatfield, D. R., and Wilson, T. D. 1982. Information innovations in social services departments: A third report on Project INISS. *Journal of Documentation* 38(4): 273–281.

Suchman, L. A. 1987. *Plans and situated actions: The problem of human-machine communication*. Cambridge: Cambridge University Press.

Suchman, L. A. 2002. Practice-based design of information systems: Notes from the hyperdeveloped world. *Information Society* 18(2): 139–144.

Sundin, O., and Johannisson, J. 2005. Pragmatism, neo-pragmatism and socialcultural theory: Communicative participation as a perspective in LIS. *Journal of Documentation* 61(1): 23–43.

Sutton, S. A. 2004. Digital library infrastructure: Metadata and the education domain. In D. Hillmann and E. Westbrooks, eds., Metadata in practice, 1–16. Chicago: American Library Association.

Tagliacozzo, R., and Kochen, M. 1970. Information-seeking behavior of catalog users. *Information Storage and Retrieval* 6: 363–381.

Talja, S., Keso, H., and Pietiläinen, T. 1999. The production of "context" in information seeking research: A metatheoretical view. *Information Processing and Management* 35: 751–763.

Talja, S., Tuominen, K., and Savolainen, R. 2005. "Isms" in information science: Constructivism, collectivism and constructionism. *Journal of Documentation* 61(1): 79–101.

Taylor, R. 1968. Question-negotiation and information seeking in libraries. *College and Research Libraries* 29(3): 178–194.

Taylor, R. 1982. Value-added processes in the information life cycle. *Journal of the American Society for Information Science* 33(5): 341–346.

Taylor, R. S. 1991. Information use environments. In B. Dervin and M. J. Voigt, eds., Progress in communication sciences, 217–255. Norwood, NJ: Ablex.

Teevan, J., Jones, W., and Bederson, B. B. 2006. Personal information management. *Communications of the ACM* 49(1): 40–43.

Thatcher, A. 2006. Information seeking behaviors and cognitive strategies in different search tasks on the WWW. *International Journal of Industrial Ergonomics* 36(12): 1055–1068.

Thatcher, A. 2008. Web search strategies: The influence of Web experience task type. *Information Processing and Management* 44(3): 1308–1329.

Thomas, N. P. 1993. Information-seeking and the nature of relevance: Ph.D. student orientation as an exercise in information retrieval. *Proceedings of the American Society for Information Science* 30: 126–130.

Todd, R. J. 1999. Back to our beginnings: Information utilization, Bertram Brookes and the fundamental equation of information science. *Information Processing and Management* 35(6): 851–870.

Todd, R. J. 2005. Information intents. In K. E. Fisher, S. Erdelez, and E. F. McKechnie, eds., Theories of information behavior, 198–203. Medford, NJ: Information Today.

Tombros, A., Ruthven, I., and Jose, J. M. 2005. How users assess web pages for information seeking. *Journal of the American Society for Information Science and Technology* 56(4): 327–344.

Toms, E. G. 2000. Understanding and facilitating the browsing of electronic text. *International Journal of Human-Computer Studies* 52(3): 423–452.

Torenvliet, G. L., Jamieson, G. A., and Vicente, K. J. 2000. Making the most of ecological interface design: The role of individual differences. *Applied Ergonomics* 31(4): 395–408.

Tufte, E. R. 2001. The visual display of quantitative information. 2d ed. Cheshire, CT: Graphics Press.

Tuominen, K., and Savolainen, R. 1997. A social constructionist approach to the study of information use as discursive action. In P. Vakkari, R. Savolainen, and B. Dervin, eds., Information seeking in context: Proceedings of the International Conference on Research in Information Needs, Seeking and Use in Different Contexts, 81–96. London: Graham Taylor.

Tuominen, K., Talja, S., and Savolainen, R. 2002. Discourse, cognition and reality: Towards a social constructionist metatheory for library and information science. In H. Bruce, R. Fidel, P. Ingwersen, and P. Vakkari, eds., *Emerging frameworks and methods: Proceedings of the Fourth*

International Conference on Conceptions of Library and Information Science (CoLIS 4), 271–283. Greenwood Village, CO: Libraries Unlimited.

Urquhart, C., and Yeoman, A. 2010. Information behaviour of women: Theoretical perspectives on gender. *Journal of Documentation* 66(1): 113–139.

Vakkari, P. 1997. Information seeking in context: A challenging metatheory. In P. Vakkari, R. Savolainen, and B. Dervin, eds., *Information seeking in context: Proceedings of the International Conference on Research in Information Needs, Seeking, and Use in Different Contexts*, 451–464. London: Taylor Graham.

Vakkari, P. 1999. Task complexity, problem structure and information actions: Integrating studies on information seeking and retrieval. *Information Processing and Management* 35(6): 819–837.

Vakkari, P. 2001. Changes in search tactics and relevance judgment when preparing a research proposal: A summary of findings of a longitudinal study. *Information Retrieval* 4(3): 295–310.

Vakkari, P. 2003. Task-based information searching. *Annual Review of Information Science and Technology* 37: 413–464.

Vakkari, P. 2008. Trends and approaches in information behaviour research. *Information Research* 13(4), paper 361. Retrieved from http://InformationR.net/ir/13-4/paper361.html

Vakkari, P., and Hakala, H. 2000. Changes in relevance criteria and problem stages in task performance. *Journal of Documentation* 56(5): 540–562.

Vakkari, P., Savolainen, R., and Dervin, B., eds. 1997. *Information seeking in context: Proceedings of the International Conference on Research in Information Needs, Seeking, and Use in Different Contexts*. London: Taylor Graham.

Vakkari, P., and Sormunen, E. 2004. The influence of relevant levels on the effectiveness of interactive information retrieval. *Journal of the American Society for Information Science and Technology* 55(11): 963–969.

Vakkari, P., and S. Talja. 2006. Searching for electronic journal articles to support academic tasks: A case study of the use of the Finnish National Electronic Library (FinELib). *Information Research* 12(1), paper 285. Retrieved from http://InformationR.net/ir/12-1/paper285.html

Vicente, K. J. 1990. Coherence- and correspondence-driven work domains: Implications for systems design. *Behaviour and Information Technology* 9(6): 493–502.

Vicente, K. J. 1999. *Cognitive work analysis: Towards safe, productive, and healthy computer-based work*. Mahwah, NJ: Lawrence Erlbaum.

Vickery, B. C. 1973. *Information systems*. Hamden, CT: Archon Book.

Vickery, B. 1997. Metatheory and information science. *Journal of Documentation* 53(5): 457–476.

Vilar, P., and Zumer, M. 2008. Perceptions and importance of user friendliness of IR systems according to users' individual characteristics and academic discipline. *Journal of the American Society for Information Science and Technology* 59(12): 1995–2007.

Voorhees, E. M., and Harman, D. K., eds. 2005. TREC: Experiment and evaluation in information retrieval. Cambridge, MA: MIT Press.

Walsh, J. P., and Ungson, G. R. 1991. Organizational memory. *Academy of Management Review* 16: 57–91.

Wang, P. 1997. The design of document retrieval systems for academic users: Implications of studies on users' relevance criteria. *Proceedings of the American Society for Information Science* 34: 162–173.

Wang, P. 1999. Methodologies and methods for user behavioral research. *Annual Review of Information Science and Technology* 34: 53–99.

Wang, P., Hawk, W. B., and Tenopir, C. 2000. Users' interaction with World Wide Web resources: An exploratory study using holistic approach. *Information Processing and Management* 36: 229–251.

Wang, P., and Soergel, D. 1998. A cognitive model of document use during a research project: Study I. Document selection. *Journal of the American Society for Information Science* 49(2): 115–133.

Wang, P., and White, M. D. 1995. Document use during a research project: A longitudinal study. *Proceedings of the American Society for Information Science* 32: 181–188.

Wathen, C. N., and Harris, R. M. 2006. An examination of the health information seeking experiences of women in rural Ontario, Canada. Information Research 11(4), paper 267. Retrieved from http://InformationR.net/ir/11-4/paper267.html

Watson, M., Russell, W. J., and Sanderson, P. 2000. Anaesthesia monitoring, alarm proliferation, and ecological interface design. *Australian Journal of Information Systems* 7(2): 109–114.

Weber, M. 1947. The theory of social and economic organization. New York: Oxford University Press. (Cited by Benton and Craib 2001.)

Wersig, G. 1993. Information science: The study of postmodern knowledge usage. *Information Processing and Management* 29: 229–239.

Westbrook, L. 2009. Crisis information concerns: Information needs of domestic violence survivors. *Information Processing and Management* 45(1): 98–114.

Wikgren, M. 2005. Critical realism as a philosophy and social theory in information science? *Journal of Documentation* 61(1): 11–22.

Williamson, K. 1998. Discovered by chance: The role of incidental information acquisition in an ecological model of information use. *Library and Information Science Research* 20(1): 23–40.

Williamson, K. 2005. Ecological theory of human information behavior. In K. E. Fisher, S. Erdelez, and E. F. McKechnie, eds., Theories of information behavior, 128–132. Medford, NJ: Information Today.

Williamson, K., and Asla, T. 2009. Information behavior of people in the fourth age: Implications for the conceptualization of information literacy. *Library and Information Science Research* 31(2): 76–83.

Williamson, K., and McGregor, J. 2006. Information use and secondary school students: A model for understanding plagiarism. *Information Research* 12(1), paper 288. Retrieved from http://InformationR.net/ir/12-1/paper288.html

Wilson, P. 1995. Unused relevant information in research and development. *Journal of the American Society for Information Science* 46(1): 45–51.

Wilson, T. D. 1981. On user studies and information needs. *Journal of Documentation* 37(1): 3–15.

Wilson, T. D. 1994. Information needs and uses: Fifty years of progress? In B. C. Vickery, ed., Fifty years of information progress: A Journal of Documentation review, 15–51. London: Aslib. Retrieved from http://informationr.net/tdw/publ/papers/1994FiftyYears.html

Wilson, T. D. 1997. Information behaviour: An interdisciplinary perspective. *Information Processing and Management* 33(4): 551–572.

Wilson, T. D. 1999. Models in information behaviour research. *Journal of Documentation* 55(3): 249–270.

Wilson, T. D. 2003. Philosophical foundations and research relevance: Issues for information research. *Journal of Information Science* 29(6): 445–452.

Wilson, T. D. 2005. Evolution in information behavior modeling: Wilson's model. In K. E. Fisher, S. Erdelez, and E. F. McKechnie, eds., Theories of information behavior, 31–36. Medford, NJ: Information Today.

Wilson, T. D. 2006. On user studies and information needs. *Journal of Documentation* 62(6): 658–670.

Wilson, T. D. 2008. Activity theory and information seeking. *Annual Review of Information Science and Technology* 42: 119–161.

Wilson, T. D., Ford, N. J., Ellis, D., Foster, A. E., and Spink, A. 2000. Uncertainty and its correlates. *New Review of Information Behaviour Research* 1: 69–84.

Wilson, T. D., and Streatfield, D. R. 1977. Information needs in local authority social services department: An interim report on Project INISS. *Journal of Documentation* 33: 277–293.

Wilson, T. D., Streatfield, D. R., and Mullings, C. 1979. Information needs in local authority social services department: A second report on Project INISS. *Journal of Documentation* 35(2): 120–136.

Wyllie, J., Skyrme, D. J., and Lelic, S. 2003. *Taxonomies: Frameworks for corporate knowledge: The shape of things to come?* London: Ark Group.

Xie, I. 2006. Evaluation of digital libraries: Criteria and problems from users' perspectives. *Library and Information Science Research* 28(3): 433–452.

Xie, I. 2007. Shifts in information-seeking strategies in information retrieval in the digital age: Planned-situational model. *Information Research* 12(4), paper colis22. Retrieved from http://InformationR.net/ir/12-4/colis/colis22.html

Xie, I. 2008. *Interactive information retrieval in digital environments*. Hershey, NY: IGI Publishing.

Xie, I. 2009. Dimensions of tasks: Influences on information-seeking and retrieving process. *Journal of Documentation* 65(3): 339–366.

Xu, Y. 2007. Relevance judgment and hedonic information searches. *Journal of the American Society for Information Science and Technology* 58(2): 178–189.

Yeh, N.-C. 2008. The social constructionist viewpoint on gays and lesbians, and their information behaviour. *Information Research* 13(4), paper 364. Retrieved from http://InformationR.net/ir/13-4/paper364.html

Zhang, Y. 2008. The influence of mental models on undergraduate students' searching behavior on the Web. *Information Processing and Management* 44(3): 1330–1345.

Zhao, L., and Reisman, A. 1992. Toward meta research on technology transfer. *IEEE Transactions on Engineering Management* 39(1): 13–21.

Zwadlo, J. 1997. We don't need a philosophy of library and information science—We're confused enough already. *Library Quarterly* 67(2): 103–121.

Index of Authors

Index of Topics